Warfare in History

THE
BATTLE OF THE GOLDEN SPURS
(COURTRAI, 11 JULY 1302)

Warfare in History

General Editors
Matthew Bennett
David Parrott
Hugh Strachan

ISSN 1358–779X

Already published

The Battle of Hastings: Sources and Interpretations
edited and introduced by Stephen Morillo

Infantry Warfare in the Early Fourteenth Century:
Discipline, Tactics, and Technology
Kelly DeVries

The Art of Warfare in Western Europe during
the Middle Ages, from the Eighth Century to 1340 (second edition)
J. F. Verbruggen

Knights and Peasants:
The Hundred Years War in the French Countryside
Nicholas Wright

Society at War:
The Experience of England and France during the Hundred Years War
edited by Christopher Allmand

The Circle of War in the Middle Ages:
Essays on Medieval Military and Naval History
edited by Donald J. Kagay and L. J. Andrew Villalon

The Anglo-Scots Wars, 1513–1550: A Military History
Gervase Phillips

The Norwegian Invasion of England in 1066
Kelly DeVries

The Wars of Edward III: Sources and Interpretations
edited and introduced by Clifford J. Rogers

War Cruel and Sharp:
English Strategy under Edward III, 1327–1360
Clifford J. Rogers

The Normans and their Adversaries at War:
Essays in Memory of C. Warren Hollister
edited by Richard P. Abels and Bernard S. Bachrach

THE
BATTLE OF THE GOLDEN SPURS
(COURTRAI, 11 JULY 1302)

A CONTRIBUTION TO THE HISTORY OF FLANDERS' WAR
OF LIBERATION, 1297–1305

J. F. Verbruggen

Edited by
Kelly DeVries

Translated by
David Richard Ferguson

THE BOYDELL PRESS

© J. F. Verbruggen 2002
Translation © David Richard Ferguson 2002

All Rights Reserved. Except as permitted under current legislation
no part of this work may be photocopied, stored in a retrieval system,
published, performed in public, adapted, broadcast,
transmitted, recorded or reproduced in any form or by any means,
without the prior permission of the copyright owner

First published in 1952 as
De Slag der Guldensporen
Bijdrage tot de geschiedenis van Vlaanderens
Vrijheidsoorlog, 1297–1305
Standaard-Boekhandel Publishers, Antwerp and Amsterdam

Revised version in English translation 2002
The Boydell Press, Woodbridge

ISBN 0 85115 888 9

The Boydell Press is an imprint of Boydell & Brewer Ltd
PO Box 9, Woodbridge, Suffolk IP12 3DF, UK
and of Boydell & Brewer Inc.
PO Box 41026, Rochester, NY 14604–4126, USA
website: www.boydell.co.uk

A catalogue record for this book is available
from the British Library

Library of Congress Cataloging-in-Publication Data
Verbruggen, J. F.
  [Slag der Guldensporen. English]
  The Battle of the Golden Spurs (Courtrai, 11 July 1302) : a contribution
to the history of Flanders' war of liberty, 1297–1305 / J.F. Verbruggen ;
translated by David Richard Ferguson ; edited by Kelly DeVries. – Rev.
version in English translation.
    p. cm. – (Warfare in history, ISSN 1358–779X)
  Includes bibliographical references.
  ISBN 0–85115–888–9 (alk. paper)
  1. Kortrijk (Belgium), Battle of, 1302. 2. Flanders (Belgium) –
History. 3. France – History – Philip IV, 1285–1314. I. DeVries, Kelly, 1956–
II. Title. III. Series.
DC92 .V413 2002
949.3'01 – dc21   2002003531

This publication is printed on acid-free paper

Printed in Great Britain by
St Edmundsbury Press Ltd, Bury St Edmunds, Suffolk

Contents

List of Illustrations	vii
General Editor's Preface	ix
Editor's Introduction to the 2002 edition	xi
Foreword to the 1952 edition	xvii
Acknowledgements (to the 1952 edition)	xix
Preface: 'An almost impossible event . . .'	xxiii
Introduction	1
Flanders at the end of the thirteenth century	1
The war	15
Philip the Fair: Prince of Flanders	19

Part One:
Historiography and the Study of the Sources

1	A Problem for Historical Methodology	29
	Summary	38
2	The Sources	40
	The emergence of Flemish and French versions	40
	The sources of the French version	45
	The sources of the Flemish version	83
	Conclusion: the Flemish and French versions	113

Part Two:
Historical Overview of the 1302 Campaign

3	The Terrain at Courtrai	127
	The battlefield according to accounts of the period	130
	The terrain according to deeds, records and old maps	135
	General conclusion on the terrain	150
4	The Two Armies	152
	The numerical strength of the two armies	152

	The carved Flemish chest at New College, Oxford, and the equipment and arms of the Flemish troops	195
5	From the Bruges Matins to the Battle of the Spurs for freedom, equality and fraternity	211
	The strategic problem	218
6	11 July 1302	222
	The council of war held in the French camp	224
	Preparations in the Flemish army	226
	The battle array chosen by the French forces	230
	The battle of the crossbowmen	231
	The charge of the French left wing	232
	The charge of the French right wing	235
	The intervention of Jan van Renesse	236
	The charge led by Robert d'Artois	237
	Crisis and conclusion	238
	The flight of the French rearguard and the pursuit	240
General Conclusion		244
Bibliography		251
Index		261

Illustrations

Plan of the battle of Courtrai		xxii
1.	Figure on Page 174 of original	134
2.	Jacob van Deventer's map	141
3.	Louis de Bersaques' map	143
4 & 5.	Two maps of the town of Courtrai from Petit Beaulieu	144–45
6.	Ferraris' map	146
7.	Map of Courtrai as it is today showing the Groeninge stream	148

Plates

The Courtrai Chest, New College, Oxford		196
I.	The Bruges Matins	198
II.	The arrival of Guy de Namur and Willem van Jülich in Bruges	200
III.	Taking the castle of Wijnendale	202
IV.	Flemish townsmen with banners of their guilds	204
V.	The Flemish battle array on the Groeninge field	205
VI.	The sortie of the French knights out of the castle of Courtrai	207
VII.	Collecting the booty after the battle	208

General Editor's Preface

'The Flemings stand there as hopelessly determined men.'
Giovanni Vilani, *Historie fiorentine* (cited p. 230)

Anniversaries obviously matter. Exactly seven hundred years ago, Flemish townsmen crushed the chivalry of their French overlord in a dramatic and bloody encounter. Precisely half a century has passed since the best military historian of his era published this study in his native Flemish. J.F. Verbruggen's *The Art of Warfare in Western Europe during the Middle Ages*, published in English translation in 1997, the third book in this series, captures the broad sweep of his subject, while this present volume is a detailed case study. As my old tutor, R. Allen Brown, used to say, 'All history is local history', and Verbruggen's analysis supports this dictum perfectly.

For, to really understand a battle, it is essential to have a clear and accurate understanding of the ground over which it was fought. The author's close investigation of this matter enables him to draw conclusions about why and how the opposing commanders drew up their forces in the way that they did. Flowing from that is the issue of the tactics used by both sides – and flowing is an appropriate word because of the significance of the water-filled ditches and marshy areas which provided the Flemish foot-soldiers with a strong position to defend. But, contrary to frequently over-simplified views of the battle, the French did not charge heedlessly into a trap. True, in retrospect, Robert of Artois would have been better advised not to attack, although, as Verbruggen explains, he was able to get his mounted troops across the ditches with relatively little loss and into position to launch a charge on the enemy's infantry. Rather, he had underestimated the determination of the lightly-armoured and simply-armed footmen in opposing his own heavily-equipped cavalry. This may well have been the result of aristocratic arrogance. Yet the resistance of an army of the low-born was not a new thing, although some historians still write of an 'infantry revolution' in the fourteenth century. Nor again were the knightly commanders incapable of learning from their defeats, as the French showed at the battle of Mons-en-Pévèle two years later, when they exercised considerable caution in the assault and came away the better party of a hard-fought draw.[1] All these matters Verbruggen explores in such a way that it might seem surprising that his interpretations have not been picked-up more by the 'Anglo-Saxon' historical world. The issue is, of course, that of the availability of his conclusions, originally published in the language generically known as Dutch and

---

[1] See Matthew Bennett, 'The Myth of the Supremacy of Knightly Cavalry' in *Armies, Chivalry and Warfare in Medieval Britain and France: Proceedings of the 1995 Harlaxton conference*, ed. M. Strickland, New Series vol. 7 (Paul Watkins, 1998), pp. 304–16.

little read by English-speakers. It is therefore to the credit of Kelly DeVries, whose ethnic heritage gives him an understanding of the language, that he has brought this volume to light via the equally valuable work of translation by David Ferguson.

Knowledge of language, and hence of sources, is an essential skill for an historian, and here again Verbruggen excels. While French and Latin accounts make useful reading for his analysis, it is the Flemish poem of a Brabançon priest, Lodewijk van Velthem, which takes centre stage and provides the most detailed and instructive guide to events. Verbruggen shares with this spiritual ancestor an immense pride in the achievements of the 'common people', their hands hardened by work and apparently prone to a nationalism that, to some observers, seems more redolent of the nineteenth century than the period of the Flemish Revolt itself. Similarly, his interpretation of the portrayal of the Flemish leaders on that unique survival, the 'Courtrai Chest', as bare-faced (while their bodyguard of knights ride in closed helms) as a deliberate attempt to create a common identity with the footmen, protected merely by steel caps, may not reflect the only iconographic intention of the artist.

Indeed, it is very hard, when analysing a medieval battle, to get close to the men who made the event, not just what they thought (which must always be an exercise of historical imagination) but who they were and how many there were of them. If the size of armies in chroniclers' accounts often seems hopelessly exaggerated, it is partly because they are, and partly because numbers had a different meaning (often with Biblical connotations) than the 'perfect' data expected by a modern audience. (Although they too may often be deceived by journalistic accounts of wars and other tragedies.) So, Verbruggen's careful interpretation of the sketchy information available from which to work out how many men – roughly 8–10,000 Flemings against some 2,500 knights (with an unknowable number of support troops) – is also a model of its kind. In simple terms odds of three- or four-to-one might seem more than adequate to enable the foot-soldiers to triumph, were it not for the disparity in equipment and sense of moral ascendancy which so benefited the knights and squires of the French army. Had the Flemings' nerve failed, then there can be no doubt that it would have been them who would have been massacred. The descriptions of men unable to release their simple weapons – pikes and iron-bound clubs – after the battle, because they had been gripping them so tightly, bear simple witness to the terror that they faced in opposing men whose craft was war, while they were mere craftsmen. The important factor of leadership, combined with fellow-feeling and a desperate need to survive, also played a crucial role in the outcome of the battle.

Some might say that battle-history is an old-fashioned form of military history, yet when it is done supremely well (as it is here), it is as an compelling and perceptive an analysis of a past event as it is possible to achieve.

Matthew Bennett
Royal Military Academy Sandhurst

Editor's Introduction

I first heard of the battle of Courtrai when I lived in Belgium in 1976–78. Interested in that nation's history, principally its medieval past, I read Patricia Carson's extremely well-written popular history, *The Fair Face of Flanders*.[1] With its historical description of Belgium as the 'slagveld van Europa' (battlefield of Europe), Carson's book became, for me, a military history. Unfortunately for the Belgians, such a history does not have many high-points. They often participated in the wars fought in their country. But rarely were they victorious. One of their greatest victories, indeed one which is still celebrated today, was fought on July 11, 1302, and became known as the Battle of the Golden Spurs, based on the extremely large number of golden spurs captured there – between five and seven hundred, spurs given to knights as tournament prizes. These were taken by their Flemish captors to the nearby Church of the Virgin at Courtrai where they would hang as trophies for eighty years until removed by descendants of those original knights after the Flemish defeat at the battle of Westrozebeke.[2]

The knights in question were French. Titularly the King of France, Philip IV (the Fair) at the time of Courtrai), was the king also of the Flemings. But it had rarely been a happy sovereignty, especially in the century prior to the Battle of the Golden Spurs. Both the count of Flanders and the large towns of the county rebelled frequently against their king. Indeed, two Flemish counts, Ferrand of Portugal and Guy de Dampierre, had been imprisoned after rebelling against (and losing to) the French king during the thirteenth century.[3] Still, before 1302, any rebellion which was made against the French was quickly and violently put down by their armies, with little or no penalty against the king or his people. In fact, more often than not, the French kingdom grew in size, with land frequently surrendered to the king as reparations for Flemish military losses; at one time, during the eleventh century, the county of Flanders stretched as far into modern France as St. Omer.[4]

But, in 1302, the previously justified confidence of the French was dashed by the Flemings at Courtrai. Flemish townspeople from throughout the county were told by their generals, sons and grandsons of the previous count, Guy de

---

[1] Patricia Carson, *The Fair Face of Flanders* (Ghent, 1974).
[2] See Jean Froissart, *Chroniques*, in *Oeuvres de Froissart*, ed. Kervyn de Lettenhove (Brussels, 1870), XIII:177–78.
[3] Ferrand was captured after being on the losing side of the battle of Bouvines, fought in 1214. See E. Warlop, *De Vlaamse edel voor 1300*, vol. 1 (Handzame, 1968), p. 404. Guy was captured in 1300. See David Nicholas, *Medieval Flanders* (London, 1992), pp. 188–91.
[4] On the decreasing size of Flanders from the eleventh to the fourteenth century see Nicholas; and Henri Pirenne, *Histoire de Belgique*, vol. I: *Des origines au commencement du XIVe siècle* (Brussels, 1902).

Dampierre, who was then languishing in French imprisonment, that they needed to gather their forces and defend their 'lands, livelihoods, and families.' Such rhetoric became reality when an army of townsmen gathered at Courtrai, stood powerfully in a massive solid line, and defeated wave upon wave of French knights and other cavalry.

The defeat at Courtrai was devastating to the French kingdom. Not only was their international reputation diminished, and the size of their forces depleted, but the French kingdom had to contend with the continuation of rebellion for more than two years. And, driven by this success, further Flemish and other southern Low Countries' rebellions would follow throughout the next two centuries.[5] The defeat at Courtrai may also have led indirectly to the Hundred Years War, with their English enemy more certain of contending against the French than before their 1302 debacle.[6]

My interest roused by Carson's brief description of the battle of Courtrai, I began researching the battle as an undergraduate student at Brigham Young University and as a graduate student at the University of Toronto's Centre for Medieval Studies – a discussion of the battle opened my PhD dissertation, Perceptions of Victory and Defeat in the Southern Low Countries during the Fourteenth Century: A Historiographical Comparison (1987) – I soon discovered the works of J.F. Verbruggen. Initially, this was his chapter on the battle which I first read in the 1977 English translation, *The Art of Warfare in Western Europe During the Middle Ages from the Eighth Century to 1340*.[7] This led me to his earlier, more complete study of the battle, *De slag der guldensporen: Bijdrage tot de geschiedenis van Vlaanderens vrijheidsoorlog, 1297–1305* (Antwerp, 1952), the book translated here.

To knowing medieval military historians, there is no doubt that Jan Frans Verbruggen, in his scholarly achievements, stands in select company with the greats of the field, Charles Oman, Hans Delbrück, Philippe Contamine, and Bernard S. Bachrach. Yet, because his principal choice of publishing languages, Dutch, is not read by most scholars, his scholarship has been known only in the few articles written by him in French or German, and the even fewer translations of his writings.[8] Needless to say, this must change! In the words of Claude Gaier, himself

---

5 See Kelly DeVries, 'Observations on the Rebellions of Southern Low Countries' Towns During the Fourteenth and Fifteenth Centuries' (forthcoming).
6 See Kelly DeVries, *The Hundred Years Wars, 1302–1485* (London, forthcoming).
7 This was translated by General Sumner Willard and Lady S.C.M. Southern and was published by North-Holland Publishing Company of Amsterdam in 1977. It has since been republished in a second edition by The Boydell Press in 1997. The original is *De krijgkunst in west-Europa in de middeleeuwen (IXe tot XIVe eeuw)* (Brussels, 1954).
8 This latter situation should change in the future, not only with the publication of this translation, but also from the annual appearance of translated articles which are to appear in *The Journal of Medieval Military History*. The first of these articles, 'Flemish Urban Militias Against French Cavalry Armies in the Fourteenth and Fifteenth Centuries', translated by myself, will be published in 2002. (The original of this article, 'Vlaamse gemeentelegers tegen Franse ridderlegers in de 14de en 15de eeuw', appeared in the *Revue Belge d'histoire militaire* 24 (1981), 359–82.)

an impressive Belgian military historian, we need not only 'lire' (read) Verbruggen's works, but also 'relire' (reread) them.

J.F. Verbruggen was born in Tisselt on November 13, 1920. As a youth he was educated in the traditional Greco-Latin Humanities education at the *Koninklijk Atheneum* in Mechelen (Malines), after which he studied at the *Cadettenschool* (Military Academy) at Saffraanberg near Sint-Truiden (Saint-Trond) and at the *Koninklijke Militaire School* (Royal Military Academy) in Brussels, from where he graduated in 1939 and was commissioned as an officer in the Belgian army. His military service disrupted by the Nazi occupation of his homeland, Jan Verbruggen entered the University of Ghent where, in July 1944, he received a licentiate in arts and letters (history). Later study at the University of Ghent resulted in a Doctorate of Arts (*summa cum laude*) in 1951, and numerous academic awards and honors.

It was during this phase of his education, that J.F. Verbruggen began to teach others. His first assignment came in 1948 when he was engaged as a *repetitor* (instructor) in military history at the same Koninklijke Militaire School that he had graduated from almost ten years previously. In December 1954, he was raised there to the position of *docent* (teacher). Two years later, in September 1956, Jan Verbruggen was named a *gewoon hogeleraar* (regular professor) at the *Officiële Universiteit* (Official University) of the Belgian Congo, Rwanda, and Burundi in Elizabethstad. For the remainder of his academic career he lived in Africa. He taught at the *Officiële Universiteit* until July 1967, and, after those former Belgian colonies achieved their independence, he moved to the *Officiële Universiteit* of Burundi in Bujumbura, where he continued to teach until 1975. He also taught at the *Institut supérieur des cadres militaires* (the Greater Institute for Military Cadets) in Bujumbura from 1974 to 1976. Besides teaching at all of these institutions, Dr Verbruggen served as Dean of Arts and Sciences from 1056 to 1959 and 1963 to 1966 (in Elizabethstad) and from 1969 to 1971 (in Bujumbura).

While teaching in and administering at these institutions, J.F. Verbruggen continued to research and write medieval military history. He was assisted in these endeavors by grants from the *Koninklijke Militaire School*, in 1951, and the *Koninklijke Vlaamse Academie* (the Royal Flemish Academy), in 1953. And, in 1956–59, he received the very prestigious three-year prize for Belgian military history, awarded by the Department of Defense of Belgium. His numerous books also reflect this scholarly interest. They include (beyond the original of this volume): *De krijgkunst in west-Europa in de middeleeuwen (IXe tot XIVe eeuw)* [The Art of Warfare in Western Europe During the Middle Ages from the Eighth Century to 1340] (1954), which was translated first into English in 1977 and also in 1997); *Het leger en de vloot van de graven van Vlaanderen vanaf het ontstaan tot in 1305* [The Army and Navy of the Counts of Flanders from the Beginning to 1305] (1960); *Het gemeenteleger van Brugge van 1338 tot 1340 en de namen van de weerbare mannen* [The Town Militia of Bruges from 1338 to 1340 and the Names of the Able-Bodied Men] (1962); *1302 in Vlaanderen: De guldensporenslag* [1302 in Flanders: The Battle of the Golden Spurs] (1977); *De kist van Oxford* [The Oxford Chest], written with B. Dewilde, A. Pauwels, and F. Warlop (1980); *Vlaanderen na de Guldensporenslag* [Flanders after the Battle of the Golden Spurs] (1991); and *De slag bij Guinegate, 7 augustus 1479: De verdediging van het graafschap Vlaanderen tegen de koning van Frankrijk, 1477–1480* [The Battle of Guinegate, 7 August 1479: The Defense of the County of Flanders against the King of France, 1477–1480] (1993). In 1953, he also co-edited (with A.F.C. Koch) *De Annales Aldenburgenses over de gebeurtenissen in Vlaanderen tussen 11 juli 1302 en 25 April 1303* [The Annales of Aldenburg Concerning the Events in Flanders between 11 July1302 and April 25 1303].

Yet, his interest in military history, in particular Low Countries' military history, does not stop with the Middle Ages. Being a scholarly product of Belgian military academies during the twentieth century, Verbruggen has naturally also turned his thoughts to the conflicts which occurred in his homeland during the last hundred years, namely World War I and II. This has led to an additional number of academic books, including among others: *Ronsele (24 et 25 mai 1940): La surprise allemande du 24 mai et la contreattaque belge du 25 mai* [Ronsele (24–25 May 1940): The German Surprise of May 24 and the Belgian Counterattack of May 25] (1966); *La bataille de Merkem, 17 avril 1918* [The Battle of Merkem, April 17, 1918] (1977); *Inval van de Duitsers en bezetting, 1914–1918, 1940–1944* [The Invasion and Occupation of the Germans, 1914–1918, 1940–1944] (1985); and *Van Sarajevo tot Versailles: Herdenkingsuitgave 75 jaar wapenstilstand, 1918–1993* [From Sarajevo to Versailles: A Commemorative Publication at the 75th Anniversary of the Peace Treaty, 1918–1993] (1993).

The number of J.F. Verbruggen's articles in all chronological fields and genres of history is equally imposing.[9]

Such a bibliography is impressive. What is perhaps even more impressive than the numbers of works in his bibliography, is that so many of these books and articles have had a significant impact on historical scholarship. Several medieval military historians have learned the Dutch language solely to read Verbruggen's texts. Numerous libraries and interlibrary loan offices within them have been inundated by requests to find his less easily accessible books and articles. A Book Prize, for the Best Book in Medieval Military History, has also been established in his name by De Re Militari, the society of Medieval Military History. No serious medieval military historian can even begin to think about the subject without first acquainting themselves with his writings. It would be nice to see this translation as the beginning of a trend in academic publishing which would see the translation of the rest of Verbruggen's impressive literature. I remember, however, in talking with the late General Sumner Willard, who, together with Lady Southern, translated *The Art of Warfare in Western Europe During the Middle Ages from the Eighth Century to 1340*, that he had expressed a similar feeling when he first translated that book in 1977. So maybe it will not happen; but it should, and I would be happy to spearhead such an effort.

---

[9] Among Dr Verbruggen's current activities is his editorship of the journal of the Genootschap voor geschied- en oudheidkunde te Vilvoorde [Society for the History and Antiquity of Vilvoorde], which appears several times a year. He has also written a number of this local journal's issues, devoting his research and writing to many non-military events.

Editor's Introduction xv

Of course the question must be asked: why is this book translated here? Why translate a book written solely about what seems from the outset to be a relatively unimportant medieval engagement. Certainly, it does not carry the weight of an Milvian Bridge, Adrianople, Hastings, Manzikert, Bouvines, Crécy, or Agincourt. Or does it? Hopefully, I have answered that question at the beginning of this introduction. But if not, read on. Undoubtedly, you will understand what I, Dr J.F. Verbruggen, and numerous other medieval and military historians have: Courtrai, the Battle of the Golden Spurs, is incredibly important for the entire history of the later Middle Ages, especially for what was to follow between the Low Countries and France throughout the next two centuries, and, by extension, what was to follow between England, the Low Countries, and France during the Hundred Years War.

I know that should be the end of this introduction, but I cannot pass up the opportunity of adding a personal note. Although I had long come to know Dr J.F. Verbruggen through his bibliography on which I had feasted for more than two decades, it was not until I became involved in this project that I came to know him personally. I can truthfully say, through my correspondences and meetings with him, that there is no more astute and sharp a scholar and no more generous and kind a man as I have found anywhere in my dealings with fellow-academics. I have enjoyed his and his wife's hospitality, and I have profited from his intelligence and hard work.

Kelly DeVries
April 2002

Foreword to the 1952 Edition

Stripped of all simplistic romanticism, the Battle of the Spurs still retains its prime importance in our history. One barely needs to be reminded of this: it is something that every Fleming is aware of. The event also had far-reaching consequences for the course of world history: the hegemonic position that France had attained in Western Europe during the thirteenth century received its first powerful blow.

For those interested in the study of history, conceived, first and foremost, as an attempt to understand past events, such an unforeseen and, for those living at the time, almost unbelievable occurrence demands explication. And this presumes serious historical research. Certainly, much has been written about the Battle of the Spurs. Amid the works and articles in journals devoted to the subject there are some very thorough scientific contributions. A few have even opened the way for further study, among them two critical studies by Henri Pirenne and the two works by Victor Fris.[1] Nevertheless, many significant problems remained unsolved and certain conceptions of the events continued to be held as valid, even if difficult to reconcile with what is known of the art of warfare in the Middle Ages. Furthermore, our knowledge of the history of Flanders, France and the Low Countries in the thirteenth and fourteenth centuries has progressed markedly in recent years. Common perceptions concerning the Battle of the Spurs, and the events with which the battle is associated, need to be corroborated with results gained.

Dr J. Verbruggen had the courage to take up this most difficult task. His technical experience gained as an officer and his well-grounded knowledge of the sources and of scholarly contributions have enabled him to finally construct an acceptable version of the events. Dr Verbruggen was also aided by his equally well-founded knowledge of army organisation and tactics in the Middle Ages that has been demonstrated in a series of remarkable preparative studies. The work that he is now presenting to the public builds on new research into all the narrative and non-narrative sources, published or unpublished, and even on iconographic sources. The research has done full justice to the mutual relations between the accounts of the battle. This enables the authority of evidence given and information about the events to be determined with a degree of certainty or probability that has not been attained before. What is more, due to lengthy research on the tactics employed by cavalry and foot-soldiers in the Middle Ages, the author is better able

---

[1] Henri Pirenne, 'La Version flamande et la version française de la bataille de Courtrai', *Bulletin de la commission royale* [henceforth *BCRH*], 4th ser., 17 (1890), 11–50; Pirenne, 'La Version flamande et la version française de la bataille de Courtrai – Note supplementaire', *BCRH*, 5th ser., 2 (1892), 85–123; V. Fris, *De slag bij Kortrijk* (Ghent, 1902); and Fris, *Vlaanderens vrijmaking in 1302* (Ghent, 1902).

than his predecessors to understand and determine the various operations as well as localising them in time and space.

I believe that every Fleming – and for that matter even Belgian too – will be grateful to Dr Verbruggen for what he has achieved in making better known one of the most important as well as one of the most glorious events of our national history. However, I admit that I attach even more importance to the author's elucidation, through the completion of his task, of our knowledge of world history, as well as to his never deviating from the most strict standards of objectivity. He has remained true to that principle laid down by Cicero which remains the condition of any true history: *ne quid falsi dicere audeat, ne quid veri non audeat historia.*

Prof. Dr F. L. Ganshof

Acknowledgements
(to the 1952 edition)

Although many works have already been devoted to the Battle of the Spurs, much concerning the period 1297–1305 still remains unknown. There is, indeed, no complete scientific study of the war from the viewpoint of the history of Flanders. A French scholar, Funck-Brentano, dealt with this period in a lengthy work, *Philippe le Bel en Flandre*, that, unfortunately, approached the subject from the French perspective. Despite the overwhelming mass of documents of which this historian made use, the work was misconceived at the very outset. Funck-Brentano was too favourable to the King, part of whose activities he then related. What is worse, much about the conditions and circumstances of Flanders was either misunderstood or completely distorted. One suspects that his rash generalisations were, at times, intentional. Although many corrections to the work have already been published, numerous misapprehensions continue to have an insidious effect upon our own historiography.

Fully recapturing the history of Flanders' War of Liberation requires lengthy research. This is especially so, and ultimately essential, if one seeks to consult all unpublished documents on this period as well as taking account of the key aspects of life throughout the Principality of Flanders. Readers will be aware of the problems thrown up by the most well-known events in the war and will thus understand the work required in detailing the whole war. While elucidating the Battle of Courtrai here, in other works I have detailed the equally interesting battle that took place at Mons-en-Pévèle.[1]

This book approaches the subject from the viewpoint of military history. However, in order to draw up a scientifically valid work in this area, it was naturally not sufficient to limit myself to strictly military aspects. Readers will understand that my research has been undertaken as liberally as possible, since, ultimately, the army, and most of all the armed forces of 1302, presented a reliable picture of society at that time. The social circumstances of those living in that period must first be understood before making statements on the military aspects.

Some of the results of my research may perhaps appear surprising to many readers. I have always striven to reproduce this episode in history with the strictest objectivity. I have neither allowed myself to be led by any preconceived idea, nor by a socio-economic interpretation of the events, nor by any tendency to stress the

---

[1] Published as 'De slag bij de Pevelenberg (18 aug. 1304)', *Bijdragen voor de geschiedenis der Nederlanden* 6 (1952), 169–98 and *Het Leger. De Natie*, 7 (1952), 258–62, 338–42. [Translator's note: the Battle of Mons-en-Pévèle is referred to in Dutch as the Battle of Pevelenberg.] See also J. F. Verbruggen, *The Art of Warfare in Western Europe during the Middle Ages from the Eighth Century to 1340*, 2nd edn., trans. S. Willard and R. W. Southern (Woodbridge, 1997), 198–203.

role of specific figures. Furthermore, I have not kept overstressing the national importance or a national interpretation of the war. On several occasions in the course of editing, the sources employed obliged me to correct an earlier opinion as well as making significant changes to previous interpretations. I was confronted with very complex ideological movements and impelling forces in the minds of the combatants of 1302 that cannot be reduced to a simple schema. I have constantly endeavoured to avoid that danger referred to by Dr Blockmans as generalising in this 'fragment of convulsive Flemish life and strife of the past'.

There were already many works on the battle of 11 July 1302. Although I felt obliged to offer a different presentation of events from that given in such studies, it is undeniable that most of them were of great service to me. I was able to avoid certain mistakes as a result of predecessors dealing with the same problem. Thus, I apologise in advance for criticism given and am grateful for all the useful material I gained from the studies. I take complete responsibility for my own personal opinions and mistakes.

It is with great pleasure that I am able to thank all who helped me. My teacher, Prof. Dr F. L. Ganshof, agreed to enrich this work with his foreword, for which I am most grateful. I am, however, infinitely more indebted to him for the historical training he gave me as well as the sympathetic approach and encouragement with which he constantly followed and motivated my research. I was always able to rely upon his help in overcoming difficulties.

I have dedicated this work to Prof. Dr H. van Werveke, one of my professors at the University of Ghent. During his seminars he gave me a full initiation in the sources and works on the Battle of Courtrai. In addition to this, he took the trouble to carefully examine my preparatory studies and helped me by providing much useful additional material and ideas.

I am also much indebted to Prof. Dr J. Dhondt who continually supported me with advice and encouragement. The discussions that I had with him on the results of my research were always most beneficial to me.

I also thank Prof. Dr E. Strubbe who helped me on numerous occasions during my research in Bruges. His suggestions were of great importance to me.

At the Royal Military School I am, equally, very much indebted to Colonel S. B. H. H. Bernard, professor of military history. He gave me constant encouragement and all manner of support; and at the same time, he ensured that I had the necessary free time for research, and for revising and correcting this present work. I also give warm thanks for their willing help to my colleagues and friends, Captain A. Broekmans and Commander E. van der Molen, both tutors at the Royal Military School.

Dr Jos De Smet, assistant curator of the Algemeen Rijksarchief in Bruges, never failed to support me with his extensive and first-rate knowledge of the history of Bruges. Furthermore, he allowed me to make repeated and lengthy use of his copy of the unpublished town accounts of Bruges in the period prior to 1302. This was an invaluable help to me. Mr C. Didier, Master of Philosophy and Literature, permitted me to read his unpublished dissertation on the Bruges communal army. Thanks to his work, I immediately had at my disposal a solid basis that was of very

Acknowledgements (to the 1952 edition)

great service in my research into the army of the Count in Flanders. In identifying the coats of arms on the carved Flemish chest at New College, Oxford, I was always able to rely upon the willing help of Dr J. Bolsée, curator of the Algemeen Rijksarchief in Brussels. Mr Piétresson de St Aubin at the Archives départementales in Lille gave me much support with his customary willingness. At the Algemeen Rijksarchief in Ghent I was aided by my friends, Dr M. Gysseling and Dr C. Wyffels. In Bruges, I am much indebted to Mr R. A. Parmentier, curator of the town archives and his assistant, Mr A. Schouteet. In Courtrai, the librarian, Dr J. Soete, and his assistant, Mr J. M. Berteele, helped me in scrutinising the archives so badly damaged during the war. I am especially grateful to the town engineer, Mr J. M. L. Demeyere, who, in addition to many interesting details, provided me with two maps of the Groeninge stream. One map indicated the situation before 1950 and the second presented the current course of the stream. My friend, Mr H. Thomassen, teacher at the Royal Cadet School, took the trouble to read my manuscript and helped me with numerous corrections in language and form. I would like to thank all of them most heartily.

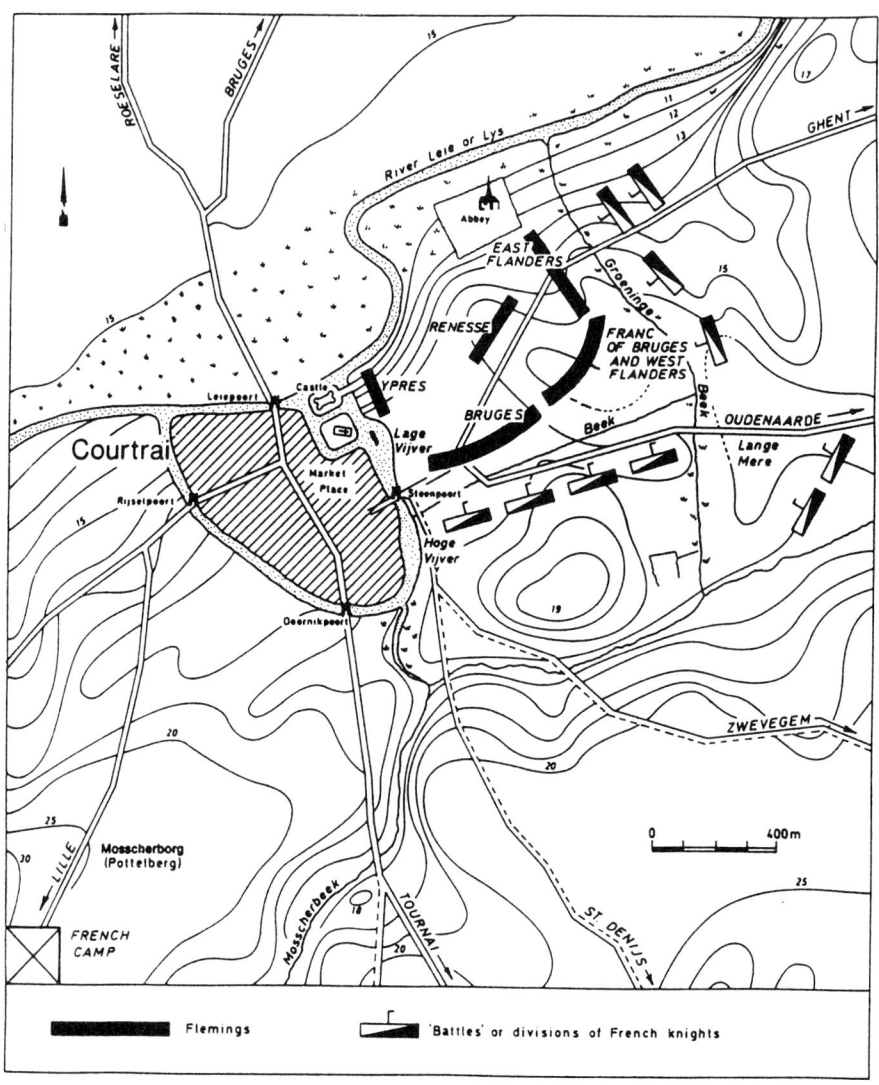

Plan of the battle of Courtrai

Preface: 'An almost impossible event...'[1]

On 11 July 1302, beneath the town walls of Courtrai, the most splendid army of knights in all Christianity, the flower of French nobility, was thoroughly defeated by Flemish rebels, by common workers and peasants. The superbly trained noblemen who had devoted their whole life to the military profession and were fully experienced in fighting on horseback in close ranks were led by an able commander, the Count of Artois, victor of various campaigns. They were defeated in three hours by men who had little experience of warfare and belonged to the lowest classes of society at that time, men who lived by the unremitting labour of their hands. This army of brave and robust workers – men with 'dirty fingernails': weavers, fullers, and peasants – all fighting on foot, was under the command of able leaders and possessed excellent weapons. They put a sudden end to the centuries-old myth of the invincibility of proud and wealthy knights. It was a major blow to the honour and glory of the French noblemen. They were the finest knights of that time, belonging to the most powerful state in Europe, and had not known defeat in the West since before their victory at Bouvines (1214).

'It was an almost impossible event' noted the Florentine banker, Villani, who deemed it necessary to detail closely this military exploit, as it was both new and remarkable.[2] When the news of the Flemish victory reached Rome, Pope Boniface VIII was awakened in the middle of the night to read the report.[3]

Not only was this most astonishing news recounted in Italy, but also in Tyrol, in Austria near the Swiss border, in Germany, in England and in Scotland. In England, the Flemish victory was even put to music in a folk song.[4] Memory of this splendid military exploit remained so vivid that when Scottish foot-soldiers crushed an English army of knights in similar circumstances at Bannockburn in 1314, two English chroniclers compared the victory to the Battle of the Spurs.[5] Sir Thomas Gray of Heton simply claimed that the Scots followed the example of the Flemings in fighting on foot at Bannockburn. Later, a third English chronicler,

---

[1] Giovanni Villani, *Historie fiorentine*, in *Rerum Italicarum Scriptores*, xiii, ed. L. Muratori (Rome, 1728), col. 388.
[2] Villani, cols. 388 and 391.
[3] Gilles le Muisit, *Chronique et annales*, ed. H. Lemaître, Société de l'histoire de France [henceforth SHF] (Paris, 1905), 68.
[4] There are several editions of this poem: Rossell Hope Robbins, *Historical Poems of the XIVth and XVth Centuries* (New York, 1959), 9–13; *Political Songs of England*, Camden Society, vi, ed. Thomas Wright (London, 1839), 187–95; *Chants historiques de la Flandre, 400–1650*, ed. Louis de Baecker (Lille, 1855), 161–72; and Monumenta Germaniae Historica, Scriptores [henceforth MGH SS], vol. 28 (Hanover, 1888), 496–9.
[5] Thomas Gray of Heton, *Scalachronica*, ed. J. Stevenson, Maitland Club, vol. 40 (Edinburgh, 1836), 142; and *Vita Edwardi Secundi Auctore Malmesburiensi*, ed. W. Stubbs, in *Chronicles of the Reign of Edward I and Edward II*, Rolls Series, 2 (London, 1883), 206.

who had a clear view of the evolution of the art of warfare, likewise referred to the similarity of the Battle of the Spurs to the Battle of Bannockburn.[6] Furthermore, the superb Liégeois historian, Jean le Bel, placed Benevento (1266), Courtrai (1302) and Crécy (1346) as being on a par with respect to the great number of princes killed in a day.[7]

In this time and age it is only with difficulty that an idea can be formed about the effect of this glorious event upon the minds of the impressionable people of that period. In countries that were not involved in the war it was noted mockingly, and with thinly disguised pleasure, that the honour and glory of the illustrious French knighthood had sunk dramatically.[8] 'The shame of this shall last for centuries!'[9] It was an immense loss of prestige for the mighty kingdom.

In France itself amazement and despair dominated. In 1300 one of the most adamant supporters of the policy of conquest, a royal advocate, had written a treatise aimed at shortening the wars against neighbours and rebellious vassals: 'One cannot believe that a prince, now alive and in possession of full powers of comprehension, would dare lie in wait for the royal army in order to enjoin in pitched battle. This would be even less the case with a count or lord who knows the knightly army of France.'[10] However, around 1305, the same advocate, Pierre Dubois, was to remark 'I do not believe that a person with full powers of understanding could believe it possible today, for a single prince to rule the whole world, and for everyone to obey him. If one were to strive for this then innumerable wars, rebellions and disputes would break out and it would be impossible to control them.'[11] Between 1300 and 1305 a great deal had occurred: the county of Flanders, having been seized, had its own prince once again. The defeat of 11 July 1302 had made the French leadership so uncertain that, for the time being, they avoided battles in the open field. They retreated on several occasions without fighting (at the end of September 1302 and on 10 July 1303) and, finally, had a battle forced upon them at Mons-en-Pévèle (18 August 1304).

---

[6] Geoffrey le Baker, *Chronicon*, ed. E. M. Thompson (Oxford, 1889), 7–9. On this subject see Sir Charles Oman, *A History of the Art of War in the Middle Ages*, 2nd edn (London, 1924), II:113; T. F. Tout, *The Place of the Reign of Edward II in English History*, 2nd edn (Manchester, 1936), 226; and the same author's understanding of developments in military strategy, 'The Tactics of the Battles of Boroughbridge and Morlaix', *English Historical Review*, 19 (1904), 225.
[7] J. le Bel, *Chronique*, ed. J. Viard and E. Depréz, SHF (Paris, 1904–5), II:109.
[8] Villani, col. 388.
[9] Petrus de Langtoft, *Ex Chronico Rythmico*, ed. F. Liebermann, in MGH SS, 28 (Hanover, 1888), 660.
[10] Natalis de Wailly, 'Mémoire sur un opuscule, intitulé: Summaria Brevis et Compendiosa Doctrina Felicis Expeditionis et Abbreviationis Guerrarum ac Litium Regni Francorum', *Mémoires de l'Académie des inscriptions et belles-lettres*, 18.2 (1855), 441; and Paris: Bibliothèque nationale, MS Lat. 6222c, ff. 5–5v.
[11] Pierre Dubois, *De Recuperatione Terre Sancte. Traité de politique générale*, ed. C. V. Langlois, in Collection de textes pour servir à l'étude et à l'enseignement de l'histoire [henceforth CTEH], 9 (Paris, 1891), 54. For the quotations see also L. Delfos, *1302 door tijdgenooten verteld* (Antwerp, 1931), 79, 111 n. 58.

Thus, it is not surprising that immediately following the events a French explanation of the terrible defeat arose that was intended to save the honour and glory of French nobility. In Flanders the great victory was glorified and presented as a just reward for the boldness of the townsmen and the competence of the commanders. In both camps preparations were under way for further battles and it was most important that all subjects were made to contribute. Both opponents, therefore, presented the events in the most favourable light in such a way that victor and vanquished contradict each other at times. Unfortunately there were no witnesses who could have functioned as adjudicators in this awkward dispute by resolving the matter on account of their authority.

However, this famous battle does not just pose problems for military and national history. The battle is a milestone, politically and socially, which secured the autonomy of Flanders. In the towns the patricians lost power and democratic government was instituted. Furthermore, the great victors of 11 July were, without a doubt, the lowly members of the guilds. By then they were accustomed to defending their rights with weapons in their hands, and, as time went by, they increasingly resorted to them if they were not able to attain their goals by other means. Later, social disturbances were to take on a more bloody character as a result of this.

The Flemish revolt and the Battle of Courtrai had both a direct and indirect influence on such matters in other principalities in the Low Countries. In Tournai, in cities in Brabant, in Liège: everywhere the guildsmen sought recognition as political bodies as well as a say in the administration of the towns. Weavers in Tournai corresponded secretly with those in Ghent and Lille. In Namur, a charter was granted to the butchers, thus recognising the trade. There were revolts in Brabant, in Brussels, Louvain, Zoutleeuw and 's Hertogenbosch with the common people coming to power for a while.[12] In Liège the sons of the patricians were called the 'enfants de France'; the Leliaarts of Flanders, those Flemish supporters of the King of France, and the Liégeois tradesmen rebelled against the collection of a tax.[13] Finally, the Flemish invasion of Holland (1304) brought the guilds to power in Utrecht,[14] this being an indirect consequence of the victory of 11 July 1302.

The Battle of the Spurs, as such a surprising and tumultuous event, gave rise to contradictory accounts and explanations. Due to its national, political and social importance one should, in approaching explanations given by those living at the time, pay careful attention to the personality of the chronicler, to his nationality, to his political and social conceptions as well as to his personal sympathies.

Even today scholars do not completely avoid such manifold influences in illustrating the importance of the battle or in judging its political effects and deter-

---

[12] See, among others, Hans van Werveke, 'De steden', in *Algemene geschiedenis der Nederlanden*, II:414.
[13] F. Vercauteren, *Luttes sociales à Liège (XIIIe et XIVe siècles)* (Brussels, 1943), 66, 70; and Vercauteren, 'Het prinsbisdom Luik tot 1316', in *Algemene geschiedenis der Nederlanden*, II:348–9.
[14] Van Werveke, 'De steden', 414; and J. F. Niermeyer, 'Het sticht Utrecht en het Graafschap Holland in de dertiende eeuw', in *Algemene geschiedenis der Nederlanden*, II:304–5.

mining the numbers of participants from the different classes in society at that time. As a result, a difficult problem arises over historical methodology, not only with respect to the sources, but also to the historical works.

This work will proceed as follows: a general introduction will detail the circumstances prevalent in the county of Flanders at the end of the thirteenth century, the war between Guy de Dampierre and Philip the Fair and the rebellion of 1302. Following this, the battle at Courtrai will be examined. A first part will discuss the historical studies devoted to the battle, and the sources available. After listing the chronicles, the work will explore how accounts given by those living at that time were examined and used by historians from the end of the nineteenth century until the present day: how they were interpreted; how a critical account was drawn up on the basis of the information they had acquired. This will lead to an account of the approach taken in researching this subject. At the same time, the reader will gain insight into the nature of historical sources as well as the difficulties with which a researcher is confronted when using chronicles from the Middle Ages.

Following the examination of the methodologies used by predecessors and an explanation of the current method of research, a detailed study will be given of the sources looking at how a Flemish and French version of the battle arose. Subsequently, each source is examined separately.

The second part looks at the history of the events of 1302. The terrain at Courtrai, the composition and numerical strengths of both armies, the events following the Bruges Matins (18 May 1302) until 11 July, or the first phase in the war of liberation of 1302, will be examined. Finally, the culminating point of the campaign will be analysed: the Battle of the Spurs. This is then followed by a general conclusion.

Introduction

Flanders at the End of the Thirteenth Century

From the tenth century to the beginning of the fourteenth century, Western Europe experienced steady progress in all spheres of the economy. The population grew steadily, thus increasing the number of both consumers and workers, as well as encouraging trade and industry. At the beginning of the period, almost all of the population lived from agriculture and was settled in the countryside; at the end, a considerable number lived in the towns. Trade and industry had grown markedly since the eleventh century, giving rise to increased prosperity in which the inhabitants of the small towns, villages and countryside shared. Land was continually being won from the sea, marshes drained, desolate ground and pasture cultivated. Where once there had been forests, there was now arable land; much progress had been made in agriculture. These four centuries of continual advance did have their crises: famines, epidemics, floods, and so on, but the disasters were, nevertheless, limited geographically and could not interrupt the general course of progress.

The fourteenth century contrasted sharply with this. Repeated famines and epidemics devastated the whole of Western Europe. A widespread famine arose in 1315 and raged until 1317. The Black Death claimed thousands of victims from 1347 until 1351. Only a few regions avoided the direct consequences of such disasters. The general crisis that thus arose was felt everywhere. Unlike in earlier periods, there was no growth in population, not even in the towns; and scarcely any new arable land was won.[1]

All indicators point to the fact that the economy, at the end of the thirteenth and beginning of the fourteenth century, had reached its highest point of development with the limited technical means which artisans and farmers possessed at that time. It is during this period of prosperity that Flanders experienced one of the most important phases in its history.

General conditions in the county of Flanders

The favourable geographical position, the industry of its people and the enterprising spirit of its merchants ensured for the county of Flanders, under the wise government of several powerful princes, a very special position in Western Europe. It became an example of a land with towns comparable to Italy, a situation not to be found elsewhere north of the Alps. Ghent and Bruges were among the largest towns of that time, second only to Paris. Having their origins in a first enclosure, of eighty hectares in Ghent and seventy hectares in Bruges, both towns grew by the late thir-

---

[1] E. Perroy, 'Les Crises du XIVe siècle', *Annales: économies, sociétés, civilisations*, 4 (1949), 167–82; and H. van Werveke, 'Inleiding', in *Algemene geschiedenis der Nederlanden*, II:xi.

teenth to early fourteenth century to towns of, respectively, 644 hectares and 430 hectares. From an earlier population of a few thousand, the number of inhabitants increased by the middle of the fourteenth century – or even, it appears, by the end of the thirteenth – to 56,000 in Ghent and 36,000 in Bruges. There may even have been somewhat more than 36,000 inhabitants in Bruges, since the figure for the middle of the fourteenth century was heavily influenced by the high death rates in 1316. In Ypres the population was estimated at 20,000 to 30,000 at the beginning of the fourteenth century.[2]

The five larger Flemish towns, Ghent, Bruges, Ypres, Lille and Douai, owed their prosperity to commerce and industry. Precious types of woollen cloth were produced and exported to five major areas: England, the Rhine region, north Germany, the east of France and Italy, the west of France and the Iberian peninsula. From there the splendid materials were distributed to a great part of the world as known at that time. At the end of the thirteenth century, important changes took place in the trading activities of Flemish merchants. Occasionally, they were pushed to the side by foreign merchants who came to collect the woollen cloth themselves or brought wool to Flanders. In comparison with the thirteenth century, Flemish merchants in the fourteenth century travelled much less frequently to far-away regions.[3]

This did not stop there being a great degree of prosperity in Flanders at the end of the thirteenth century as a consequence of the cloth industry. Primarily located in the five major towns, the industry also allowed smaller towns to flourish and, furthermore, was widespread throughout the countryside. Woollen cloth was, during these centuries, one of the most particular export articles, and was in demand everywhere. In addition, Flemish towns possessed an advantage in that they were complementary in the production of various types of cloth and did not compete with each other. At the same time, production was carefully controlled by the town authorities, ensuring that materials possessed a highly regarded quality. Continual emphasis was placed on the fact that the cloth ought to contribute to the town's honour. However, towards the end of the thirteenth century, Flanders gradually lost the great lead it had enjoyed over other principalities in the Low Countries. The cloth industry and the manner in which trade was conducted were of great social and political influence.

---

[2] F. L. Ganshof, *Over stadsontwikkeling tusschen Loire en Rijn gedurende de middeleeuwen*, Verhandelingen van de Koninklijke Vlaamsche Academie (Antwerp, 1941), 44, 58; van Werveke, 'De steden', 402; van Werveke, 'Het bevolkingscijfer van de stad Gent in de veertiende eeuw', in *Miscellanea L. van der Essen* (Brussels, 1947), 345–54; van Werveke, *De omvang van de Ieperse lakenproductie in de veertiende eeuw*, Mededelingen Koninklijke Vlaamsche Academie (Antwerp, 1947), 13; J. Demey, 'Proeve tot raming van de bevolking en de weefgetouwen te Ieper van de XIIIe tot de XVIIe eeuw', *Belgisch tijdschrift voor philologie en geschiedenis*, 28 (1950), 1040; and J. De Smet, 'L'Effectifs des milices brugeoises et la population de la ville en 1340', *Revue belge de philologie et d'histoire*, 12 (1933), 636.
[3] Van Werveke, 'De opbloei van handel en nijverheid', in *Algemene geschiedenis der Nederlanden*, II:417–26.

The social and political consequences of trade and industry

The influence of the cloth industry upon town life in Flanders was so great that artisans working in the wool industry constituted more than half the male population in predominantly industrial towns such as Ghent and Ypres. In a trading centre such as Bruges, where merchants from many nations met, wool artisans – weavers, fullers, wool shearers and so forth – made up approximately one third of the male population. The emergence of such a class of specialised artisans also encouraged the development of other crafts whose members worked to fulfil local needs – they included the bakers, butchers, carpenters and so on. Alongside this, in certain towns, the shipping industry developed, and its importance grew to the extent that Flemish merchants were increasingly less likely to sell their goods themselves in distant regions; they preferred to entrust the precious cargo to shippers. Bruges also flourished with brokerage which was the most important craft after the weavers and fullers in terms of numbers employed in it.[4]

During the course of the thirteenth century the people, referred to as the *gemeen*, the commoners, attained an ever greater degree of prosperity and became aware of its power in the towns. Accordingly, they came into conflict with the political rulers, the patricians who, at the same time, were their employers and often their landlords. Such rich burghers (*poorters*) owed their privileged position in law to full rights of ownership of part of the town territory, such as Ghent, or to the fact that they belonged to the merchants' guild, such as the London Hanseatic league in Bruges. At the end of the thirteenth century, one would have to include those burghers who possessed three hundred pounds, although five hundred pounds was required in Ypres.[5] This privileged class had succeeded in making the office of alderman hereditary among its members. They did not just possess power with respect to the town administration, but also to the regulation of work and production. Almost all of them were not only merchants, but also entrepreneurs. As merchant-entrepreneurs the patricians employed workers in the wool industry. They provided the wool that was used by artisans, and subsequently took back the cloth produced to sell it. Workers were mere wage labourers. A merchant-entrepreneur used all means available to hold prices at a minimum, while keeping down wages and exploiting workers. On occasion, stones were put in the wool sacks so that workers would not receive the amount of material ordered and could not deliver the desired quantity of cloth. At times, the wool at the bottom of the sack was of lower quality than that at the top. Merchants sometimes paid workmen in kind, with wool, grain and other products. Some workers only received part of their wages with complaints made by workers going unheard as town judges belonged to the

---

[4] Van Werveke, 'De steden', 408–9; and J. A. van Houtte, 'Makelaars en waarden te Brugge van de 13e tot de 16e eeuw', *Bijdragen voor de geschiedenis der Nederlanden*, 5 (1950), 1–30, 177–97.

[5] F. Blockmans, *Het Gentsche stadspatriciaat tot omstreeks 1302*, Rijksuniversiteit Gent: Werken uitgegeven door de Faculteit Wijsbegeerte en Letteren, no. 85 (Antwerp, 1938). See also J. De Smet, 'Rond een Brugs poortersgeslacht van de XIIIe eeuw', *Biekorf*, 51 (1950), 10–11.

patrician class. It was sufficient for the merchant to reject the complaint under oath in order to ensure that the proceedings were unsuccessful.[6]

The lower classes were economically exploited, did not have any say in political matters, and had no access to a just judicial system. In addition to this they were obliged to pay the greater part of the taxes levied to finance town expenditure that was managed by patricians who never gave account of the monies spent. Town taxes weighed heavily upon consumer goods: 'My lord', said the members of the commonalty at Damme in 1280, 'the *assise*, or tax, weighs heavily upon bread, wine, beer and mead . . . for this reason the poor people who have to earn their living by labour pay more than the rich.' Such a taxation system had already been in operation for fourteen years at Damme. The rich had only been paying a tax for two years on their income or on their business activities as merchants.[7] Moreover, the lower classes accused patricians everywhere of being quite arbitrary in their use of taxes collected.

This resulted in social unrest in 1280, not only in Flanders, but also in Tournai (as early as 1279) and in the Brabant towns from 1280. Everywhere the lower classes, who had become more powerful, sought to throw off the hated yoke. They strove for control over the town finances, for participation in the administration and the establishment of their professional associations as recognised bodies with political power.

The patricians maintained their position for a time, although in the period 1270–1300 they were confronted with many difficulties. Abroad they were gradually pushed out of the local markets, that is in England and north Germany, as well as experiencing difficulties at the annual fairs of Champagne. Within their own circles they faced opponents who did not belong to those families that had appropriated the office of alderman, as in Ghent. Furthermore, the richest members of the lower classes wanted to be admitted to the privileged class. Merchant-entrepreneurs had to cede part of their activities, the production of cloth, to cloth-makers, often weavers who had become wealthy. At least in Ypres they formed a class between the common people and the patricians.[8] Moreover, politically, the patricians were forced to come to terms with the Count of Flanders who sought to make his own power felt in the towns themselves, subjecting them to closer control.

At the same time as the patricians were being confronted with such difficulties, artisans became more closely associated with each other and, by means of professional associations, they strove to attain political and military power. Over time they gained limited rights to gather under the supervision of patricians who were

---

[6] Blockmans, *Het Gentsche stadspatriciaat*, 249; van Werveke, 'De steden', 404; C. Wyffels, *De oorsprong der ambachten in Vlaanderen en Brabant*, Verhandelingen Koninklijke Vlaamse Academie (Brussels, 1951); and Wyffels, 'Les Corporations flamandes et l'origine des corporations de métier', *Revue du nord*, 32 (1950), 202.
[7] Ant. De Smet, 'De Klacht van de "Ghemeente" van Damme in 1280', *BCRH*, 115 (1950), 9.
[8] Van Werveke, 'De steden', 405; Demey, *De Vlaamse ondernemer in de middeleeuwse nijverheid*, 3–6; and van Werveke, *De koopman-ondernemer en de ondernemer in de Vlaamsche lakennijverheid van de middeleeuwen*, Mededelingen Koninklijke Vlaamsche Academie (Antwerp, 1946), 10–16.

appointed by the town magistrate. A parallel development was that of the increasing military organisation of the artisans. Previously the communal army had been subdivided according to areas of the town. From 1280 onwards, at least in Bruges, dues paid by new apprentices, artisans and masters in the guilds of the cloth industry were used to make and maintain tents and banners.[9] Guilds thus received their own insignia which were a means of bringing members together and encouraging group consciousness. It is here that the origins can be found of the new organisation behind the communal armies as well as the base of their military power.

The situation in the countryside
In the countryside, nobility still played a prominent role. The castles of the more important noblemen looked down upon the villages around them and their power was still very significant. Knights and squires formed a privileged caste that was, however, not completely closed in Flanders. And, indeed, one notes that the Count, Guy de Dampierre, also knighted persons who were not noblemen, thus ennobling them, even though such a practice was forbidden by the King of France.[10] Still, at the end of the thirteenth century, the economic situation of the nobility was not very promising. Since the beginning of the century they had experienced numerous financial problems, and the golden era had already passed by the second half of the twelfth century. The number of knights had sunk dramatically and most members of the nobility were merely squires. At the same time, however, population growth of other social classes had been marked. A knight was still a distinguished person at the end of the thirteenth century, and he very often held a village from the Count as part of the fief. Thus, one notes that, at the beginning of the fourteenth century, the Lord of Gruuthuus had an annual income of 1140 Parisian pounds from the fiefs held from the feudal court of Bruges. The Lord of Praat had an even higher income.[11] In 1297, the knight, Gerald de Moor, Lord of Wessegem, joined the Count's army with seven horses representing a value of 960 Parisian pounds.[12] They were, however, wealthy noblemen. Bailiff Simon Lauwaerd, who was robbed of his possessions by Count Guy de Dampierre, had a fortune estimated at 4149 pounds. This equals that of the richest Brugeois burghers at the same time. One may assume an annual income of two to five hundred pounds for a normal knight although many squires had to survive on a hundred pounds or less. Poorer noblemen who entered the Count's service as bailiffs sought to raise their income

---

[9] Wyffels, *De oorsprong der ambachten*, 99.
[10] P. Thomas, *Textes historiques sur Lille et le nord de la France avant 1789*, Bibliothèque de la société d'histoire du droit des pays flamands, picards et wallons, II (Lille. 1936), 230–6.
[11] J. De Smet, 'Le Plus Ancien Livre de fiefs du Bourg de Bruges vers 1325', *Tablettes des Flandres* (1950), 7. However, for the Lord of Praet, see Register 45.925, Brussels, Rijksarchief, ff. 3–3v.
[12] J. de St Genois, *Inventaire analytique des chartes des comtes de Flandre . . . autrefois déposées au château de Rupelmonde* (Ghent, 1843–6), nos. 902, 263, with the incorrect value of 240 pounds instead of 140 pounds for one of the horses. The total equalled 1200 pounds *tournois* or 960 pounds *parisis*.

by extorting money from local inhabitants. The numerous complaints against bailiffs at the end of the thirteenth and the beginning of the fourteenth century provide clear proof of this.[13]

Aside from a few rich families, the nobility could only just live in the fashion of rich patricians from the towns. It is not surprising then that one notes marriages between daughters of rich burghers and young noblemen as well as daughters of nobles who also married burghers.[14]

Politically, the Flemish nobility had a less important role to play. This had been the case from 1128 onwards, and only sporadic increases in power are to be noted in the following period. Some noblemen had somewhat more power as counsellors to the Count. Bailiffs also had influence as officials while other noblemen functioned as aldermen in the castellanies.

The importance of the nobility lay, however, in the military sphere: as a heavily armoured cavalry, the noblemen formed the principal part of the Count's army until 1300 and militarily they had the full confidence of the Count. Nevertheless, the old feudal system was in full decline. Fiefs had been carved up, except those of more important lords, and many vassals did not themselves have to perform military duties. Very often a vassal only had to provide a horse of minimal value. Thus, one also notes, in 1297 military service of knights and squires took place at the expense of the Count. Even important vassals received considerable payments. This, however, led to a new incentive for numerous knights and squires to join the Count's army. It was then possible, once again, as in the twelfth century, to raise an army of almost a thousand noblemen in Flanders.[15]

In the second half of the thirteenth century some noblemen accompanied Guy de Dampierre on his crusade with St Louis to Tunis,[16] Robert de Bethune in the army of Charles of Anjou[17] and Guy de Dampierre in the crusade to Castile (1276), or took part in the expedition to Aragon (1285).[18] It increasingly became a custom for Flemish noblemen to serve in the army of the French King. This was the case, among others, for Robrecht van Wavrin, Lord of St Venant, who fought in Aquitaine in 1296 and became seneschal of Guyenne. Gilbert, Viscount of St Winoksbergen, also fought in the French army at this time.[19]

In the countryside one must also take account of the free men, not just the nobility. Serfdom had, to a great extent, disappeared in Flanders. There were still

---

[13] H. Nowé, 'Les Baillis comtaux de Flandre', *Académie royale de Belgique, Classe des lettres, mémoires*, 25 (1929), 82–3, 86, 426 ff.
[14] J. De Smet, 'Le Plus Ancien Livre', 8.
[15] J. F. Verbruggen, 'Le Problème des effectifs et de la tactique à la bataille de Bouvines (1214)', *Revue du nord*, 31 (1949), 186.
[16] For this see J. Buntinx, *Het memoriaal van Jehan Makiel*, Commission royale d'histoire [henceforth CRH] (Brussels, 1944).
[17] See, among others, le Muisit, 8.
[18] In *Recueil des historiens de France* (henceforth RHF), 22, ed. N. de Wailly and L. Delisle (Paris, n.d.), 688, 692, 696, 700, 703.
[19] F. Funck-Brentano, *Philippe le Bel en Flandre: les origines de la guerre de cent ans* (Paris, 1896), 220 and n. 1; and F. Lot, *L'Art militaire et les armées au moyen âge en Europe et dans le proche orient* (Paris, 1946), I:248.

serfs in the Land of Aalst and the Land of Termonde, but in a colonised area such as maritime Flanders, with its polder areas won back from the sea, the local population was practically free. There they developed into a peasant class that, for a long time, had been known for their coarse manners and tumultuous behaviour. This character expressed itself clearly during the great rebellion of 1323–8. The area was heavily populated and had to be constantly protected against the sea. The peasants had attained a high degree of self-administration, especially since the nobility, due to the economic crisis, lost some of its earlier power. Still, the material circumstance of such peasants, although comparing well with that of farmers in other principalities, was less attractive than that of artisans in the towns.

Land was mostly in the hands of noblemen, burghers and the abbeys. At the end of the thirteenth century one mainly finds the tributary system. Peasants paid rent per year, in money or kind, for the land they farmed. In addition to this, there was the 'helftwinning' system, or half-tenancy, where the lord paid part of the costs and then received half of the harvest. Furthermore, there was 'tenure' or hereditary land (*hereditas*): the land was hereditary, but death duties had to be paid. The peasant could also sell the land, but then had to pay a transfer fee. Duties were listed in detail, and hereditary land was in fact very similar to property. Furthermore, the number of peasants who had, in the mean time, acquired land as their own property increased in this period. Still, their number remained small.

Although there were improvements in agriculture, techniques remained rather rudimentary. For this reason grain had to be imported into a heavily populated area such as Flanders. The three-field system was most common in the county. Farmland was divided into three parts with one being used for intensive cultivation (wheat, winter cereals), the other for less intensive cultivation (spring or summer cereals) with the third part being left fallow. The following year land left fallow the previous season would be used for intensive cultivation and so on. In the thirteenth century, however, fallow land began to be used in Flanders to grow foodstuff for animals, above all turnips. The soil improved as a result and at the same time this enabled animals to be kept in the sheds and stables in winter time which in its turn produced more animal waste that could then be used to make the land more fertile.[20]

From the events of 1302 to 1304 one sees that free peasants, as well as artisans from the towns, were wealthy enough to purchase sturdy weapons and that they were very able-bodied.

In addition to agriculture, the fishing economy should also be noted; this was found above all on the western coast. It lent prosperity to the following towns in the twelfth and thirteenth centuries (given here in order of the importance in 1324): Nieuwpoort, Dunkirk, Blankenberge, Ostende, Gravelines, Lombardzijde, Mardijk. Along the River Zwin the smaller towns were, more or less, trading ports in earlier

---

[20] L. Voet, 'Het Platteland maatschappelijk en economisch', in *Algemene geschiedenis der Nederlanden*, II:472–82. See also F. L. Ganshof, 'Medieval Agrarian Society in its Prime. France, the Low Countries and Western Gerrmany', in *The Cambridge Economic History of Europe*, I (Cambridge, 1942), 278–322.

times. According to order of importance, they were as follows: Sluys, Aardenburg, Damme, Oostburg, Monnikenreede, Hoeke and Muide. And along the River Honte there were these towns: Hugevliet, Biervliet, Boechoute, Axel and Hulst.[21] At the same time, villages, such as Kieldrecht and Saaftinge had become so important, as early as 1304, that together they were able to provide 68 shipmasters and sailors with 16 small ships for the war fleet.

Shipmasters from the coastal area of the Zwin river, and along the Scheldt, were, in 1303 and 1304, to form the fleets, powerful for that time, used in waging the war in Zeeland and Holland.[22] In 1302 they were to help defend the northern border of the county while the armies on the southern border fought against the King of France.

Count Guy de Dampierre and his policies
Guy was already forty-nine years old when, in 1278, he became Count of Flanders. From his first marriage, to Mathilde of Bethune, he had eight children, and from his second marriage, to Isabelle of Luxembourg, there were as many surviving children. The Count had acquired the seigniory of Bethune as well as having bought the county of Namur. Therefore, he was justified in considering himself to be the most powerful and richest prince in the Low Countries. As father of this family, he had succeeded in finding good matches for most of his children: the eldest, Robert, Lord of Bethune, was to succeed Guy as Count of Flanders; Willem became Lord of Termonde and of Crèvecoeur, marrying a daughter of the French family, de Nesle; Baldwin died in 1296; John became bishop of Liège (1282–91); Philippe married an Italian princess, becoming the Count of Chieti and of Loreto; Margaret married Jan I, Duke of Brabant; Beatrice married Floris V, Count of Holland; and Maria married Willem, Count of Jülich. Two of Maria's sons were to sacrifice their young lives for Flanders: Willem van Jülich, the elder, died in 1297 after the Battle of Furnes, and Willem van Jülich, the younger, became the hero of 1302 and fell in the Battle of Mons-en-Pévèle (1304). And the children from Guy's second marriage: Jean de Namur, margrave of that principality; and Guy de Namur, with both playing a very significant role in 1302; Henry, Count of Lodi; Margaret, first married to the son of the King of Scotland and then to Reinout, Count of Guelders; Johanna entered a cloister; Beatrice married Hugues IV of St Pol; Philippina was engaged to Edward II of England, although afterwards she was kept captive at the French court; Isabella married the Viscount of Broekburg. Three children from this second marriage died at a tender age.

The actual character of Guy de Dampierre remains somewhat mysterious. As of yet, no complete study has been devoted to him or his government. The Count certainly thirsted for power: all his policies point in this direction. He was also easily tempted to use violence, with Ghentenaar aldermen experiencing this on several occasions. He could be sly and cunning, at times clearly acting in bad faith,

---

[21] R. Degrijse, *Vlaanderens haringbedrijf in de middeleeuwen*, De Seizoenen, 49 (Antwerp, 1944), 24.
[22] J. F. Verbruggen, *Vlaanderen na de Guldensporenslag* (Bruges, 1991), 41–8, 79–102.

among others against Floris V of Holland in 1290.[23] He also cannot be absolved of the charge of being self-seeking, since he constantly strove to fill his treasury. Thus he imposed heavy fines after the uprising in Bruges in 1280 and 1281 which for the most part fell upon the lower orders of his then allies. In order to make a financial gain as well as to win the favour of the King of France, he was very brutal in introducing the fiftieth penny in his principality. Guy was enraged at Philip IV when he seized goods of the Lombards in the county in the face of Guy's entitlement to such returns.[24] He distanced himself from his earlier ally, Reinout van Guelders, by meticulously stripping bare the county of Guelders that had been, temporarily, placed under his administration. This finally drove Guelders into the arms of Philip the Fair.[25] Even though he knew perfectly well that he disadvantaged his subjects by forbidding the importation of English wool, he was nevertheless extremely vigilant in executing the royal decrees since he profited personally from them.[26] After taking out large sums in loan from the Artesian money-lenders, the Crespins, he appealed to the Pope to have himself dispensed from interest on the loan, as the Church regarded all interest as usury.[27]

Guy did not have an accurate idea of what actually formed the power base of his state. As did most feudal princes of his time, he did not understand what could be gained from the lower orders. He was not very favourable to these classes, even though he often presented himself as their ally, abandoning them as soon as he could reach an agreement with the patricians who were financially profitable for him. At the beginning of the war, to a large extent he made an accommodation with the lower classes. But in 1298, as soon as he thought that the advantages gained were not proportionate to what he had granted, he wrote to his sons, asking them to attempt to gain the Pope's permission for him to retract those previously given concessions.[28]

After he had so often allowed himself to be ensnared by the King's shrewder politics, Guy himself was very cunning in deciding to engineer a breach of contract by his lord. He succeeded in having the law on his side by causing a denial of justice to be effected: Philip IV had not allowed him to bring his dispute before the peers of France, thus breaking the Treaty of Melun (1226). During the armistice negotiations in Rome (1299), his representatives very skilfully appealed to the Pope. They noted that he was a refuge against kings who did not recognise any power other than their own, and that the Pope possessed the ultimate power with the right to remove the King of France and the emperor of the Holy Roman Empire

---

[23] H. Obreen, *Floris V, Graaf van Holland en Zeeland, Heer van Friesland (1256–1296)*, Université de Gand, Recueil de travaux publiés par la Faculté de philosophie et lettres, fasc. 34 (Ghent, 1907), 129–43.
[24] See Guy's declaration to the King in Kervyn de Lettenhove, *Histoire de Flandre* (Brussels, 1847), II:563, 565.
[25] Niermeyer, 267–8.
[26] Funck-Brentano, *Philippe le Bel*, 134–5.
[27] Ibid., 79–80.
[28] Ibid., 245; and Delfos, *1302 door tijdgenooten verteld*, 98 n. 16.

from their thrones.[29] This appeal to the Pope was only to bear fruit in 1302 when Philip IV came into conflict with Boniface VIII.

As seen above, Guy de Dampierre cannot simply be seen as a martyr, as a victim of Philip the Fair. As far as can be known, and that only provisionally due to insufficient knowledge about his personality, the Count had much responsibility in the failure of his politics, both in Flanders and abroad. Still, there is also the question about how far Guy felt he was obliged to act as he did as a result of the lack of financial resources for his responsibilities as prince.

Indeed, various suggestions have already been made, indicating that the counts of Flanders in the thirteenth and fourteenth centuries no longer had access to sufficient resources to finance the growing expenses of their state. They continually had to ask for grants from the towns and, for this reason, Guy sought to make his power felt in the five larger towns. The Count took out loans almost everywhere: in Arras, from his towns, his knights, merchants and so on. Very often his towns took out loans in his name or their own, albeit still for the impoverished Count. Naturally, this grew even worse during the war. However, one should not go too far in this direction. Guy's policies required enormous sums of money that very often led to pure squander. This was the case with the numerous money-fiefs, or *fiefs-rentes*, granted to important French noblemen who, of course, did not support him during the war.[30]

At home, Guy strove to bring the towns increasingly under his control. The five larger towns were practically independent from the Count, as far as the town administration was concerned, since the benches of aldermen had become hereditary. Guy wanted to oblige aldermen to give account of their administration of town finances. This was one of the demands of the common people who had made serious complaints against mismanagement by the town administration in Ghent in 1275. At that time, together with his mother, Guy administered the county. As soon as he had removed the aldermen from office, despite the charter of Count Ferrand of 1226, they appealed to Philip III who set up an investigatory committee which came to the conclusion that only eight aldermen had abused their power and, therefore, not all of them could be removed.[31] The Ghent aldermen were divided into three groups of thirteen. Two of them occupied in turn the two active aldermen's benches, while the third group remained out of office. They were constantly appealing to the King.

During the uprisings of 1280–1, Guy was able to increase his power in Bruges,

---

[29] Funck-Brentano, *Philippe le Bel*, 328–9; Fris, *Vlaanderens vrijmaking in 1302*, 98; and Delfos, *1302 door tijdgenooten verteld*, 13.

[30] For the numerous money-fiefs given by Guy de Dampierre to French and other foreign vassals see, among others, D. J. Godefroy, *Inventaire chronologique et détaillé de toutes les chartes qui se trouvent dans les archives des comtes de Flandre déposées dans l'ancienne chambre des comptes du Roy à Lille*, manuscript at the Archives départementales du nord, Lille, vols. IV–V.

[31] H. van Werveke, 'Avesnes en Dampierre. Vlaanderens Vrijheidsoorlog, 1244–1305', in *Algemene geschiedenis der Nederlanden*, II:313–14; and Fris, *Vlaanderens vrijmaking in 1302*, 44–5.

Ypres and Douai. At the same time he did not show much political competence since he not only imposed heavy fines in Bruges, but also refused to renew the charter of town privileges that had been destroyed by the fire in the belfry in 1280. The Count only returned them in 1297 in order to have the town on his side in the war against Philip the Fair. It was, by then, too late.

Guy de Dampierre against Philip the Fair

In 1285 a new King came to the throne in France, Philip IV, the Fair. This brought a change in the policy of French kings with regard to Flanders. Until that time, kings had not interfered much with internal matters. Interference now became the standard, and it constantly put Guy de Dampierre at a disadvantage. Intervention on the part of the King was made possible by the actions of the thirty-nine Ghent aldermen as well as Guy's inept conduct.

In fact, both princes followed the same policies, each in his own principality. While the Count wanted to increase his authority in Flanders, above all in the five larger towns, the King wanted to impose his authority upon the two powerful fiefs left: Flanders in the north and Guyenne in the south-west, held as a fief by the King of England. However, was it the intention of Philip IV to annex and fully absorb the county? Was it not sufficient for him to have his authority recognised by the Count and the towns?

This last position has, indeed, been defended by French historians. They view Philip the Fair as a feudal prince who did not intend to annex the larger fiefs. For him, it was sufficient that his authority was recognised and that his officials were able to carry out exact control. Such officials did, at times, go further than the King desired.[32] A variety of elements is seen as pointing to the fact that Philip was actually still a feudal prince; hence, one may ask, to what degree were his policies his own? He was surrounded by lawyers, legal counsellors of minor nobility who sought to introduce royal absolutism on the basis of Roman law. Philip the Fair had full confidence in those advising him: Pierre Flote, Guillaume de Plasian, Guillaume de Nogaret, Enguerrand de Marigny. They remained in power as long as he ruled, with all being low characters with no conscience. They did not shrink from falsification, and any means were good if they could lead to the realisation of their goals. Guillaume de Nogaret even went so far as to arrest Pope Boniface VIII at Anagni on 7 September 1303 during the Pope's conflict with Philip the Fair. These jurists carried out policies that barely showed any feudal characteristics.[33] During the negotiations with Pope Boniface VIII in 1298, the Pope asked Pierre Flote, delegate of Philip IV and Keeper of the Seals: 'You have taken Normandy from the King of England, yet you want to take all that he has [in the kingdom of France].' Pierre Flote answered: 'Surely, Sir, you speak truth.'[34] At Tournai in

---

[32] See, among others, E. Perroy, *The Hundred Years War*, trans. W. B. Wells (Oxford, 1951), 43–4.
[33] F. Lot, *La France des origines à la guerre de cent ans* (Paris, 1941), 151, 160.
[34] R. Fawtier, 'L'Europe occidentale de 1270 à 1328', in *Histoire générale*, ed. G. Glotz (Paris, 1940), 325; and J. Favier, *Philippe le Bel* (Paris, 1978), 231.

September 1311, Marigny declared that the King had been unnecessarily merciful in giving back Flanders to the Count – a manifest traitor. Someone speaking for the King, probably Marigny, told the delegates of the towns of Flanders: 'Let the people remember the fate of the Duke of Normandy and the Count of Toulouse, greater men than the Count of Flanders, who lost their lands because they defied the King.'[35]

French historians write that Philip IV had no intention of annexing Aquitaine and Flanders. But they can find no good reason for the war in Aquitaine and cannot explain why the King returned Aquitaine to the King of England. These historians cannot explain it, because their analysis is not complete and is biased. Philip IV changed his plans: he realised that he had made a big mistake. The King had not been told that his policies were wrong. In August 1304, Philip IV knew that he had won the battle at Mons-en-Pévèle by good luck, that he was nearly killed and that it was better to make peace and give Flanders back to the Count. There is sufficient evidence that the King was striving for annexation. Flemish and Brabantese chroniclers were convinced that the King wanted to annex Flanders as part of the royal territory. Furthermore, from 1300 to 1302, when Flanders was under French control, the King did not appoint a new prince but merely representatives. Everywhere he acted as a direct or immediate sovereign.[36]

Jacques de Châtillon was 'garde de par nostre sire le roi de sa terre de Flandre', 'guardian in the name of our Lord the King of his country of Flanders'.[37] The King did not just occupy the part of Flanders that belonged to the kingdom of France. The small garrisons in the castles and fortresses of Flanders were paid by the King; most of the soldiers were French. Three big new castles were erected by the King at his own cost, at Bruges, Courtrai and Lille in 1300, but the castle at Bruges was never finished. In 1302 the new castle at Courtrai received a garrison of 334 persons and was strong enough to hold out against besiegers from 23 June until 13 July 1302. The castle of Rupelmonde held out until November 1302. The Flemings of that time regarded the occupation of the county as an annexation and reacted accordingly. This is above all what matters, since Philip IV did not expose his personal plans. The fact that the government of Philip the Fair was no longer feudal is also indicated by the strong reaction on the part of the French nobility and burghers at the end of the reign and following the King's death in 1314. This was also a consequence of the many 'osts de Flandre', royal expeditions against the Flemings: two 'osts' in 1302, one in 1303, an 'ost' and a fleet in 1304, an 'ost' in 1312, 1313, 1314; and, under his sons, in 1315, 1316, 1318, 1319. Such an 'host sans rien faire', an army that did not dare give battle, gave rise to anger and indignation among the French burghers and chroniclers.

Philip IV 'had an acute, probably too acute, sense of his royal dignity'. His reign marks the culmination of the medieval French monarchy. From 1285 to 1314, all

---

[35] J. R. Strayer, *The Reign of Philip the Fair* (Princeton, 1980), 340–1.
[36] For Lille see R. Monier, *Les Institutions centrales du comté de Flandre* (Paris, 1943), 102. See also van Werveke, 'Avesnes en Dampierre', 327.
[37] Funck-Brentano, *Philippe le Bel*, 356 n. 1.

his enterprises were executed with an extraordinary constancy, leading to an increase of the royal might and the destruction of the persons, groups and institutions that opposed or obstructed it. To attain these results, all means were good: obstinate war against the Flemings till the end of the reign, and spectacular trials, well ordered, the accused going from interrogation to torture, accused of sorcery, heresy, crimes against nature, and eventually going to the stake.

Everything points in the direction of a French policy of expansion. From the tenth to the twelfth century the kingdom of France had lost territory to the Holy Roman Empire during a period of weakness. Now these areas were being taken back, among others Ostrevant to the west of the Scheldt, from the Count of Hainault; elsewhere the Meuse River became the border once again: in the county of Bar those areas that lay on the left bank of the river. This was also the case with Lyon on the left bank of the Saône River.[38] The power of the King was in fact so great that, in 1300, Pierre Dubois suggested subjecting the whole world to the rule of the French king. Even later, he was still an advocate of a union of peoples under the leadership of Philip IV.[39] For Jan van Heelu, the Brabantese chronicler, the King was 'the most noble and powerful man to be found in the world'.[40] Territorial expansion, above all into those larger fiefs still in existence was thus completely in line with the development of the kingdom. Anything else ought to provoke astonishment. French influence had indeed already progressed so far in the Netherlands that, in 1289, Philip the Fair settled the dispute between Jan I of Brabant and Reinout van Guelders.[41]

Guy de Dampierre was defeated by Philip IV everywhere.[42] It began with the conflict between the Count and the thirty-nine Ghent aldermen, with this dispute dragging on until the definitive break. As early as 1289, there was a royal representative in Ghent who had to protect the city against the Count's arbitrariness. The latter tried in vain to settle the dispute by putting the matter, with the agreement of the thirty-nine aldermen, to the aldermen of St Omer (1290). Nevertheless, somewhat later (1291), Philip IV declared this to be invalid.[43] In that year, a new conflict arose concerning the presentation of the town accounts. Guy took several aldermen captive, sending them to Holland. Further intervention by the King and his parliament did not, however, resolve the problem (August 1292).[44]

Following this, the patricians in the town of Valenciennes rebelled against Jean d'Avesnes, Count of Hainault. Guy de Dampierre hoped to conquer part of

---

[38] Lot, *La France des origines*, 153–4.
[39] Dubois, *De Recuperatione Terre Sancte*, 54 and the introduction.
[40] H. Pirenne, *Histoire de Belgique* (illustrated edition) (Brussels, 1948), I:164.
[41] Funck-Brentano, *Philippe le Bel*, 115–16.
[42] F. Blockmans, *1302 vóór en na: Vlaanderen op een keerpunt van zijn geschiedenis*, De Seizoenen, 9 (Antwerp, 1941), 26–34. For the following pages see also H. Nowé, *La Bataille des éperons d'or*, Collection Notre Passé (Brussels, 1945), 26–44.
[43] Funck-Brentano, *Philippe le Bel*, 118–19.
[44] J. Vuylsteke, *Uitleggingen tot de Gentsche Stads- en Baljuwrekeningen, 1280–1315*, ed. V. van der Haeghen and A. van Werveke, *Oorkondenboek der stad Gent, 1e afd.: Rekeningen*, II (Ghent 1906), 26–31; Funck-Brentano, *Philippe le Bel*, 122–3; van Werveke, 'Avesnes en Dampierre', 319.

Ostrevant and Valenciennes, since Philip had advised the rebels to turn to the Count of Flanders. In fact, the King had set his eyes on Ostrevant, something that Guy had not understood, and that was to lead to all his labours failing.[45]

In the meantime, the Count waged war, in 1290 and 1292, against Count Floris V of Holland who wanted to wrest Zeeland to the west of the Scheldt river from feudal dependency on Guy. In April–May 1292, he had talks with Edward I of England in order to put an end to the innumerable maritime disputes between fishermen and shipmasters from both countries. However, in 1293 he went a step further: negotiations were begun that, on 31 August 1294, led to the engagement of Guy's daughter, Philippina, to the future Edward II of England. But England had been at war with France since 12 May 1294, and thus Guy had engaged his daughter to the son of the enemy of Philip the Fair. The French King intervened: Guy was held captive in Paris and had to hand over his daughter.[46] From this time onwards Philippina remained at the French court, dying there in 1304.

Guy succeeded in reaching an agreement with the thirty-nine aldermen in Ghent, but this occurred to the disadvantage of the common people who appealed to the King themselves. The King then supported the common people against the Count and the aldermen.[47] At the same time, Philip sent fresh guardsmen to Ghent, tightened the prohibition on trade with England and had his decrees with regard to money strictly followed. Such decrees forbade the circulation of foreign currencies in Flanders, this being very negative for trade in the county. Furthermore, the King imposed a higher exchange rate for his own currency than it was worth.[48] Guy protested heavily, and this time Philip the Fair made a few small concessions on 6 January 1296 that were used to make a fool of the Count. Guy de Dampierre was to collect a fiftieth of all his subjects' possessions, receiving half of the sums collected. The bait was sufficient to have the Count mishandling and using violence against defiant taxpayers. He went so far that the citizens of Bruges, Lille, Douai and Ypres proposed paying the tax to the King. Philip greedily accepted, pocketing the money behind the Count's back. Of course, he did not share the returns, although he ordered the Count to pay back those sums he had already collected in the above towns. He even tried to take half of the returns in Ghent since, as a result of the ruling of 6 January 1296, the thirty-nine aldermen had been suspended and Guy had already collected the tax.[49] The King reinstated the thirty-nine aldermen in their offices, allegedly on Guy's request, although Guy together with the common people protested immediately. Philip retorted by deposing the Count from his position of authority in Ghent and by once again sending a French official to the town.[50]

In the meantime, royal policies were also successful abroad, even though he had

---

[45] Van Werveke, 'Avesnes en Dampierre', 317–18.
[46] Ibid., 319–20.
[47] Vuylsteke, 31–9.
[48] Funck-Brentano, *Philippe le Bel*, 128.
[49] Vuylsteke, 39–48, 58–62.
[50] Ibid., 62–5.

taken Ostrevant from Jean d'Avesnes, the King still possessed a powerful trump card: Valenciennes. From this point onwards, the Count of Hainault gradually went over to the French side: in 1295 he negotiated between the King and Floris V of Holland, who succumbed to French gold, leaving the English camp on 9 January 1296.[51] This happened three days after the King's agreement with Guy, and Philip made a pact with his vassal's enemy. Floris was murdered five months later by Dutch noblemen with Guy de Dampierre and Jan II of Brabant, as well as Edward I of England appearing to be involved in the conspiracy.[52]

Jean d'Avesnes also became an ally of Philip the Fair as soon as the latter had returned the town of Valenciennes to him. Nevertheless, the townspeople appealed to Guy who hoped to be able to keep the town based on the agreement of 6 January 1296. Once again, the Count had the experience of having proclaimed his rights too early: Philip forbade the five more important towns from allowing their militias to serve in the Empire.

For the umpteenth time, Guy had to appear before the King's parliament, obliged to transfer Valenciennes to the King who then returned the town to Jean d'Avesnes. Officially, however, the alliance of Philip IV with Hainault was only concluded in May 1297. On 28 August 1296, the parliament repealed any minor privileges that Guy had obtained on 6 January. In the presence of delegates from the Flemish towns the Count was even obliged to transfer possession or the *weer* of the five larger towns to the King. However, this time Guy demanded that a decision be made by the French court of peers and refused to reply any more since, in fact, his county was no longer in his possession. Four towns were then returned to him, but the King kept Ghent for himself. Guy's decision, however, had been taken: his request for the jurisdiction of the Court of Peers had been rejected, which could be invoked in breaking the feudal ties with his prince. In September 1296, after a further summons, he did not appear. The threat of an alliance with Edward I was clearly present in 1294 following the engagement of his daughter, Philippina. It now became reality. On 7 January 1297, the alliance was made, and on 9 January he broke with Philip IV.

The War

Guy's renunciation of feudal ties of 9 January 1297 was transmitted to the King on 20 January. The letter listed the numerous complaints of the Count and pointed to the losses caused by the currency decrees and hindrance to trade. Guy also pointed to the fact that the refusal of the King to allow him to appear before his equals, the peers of France, had freed him from any feudal obligation. This was very important since relations between Flanders and France were then governed by the Treaty of Melun (1226), stipulating, in the event of a rebellion on the part of the Count, that Flemish vassals and subjects were to support the King. However, this was only

---

[51] Van Werveke, 'Avesnes en Dampierre', 322–3.
[52] Niermeyer, 295–6.

applicable if the prince had submitted the dispute to the court of peers. Philip the Fair understood perfectly well that Guy de Dampierre had the law on his side and put exceptional effort into eliminating such valid grounds. As early as 18 February, royal envoys were in Courtrai, proposing the settlement of the dispute by the Court of Peers. By that time, however, the Count rejected the untimely concession.[53]

Preparations began being made on both sides for an armed conflict. With only a few exceptions, Flemish noblemen rallied to Guy's side. Indeed, during the first military operations, a number of those who would later support the French King, the 'Leliaarts', were to be found in the Count's army. The defection of the King's Flemish allies, the Leliaarts, only commenced following the capitulation of Lille and increased according to the prospects of the King winning.[54] As soon as Philip IV had conquered part of Flanders, he began to let his power be felt: there were numerous confiscations of estates belonging to Guy's supporters, the so-called 'Liebaarts'. Such estates, used as guarantees together with French gold, could induce pro-French sentiments in former supporters of the Count. Gradually, supporters of the King of France in Flanders grew in number. Still, despite what has generally been assumed until now, they never formed the majority of Flemish noblemen.[55] Most of them remained loyal to Guy even if, at certain moments, there were rather significant numbers of defections.

Aside from his alliance with the King of England and support he expected from King Adolph of Nassau, Guy had also engaged many knights from the Rhine area and from Brabant. An undated document, probably from the first half of 1297, shows that he was by that time counting on 602 heavy horsemen who had already been paid. He hoped to increase this number to 732. Furthermore, the Count also tried to engage another 490 heavy horsemen from the same region, as well as from Luxembourg and Namur. The extent to which the noblemen had strengthened his army cannot be determined for the moment. However, there are numerous indications that he had at his disposal over six hundred allies, perhaps even more.[56]

As to the position of the towns, much, perhaps even everything, depended on the town magistrates. Thus Guy took steps here, replacing pro-French aldermen with those favourable to himself. At the same time, he granted concessions to demands made by the common people. This was the case in Ghent where some of the thirty-nine aldermen were able to escape, although the remaining aldermen were arrested. Their property was seized and in part divided among noblemen favour-

---

[53] Van Werveke, 'Avesnes en Dampierre', 323–4; Nowé, *La Bataille des Éperons d'or*, 44–5; and Funck-Brentano, *Philippe le Bel*, 209.
[54] See in this respect the numerical strengths of noblemen at the Battle of Courtrai in chapter II.
[55] This is based on research into the political persuasion and convictions of noblemen in the period 1297–1304. Relevant information on approximately five hundred noblemen has been gathered, and a concise overview is given in the numerical strengths of noblemen as of 11 July 1302 in chapter II.
[56] This document has been published in L. A. Warnkoenig and A. E. Gheldolf, *Histoire de la Flandre et de ses institutions civiles et politiques jusqu'a l'année 1305* (Brussels, 1835–64), II:516–18, no. 36. However, the publisher omitted the interesting text which indicated who had already been enrolled and paid and who had not. The text is to be found in the Archives départementales at Lille, Chambre des comptes, B. 1266, 235.

able to the Count.⁵⁷ The Count finally returned and extended the privileges in Bruges. There, some burghers were arrested, but it cannot be known whether he replaced the aldermen by others.⁵⁸ In Douai, pro-French aldermen were replaced by men favourable to the Count.⁵⁹ Thus, the Count had good control of his towns with Lille, Douai, Ypres and Ghent continuing to support him, although in Bruges the plans went amiss. However, in the mean time, Philip the Fair had gained the support of the Pope, who promulgated an interdict on Flanders. Guy appealed to Rome, and the measure was rescinded.

In waiting for the King of England, who had not yet arrived with his army, the Count attempted to maintain control of his more important towns: Lille, Douai and Ypres were prepared for defence. The royal army lay siege to Lille, and a division under the command of Robert d'Artois defeated one of the Count's armies at Furnes. On 1 September, Lille was forced to surrender; one of the conditions of the surrender was that the noblemen could choose the party of the King or of the Count. From this point onwards, the number of Flemish noblemen who supported the King grew rapidly.

In the meantime, Edward I had arrived in Flanders with an army of 670 heavy horsemen and around seven thousand foot-soldiers. The number of noblemen was rather low, since the English King was in conflict with the noblemen at that time.⁶⁰ In Bruges, Edward took note of the fact that the town magistrates had little desire to defend the town, even though an obligatory loan had been collected in June 1297 for fortifications.⁶¹ The town magistrates did not accept a proposal made by the English King to share in the fortification costs.⁶² Following this, Edward left for Ghent where he helped the town in strengthening its defences.⁶³

After his conquest of Lille, Philip the Fair and his army advanced deep into Flanders. He reached Ingelmunster on 7 September. He then held back somewhat, waiting for the reaction of his enemies who, nevertheless, did not dare engage in open combat. However, even though they had not been attacked on 18 September the men of Bruges sent representatives to Ingelmunster concluding an agreement with the King of France.⁶⁴ The French took Bruges as well as the port, Damme. In the town, men loyal to the King were in power so that the French could act in line with the town.⁶⁵ Brugeois aldermen, who previously had done nothing for the

---

⁵⁷ Blockmans, *Het Gentsche stadspatriciaat*, 363–7, 512–15.
⁵⁸ C. Wyffels and J. De Smet, *De rekeningen van de stad Brugge (1280–1319): Eerste deel (1280–1302)*. CRH (Brussels, 1965), I:561.
⁵⁹ G. Espinas, *La Vie urbaine de Douai* (Paris, 1913), I:232–7.
⁶⁰ N. B. Lewis, 'The English Forces in Flanders, August–November 1297', in *Studies in Medieval History Presented to F. M. Powicke*, ed. R. W. Hunt (Oxford, 1948), 311–13.
⁶¹ Wyffels and De Smet, I:524–35, 578–94.
⁶² Funck-Brentano, *Philippe le Bel*, 259–60.
⁶³ Lewis, 315 n. 2. These labours began on 12 September, with several workmen whose numbers, on 21 September, had grown to four hundred, working under four masters.
⁶⁴ Gilliodts-van Severen, I:54 n; Wyffels and De Smet, I:551–3; and Funck-Brentano, *Philippe le Bel*, 260–1.
⁶⁵ T. de Limburg-Stirum, *Codex Diplomaticus Flandriae (1296–1325)*, Société d'émulation (Bruges, 1878–89), I:329, no. 140.

Count, now began to build the fortifications of their town. Until the moat was complete, iron chains were placed in the narrow streets as a means of protection against attacks by the Count or by the English.[66] They sent auxiliary troops to Damme; very cleverly the King of France had a thousand pounds distributed among the guilds, and subsequently crossbowmen and tradesmen left for Damme to defend the town against the Count. By 22 September, 25 crossbowmen had left; on 25 September, 56 crossbowmen and as many helpers; on 3 October, 131 crossbowmen and 24 helpers, 69 weavers, 62 fullers and 34 shearers. All of them were paid by the town itself.[67] In Damme, however, the Count still had loyal followers including, among others, Clais de Leu, Dierk f. Dierk, Willem de Witte and Peter Winne. On 10 October they helped the Count and the English troops in retaking the town, which had not been sufficiently fortified. Following this, they were appointed aldermen.[68]

With this, the military operations ended. An armistice was concluded, eventually being prolonged until 6 January 1300 due to mediation by the Pope. The Pope brought about a peace agreement between the two kings which, however, did not include Guy, despite efforts made by Flemish envoys sent to Rome. Philip the Fair with his gold had almost completely won over the papal court for the French cause. The paltry resources available to Flemish envoys were insufficient. When change came in papal politics towards the end of 1299, as a result of the alliance between Philip the Fair and Albert of Austria, it was too late for Guy de Dampierre and Robert de Bethune.[69]

In Holland and Zeeland Guy also lost his ally. The son of the murdered Floris V, Jan I, was at first under the authority of Jan van Renesse, who ruled with the help of the English. Later, however, Wolfert of Borselen took power until he was murdered on 1 August 1299. Since Count Jan I died shortly afterwards, on 10 November, Jean d'Avesnes, Count of Hainault and the most direct heir, subsequently acquired both Holland and Zeeland.[70] Guy de Dampierre and his successor, Robert de Bethune, now stood alone while the French sphere of influence had spread to include Hainault, Holland and Zeeland.

When the period of armistice came to an end, on 6 January 1300, the situation in Flanders was desperate. Douai surrendered immediately: and indeed the town had been completely isolated. With the help of Bruges, Charles of Valois besieged Damme whose fall brought with it the surrender also of the other towns along the Zwin river. Ghent was also forced to capitulate, while Ypres, under the command of

---

[66] After the town defences had been fortified sufficiently, the chains were removed: Wyffels and De Smet, I:560: 'pro cathenis per vicos in villa amovendis, 3 lb. 10 s.' For the use of chains in Tournai during the construction of defences in 1295, see le Muisit, 39: 'Et tunc facte sunt cathene et posite in vicis ubique, ut in necessitate tenderentur.'
[67] Wyffels and De Smet, I:551–3.
[68] De Limburg-Stirum, I:329, no. 140; and Funck-Brentano, *Philippe le Bel*, 268–9.
[69] Funck-Brentano, *Philippe le Bel*, 280–304, 327–9; and van Werveke, 'Avesnes en Dampierre', 326–7.
[70] Niermeyer, 300–2.

the young Guy de Namur, held out the longest.[71] Guy de Dampierre, Robert de Bethune, Willem of Termond, Lord of Crèvecoeur and a hundred or so noblemen who had remained loyal to the Count surrendered.[72] They were imprisoned in French castles.

Philip the Fair: Prince of Flanders

The occupation of a substantial part of Flanders in 1297 and the ensuing armistice in 1298 and 1299 had given rise to the most trying circumstances in the county. While Guy de Dampierre paid or compensated those who had remained loyal to him with the scarce resources at hand, Raoul de Nesle, the King's governor of the occupied parts, seized his supporters' properties. This fell heaviest on nobles and other followers of the Count, and the camp of those favourable to the King of France consequently grew just as the number of those favourable to the Count declined. There were various noblemen, for example Baudoin d'Auberchicourt and the squire, Rogier van Oxelaere, who were first robbed of their possessions until they surrendered unconditionally to the King and joined the French.[73] Flanders had, then, been completely conquered, and Flemish noblemen became direct vassals of the King as the prince of Flanders whom they were obliged to serve.

Furthermore, much confusion had arisen in the countryside. Land seized by the Count from noblemen favourable to the French was, in the mean time, being farmed by peasants. During the first armistice such noblemen, the Leliaarts, carried out incursions into their former estates[74] and returned as the great victors in 1300. They took revenge, not only upon those loyal to the Count, relatives of imprisoned noblemen, but also upon the peasants, who were much oppressed.[75]

In the towns, the French were faced with even thornier problems. How were they to settle the conflict between the common people and the patricians without speaking of the differences between the pro-French aldermen (Leliaarts) who had returned and their successors? The dispute between the masses and the rich burghers would in any case flare up once again. The commoners had indeed not overly devoted themselves to the Count's cause in 1297 and 1300. At most they helped in the defence of towns such as Ghent, Ypres and Damme where the garrisons were, however, for the most part composed of noblemen. Furthermore, one even notes that in 1298 Guy de Dampierre was not alone in being disappointed with the attitude and reactions of the common people. On 22 April 1300, his son Willem also complained bitterly about the commoners of the Land of Waas and of

---

[71] Funck-Brentano, *Philippe le Bel*, 333–4.
[72] See the numerical strength of the two armies found in the list in chapter II.
[73] *Les Journaux du trésor de Philippe le Bel*, ed. J. Viard, in *Collection de documents inédits sur l'histoire de France* (Paris, 1940), 188, c. 1171; Funck-Brentano, *Philippe le Bel*, 304 n. 3; and E. de Coussemaker, 'Confiscations dans la Flandre maritime', *Bulletin du comité flamand de France*, VI (1872–5), 111, 146–7.
[74] De Limburg-Stirum, I:238–9, no. 86.
[75] *Annales Gandenses*, ed. and trans. H. Johnstone (London, 1951), 11–12.

Beveren who did not wish to join the defenders of Damme.[76] Still, the lower orders did participate, and this appears most importantly in Bruges where in 1297 artisans grouped together in their guilds, taking part in the defence of Damme on the French side. In 1300, they also took part in the conflict, thus improving their organisation. It can be assumed that the communal army already had the organisation that was to become characteristic in the fourteenth century.[77] The commoners had thus gained an excellent weapon, becoming even more conscious of their power than previously.

To this one should add that all the towns had incurred enormous costs for their fortifications, for payments to Flemish and foreign knights and so on. Town debts had, in this manner, increased disturbingly. How were they to be settled? According to custom, this was normally effected, above all, by the masses, due to the nature of the taxes. Ypres and smaller towns, such as Furnes, and even Pamele, were also punished by the King for their opposition,[78] or for leaving the French and joining the Flemish camp as at Damme.[79]

The new governor, Jacques de St Pol, known as Jacques de Châtillon, was therefore faced with a difficult task. However, reference is rightly made to the fact that the King could not actually find any suitable governor in his entourage as French noblemen did not understand the social circumstances of the Flemish towns nor did they speak the language. They also had too many prejudices against the lower orders to be able to understand their aspirations.[80] Moreover, Jacques de St Pol took over in a situation which had been seriously aggravated by his predecessor, Raoul de Nesle. Although confiscation of the property of noblemen ceased, many knights were still in prison in France. Flemish nobles who supported the King persecuted their families and oppressed the peasants. Since St Pol gave support to the pro-French noblemen he was soon not overly popular in the countryside.[81]

Finally, one ought not to overlook the fact that the imprisonment of the old Count Guy, and his successor, Robert, would lead to many grievances being forgotten, since they did ultimately form the legal authority in the county. The common people regarded them as martyrs, and there were soon rumours that the King was being deceitful to them by annulling the favourable conditions that had been granted by his brother, Charles of Valois.[82] The defeat of a powerful prince provoked much sympathy on the part of the people whose bonds of attachment to the Count and family were thereby strengthened. As for the more cultured, national

---

[76] De Limburg-Stirum, I:297, no. 116.
[77] J. F. Verbruggen, 'De organisatie van de militie te Brugge in de XIVe eeuw', *Handelingen société d'emulation de Bruges*, 87 (1950), 170.
[78] Funck-Brentano, *Philippe le Bel*, 363–4.
[79] Ibid., 355–6.
[80] Van Werveke, 'Avesnes en Dampierre', 328.
[81] *Annales Gandenses*, 12–13.
[82] This misconception can be found in later sources: le Muisit, 58; Villani, col. 363; *Istore et croniques de Flandres*, ed. Kervyn de Lettenhove, CRH (Brussels, 1879–80), I:223 n. 2; *Chronographia Regum Francorum*, ed. H. Moranvillé, SHF, 3 vols. (Paris, 1891–7), I:87–8; *Chronique normande du XIVe siècle*, ed. A. and E. Molinier, SHF (Paris, 1886), 15. See also Delfos, *1302 door tijdgenooten verteld*, 101 n. 21.

sentiments were certainly heightened: Master Gilbert van Outere probably wrote the following as early as 1297:

> Flanders, once guided by an auspicious star,
> Now unrigged by storms, a drifting wreck,
> Flanders, that once glittered with opulence,
> Now sunk and mourns in mire and ash,
> Flanders, that was always able to rule,
> Now resembles a slave in rags!
> How deep have you fallen!
> And still! We hope that you will stand up once again and will find solace. Say with us: Let it be so!
> . . .
> France rejoices! But times change, Fate is but an unsettled thing.[83]

This is not to say that a Flemish rebellion was unavoidable. An able administrator would have been able to make good very many things. However, the King of France appears not to have had much confidence in Flemish sentiments and, as early as 1300, he began, at his own cost, to construct fortresses in Lille, Courtrai and Bruges.[84]

What was extraordinary about the uprising is the fact that it began in a town, Bruges, that as of 18 September 1297 stood on the side of the King. The fact that Ypres did not rebel is understandable: the town had at least made a thorough effort, and Robert de Bethune had shown his gratitude for this.[85] It was then punished very severely with an enormous fine of 120,000 Parisian *livres* and an annual tax of 3000 Parisian *livres*.[86] The patricians were both richer and more powerful in Ypres than in other Flemish towns which meant that the common people could be kept under control. Ghent did not lead the rebellion due to a series of events as well as to actions on the part of St Pol.

One year after the conquest, the King and Queen visited Flanders. They were given a splendid reception in Ghent, where the patricians spent an enormous sum on the festivities. The commoners welcomed and cheered the prince, beseeching him to abolish the tax on beer and mead. Philip conceded this with the noble gesture of a King in high spirits during his glorious entry. The town council, however, were horrified, wondering how they could ever pay back the town debts without such a tax.[87] When the Bruges town council heard this, they forbade the common people from making such a plea to the King upon pain of death. The commoners were so displeased with the prohibition that they did not wish to cheer the King, keeping silent while attending the ceremonies. This appeared to have been most remarkable for the King. After the King had left, the burghers wished to

---

[83] Delfos, *1302 door tijdgenooten verteld*, 19. See MGH SS, 25:547.
[84] *Annales Gandenses*, 16. Even before 18 July 1300, land had been expropriated in Bruges: Godefroy, V, no. 4315.
[85] Funck-Brentano, *Philippe le Bel*, 337 n.
[86] Ibid., 363.
[87] *Annales Gandenses*, 12–13.

have the town pay for the new clothes which they purchased for the royal visit while the common people would have to pay for their own clothes themselves. This led to protest and disturbances provoked by a weaver, Pieter de Coninc.[88]

> Pieter was small in stature and of lowly origins. He had, as weaver, always been obliged to earn his living and had never possessed more than 10 *livres*, nor had anyone else in his family. Still, he was well-spoken and could speak so eloquently that it appeared as a wonder. For this reason he was held so dearly by the weavers, fullers and shearers (the principal guilds of the drapery) that his wishes were law for them.[89]

The Brugeois burghers and aldermen, however, sought by means of an artful trick to silence the commoners, instilling fear in the hearts of the trouble-makers. They advised the royal bailiff, Pieter du Breucq, a Flemish follower of the King of France, to imprison Pieter de Coninc and twenty-five other leaders in the Steen, the former prison of the Count that had become a royal prison. The people saw this as a direct provocation, and took up arms, freeing Pieter and his followers. Order was re-established, although the commoners feared the evil intentions of the rich burghers.[90]

Jacques de St Pol, however, regarded the riots as *lèse majesté*, since the royal prison had been broken open. With the help of a Flemish supporter of the King, the knight, Jan van Gistel, he contrived a plan against the guildsmen. The rich burghers were to attack the commoners in the town, following a given sign, then open the gates to let in St Pol with an army of five hundred knights. The plan failed. The guildsmen took up their weapons just in time and subsequently defeated the burghers. Jan van Gistel fled and Jacques de St Pol did not dare enter the town with his small army. The event took place on a Thursday in the middle of July 1301.[91]

The governor then called upon his brother, the Count of St Pol, for help in drawing up a powerful army consisting of Flemish noblemen and patricians from other large towns. However, an agreement was concluded: those guilty were banished from the town and could never return. Pieter de Coninc and his followers left, and St Pol subsequently entered the town. He immediately had several of the gate towers demolished, gates removed, the town ramparts broken down in several places and a section of the moat filled. After this he made a much more important decision: all privileges were to be rescinded,[92] with Bruges having to deliver 468 hostages to be imprisoned in Tournai.[93] There were among the hostages five

---

[88] Ibid., 13.
[89] *Chronique artésienne et chronique tournaisienne*, ed. F. Funck-Brentano, CTEH, 25 (Paris, 1899), 37–8.
[90] *Annales Gandenses*, 13–14.
[91] Ibid., 14–15.
[92] Ibid., 15–16. The Flemish noble and supporter of the King, Baudouin de le Planke, led the work of demolishing the fortifications: *Journaux du trésor*, 780, c. 5361.
[93] L. Verriest, 'Le Registre de la "Loi" de Tournai, de 1302 et listes des otages de Bruges (1301) et de Courtrai', *BCRH*, 80 (1911), 485 ff.

pro-French burghers and two sons of the pro-French party, as well as eleven burghers favourable to the Count.[94]

The punishment was disproportionate to the offence, and St Pol's severe response gave rise to a general feeling of discontent among both the burghers and the commoners. The Bruges town council, which was composed almost entirely of Flemish supporters of France, appealed to the King in vain.[95] Immediately following this the council also appealed to the King's parliament where previously it had always won out against the Count.[96]

A simple dispute between commoners and burghers, normal in the period between 1280 and 1297, gave rise to a serious crisis whereby the governor alienated himself from a town that had taken the French side since 1297. Jean de Namur and his brother, Guy, took note of this, both having retreated to their county of Namur. Together with a nephew, Willem van Jülich the younger, who had lost his brother in Flanders in 1297, they began to make plans. During the winter they sent representatives to Flanders, establishing contacts with those favourable to the Count and succeeded in having Pieter de Coninc and his followers returned to Bruges. Immediately, Pieter became popular there once again: weavers, fullers, and also guildsmen of other trades rallied around him. On account of the general discontent at St Pol's actions the royal bailiff and the aldermen did not dare trouble Pieter de Coninc thus allowing the influence of the people's leader to grow from day to day. His authority also increased when the Brugeois envoys returned from Paris with the news that the appeal had had no effect. Pieter de Coninc became so powerful that he forbade those workmen carrying out the demolition of the fortifications to continue filling in the town moat. Meanwhile, the construction of a royal fortress had not materialised. The royal bailiff and the aldermen, as well as some of the pro-French burghers, fled, considering themselves no longer safe in the town.[97]

In Ghent, the aldermen obtained the permission of Jacques de St Pol, allowing them after all to put a tax on beer and mead, and this despite the absolution given by the King. The following day this led to a strike by the commoners. As the patricians together with the royal bailiff, a Flemish supporter of the King, Jan Lauwaerd, attempted to force the commoners back to work, a riot broke out at which the patricians were defeated. Once again, Jacques de St Pol was prepared to take severe action.[98]

However, by the beginning of the month of May, the Count's sons felt that the

---

[94] Ibid., 485, 491–2: Jacob van Hertsberghe, Robrecht die Ruddere, Robrecht van Curtrike, Lamsin Bonin, burghers, and the broker, Jan die Grant. Also, Pieter, son of the Flemish ally of the King, Jan van Hertsberghe, and Gillis, son of Symon van Artrike. See also J. De Smet, 'De inrichting van de poorterlijke ruiterij te Brugge in 1292 en haar indeeling in gezindheden in 1302', *Verslagen en mededelingen van de Koninklijke Vlaamsche Academie* (Aug.–Sept. 1930), 500–4.
[95] Wyffels and De Smet, I:1027–8.
[96] *Annales Gandenses*, 16.
[97] Ibid., 16–17.
[98] Ibid., 17–18; *Chronique artésienne*, 35–7; and Lodewijk van Velthem, *Voortzetting van de Spiegel historiael (1248–1316)*, ed. H. Vander Linden, W. de Vreese. P. de Keyser, and A. van Loey, CRH (Brussels, 1906–38), II.1.IV:251–4, cc. 7–8.

conflict had ripened sufficiently to allow for intervention. They sent the young Willem van Jülich to Bruges where he was received as a ministering angel. This nobleman had been predestined for a promising career in the church, but eventually turned out to be a born man of war. On account of his impressive appearance he immediately won the hearts of the masses. Like Pieter de Coninc, Willem van Jülich was also an excellent speaker and, moreover, young, handsome and brave with a clear understanding of the situation. He knew what had to be done in order for the uprising to spread. Willem was recognised as the leader, not only in Bruges, but also in Damme and Aardenburg. At once he sent the guildsmen of Bruges to the fortified castles of pro-French noblemen where French garrisons were located. By this action he attained two goals: driving out the oppressors of the local people and initiating the struggle against the French. The house of the Flemish supporter of the King of France, Jan van Sijsele, and the Count's castle at Male were attacked and taken. At Male, all members of the French garrison were killed. The people of Ghent then sent representatives to Bruges in order to conclude an alliance. All the above had been accomplished masterfully.[99]

Nevertheless, the pro-French burghers of Ghent, and the richer commoners who feared the loss of their possessions in an uprising, were able to convince St Pol that he had to restore order in Ghent, since otherwise they would join Bruges, then being led by Willem van Jülich. St Pol understood that he had to make concessions, and he concluded an agreement with the people of Ghent on 11 May 1302. At the same time, however, he had gathered together an army in order to subject Bruges.[100]

Ghent now remained on the side of the King. Pieter de Coninc made a vain attempt on 12 May to win over the people of the town. He approached Ghent with an army, but retreated when the pro-French Flemish forces and the bailiff moved against the people of Bruges.[101] Nevertheless, by the time Guy de Namur arrived in Flanders, all efforts had in the end failed. In Aardenburg and Bruges, public opinion turned around: Flemish burghers, favourable to the King, and the richest commoners, who were also fearful of their possessions, both manipulated the people. Willem van Jülich understood that the rich had only taken common cause with the lower orders out of necessity. Furthermore, he was also informed that St Pol was gathering together an army. No longer considering his person safe in Bruges he retreated to the Four Ambachten.[102]

The situation appeared to be desperate when Pieter de Coninc returned to Bruges having first restored to power those favourable to the Count at Aardenburg. Ghent had not rebelled, Willem van Jülich had left Bruges and, together with Guy, was to leave Flanders. The leader of the commoners was held responsible for the failure, and his life was at risk. He in turn was obliged to flee.[103]

---

[99] *Annales Gandenses*, 19–20.
[100] Ibid., 20–1; and *Chronique artésienne*, 38.
[101] *Annales Gandenses*, 21; and Lodewijk, II.1.IV:265–7, c. 14, v. 937 ff.
[102] The *Vier Ambachten*, or four shires, were Axel, Hulst, Assenede and Boechoute.
[103] Lodewijk, II.1.IV:267–8, c. 15; and *Annales Gandenses*, 21–2.

Panic arose in Bruges: everyone had compromised themselves, and both the burghers and the commoners tried to save what could still be saved. St Pol moved from Courtrai with his army of Artesian, Hainaulter and Flemish noblemen. The army was composed of eight hundred noblemen, of whom a hundred and twenty were knights with the rest being composed of squires, three hundred foot-soldiers and crossbowmen.[104] A delegation from Bruges left to meet St Pol accompanied by one of the King's councillors, the chancellor, Pierre Flote. An agreement was reached that those offenders from the lower orders were to leave Bruges. This took place on 16 and 17 May, with several thousand men leaving for Damme, Aardenburg, Oostburg and along the coastal area around the River Zwin. Their anger was immediate when they passed carriages carrying provisions to the army along the Zwin River. The exiled overpowered the accompanying troops, replenishing themselves fully with the wine and food.[105]

On 17 May, St Pol entered Bruges. At the very last moment, the burghers warned him against this most insistently. They exhorted him not to enter the town in person since the commoners hated him so much that violence was feared.[106] The harsh man of war, however, did not wish to let any apprehension be seen and ignored the wise counsel, entering the town with bodies of soldiers in formation. The inhabitants were already very anxious, and such a display of power made the masses only more fearful. The governor appeared to be furious, and all kinds of rumours were soon circulating that the French soldiers intended to attack the inhabitants at night. Panic arose and the desperate commoners sent messengers to those who had left the town, calling them back before it was too late. Together, they would all attack St Pol's soldiers with the battle cry 'Scilt ende vrient' (Shield and friend).[107] While the soldiers of the governor had been given quarters in the hotels and hostels, only a small number of troops remained behind to keep guard over the partially demolished walls and gates. In the early hours, still before dawn, the French were suddenly attacked. Commoners in Bruges immediately took up arms and joined the returned exiles. The French noblemen attempted in vain to give the battle cry, but they could not pronounce the word *scilt*; they pronounced it *escilt*.[108] St Pol, Pierre Flote, the Viscount of Lille, the royal bailiff, Pierre du Breucq, were still able to escape. However, in the fighting in the streets and hotels, the French lost a hundred and twenty men, noblemen and foot-soldiers, and certainly eighty-five noblemen were taken captive of whom more than half were Flemish.[109]

---

[104] *Chronique artésienne*, 40.
[105] *Annales Gandenses*, 22 3.
[106] *Chronique artésienne*, 41–2.
[107] *Annales Gandenses*, 24; Lodewijk, II.1.IV:269–70, c. 15, vv. 1019–70; le Muisit, 63; and *Chronique tournaisienne*, in *Chronique artésienne et chronique tournaisienne*, ed. F. Funck-Brentano, CTEH, 25 (Paris, 1899), 43 n.3.
[108] F. Debrabandere, 'Scilt en vrient', *De Leiegouw*, 19 (1977), 361–6. The Flemish pronunciation of these words is difficult for a French speaker. See also J. F. Verbruggen, 'Scilt ende vrient', *Revue belge d'histoire militaire*, 23 (1979–80), 311–22.
[109] C. Wyffels and A. Vandewalle, *De rekeningen van de stad Brugge (1280–1319): Tweede deel (1302–1319), eerste stuk (1302–1306)*. CRH (Brussels, 1995), 56–8.

The event of 'Bruges Friday' had tremendous consequences. In Tournai, people said that from that day onwards the Holy Blood kept in Bruges never flowed again as it had every Friday.[110] In France, the attack was regarded as sordid betrayal, as an atrocious conspiracy. It is interesting to note how the royal entourage presented the event in November 1302:

> The inhabitants of Bruges had a dispute among themselves, and the commoners had killed several important men. The King did not wish to take any harsh action, but treated them good-naturedly as befitting a good lord. In order to re-establish lasting peace between them, he sent prelates, clerks and knights in order to bring about reconciliation and to deal with the matter. The men of Bruges let various knights and other men into Bruges who had been sent to bring peace after they had assured them that they could enter in safety since the villains had left. After they had entered and had been pleasantly received, the Flemish attacked at dawn at a moment that the King's men were not suspecting. They killed some of them in their beds; others fled fearing for their lives. The people of Bruges kept all that the King's men had brought to the town, men who had come for their own good. It was a most treasonable and perfidious act, as is clear to all.[111]

Of course, one can, in objecting to the above, note that St Pol came with an army and went much further than the royal entourage presented it above.

For their part, the Flemings claimed that Pierre Flote had promised that St Pol would enter the town with three hundred unarmoured knights.[112] This would correspond well with the role of a mediator and investigator to bring about reconciliation and to act as a friend of the town in order to restore order and peace. The people of Bruges, however, feared that he would not keep that promise.

The Ghentenaar Friar Minor of the *Annales Gandenses* initiated an examination with his contemporaries that was to determine whether or not the people of Bruges had conspired to attack the French. According to him this was not the case, or if so, then very few people knew of it, 'and indeed, I found no sure proof of this'.[113]

The attack shows how very much St Pol had come to be hated by the common people after scarcely two years in power in the county. It shows also that the French commander did not keep the agreement. A terrible act had been committed against Philip IV. War broke out once again, although now, according to the reports of that time, between the people of Flanders and the King.[114]

---

[110] Le Muisit, 65.
[111] Funck-Brentano, *Philippe le Bel*, 393.
[112] *Annales Gandenses*, 22.
[113] Ibid., 24.
[114] De Limburg-Stirum, I:330, no. 140: 'Et quant li communs de Flandre se mist encontre le roy.' See also de Limburg-Stirum, II, no. 307. *Annales Gandenses*, 19, on the people of Flanders and the sons of the Count.

Part One

**HISTORIOGRAPHY AND
THE STUDY OF THE SOURCES**

1

A Problem for Historians

A Problem for Historical Methodology

Although there is not a single description of the battle drawn up by a participant, there are rich sources of documentation that have been left by contemporaries of the warring parties. A list of these descriptions, in chronological order of composition, allows an initial approach to the sources. Only those chronicles from the period itself have been included where the authors may have known specific participants in the battle. Many short commentaries or simple records of the events have been ignored, since they do not present any new facts, merely forming a narrative based on general information. As the sources will be discussed thoroughly below, it is sufficient here merely to note who wrote them and when.

The Battle of the Spurs is reported fully in the following works:

In a chronicle written by a burgher of Arras and, accordingly, referred to as the *Chronique artésienne*. The account was written as early as the end of 1304.[1]

In a rhymed chronicle of 1306–7 dedicated to the King of France: *La Branche des royaus lingnages*, written by a burgher of Orléans, Guillaume Guiart.[2]

A Ghentenaar Friar Minor began, in 1308, to compile the *Annales Gandenses*. Two years later, in 1310, he had finished the account of events for the period 1297–1308 and was later to continue the historical work up to 1310.[3]

Between 1313 and 1316 a Brabantese parson, Lodewijk van Velthem, gave a very lively account of the Battle of the Spurs in his *Voortzetting van de Spiegel historiael*.[4]

Between 1313 and 1317 a burgher of Paris, Geoffroy de Paris, also gave an account of the events in his *Chronique rimée*.[5]

Around 1317 the events were detailed in the sequel to the chronicle of

---

[1] *Chronique artésienne et chronique tournaisienne*, ed. F. Funck-Brentano, CTEH, 25 (Paris, 1899).
[2] Guillaume Guiart, *La Branche des royaus lingnages*, in RHF, 22, ed. N. de Wailly and L. Delisle (Paris, n.d.).
[3] *Annales Gandenses*, ed. Hilda Johnstone (London, 1951). *Annales Gandenses*, ed. F. Funck-Brentano, CTEH, 18 (Paris, 1896).
[4] Lodewijk van Velthem, *Voortzetting*.
[5] Geoffroy de Paris, *Chronique rimée*, in RHF, 22, ed. N. de Wailly and L. Delisle (Paris, n.d.).

Guillaume de Nangis: *Continuatio Prima Guilelmi de Nangiaco Chronici* by a monk of the abbey of St Denis near Paris.[6]

Again, in the same period (1316–18), perhaps somewhat earlier, the account of Ottokar von Stiermarken was drawn up in his *Oesterreichische Reimchronik*.[7]

A monk of the abbey of Clairmarais near St Omer, Bernard of Ypres recounted the battle of 11 July in the *Chronicon Comitum Flandrensium*, also known as the *Genealogiae Comitum Flandriae Continuatio Clarismariscensis*.[8]

Willem Procurator, a monk from the abbey of Egmond in Holland, also reported the battle in his *Chronicon* written before 1323.[9]

By 1342, the battle of 11 July had also been recounted in a French chronicle, now lost, although it was used by those living at that time. This was the case for the burgher of St Omer who reproduced this lost source, in concise form, in his old chronicle of Flanders published by Kervyn de Lettenhove under the title *Istore et croniques de Flandres*.[10] (This work will consistently be referred to using the above title.) The lost source was also employed by the *Chronique normande du XIVe siècle*,[11] as well as by the *Anciennes chroniques de Flandre*, published in the *Recueil des historiens de France*.[12] Between 1415 and 1422 a monk from St Denis made use of both the lost source as well as of the *Chronique normande*. The monk gave a more detailed account of the Battle of the Spurs than the three previous versions in the *Chronographia Regum Francorum*.[13]

Although these four chronicles, *Istore et croniques*, *Chronique normande*, *Anciennes chroniques* and *Chronographia*, have their origins in a common source they nevertheless do not give exactly the same account of the battle. An account must be taken of the differences in minor details.

Before 1348, and perhaps as early as 1306, a Florentine, Giovanni Villani, had also given a long description of the Battle of Courtrai.[14]

Gilles le Muisit, of Tournai, dictated his chronicle from 1347 to 1349,[15] and around the year 1348 Jean de Winterthur also wrote his.[16]

---

[6] Guillaume de Nangis, *Continuatio Chronici Guillelmi de Nangiaco*, in RHF, 20, ed. Daunou and Naudet (Paris, 1840).
[7] Ottokar von Stiermarken, *Oesterreichische Reimchronik*, ed. J. Seemuller, Monumenta Germaniae Historica, Deutsche Chroniken, V:1, 2 (Hanover, 1890–3).
[8] *Chronicon Comitum Flandrensium*, ed. J. J. De Smet, *Corpus Chronicorum Flandriae*, 1, CRH (Brussels, 1837).
[9] Willelmus Procurator, *Chronicon*, ed. C. Pijnacker Hordijk, Werken uitgegeven door het Historisch Genootschap (gevestigd te Utrecht), 3rd ser., 20 (Amsterdam, 1904).
[10] Ed. A. and E. Molinier, SHF (Paris, 1886). Published prior to this as *Istore et croniques de Flandres*, ed. Kervyn de Lettenhove, CRH, 2 vols. (Brussels, 1879–80).
[11] *Chronique normande du XIVe siècle*, ed. A. and E. Molinier, SHF (Paris, 1886).
[12] *Anciennes chroniques de Flandre*, in RHF, 22, ed. N. de Wailly and L. Delisle (Paris, n.d.).
[13] *Chronographia Regum Francorum*, ed. H. Moranvillé, SHF, 3 vols. (Paris, 1891–7).
[14] Giovanni Villani, *Historie fiorentine*, in *Rerum Italicarum Scriptores*, XIII. ed. L. A. Muratori (Rome, 1728).
[15] Gilles le Muisit, *Chronique et annales*, ed. H. Lemaître, SHF (Paris, 1905).
[16] Johannes Vitoduranus, *Chronicon*, ed. F. Baethgen, Monumenta Germaniae Historica, nova series, III (Hanover, 1924).

From all these sources there are three that presented the events in a light favourable to the victors: the Friar Minor from Ghent of the *Annales Gandenses*, Lodewijk van Velthem, and the author of the *Chronicon Comitum Flandrensium*. All the other authors give a version of events aimed at defending the vanquished. At the very important points the pro-French accounts contradict the pro-Flemish. First of all, how historians dealt with this problem, how they interpreted and criticised the sources will be examined in order to be able to draw up a critical account of the battle.

The oldest studies can be fairly quickly dealt with. They were characterised by a lack of a systematic and historical methodology,[17] and this includes the study by G. Köhler.[18] The first historians nevertheless did make use of all the information in the listed sources to present a complete narrative. In doing so, however, they forgot to take account of the fact that the sources they used radically contradict each other. It is true that the Prussian general Köhler made a distinct choice of sources by giving preference to pro-Flemish writers, above all to Lodewijk van Velthem. Still, this does not alter the fact that he did not make sufficient distinctions between sources written by those living at that time and those written at a much later date with numerous unreliable additions to the original account. His insufficient knowledge of the relative value of the texts used led to him giving a mosaic of excerpts from all the chronicles, of the most varying quality. Köhler's study has been very much over-valued up to now because his work inspired Pirenne in his notable study of the French and Flemish versions of the battle,[19] and because he followed the great Belgian historian in his account of his.[20]

The same deficiency in methodology is also to be found in the work of de Maere d'Aertrycke.[21] True, he did attempt to reconcile the most contradictory elements from all the sources, but ended up coming to untenable conclusions. Moreover, the account given in the sources was compromised with unjustifiable changes and erroneous interpretations. Thus, the author in the end presented a rather contrived account instead of a historically justified picture of the Battle of the Spurs.[22]

---

[17] Lot, *L'Art militaire*, I:253.
[18] G. Köhler, *Die Entwickelung des Kriegswesens und der Kriegführung in der Ritterzeit von Mitte des 11. Jahrhunderts bis zu den Hussitenkriegen* (Breslau, 1886), II:216–49.
[19] Pirenne, 'La Version flamande', 11–50.
[20] G. Köhler, *Ergänzungsheft die Schlachten von Tagliacozzo und Courtrai betreffend* (Breslau, 1893).
[21] M. de Maere d'Aertrycke, *La Bataille des éperons d'or* (Namur, 1933).
[22] In this respect, his attempt to determine the exact duration of each of the attacks should be noted (*La Bataille des éperons d'or*, 45–6). He sought to be too accurate while the sources do not permit this. De Maere d'Aertrycke attributes special reserve troops to each of the three larger Flemish corps, something that the sources did not report (53). Contrary to almost all the texts, he did not portray the Flemish front as being protected by a stream or brook. Ottokar von Stiermarken's pits become latrines in his account. The author also accepted all figures regarding the numerical strengths given in the sources and is most arbitrary in his use of such figures, e.g. 60,000 Flemish soldiers given by the *Annales Gandenses* (33). Furthermore, the author claims that there were 20,000 Flemish troops at Courtrai. According to him therefore the figure of 60,000 men ought to be regarded as the total number of Flemish forces. Approximately 10,000 Frenchmen had been left behind in the castles. Those laying siege, however, needed a fourfold

In an excellent study Pirenne clearly indicated how Flemish and French versions were formed immediately after the battle. Funck-Brentano, however, appeared to advocate a different approach to the matter. Since none of the sources were written by eye-witnesses, Funck-Brentano was of the opinion that the value of the accounts had to be judged according to when they were written as well as the place of origin of the author. This allows one to determine who could have consulted eye-witnesses and who could not. Furthermore, he attempted, rather too pedantically, to prove that there was only one version, the French one. The Flemish victory was attributed to a ruse or to dishonourable stratagem. In his opinion the most reliable source was the *Chronique artésienne*, and he fully accepted its account.[23]

Pirenne was able to show the defects of such a method.[24] It is insufficient to merely classify the sources according to the date they were written and the place of origin of the author. Even when the author comes from the area itself and interviewed witnesses, he can mislead us due to the influence of national pride,[25] social attitudes,[26] personal sympathy or antipathy for a country or leader,[27] or in reaction to an account by an opponent.[28] One should not be surprised, in dealing with a victory or defeat of such importance as the Battle of Courtrai, at the great differences between the versions. The victor seeks to increase the merit of his soldiers, while the vanquished is inclined to ascribe a crushing defeat to betrayal, conspiracy or fatal accident, or to the unfavourable terrain or the inability of political or social opponents. In such cases, those sources written at a time closest to the event appear to be the most unreliable. This is so because the authors from the vanquished side are more sensitive to the national catastrophe and are still unable to make a neutral judgement, while the victors seek to increase their own glory. The account given by the *Chronique artésienne* presented all these failings in a work that had been written too soon after events and also ignored certain important details. There is no reason whatsoever to regard it as being the best account.[29]

Following Pirenne, who had clearly distinguished between the sources according to the version they belonged to, it then appeared possible to draw up a new historically valid and critical account. Frederichs attempted to compile a definitive account from the studies by Köhler, Funck-Brentano and Pirenne. In doing so, he followed a new method with some exaggeration, incorrectly applying a meticulous

---

numerical superiority. The Frenchmen were, then, besieged by 40,000 Flemish troops, and there were 20,000 Flemish soldiers left at Courtrai.

[23] F. Funck-Brentano, 'Mémoire sur la bataille de Courtrai (1302, 11 juillet) et les chroniqueurs qui en ont traité pour servir à l'historiographie du règne de Philippe le Bel', *Mémoires de l'Académie des inscriptions et belles-lettres (Savants étrangers)*, 1st ser., 10.1 (1891).
[24] Pirenne, 'Note supplementaire', 85–123, esp. 92–3.
[25] Flemish and French versions.
[26] Did the Flemish sources not perhaps ignore the role of the Flemish knights? Did the burgher, Geoffroy de Paris, not unfairly put the blame for defeat on the shoulders of the knights? Did Villani not write contemptuously of Flemish guildsmen?
[27] Villani was not favourable to Philip the Fair, nor to the Count of Artois; Ottokar von Stiermarken despised the French King.
[28] Lodewijk and Guiart reacted against the enemy's account of events.
[29] Pirenne, 'Note supplementaire', 102–4.

differentiation between the Flemish and the French versions. Frederichs made a choice between the sources, after a critical discussion of them, and then he followed what he felt to be the most reliable texts. He used the account of the Frenchman, Guiart, to detail preliminary movements and positions. For the battle itself he once again used French sources, above all Guiart and Geoffroy de Paris, in describing the crossbow battle. In giving an account of the battle between the French knights and the Flemish foot-soldiers he made use of Lodewijk's text. The *Annales Gandenses*, as well as the *Chronicon Comitum Flandrensium* and the continuation of the chronicle by Guillaume de Nangis provided additional details, as did the other French sources in as much as their accounts were not contradictory to those of the aforementioned chroniclers.[30]

This method is, however, in error since on the one hand it was completely based on the accounts by Guiart and Geoffroy de Paris in depicting the initial stages of the battle, and on the other hand, in detailing the battle itself Lodewijk's account was accepted both exclusively and completely. This was due to an insufficiently critical analysis of each of the accounts. It is a simple matter to refute Guiart and Geoffroy de Paris, for example, by making use of the pro-Flemish Lodewijk or the French *Chronographia* in giving an account of the role of crossbowmen and light foot-soldiers in the battle. Moreover, the latter sources derive their material from both versions, which is not the case for Guiart and Geoffroy de Paris. Even though Lodewijk's account of the battle between the French knights and Flemish foot-soldiers surpasses the others, this does not alter the fact that, without a doubt, Lodewijk van Velthem exaggerated several times in his account. On occasions, Frederichs follows Lodewijk's account too literally, which goes against the principles of a critical historiography that seeks to eliminate exaggerated elements in both versions. Furthermore, Frederichs made a serious methodological mistake. Even though Guiart was alone in depicting a sweeping movement of the French army from the Groeninge stream to the Grote Beek stream, and the other sources make no mention of this, Frederichs still accepted it and, what is more, he adapted Lodewijk's text to that of Guiart. In doing so he had the Brabantese clergyman differentiating between different types of ditches.[31] This differentiation between types of streams or waterways is not substantiated whatsoever and even contradicts the correct meaning of some of Lodewijk's verses.[32] In addition to this, Frederichs was still influenced by Köhler's study, even though he corrected the study. Thus, on the basis of evidence given by a sole account written at a later date in one of the versions of *Istore et croniques*, he erroneously assumed that it suddenly began to rain before the battle.[33]

Although Fris developed and significantly improved upon Frederichs's work, he

---

[30] J. Frederichs, 'De slag van Kortrijk', *Nederlandsch museum*, 36 (1893), 257–95. Quotations come from the offprint, 41–2. Frederichs, 'Les Derniers Travaux sur l'histoire et l'historiographie de la bataille de Courtrai', *Messager des sciences historiques de Belgique* 67 (1893), 163–82.
[31] Frederichs, 'Les Derniers Travaux', 180–2.
[32] See the discussion of Lodewijk's account below.
[33] Frederichs, 'De slag van Kortrijk', 29 n. 3.

still followed the same methodology.³⁴ Part of the above criticism is therefore also applicable to his comprehensive work. That is the assumption of a sweeping movement, of which Guiart spoke, and the adaptation of Lodewijk's account to such a movement, whereby he, like Frederichs, differentiated between the waterways mentioned by Lodewijk. In addition to this, he also in this respect follows Guiart and Geoffroy de Paris too closely in the description of the light foot-soldiers' battle, and Lodewijk in the description of the battle itself, and this without eliminating the exaggerated elements in the passages.

Delfos's work is open to the same criticism, since the author presented a sequence of excerpts from the sources without sufficient criticism of them.³⁵ Moreover, he succumbed at numerous points to the temptation to place national feeling at the forefront. Delfos exaggerated his reaction to Pirenne, who went too far in his neglect of national identity *before* 11 July 1302. Delfos has the merit of pointing to the fact that a national identity existed in the county of Flanders in 1127–8.³⁶ This was before Petrus Pictor added a completely convincing proof to such a view.³⁷ Recently, the fact that a feeling of national consciousness existed in Flanders at the beginning of the twelfth century was made even clearer.³⁸ Still, the existence of a national consciousness does not necessarily lead to armed conflict with, and rebellion against, the conqueror and occupier of the country. It is here that Pirenne was correct in stating that the Flemish rebellion against Philip the Fair was not a spontaneous upsurge of national identity. Delfos did not take sufficient account of the fact that the feelings, thoughts and opinions of people living at that time differed *before* and *after* significant events such as the Bruges Matins and the Battle of the Spurs. Obviously, people's minds changed. This is evident from actions on the part of certain noblemen who, following the Bruges Matins, came to assist the rebellious commoners of Bruges, or, after 11 July, from the actions of certain Flemish nobles, previously supporters of the King, who from that point on joined the battle in the rebel ranks.³⁹ Since those authors adhering to both the French and to the Flemish versions wrote after 1302, and some of them very much later, after many years of war against the French, they at times forgot when a change in public opinion, and in

---

³⁴ Fris, *De slag bij Kortrijk*, 244–60, esp. 254–5, for the four types of waterway, and 259 with the sources he followed in his critical account. Pirenne, 'Note supplementaire', 98 n. 1, was of the opinion that Lodewijk used the words 'gracht' or 'grachten' (moat, ditch, trench), according to the requirements of the verse and rhyme.
³⁵ Delfos, *1302 door tijdgenooten verteld*.
³⁶ L. Delfos, 'De omwenteling uit 1302 en het begrip "Vlaanderens eere" ', published in 1936 and included in L. Delfos, *Verkenningen door onze geschiedenis* (Bruges–Utrecht, 1944), 22–32.
³⁷ For this poem see A. Boutemy, *Recueil de textes historiques latins du moyen âge, Coll. Lebègue* (Brussels, 1943), 53–5; and Petrus Pictor, *Delaude Flandriae*, ed. J. van Mierlo, SJ (Brussels, 1944).
³⁸ J. Dhondt, *Les Origines des états de Flandre* (Louvain, 1950), 6 and notes.
³⁹ The Brugeois rebels were abandoned even before the Bruges Matins by members of the Count's family. Following the events, they rushed to their help once again, as did many noblemen. For the Flemish nobles who supported the King after 11 July see *Annales Gandenses*, 33.

feelings of national identity, actually had taken place.[40] Foreign sources were not aware of such shades of difference, and their value as evidence is, therefore, rather suspect in this regard.

In a notable article the French linguist Wagner also dealt with the study of French sources and in passing he presented his ideas as to what method should be followed. He merely had access to Köhler's substantial work, Funck-Brentano's *Mémoire* and Pirenne's first article on the Flemish and French version of events. For this reason, Wagner's work is first and foremost a critique of Funck-Brentano's methodology and at times that of Köhler. Wagner was correct in his explanation of how the two versions arose. The French reworked the defeat according to two popular patterns: treachery or ruse, and incompetence on the part of their commanders.[41] Wagner carefully refuted Funck-Brentano's arguments indicating how the *Chronique artésienne*, precisely due to it being written so shortly after the event, propagated rumours about artificial ditches[42] into which French knights were alleged to have fallen. He also proved, beyond doubt, that Ottokar von Stiermarken was informed by a French participant in the battle.[43] He rightly emphasised that choosing and following one single source as the most important, and excluding other sources, is in the end the reflection of pure sentiment.[44] His essay does for a major part correspond to that of Pirenne in his 'Note supplémentaire'. Still, when Wagner proceeded to depict the battle, he used as his base the rather unreliable account by Geoffroy de Paris. This was a serious methodological mistake. Indeed, Wagner had carefully proven that the French sources form an apology of the defeat; following this he employed them himself without being sufficiently critical, and without consulting the Flemish sources. Furthermore, Geoffroy de Paris was in all respects a secondary witness. It is true that he strove for a certain veracity, but this still does not alter the fact that he was badly informed and that his historical method is open, and rightly so, to serious criticism. Wagner criticised Lodewijk, yet he still repeated Funck-Brentano without himself having read Lodewijk's account. Thus, he once again made a very serious methodological mistake, all the more so since he had shown how one-sided Funck-Brentano was in his handling of the French sources. With an unreliable source as his base, moreover, he incorporated information from texts of questionable value. Finally, he put his full and blind trust in Köhler's study 'whose competence is indisputable'.[45] He concluded that there were almost no concrete details on

---

[40] Typical of this are the speeches made before the battle by the Flemish leaders. In Lodewijk's account and in the *Annales Gandenses*, as well as in the *Chronographia*, it was a question of rather practical advice. In the *Chronicon Comitum Flandrensium*, however, it was a question of the laws and freedoms of the county. Patriotic observations were added to purely military advice by an author who was only writing in 1329.
[41] R. L. Wagner, 'La Bataille de Courtrai (1302): essai de critique des sources françaises', *Mémoires de l'Académie nationale des sciences, arts et belles-lettres de Caen*, n.s. 10 (1942), 396, 406.
[42] Ibid., 410.
[43] Ibid., 411.
[44] Ibid., 364.
[45] Ibid., 379.

the battle. For this reason the battle lay outside the grasp of military history,[46] a point that may be defended on the basis of the French sources, yet not following a consultation of Flemish sources.

A final and most significant objection to Wagner's methodology is applicable both to the aforementioned studies and to studies such as those by Funck-Brentano, Frederichs and Fris. The criticism is that Wagner's manner of working lacked the necessary military methodology that would allow us to state, on the basis of careful study of both the military aspects as well as the art of warfare of that period, exactly what was possible and what was not. This is pertinent to the problem of troop strength on which Wagner follows Köhler, and to the account of the unlikely attack by French foot-soldiers as recounted by Guiart and Geoffroy de Paris.[47] It is also pertinent when we compare, through actions and reactions on both sides, how warfare was practised in the period between 1302 and 1304. The influence of the Battle of the Spurs on later French cavalry tactics allows us to see clearly why the Flemings won on 11 July 1302.[48]

This factual element of criticism, based on knowledge of military matters, was introduced in examining the Battle of Courtrai, following Köhler's unsuccessful attempt, by Wodsak, a student of Delbrück.[49] It cannot, however, be claimed that this was an unmitigated success.[50] Still, it did present an undoubted improvement in certain details, including a better analysis of troop strength, an improved description of the crossbow battle and a rejection of the sweeping movement mentioned by Guiart. Nevertheless, on methodology there is much to disprove of – insufficient distinction between contemporary and later sources, and completely incorrect interpretations of both sources and studies of the battle. The legend of the cunningly dug ditches was accepted. Wodsak's shortcomings drew the Belgian historian's attention away from the results actually achieved. Sir Charles Oman followed, for a major part, his account according to the summary by Delbrück, so that the English author also wrote of dug ditches. This enabled him to make a cautious comparison with Bannockburn in which the existence of such ditches has

[46] Ibid., 360, 425. This point of view is, however, not correct for all the French sources.
[47] Ibid., 376–7, on troop strength, and 394–5, on the archers' battle. There are several mistakes. On 376, Wagner states that the French army troop strengths were exaggerated by the Flemings. This also occurred in the French sources, as regards their own army as well as to the Flemish army. Indeed, this was a common occurrence in medieval sources. Guiart was allegedly the only author with significant competence in the military field (Wagner, 388). This is a rather exaggerated standpoint since the Ghentenaar Friar Minor's chronicle is of great value on tactics and strategy and at times is as good as Guiart in its descriptions. Wagner mentions (423–4) the dishonourable act of the victors in robbing the fallen soldiers. This was simply a common practice of the time that continued, as a matter of fact, until the beginning of the nineteenth century, e.g. at Waterloo in 1815.
[48] J. F. Verbruggen, 'De Gentse minderbroeder der *Annales Gandenses* en de krijgskunst in de periode 1302–1304', *Handelingen der maatschappij voor geschiedenis en oudheidkunde te Gent*, n.s. 4 (1949), 9.
[49] F. Wodsak, 'Die Schlacht bei Kortrijk', Berlin dissertation (Berlin, 1905). A summary of this can be found in H. Delbrück, *Geschichte der Kriegskunst im Rahmen der politischen Geschichte*, vol. III: *Mittelalter* (Berlin, 1907), 439–47.
[50] See Pirenne, *Histoire de Belgique*, I:256 n. 14: 'Le Travail de Wodsak n'a aucune valeur.'

been confirmed by Scottish and English sources.[51] Finally, Wodsak's and Oman's accounts were, above all, based on Villani and the *Anciennes chroniques de Flandre*.[52] A choice of such later sources is not to be justified methodologically, since Flemish sources that were written earlier contradict evidence given in the later accounts.

The last scholar who approached the problem of applying a historical methodology to the history of the Battle of Courtrai is Lot.[53] Like Pirenne, Lot accepted the existence of two versions of the battle.[54] Following this he used Funck-Brentano's division, ordering the sources according to when they were compiled as well as the place of origin of their authors, after which Lot divided them into several categories according to their value as evidence. He eliminated from the French version the explanation ascribing the defeat to treachery, since this accusation was employed by the entourage of King Philip the Fair for propaganda purposes.[55] However, on the ditches Lot did not reach a conclusion. He referred to the danger of drawing up an account of the battle based on the numerous sources that often present different versions of the events.[56] He speculated about whether it would not be better to accept a more cautious solution: a concise compilation of the principal accounts written at the time without drawing up a general narrative. However, some accounts were, to a great extent, dismissed by Lot (Guiart) or partially dismissed (Villani and Geoffroy de Paris) due to the improbability of the account. Based on this analysis, Lot concluded that Lodewijk, Villani and Ottokar, even though enemies of Philip the Fair, ascribed the success of the Flemings to a stratagem.[57] This is something that does not at all correspond to Lodewijk's and Villani's texts. Ultimately, Lot wrote an account in broad outline where both hypotheses were considered: with ditches cutting across the battlefield between the Flemish positions and both streams, and with only the Groeninge stream and the Grote Beek (the Great Brook) presenting significant obstacles.[58]

The great French medievalist thus makes use of a very cautious methodology, resulting in the conclusion that one cannot possess the necessary means of determining the historical truth. Still, his study was marred by an undeniable lack of

---

[51] Oman, II:112–18; on the Battle of Bannockburn, see Oman, II:86 n. 1–2.

[52] Wodsak, *Die Schlacht bei Kortrijk*, 77. However, one must be cautious in consulting Wodsak's work since, on numerous occasions, he went against his sources or against other historical studies: according to Pirenne (9), there were no frontal impediments, and Gilles le Muisit was Flemish (15). His pro-Flemish sentiment is evident (16); the person continuing de Nangis's chronicle (Nancy in Wodsak, 18) was also pro-Flemish; Bruges and Ypres were not defended (21); chroniclers are said to present no information about the terrain itself (32); Geoffroy de Paris is said also to have talked of dug ditches (41); Wodsak has Guiart state the contrary to what is actually in the source (52); the same for Villani and Lodewijk (63); and once again for Lodewijk (67), etc.

[53] Lot, *L'Art militaire*, I:252–64.

[54] Ibid., I:252–3.

[55] Ibid., I:255.

[56] Ibid., I:256.

[57] Ibid., I:259.

[58] Ibid., I:260.

understanding about the correct details of certain sources stemming from his not having studied the texts sufficiently. From Lodewijk's account, who was presented as a myth maker, Lot only read several excerpts that had been translated by Funck-Brentano in his *Mémoire*. He accepted the unfounded criticisms of Funck-Brentano, adding still further arguments that do not, however, appear strongly founded since they are based on an incorrect interpretation of the source. Such shortcomings seriously weaken his argumentation from the point of view of its historical methodology.

The caution shown by this great scholar does, however, provide food for thought. The merit of Wagner and Lot lies in their pointing to the risks of using one source (or a series of sources) exclusively, even if it is the most reliable source, in drawing up a critical description of the battle. The first duty of a historian is the careful elimination of exaggerated elements in both versions and, following this, to reconcile the accounts as far as is possible after rejecting all dubious explanations. Finally, one must return to the method that has been detailed brilliantly by Pirenne, whose 'Note supplémentaire' is still the most excellent work that there is in this field. Nevertheless, such a method is not sufficient, since an addition has to be made, taking account of the military history of the Middle Ages.

Summary

The first method consisted of reconstituting an account of the battle by bringing together *all* information given by the sources. This method has now been shown to go against sound historical methodology.

The second method, choosing a limited number of texts, risked ignoring certain accounts containing both correct and incorrect information. A more significant danger was that one can too readily lend wholesale credence to claims made by *one* side without eliminating the exaggerated elements.

A third method may, in part, be followed by retaining all the common elements in the sources written by those living at the time and ignoring the rest. Still, the information that has been recorded solely by a very well-informed chronicler ought not to be overlooked. A consideration must be made of the fundamental difference between the two versions that makes it most difficult to fully reconcile the texts and to reach a common conclusion. One should also not forget that some authors were seeking above all to explain a miraculous and surprising event. In doing so they have more or less given a personal opinion or explanation of the events rather than an accurate account of reality. Such a description, presented by trusting chroniclers, leads to the misrepresentation of events and to quite erroneous conceptions.

Careful comparison of the sources is essential. This allows us to see how their agenda for explaining the French defeat derives from their particular historical context. It is also possible at other points in the explanations to show mutual influences that lead to surprising results.

All the above observations lead to the following approach: first and foremost, to present an accurate study of the sources, taking account of the author's character and his opinions on national, political and social matters. At the same time, the accounts will be critically examined in order to eliminate misconceptions and exaggerated elements. In this critical treatment an account of the art of warfare in the period 1297–1304 and above all from 1302 to 1304 will be made. It was in the latter period that the great victory of 11 July 1302 exerted such a deep and determinant influence. It obliged French knights to employ new tactics which, in turn, had a determinant effect upon the art of warfare in the period. Therefore, comparisons will be made when necessary with battles in that period, and with the battle that took place at Mons-en-Pévèle. Moreover, a factual methodology will be applied, using information about troop strength, weaponry and psychological factors affecting the troops (knights, foot-soldiers, crossbowmen and other light soldiers). The significant problem of troop strength will receive special research: the numerical strength of communal armies for the whole of the fourteenth century is examined in order to gain an accurate idea on this. This will also be attempted for the French armies, for which, however, there is less conclusive information to hand. Nevertheless, this method provides a satisfactory answer to the problem.

Following this preliminary study, each phase of the battle will be examined. In doing so, all the aforementioned methods are used in a meticulous comparison of the different information from the independent sources that appear reliable. This has the aim of attaining the most logical solution. The problem facing commanders from both camps on 11 July 1302 will be confronted. In doing so, the numerical strength of both armies, their major characteristics, the equipment and morale and their use of the terrain must be accounted for. The power of each army and the characteristics of the terrain were determinant factors for commanders in seeking solutions to problems; their tactics were oriented to such factors. However, the sources will be adhered to strictly so as not to give a fictional account, not to give a modern solution to a problem of 1302. In such an examination, it is useful to compare accounts, showing how some authors contradict each other and, by doing so, it also becomes clear what was added at a later period by certain authors.

In this manner a method that is suited to the study of the art of warfare in the Middle Ages will be followed. Not only is access to texts that are free from digression or later interpolation required, but also the sources must be ordered according to rules dictated by sound historical methodology. Following this, their intrinsic value must be determined, based on the knowledge that a specific author possessed of the art of warfare, of military matters, at that time. This will allow the rejection of certain conceptions as biased that may appear quite correct to the uninitiated.[59]

---

[59] See, in this respect, Lot's excellent remarks: ibid., I:13, II:181 n. 3.

2

The Sources

The Emergence of Flemish and French Versions

The glorious Flemish victory beneath the walls of Courtrai did not bring an end to the war. It was clearly evident that the most powerful prince in the West would make an immediate attempt to wipe away the shame brought by the defeat. The Flemings understood that their defence had to be organised quickly. All considered, the victors of 11 July 1302 represented only half of the county, these being Bruges and the Bruges Franc, the coastal areas, the areas around Courtrai and Aalst. Ghent was still in the hands of Flemish followers of the King; only a few hundred of those who had been banished from the town, and had fled, took part in the battle. Ypres only sent a moderate contingent. Lille, Douai and all of those lands that later formed French Flanders were still occupied by royal troops. Would the inhabitants of such towns, and the surrounding countryside, accept the possibility of successfully resisting the powerful King of France? In order to convince them, the rebels acted very skilfully. After the merry news of the victory had driven out the patricians at Ghent and made powerless those Flemish favourable to the King, an armed delegation entered the town triumphantly. Never had such a celebration been seen before. No man worked that day. The victors had brought their armour and weapons with them: the blood-stained, damaged armour and split shields all proved how violently battle had been waged and how the townsmen had risked their lives against the Flemish supporters of the King and their French allies.[1] Had not the most splendid and bravest army that Philip the Fair had ever brought together been destroyed?[2] In the same manner the less powerful armies of the King of France could also be annihilated. God and St George had undoubtedly been on the Flemish side: a picture of the saint was to be carried on horseback during future campaigns in order to ensure the continuing support of the patron saint of soldiers.[3]

A general sentiment of national consciousness found clear expression: during the siege of Lille those supporters of the King remaining in Flanders made a notable effort to ensure their previous actions were forgotten and to win the favour

---

[1] Lodewijk, II.1.IV:353, c. 43, vv. 3084–98.
[2] *Annales Gandenses*, 32; and C. Callewaert, 'Onuitgegeven aantekening uit het jaar 1302 over den Guldensporenslag', *Annales Société d'emulation de Bruges* 60 (1910), 359.
[3] *Chronographia Regum Francorum*, I:161; and Lodewijk, II.1.IV:330–1, c. 35, vv. 2531–2.

of the Count's sons.⁴ The clergy also took part in local militias or supported the military operations financially.⁵ Artisans, whose guilds were now officially recognised, laid the basis of their power in the future. As they had gained representation in Bruges and Ghent, and had control of expenses, they thought that the period of social justice had dawned.⁶ Their enthusiasm knew no bounds. Rich burghers of Bruges, favourable to the Count, gave enormous sums to support the rebels. Patricians and noblemen taken prisoner were also forced to contribute to the war chest. The democratically administered town of Bruges controlled this war chest, into which proceeds from confiscated properties and lands flowed. The great leaders, Guy and Jean de Namur, and Willem van Jülich, as well as foreign and Flemish noblemen, were kept at the expense of the town which was to give account of income and expenses to the son of the Count.⁷ A minor town clerk noted in passing when entering an expense for Jean de Namur that this was 'to protect the country'.⁸ After the speedy conquest of Lille and Douai, where the artisans were immediately prepared to help their fellow countrymen, the 'Lion won back his country again'.⁹

From this point onwards the whole of Flanders was to send its sons to the borders; all classes were represented, even if the character of the Count's armies changed completely due to the preponderance of common people over noblemen.

'So proud and bold had the Flemings become on account of their victory at Courtrai that one Fleming with his *goedendag* [a type of short club-like pike] would have engaged in combat with two French knights on horseback.'¹⁰ This general exhilaration at the victory, as well as the steadily increasing success of the uprising, lay at the base of the most popular explanation of the Flemish victory. The picture of the common people is always that of a glorious tale of victory. Thus, it was the numerically inferior Flemish who had won the battle against the much more numerous French who lost more than 15,000 knights. The courage of a few rebels and the wise advice of their brave leaders who fought in their midst, made possible this splendid victory against the finest French noblemen. There was no single word about the very favourable terrain in this extreme version that circulated in the course of the years 1323–8 and was recorded by a monk who had little sympathy for the rebels of that time and their parents of 1302.¹¹

When, in September 1302, a fresh French army approached the border, it did not meet with a small band of troops provided for a normal military expedition by a count. It was confronted with a powerful army in which troops from all the county

---

4 *Annales Gandenses*, 33.
5 Ibid., 36. The Ghentenaar Friar Minor was in the army at Flines. See also *Chronica et Cartularium Monasterii de Dunis,* ed. F. van de Putte, Société d'emulation (Bruges, 1839), 227.
6 H. van Werveke, *Gand: esquisse d'histoire sociale*, Collection notre passé (Brussels, 1946), 49.
7 See for this chapter II on the numerical strength of the two armies.
8 Wyffels and Vandewalle, II:113.
9 Lodewijk, II.1.IV:361, c. 45, vv. 3300–1: 'heeft de Liebaard (Leeuw) zijn land weergewonnen', and *Annales Gandenses*, 34–5.
10 Villani, col. 388.
11 *Chronicon Comitum Flandrensium*, 168–70. Guiart reacted against such a Flemish version in 1304: Guiart, 173–4, vv. 118–29.

were represented. A programme of national defence had been brought into effect and even monks were conscripted in the defence of the fatherland.[12] The best chronicler of the war against Philip the Fair, the Ghentenaar Friar Minor, was in the Flemish army and gave an excellent description of the morale of the fighters.[13] The Flemings realised that the King of France would not dare attack them at Vitry and, following this, at Flines, and even accepted proposals for peace negotiations. Thus, Flemish enthusiasm grew so much that Willem van Jülich, the most popular commander, together with numerous soldiers, proposed attacking the enemy and putting an end to all the fruitless negotiations. Jean and Guy de Namur, supported by the more cautious commanders, refused, however, to accept the proposal. When the King then suddenly ended his short expedition with a rushed and disorderly retreat some of his supplies of wine had to be poured away; some of it fell into the hands of unruly Flemish soldiers who, despite the orders of their leaders, began pursuing the powerful French army.[14] The retreat of the King brought the morale of the Flemings to its highest level and was the cause of much rejoicing on their part.[15] If the King did not dare engage in battle even with a powerful army, then this was one more proof of the power of the Flemings and the influence of their victory of 11 July that is, without doubt, to be attributed to their courage.

How different was the situation in France! The Flemish uprising at the Bruges Matins was followed by the French defeat at Courtrai. The defeated noblemen, who on 11 July made a hasty escape to Tournai and Lille, had lost more than a battle. They had lost their honour, their reputation and fame had been blotted out. The destruction of such a splendid royal army had an extremely negative influence on the prestige of Philip IV, and of France itself. It is obvious that immediately following the event, excuses for this surprising and unbelievable defeat were sought. Common people could not believe that the magnificent formations of knights had been completely and utterly defeated in normal battle. It was not difficult to find a biased version of events that would leave untarnished their national pride. The battlefield was, of course, intersected by streams and very favourable to the Flemings. On the basis of this, then, the assumption arose that the knights rode blindly into unknown ditches where they were killed, without being able to defend themselves, by the Flemings, who did not even seek to take them captive. Since they had gone so far, it was but a small step to explain the defeat as being due to a base trick, treacherous actions and betrayal. Naturally, the explanation was accepted readily since one and a half months previously the men of Bruges had at night treacherously attacked and partially destroyed the French garrison in their town. Thus, the defeat was not only attributed to unknown waterways: at the same time, or somewhat later, it was being rumoured that the Flemings had secretly dug

---

[12] Lodewijk, II.1.IV:280, c. 48, vv. 3530–4; and *Annales Gandenses*, 35–6.
[13] *Annales Gandenses*, 36–7. See also Lodewijk, II.1.IV:373–4, c. 49, vv. 3606–21; II.1.IV:379, c. 51, vv. 3765–75.
[14] *Annales Gandenses*, 37; *Chronique artésienne*, 56; and Funck-Brentano, *Philippe le Bel*, 436.
[15] Le Muisit, 71.

holes and ditches, covering them with grass and wattle. The treacherous actions were then beyond doubt.

Immediately following this most embarrassing defeat, Philip the Fair prepared for a new expedition. Such an expedition required extremely high sums of money for the soldiers' pay as well as careful preparation of provisions for the troops and the garrisons near the border. The royal treasury could not produce the money required and the King was obliged to turn to his subjects for financial assistance. This was, among others, the case for the clergy of the bailiwick of Bourges (29 August 1302). Philip's letter to the clergy was noble and moving; a genuine political work of art.[16] To this class of people, the most developed intellectually, he could not, however, make use of rumours current among the common people. Nor could he attribute the victory to the power and courage of the rebels, which would have caused much amazement among his subjects. Furthermore, the King was, at that moment, ready to lead the punitive expedition in person against the victors of Courtrai. He appeared to have confidence in the outcome since 'neither by their power, nor their courage' had the Flemings won the battle 'but rather by an event of unfavourable destiny and harsh fortune'.[17]

However, upon reaching the border the King did not dare attack the powerful Flemish army. The ghost of Courtrai was still too present before the eyes of his knights. He even accepted proposals for negotiations.[18] When the Flemish representatives proposed compensation for the calamity at Courtrai, Gaucher de Châtillon answered that it was not a question of a battle such as that of Courtrai, an open battle where all could defend themselves and one of the two sides was to take victory, but of the shameful attack by night at Bruges.[19]

At that time, therefore, the King was not thinking of accusing the Flemings of treachery or perfidious cunning at the Battle of Courtrai. However, the punitive expedition of Philip the Fair ended in a chaotic retreat. The astonishment was so great in France that the most fantastic rumours were being told about the latest failure.[20] The high nobility was said to have betrayed the King. This accusation shows how low confidence in the knighthood had sunk following the defeat of Courtrai and the failed expedition to Flines. The nobility, however, accused the common people of having taken the side of the Flemish townsmen because of their hatred of the King and nobility.[21]

At a time when such a state of mind was predominant, certain chroniclers unde-

---

[16] Wagner, 412.
[17] Funck-Brentano, 'Mémoire', 318; Lot, *L'Art militaire*, I:254; Pirenne, 'Note supplementaire', 118; and Fris, *De slag bij Kortrijk*, 204.
[18] Lodewijk, II.1.IV:374–7, c. 50; *Chronographia*, I:119; *Istore et croniques de Flandres*, I:285.
[19] Lodewijk, II.1.IV:376, c. 50, vv. 3670–84.
[20] The Queen of England, the sister of Philip the Fair, heard from her husband that her brother was betrayed by his own barons and reported this immediately to the King of France: le Muisit, 70, *Les Grandes Chroniques de France*, ed. J. Viard, SHF (Paris, 1935), VIII:212; *Chronique normande*, 20–2; *Istore et croniques de Flandres*, I:256; *Chronographia*, I:117; and Villani, col. 391.
[21] The *Chronique tournaisienne*, 56 n. 3. However, the author, a man from Tournai, added that in reality both the King and the nobility were afraid of the Flemings.

niably came to the conclusion that no artificially dug ditches and waterways gave victory to the Flemings on the Groeninge field. They sought an explanation of the defeat in the inability of the nobles, of their commander, Artois, and in the arrogance of the nobility as a caste. This version is seen clearly in the accounts given by burgher chroniclers of that time, Guillaume Guiart and Geoffroy de Paris.

Philip the Fair was, however, obliged to prepare the expedition of 1303. Still, a powerful knightly army cost many times more than a militia composed of artisans and peasants. Once again he was forced to appeal to the pockets of his subjects, who, however, did not have any more confidence in royal military expeditions after the heavy defeat at Courtrai and the failure at Flines. Counsels to the King decided to make use of more effective means.[22] An official explanation for the embarrassing events was given in order to gain the financial support of his subjects and, at the same time, to explain how the war arose, the defeat on the Groeninge field and the failure in September. For this purpose clear orders were given to the King's knights who were charged with the task. They were advised to be polite and discrete. At the same time they received the substance of the conversations they were to have in order to stir up people of the 'good towns' against the Flemish 'villains'.[23] The following account was given of the Courtrai catastrophe: 'Et cil ennemi firent fosséz et fosses faussement en traïson', the Flemish 'villains' falsely and treacherously dug ditches and holes so that the Count of Artois and many of the King's men found their death by this act of treachery, this deceit and evil deed.[24] The pitiful failure of the royal expedition of September 1302 was explained in the following manner:

> The King and high lords of his army saw that the enemy was camped in such a dangerous position that the good men of the army were not able to attack the enemy without great losses and the destruction of the French soldiers. The King did not wish this at all and thus decided to make another attempt and make use of his own possessions. However, winter came, during which the horses and soldiers could not stay outside any longer without great danger. For this reason he then decided, with the approval of a council of high lords and good men of the army, that his soldiers would retreat until the weather was favourable once more.[25]

---

[22] Such methods were applied on numerous occasions. See, for example, Lot, *La France des origines*, 156–7, for the bull issued by Pope Boniface VIII, *Ausculta, fili*, that was given so concisely as to be an actual forgery. In 1296, Count Guy de Dampierre experienced difficulties on account of a falsified letter to the French court. See Funck-Brentano, *Philippe le Bel*, 148–50.
[23] Lot, *L'Art militaire*, I:254–5, is of the opinion that the document was written by Guillaume de Nogaret.
[24] Funck-Brentano, 'Mémoire', 323; Lot, *L'Art militaire*, I:255: 'Visiblement c'est de la cour de France qu'est partie l'utilisation de la traîtrise'; Wagner, 412: 'C'est un moyen de propagande visiblement destiné à frapper les esprits des Poitevins. Le ton change (et la vérité officielle avec) selon les exigences de chaque situation particulière'; Pirenne, 'Note supplémentaire', 38–9, for the same comment; and Fris, *De slag bij Kortrijk*, 204–7.
[25] Funck-Brentano, 'Mémoire', 323–4.

Philip the Fair did not, therefore, dare attack at Vitry, or at Flines, because the position of the Flemings was too strong. He did not repeat Artois's mistake, and the lesson of Courtrai was already being applied.

By such royal instructions the version of ruse and of treachery naturally circulated throughout the kingdom. Advisors to the prince were constantly true to their declaration. The counsels to King Philip the Fair, Guillaume de Nogaret and Guillaume de Plasian, drew up in 1310 a document against Pope Boniface VIII, with whom the King had a serious conflict. The document still contained the following sentence:

> It will be shown that the Pope, after he had received news of the aforementioned uprising said: 'All is going well . . .', and this same Boniface showed pleasure in public at the defeat of the French at the hands of the Flemings, a defeat that was achieved not by the power of the Flemings, but by means of treacherous and evil cunning.[26]

The foreign mercenaries in the royal armies were to spread this version of events abroad. However, the explanation given by the royal entourage was not to be accepted everywhere: the accusation of treachery by digging holes and ditches was to disappear very rapidly in France itself. This clearly indicates the artificial nature of this version and brings us to the consideration of the sources and their explanation of the defeat. A study of the French version will be made and, in doing so, an examination of the sources that remained faithful to the explanation given by the royal entourage. The best source for this is without a doubt the *Chronique artésienne*, that chronicle which is so remarkable also in other respects.

The Sources of the French Version

The *Chronique artésienne*

The excellent *Chronique artésienne* was written by a burgher of Arras who, however, was not a soldier as has on occasions wrongly been assumed.[27] The *Chronique* was written in 1304, shortly after the events, and the reader immediately senses that the author wrote very much under the influence of the defeat at Courtrai, so painful as it was for his countrymen.[28] It is also, therefore, a very biased source.

---

[26] Ibid., 304–5; and Fris, *De slag bij Kortrijk*, 93, n. 2.
[27] The text invoked by Funck-Brentano (*Chronique artésienne*, xi) does not prove that he was a soldier in the royal army: 'Et de nos gens y eut bien .1. mors de chiaux de Saint Omer, mais des nostres n'y eut mort personne qui fust de nom, ne aussi n'i eut-il de chiaux de delà, fors gens à piet' (And of our men, there were 50 killed from St Omer, but of our men (of Artois) no man of name or repute was killed, nor any of the men of the other region (the rest of France), except foot-soldiers). The author compares the men of St Omer, Arras and those of the rest of France. It can only be concluded from the text that the author lived in Arras. However, he never appears himself as an eyewitness in his account of the battles.
[28] Funck-Brentano, 'Mémoire', 252.

The author began his work with the translation and ordering of a series of irrefutable documents kept in French chancelleries which proved the suzerainty of the King of France over the county of Flanders. At the same time the documents showed that the King could legally expect the support of the subjects of the county in the event of the Count being disloyal. He carefully indicated what rights Philip the Fair possessed with respect to Flanders. Following this, the author gave a brief explanation of the beginning of the war, showing that Count Guy de Dampierre had broken his own oath by his actions.[29] The account of the military operations of 1297 is short and written from memory.[30] After this the author gave a list of dukes, princes and viscounts who accompanied the King on the expedition. He listed seventy of them and it is evident that he could only have drawn such information from diplomatic sources.[31] Thanks to papers from the bailiff's archive at Arras he was able to present a series of documents concerning the truce concluded in January 1298.[32] He then suddenly turned to the events of 1300, merely giving a summary explanation of the military operations. Nevertheless, following this he gave a list of Flemish knights who were imprisoned, together with Count Guy. The list fully corresponds with the report on the conditions in which the imprisoned noblemen were being held in France.[33] From May 1300 he suddenly turned to the end of March 1302. As regards the Bruges Matins he acquired information on the French army that was gathered together in Arras, Hainault, the castellany of Courtrai and elsewhere. The information is such that it may rightly be assumed that he also gained this information from a document relating to financial matters; and this is indeed the only point where he presents reliable troop strengths.[34] The author also gave the composition of the garrison of the Courtrai castle.[35] Following the account of the Battle of Courtrai a list follows of dukes, counts, princes and bannerets who fell on 11 July 1302. The list is not complete, since the author did not know the names of several of the fallen noblemen from Champagne or Normandy.[36] He then noted the settlement by which the garrison of the Courtrai castle surrendered.[37] All of these documents are undeniably complete or partial reproductions of official documents or lists of those who took part or lost their lives. It is only for the period following the Battle of the Spurs that the nature of the chronicle changes completely. It then becomes a truly narrative work with an accu-

---

[29] *Chronique artésienne*, xiii–xiv.
[30] Funck-Brentano, 'Mémoire', 246.
[31] *Chronique artésienne*, 21–3.
[32] Funck-Brentano, 'Mémoire', 246; and Fris, *De slag bij Kortrijk*, 16.
[33] Funck-Brentano, 'Mémoire', 247.
[34] See the poignant observation on the part of Lot, *L'Art militaire*, I:269 n. 3. The *Chronique artésienne* indicates a total of 800 cavalrymen in heavy armour, including 120 knights with the rest squires. It also includes a tally of 300 crossbowmen and foot-soldiers.
[35] *Chronique artésienne*, 44–5.
[36] Ibid., 49–51. However, two names are missing in Funck-Brentano's edition: Lord Jean de Brabant, following Geoffroy de Brabant, and Renaut de Trie, marshal (*mareschiaux*), after Guys de Neele, marshal (*mareschiaux*), a typical mistake when copying. See Koninklijke Bibliotheek, Brussels, MS 14561–4, f. 202. Fris's edition is complete (*De slag bij Kortrijk*, 22–3).
[37] *Chronique artésienne*, 52–4.

rate and detailed account of events. Without a doubt it gives the best chronological list of secondary events for the period.[38]

The account of the battle found in the *Chronique artésienne* will now be examined.[39] The Count of Artois arrived at Marquette on 2 July. He stayed there for four days, being informed while there that the garrison of Courtrai castle was in difficulty and that a powerful army of Flemish rebels was laying siege to the garrison and had entered the town. Robert d'Artois and his men decided that they could not attack their enemies where they were and turned to the fields before the monastery of Groeninge. While preparing themselves to carry out the operation the Count and the marshals gave orders to bodies of knights to be arrayed

> since the enemies were completely lined up behind the ditches outside Courtrai. They had dug the ditches skilfully with coverings at various points. There were also ditches that were covered with grass and wattle so as to injure our men. Our men were not able to fight them if they did not enter the ditches . . . and they entered with the Lord of Artois and his formation, Lord Raoul de Nesle, the constable and two marshals, Lord Jacques de St Pol and Lord Jean de Burlats and many other men who were in their formations as well as other knights and their men who did not keep order in their formations as they wished to perform bold and brave deeds that day so that they all died. And most of them killed each other since they fell into the ditches where they drowned and caused each other to suffocate. And upon seeing this disaster, at a moment that they were already showing a desire to flee, the Flemings came and killed many of our men.

The account ends with the flight of the Count of St Pol, of the Count of Boulogne and of Louis de Clermont. Subsequently the work gives a list of those who fell and those taken captive as well as the names of the Flemish leaders.

What is notable is the brevity of the account. Let us now turn to the French scholar R. L. Wagner who wrote a notable commentary on it and a sharp, although fully justified, critique:

> This text, so precise in other respects, so meticulous in its enumeration, its explanation of politics, shows a crushing poverty when the author turned to the account of the battle itself. No vivid information, no perspective makes it appear probable. It seems that the author who knew, on account of having the list, the names of the important men who fell that day, did not have a minimally accurate knowledge on the terrain and to the vicissitudes of the battle.[40]

Moreover, the chronicler was silent about certain very significant events. The author knew so well the dates of the departure of the Count of Artois from the town of Arras and of his stay at Marquette, yet did not even give the date of his arrival

---

[38] Funck-Brentano, 'Mémoire', 248. Several chronological mistakes (*Chronique artésienne*, 75–6) indicate that he was writing somewhat after the events. The only copy of the manuscript is unfortunately incomplete. Two complete sentences (*Chronique artésienne*, 63, 87) prove that the copier of the manuscript obviously omitted certain events and names.
[39] *Chronique artésienne*, 47–9.
[40] Wagner, 410.

before the gates of Courtrai. And this information is of the greatest importance as the French army appeared before the town walls from 8 July.[41] There were skirmishes in front of the gates of Courtrai.[42] It was only after these unsuccessful attacks that the Count of Artois moved to the open area in front of the monastery of Groeninge which was the only place he could reach the garrison from. And this only happened on 11 July after he had been in front of the town for two full days. Since the author was well acquainted with the nobleman, Jean de Lens, he must also have gained this information from him. Furthermore, he makes a reference to this by stating that the French could not get at their enemy easily from where they were. Yet, despite this information, he still gave the general impression that the army went directly from Marquette to the Groeninge field. Subsequently, the author wrote 'et ceci est d'une gravité qui surprend, il confond le ruisseau de Groeninge, derrière lequel s'était . . . alignée l'armée flamande, avec les fossés prétendûment creusés dans la plaine' (and this was a surprising mistake; he confuses the stream of Groeninge, behind which . . . the Flemish army was lined up, with the ditches allegedly dug in the open field).[43] He did not even mention the advice given by high noblemen to the Count of Artois when they warned their commander of the difficult nature of the terrain. No mention was given of the battle between the crossbowmen, although it is possible that he was making reference to this when claiming that the Flemings had already begun to flee.[44] He was also completely silent as regards the sortie made by soldiers under Jean de Lens, the commander of the garrison of the castle under siege.[45] This is rather suspicious since, as already stated, the author knew Jean de Lens very well. The numerous mistakes and the suppression of essential information oblige us to be cautious about the account. The preference on the part of the chronicler for official documents is apparent, and thus it is certain that the purpose of this source, written so shortly after the events, was to seek to confirm a version based on royal propaganda: 'cil ennemi firent fosséz et fosses' (the enemy had dug ditches). Wagner's conclusion is clearly appropriate: 'nous demandons si, loyalement, il est possible d'accorder une grande valeur à un texte dont l'apparente clarté, l'allure catégorique masque une si grande confusion. Soyons nets! En saine critique, il n'est pas permis de croire d'emblée au témoignage de la *Chronique artésienne*' (We ask if, honestly, it is possible to give very much value to a text whose apparent clarity and categorical nature masks so much confusion. Let us be clear! According

---

[41] See the accounts of the Count of Artois, published in Funck-Brentano, 'Mémoire', 312. See also Wagner, 378 n. 35. For the location of the French camp see *Annales Gandenses*, 28; Lodewijk, II.1.IV:287, c. 21, vv. 1484–8; and Villani, col. 383.
[42] *Annales Gandenses*, 29. A more detailed description of the attacks is given in Lodewijk, II.1.IV:286–7, c. 21, vv. 1450–92. See also le Muisit, 66: 'comes . . . combussit villas citra et suburbana de Curtraco et fecit multos insultus.'
[43] See Wagner, 410.
[44] *Chronique artésienne*, 48.
[45] *Annales Gandenses*, 30; *Chronicon Comitum Flandriae*, 169; Guiart, 240, vv. 15,141–51; and Lodewijk, II.1.IV:310, c. 28, vv. 1997–2004.

to strict methodological principles it is not possible to accept, at first sight, the testimony of the *Chronique artésienne*).[46]

The *Chronique artésienne* is, however, not the only source that mentioned holes that had been dug. In his Austrian verse chronicle, Ottokar von Stiermarken expanded upon the royal propaganda by adding all manner of detail. His account is, however, of extremely low value, as is the case with the even more fantastic account given by Jean de Winterthur who followed a similar version and elaborated still further.

Ottokar von Stiermarken's *Oesterreichische Reimchronik*
The section of this chronicle that is of most interest to us was probably written in the years 1316–18. However, it is possible that it had already been written somewhat before then. As for the author, Ottokar von Stiermarken, he was a knight in the service of Ottokar von Liechtenstein and compiled his extensive work in Tyrol.[47]

Some scholars value his account,[48] as Ottokar wrote that 'he does not want to recount how this man slew and how that man stabbed, how with a push, they broke through a formation' but how, due to his having been informed by someone who took part in the battle, he sought to convey something about it. The combatant who provided him with the account participated so fully that he did not see how they were thrusting away and how the events actually took place. Ottokar, however, reproduced the end of the battle as it was recounted to him.[49]

In reality such a claim by Ottokar is of no importance to us. The poet called upon the authority of a so-called eyewitness for a Flemish victory, that is alleged to have taken place between the Bruges Matins (18 May) and 11 July 1302.[50] As no battle took place during the period, this account of a victory is completely invented. However, in order to make his account credible, Ottokar claimed that he was informed by an eyewitness.[51]

Ottokar did use written sources for his verse chronicle; still, he was very liberal in his use of the information contained in these sources.[52] He knew very little about events in Flanders and thus made one mistake after another.[53] His account of the Battle of Courtrai is of no value: there is not one single correct and accurate piece

---

[46] Wagner, 410–11. See also Pirenne, 'Note supplementaire', 104.
[47] Ottokar von Stiermarken, cii. See Fris, *De slag bij Kortrijk*, 59–61, 65–73, for the text of this version.
[48] Pirenne, 'La Version flamande', 36 n. 2; Funck-Brentano, 'Mémoire', 292; and Delfos, *1302 door tijdgenooten verteld*, 94.
[49] Ottokar von Stiermarken, 849–50, vv. 64,071–90, especially v. 64,079.
[50] Ibid., 848–50, vv. 63,965–64,120. See also the note by Ottokar's editor, Seemuller, 848; and Fris, *De slag bij Kortrijk*, 64. Lot, *L'Art militaire*, I:259 n. 5, refers to this fictitious battle as if it contained the account of the Battle of Courtrai. Wagner, 411, did not consult this edition, but still rejected Ottokar's testimony; Lot did not do this.
[51] Ottokar von Stiermarken, 849–50, vv. 64,077–88. See also Seemuller's comment, lxx.
[52] Ottokar von Stiermarken, 848 n. 1.
[53] Fris, *De slag bij Kortrijk*, 62–4.

of information in it, except that the Flemings did not take any captives. Furthermore, it is all so vague and general that such an account can only be dismissed.

Ottokar claims that a weaver from Ghent provoked the uprising in Flanders and that this person's authority was recognised in all towns of the county. The weaver thought of a cunning plan: the digging, at night, of long, broad and deep ditches with iron-tipped poles. They were then covered with turf so as to conceal them from the French.[54]

In the French army, Ottokar had the brother of the King appear. He had led military operations in 1300, but he was not present in 1302. Also, the list of French units of knights is very incomplete.[55]

The Flemish rearguard was composed of cavalrymen.[56] The Flemish commander also sent a priest in order to initiate peace talks.[57] Finally, the battle began and the Flemings moved very skilfully behind their ditches.[58] They had divided their army into two groups and attacked the French knights as they rode into the ditches, both from behind and in front.[59] Despite all the efforts made by the French themselves to encircle the Flemings they were not able to free themselves from the fatal grip and were destroyed. This was all the more so as the Flemings had received orders not to take any prisoners.[60]

It is clear that the person who informed Ottokar was not Flemish. This is evidenced only too well by his account. Can it be accepted that a Fleming would have recounted that the rebel's rearguard was composed of cavalrymen? He would also have known that Ghent was still on the side of the King of France. Can it be accepted that the Flemings had the time, during a short summer's night, to dig ditches over an area of one kilometre, and to cover them in such a manner that the enemy did not notice anything? And after a night of tiring work in the dark this militia was supposed to have pulled back past the holes and to have carefully avoided, by day, the hidden ditches.[61]

We may, without any objections, dismiss this fabulous tale. Indeed, there is no single accurate description to be found in it: nothing about the terrain, nothing about the Flemish commanders, their troops and their positions. Ottokar gave us a vague, albeit very long-drawn account that must serve as an explanation of the cunning plan. His actual account of the battle itself was completely invented. The only point where he added some further piece of information is, naturally, the

---

[54] Ottokar von Stiermarken, 852, vv. 64,305–21.
[55] Ibid., 853, vv. 64,330–79.
[56] Ibid., 855, vv. 64,517–32.
[57] Ibid., 855–6, vv. 64,543–87.
[58] Ibid., 856, vv. 64,591–617.
[59] Ibid., 856, vv. 64,619–30.
[60] Ibid., 856–7, vv. 64,631–65; 857, vv. 64,666–74.
[61] Wagner, 411–12; and Fris, *De slag bij Kortrijk*, 65.

cunning plan: the ditches that were dug secretly. The legend was developed even further here than by the royal entourage or the *Chronique artésienne*.⁶²

Another credulous author who also lived far away from where the events took place was Jean de Winterthur. He also heard the rumours that were being put about by the royal entourage and by some of those who had fought in the defeated army. He tailored them for his public, giving the legend new form.

Jean de Winterthur

This friar of the Villingen monastery in Baden lived in Lindau from 1343 until he died around 1348. His work is of very great value with respect to events in Germany in the middle of the fourteenth century,⁶³ and the chronicle is also the main source for the conflict between the Swiss and the Austrian knights, among others for the renowned Battle of Morgarten in 1315, the first great victory for Swiss foot-soldiers.⁶⁴ The author appeared, however, to have been utterly lacking in any critical approach and accepted, with an incredible ease, numerous fabulous details. He claimed to have received information from eyewitnesses. Questions arise, then, as to whether Jean de Winterthur invoked the authority of persons in order to give his account the necessary force, making it by this means credible.

Who informed Jean de Winterthur about the Battle of Courtrai? At least two groups of people can be discerned in his account, although some gave conflicting versions. In the short account of the Battle of the Spurs Jean de Winterthur, following his explanation of the battle, speaks of the losses suffered by the French. In order to justify the figures given he invoked the authority of his sources:

> Various people who lived in the area at that time say that 25,000 brave and armoured men fell; seventy renowned and powerful lords were also killed, all of them under different banners. I know this from a reliable account by those who took part in the battle. Some, however, say that the Flemings only rode on mares for some sly purpose . . . so that the excellent and heavily armoured French warhorses would become impassioned by desires.

This happened, and the French stallions brought their riders quickly to the Flemish mares, thus entering the man-made ditches dug the night before the battle. The ditches were well hidden and in them the water of a river that flowed through the valley was channelled away. Strictly speaking he is thus only using the authority of participants concerning the number of bannerets who fell. The figure given, seventy bannerets, is actually close to the most accurate information we have on the matter. At the same time Jean de Winterthur showed that he also consulted

---

⁶² Even though Ottokar despised the King of France, as he thought that he had dishonoured Guy de Dampierre's daughter (v. 63,717), he still did not bear any animosity towards France itself (843, vv. 63,596–9). See also Fris, *De slag bij Kortrijk*, 63 n. 2.
⁶³ Jean de Winterthur, 31–2.
⁶⁴ Delbrück, 578.

other newsbearers. Some of them told him an exceptionally foolish and fabricated story that was to show how the Flemings disregarded all knightly custom by not riding on stallions. It is evident that he once again called upon the authority of an imaginary informant in order to add credibility to his claims. The account itself gives far too little information to assume it was from eyewitnesses. The account is reproduced below:

> One day the Flemings, who were in a valley, gained victory against the French. They made use of a cunning trick which the less cautious and unsuspecting opponents fell for. The night before the battle they dug holes underneath the ground covering them carefully so that they could skilfully entice the unsuspecting French into them. The day after, the French attacked and fell into the holes, which were full of water since the Flemings had diverted a waterway that runs through the valley into the holes. The Frenchmen were killed by the fall, or drowned, or else they were slain.

A list of losses then follows with indications about the persons who gave the information and, finally, on the basis of certain informants, the absurdly cunning Flemish plan.

It is clear that this account is of no value. The Flemings, about whom nothing more is told, were lined up in a valley, which naturally was self-evident for Jean de Winterthur and his readers. In a short summer night they dug underground holes into which they even diverted a waterway. It is here then that Ottokar von Stiermarken's account is made plausible for readers from what was to become Switzerland and from south Germany. The absurd and cunning plan has the Flemings on horseback. Once again, and without any doubt, there is a confrontation with a more elaborate reproduction of the French version as put about in neighbouring countries by the royal entourage and those vanquished. Remarkably, all of those elements connected to the cunning plan and the ditches were elaborated upon with new details while the rest of the battle was reported in an extremely incomplete manner.

Nevertheless, the explanation of the defeat being due to the ditches dug was not accepted everywhere. This becomes evident immediately upon examining several sources that did not originate in knightly circles. The crossbowman, Guillaume Guiart, and the burgher, Geoffroy de Paris, were critical of the explication given by the royal court and by the noblemen. Both sought their own explanations that show clearly how they were influenced by their own social environments. Townsmen in the French army suddenly came to play an important role even if before then not much had been reported about them. In this respect, Guillaume Guiart first of all deserves special and critical examination.

Guillaume Guiart
Guiart first took part in the war in the spring of 1304 along the Flemish border with a contingent of ninety townsmen sent by the town of Orléans. He was, as a sergeant, in command of his fellow townsmen and while serving suffered injuries to his right foot and left arm following a fight at La Haignerie during the advance

of the army of Philip the Fair from Tournai towards Mons-en-Pévèle.[65] His brief experience of battle allowed him, however, to give an excellent description of warfare at that time. He not only describes the customs and tactics of the French army in a remarkable, albeit verbose, manner, but the Flemish army is also expertly depicted concerning, among other things, the *goedendags*, the phalanx formation, battle techniques, etc.[66] Guiart is an excellent source for minor details on the art of warfare in the period 1302–4 and his work constitutes a sound addition to the *Annales Gandenses*. This Flemish chronicle gave a thorough account of tactical developments of that time while Guiart provides the necessary description of life in the army, movements, advances, camps, etc. While the Flemish author examined and reproduced the general context, Guiart paid attention to minor details that fill in the picture and add colour to it.[67] However, on account of the fact that the Orléans burgher only took part in the war in 1304 he did not stress the new elements in French tactics. This was something that was especially emphasised by the Ghentenaar Franciscan friar. Nevertheless, in the careful and meticulous account given by the less gifted Frenchman is found the necessary confirmation of details in the friar's explanation.

Guiart began his account of the events immediately after the military operations. After being wounded he was treated in Arras in August 1304. It was there that he had the idea of drawing up a history of the war. Naturally, he aimed at explaining the true course of events since the Flemings were glorifying their victory at Courtrai, and the rebels were not speaking of their defeats at Furnes (1297), Arques (1303), Gravelines (1304) and in Zeeland (Zierikzee, 10–11 August 1304). The Flemish version of the war was, indeed, dishonourable for the French King.[68] Guiart sought to combat this biased version of events and this induced him to write his chronicle, which he subsequently dedicated to Philip the Fair.

Such a reaction always leads to exaggeration. The platonic declaration made by the author of his love of truth is only to be accepted with strict reservations. The reliability of his account must be determined most carefully. A critical examination shows very quickly that the crossbowman from Orléans, as a subject of the King of France, not only exaggerated, but also made use himself of known falsehoods.

The campaign of Guiart was very short. He saw little fighting, perhaps only during skirmishes on 13–14 July 1304. On the first day of the invasion of Flanders,

---

[65] Guiart, 174, vv. 104–8; 285, vv. 19,876–903. The following day was 11 August (v. 19,921).
[66] Ibid., 233, vv. 14,407–37; on the *goedendags* see 287–8, vv. 20,155–69; for a good description of the phalanx see 291–2, vv. 20,573–8.
[67] Verbruggen, 'De Gentse minderbroeder', 4 ff.
[68] Guiart, 173, vv. 36–66; 174–5, vv. 100–76. Guiart spoke of a Flemish defeat in Zeeland. He was certainly referring to the Flemish defeat at sea in front of Zierikzee. He appeared to be forgetting that in August 1304 very little could be said of Zierikzee by the Flemings, since news of the event only reached the army at the border on 13 August: *Annales Gandenses*, 63. The Battle of Furnes in 1297, during the conflict between Count Guy and Philip the Fair, was certainly of minimal interest for the townsmen. Gravelines was only reported and described by Guiart. His account ought not to be accepted a priori. On the Battle of Arques see Verbruggen, 'De Gentse minderbroeder', 6–7; and Verbruggen, *The Art of Warfare in Western Europe during the Middle Ages*, 194–7.

he was wounded on the attack at La Haignerie, probably on 10 or 11 August. Because he was so quickly out of combat, the resistance which he felt physically gave him great respect for the Flemish forces. But he may never have encountered the full Flemish army in its battle array.

Furthermore, consideration ought to be given to the fact that Guiart was writing very shortly after the events, since he had already begun his work in 1304. A definitive text was drawn up in 1306, and the chronicle was finished in 1307.[69] There are always, for the non-biased explanation and judgement of events, serious disadvantages associated with writing so shortly after an event, especially when it is a question of a heavy defeat.

What sources did he use? Up to 1296 he made use of a Latin source he had consulted in the abbey of St Denis near Paris. Until that time, his chronicle is merely a rhymed adaptation of the *Chronique de St Denis*.[70] For the period 1290–1306 use was made, he stated, only of events reported to him by eyewitnesses or of which he himself had been a witness.[71] Yet, somewhat later in his introduction he contradicted this claim: he began work after deciding, in August 1304 at Arras, to write a history of the war. For events of which he did not know much, he interviewed those who took part and certainly other persons as well. However, a clerk was of the opinion that Guiart had not received enough information and advised him to go to St Denis and consult the sources there.[72] The abbey was indeed one of the great centres for history in the Middle Ages in France. There Guiart would come to know the true course of events, not fabricated tales or legends. He followed the advice and came to the conclusion that his notes made at Arras and its surrounding areas were of no value. He burnt them and, following this, began to write a real and true account.[73] On 8 May 1306, he started his work once again. This declaration clearly contradicts what he claimed above, and scholars who are interested in his work have not taken this into consideration sufficiently. One detail is not to be disputed: Guiart did not take any notes before August 1304. Consulting eyewitnesses must thus have been more difficult than one has supposed. This chronicler probably allowed himself to be influenced by documents kept in the abbey of St Denis as well as such information as he obtained there. He was, however, able to present the information in an excellent manner due to his knowledge of the terrain and of military science gained in 1304 during his brief period in action and could, of course, have visited the area after the war

---

[69] Guiart, 174–5, vv. 149–76.
[70] Ibid., 173, vv. 39–46.
[71] Ibid., 173, vv. 47–66.
[72] Ibid., 174, vv. 149–63.
[73] Ibid., 174–5, vv. 164–74: 'Bien tost après cestes paroles. / M'en vins là, et tant esploitai. / Qu'i vi ce que je convoitai. / Lors alai faus apercevant / Quanque j'avoie fait devant; / Si l'ardi, c'on ni déust croire; / Et me pris à la vraie hystoire / Jouste laquelle je me sis / En l'an M et CCC et VI, / VIII jours ainz may, qui voir enterve / Ai recommencieé ma verve.' (Shortly after those words, I went there [to St Denis] and found what I sought. I saw that all that I had done before was false. I burnt it. Nobody was to believe it. I began with true history, sitting down to write it in the year 1306, on 8 May. Seeking the truth, I began my story once more.)

towards the end of 1304 and in 1305. The problem is even more important when turning to the Battle of Mons-en-Pévèle (18 August 1304) and the naval battle near Zierikzee (10–11 August 1304). Guiart described both events so accurately and in such detail that he was thought to have been a witness. This could not have been the case for Zierikzee since he was wounded on 10 August near La Haignerie and was, perhaps, already in Arras in order to have his wounds treated before the Battle of Mons-en-Pévèle.[74]

Guiart's account of the Battle of the Spurs
The account given by the burgher of Orléans merits thorough examination since various historians of the Battle of the Spurs used information given by him in detailing a turning movement carried out by the French army. The army was alleged to have first moved across the Groeninge stream and then to have deployed its formations along the Grote Beek (the Great Brook), thus forcing the Flemings to change their original positions. The French knights were then alleged to have attacked across the Grote Beek stream after Flemish light troops had been pushed back by crossbowmen.[75] This conception of events is no doubt erroneous since Guiart's text, detailing the turning movement, is not very detailed. Furthermore, the presentation of the crossbow battle appears exaggerated.

In summary: when the Flemings left Courtrai on 11 July 1302, and were rallied together on the open field, the French formed their formations or *bataelgen*. In little time they advanced closing in upon their enemy up to two shots of the bow,[76] and they came before a long ditch full of mud where the horses sank in up to the saddle if they dared enter it.[77] Raoul de Nesle, the constable, noted that the crossing was difficult and was worried about the dangers of a battle on the other side with the stream behind them. He said to the Count of Artois: 'Lord, our soldiers would be in a dangerous position if they fight on the other side with the stream behind them. If they had to give way and the horses entered the stream then they would have difficulty getting out.'

So as to avoid this dangerous battle on the other side with the obstacle behind the army, Nesle proposed moving backwards somewhat and thus tempting the Flemish troops out of their strong position. The tempestuous and overly hasty French commander took the advice to be inappropriate. Other noblemen, however, expressed the same doubts as the constable.[78] Artois did not listen and had his knights take their positions for battle as well as the foot-soldiers. The crossbowmen

---

[74] There is nothing concerning this in Fris, *De slag bij Kortrijk*, 24, or in Funck-Brentano, 'Mémoire', 260–3, 470 n. 3.
[75] H. G. Moke, 'Mémoire sur la bataille de Courtrai', *Mémoires de l'académie royale de Belgique*, 26 (1851), 1–63; Köhler, *Die Entwickelung des Kriegswesens*, II:216–49; Pirenne, 'La Version flamande', 24; J. Frederichs, 'De slag van Kortrijk', 25–6; Fris, *De slag bij Kortrijk*, 23, 357–8; Blockmans, *1302, vóór en na*, 67; and Nowé, *La Bataille des éperons d'or*, 76. Nowé appropriately notes that Guiart is alone in detailing such a movement.
[76] Guiart, 238, vv. 15,004–8.
[77] Ibid., 238, vv. 15,009–13.
[78] Ibid., 238–9, vv. 15,014–40.

went first following the stream until they found a crossing not far from where they were. Under the command of Jean de Burlats they were deployed in the open field: the enemy was in front of them. The position of the French light troops was as deep as the length of a catapult shot. It was as wide as two lengths of a bow shot. The knights were ranged behind them.[79] The Count of Artois was to the right with Jean de Hainault who had just been knighted. Geoffrey de Brabant was also there with the counts of Aumale and of Eu, as well as the two brothers de Nesle and Jacques de St Pol with their formations. Louis de Clermont stayed on the other side of the ditch that separated them. Louis de Clermont, the Count of St Pol and the Count of Boulogne were to form the rearguard.[80]

The French crossbowmen drew their bows and shot their arrows in thick volleys. They drove their opponents back for the distance of one and a half bowshots.[81] The first ranks even threw down their bows so as to be able to storm after the enemy with their shields in one hand and their drawn swords in another. They were so confident in doing so, that some of the Flemish soldiers started to flee.[82]

A knight, Walepaièle, saw the favourable development of the battle and shouted to Artois: 'My lord, the commoners will perform such feats of arms that they will carry the honour of the battle. What have we, noblemen, come here to do if they put an end to the battle? Let us advance for it is time!'[83]

'Forwards' was the order given by the Count and he spurred his horse with the whole formation following. They advanced through the foot-soldiers, of whom many were trampled down. Then the Flemings shouted: 'Dear Count, for the sake of God let us have some space in which to fight. You will be praised highly by all who know what truly took place.' Artois agreed to this and had his standard bearers turn around in great haste. The French knights turned their backs to the Flemings who, however, suddenly attacked them.[84] At the moment that the French noblemen were retreating, Jean de Lens stayed behind with his foot-soldiers who had left the castle for the open field and were gathered together in their ranks facing Courtrai.[85] They had set fire to the town and then they began helping foot-soldiers who had been trampled down by the warhorses. However, when they saw that the knights were retreating and were being attacked from behind by the Flemings, they began to flee as fast as they could.[86]

After this Artois's banner was taken down. Jean de Hainault fell. The brave knights forced a path into the ranks of the Flemings while the frightened men fled trembling into the ditches where they tried to cross over, but only fell into chaos. Horses and knights fell into disarray, and into the mud. Artois, however, fought in the midst of the men of the Franc of Bruges. He could but do little, since the Flem-

---

[79] Ibid., 239, vv. 15,043–58.
[80] Ibid., 239, vv. 15,059–81.
[81] Ibid., 239, vv. 15,082–93.
[82] Ibid., 239, vv. 15,094–105.
[83] Ibid., 239, vv. 15,106–18.
[84] Ibid., 239–40, vv. 15,119–40.
[85] Ibid., 240, vv. 15,141–47.
[86] Ibid., 240, vv. 15,148–60.

ings were so numerous there that certainly thirty of them fought against one of Artois's soldiers. Artois's warhorse was killed beneath him, and the Count fell.[87] The following lords were killed: the Counts of Aumale and of Eu, Tancarville, Geoffrey de Brabant, Guy le Vidame, Raoul and Gui de Nesle, Jacques de St Pol and Pierre Flote. The commanders of the rearguard left the battlefield with a sorrowful heart as all their men had fled, and they were not able to rally them again.[88]

This account which was presented as fully as possible since it poses several very interesting problems will now be examined.

First of all, the fact needs to be mentioned that Guiart's account did not speak of cunningly dug ditches. His account was dedicated to the King of France, and Guiart was reacting against an exaggerated Flemish version of the events. This shows that on the Flemish border and around Arras as well as in the abbey of St Denis the account of cunningly dug ditches was not generally believed.

Aside from this, and despite his tendency to react against the Flemish account, Guiart confirmed the Flemish version at two very important points. This is the case for the advice given by Raoul de Nesle. The constable took account of the fact that it was dangerous to enjoin in battle with a deep ditch behind the French knights. In Guiart's account, however, the stream did not play a role as a frontal impediment. During the battle some of the French knights were to flee full of fear towards the stream and drown there. This corresponds fully with the account given by pro-Flemish sources such as Lodewijk and the Ghentenaar Friar Minor.[89] A second confirmation is to be found in the description of the attack by Jean de Lens and such information is not given by any other French source. However, Guiart was very vague here and it is clear that he did not have an accurate representation of the Flemish positions. He did not speak of the men of Ypres who were lined up before the gate of the castle in order to protect the Flemish rear and this gave the impression that the garrison of the castle was able to provide assistance to some of the French foot-soldiers even though this was impossible on account of the Flemish battle array still being situated between the French foot-soldiers and the men of Ypres.

After this there is the problem of the ditch and of the turning movement. The stream, or waterway, long and full of mud, was at a distance of two arrow shots away from the Flemish positions. Examining a map of the battlefield, one notes that the stream could have been the Groeninge or the Mosscher (or Klakkaerts brook or stream) which is five hundred metres from the Grote Beek (the Great Brook). It could not, however, have been that section of the Groeninge stream that runs from the Lys to the Grote Beek since the Flemish position there was supposedly closer to the French position. And it was there that the Flemish crossbowmen

---

[87] Ibid., 240, vv. 15,162–91.
[88] Ibid., 240, vv. 15,195–212.
[89] Pirenne, 'La Version flamande', 31; *Annales Gandenses*, 70; Lodewijk, II.1.IV:317, c. 31, vv. 2192–203; II.1.IV:314, c. 29, vv. 2104–5; II.1.IV:328, c. 34, vv. 2473–4. See also the examination of the Flemish version below.

were alleged to have defended the Groeninge, but Guiart made no mention whatsoever of this. It is nevertheless possible that the French reached the Groeninge to the east of the Grote Beek.

The crossbowmen crossed the ditch spreading out into the open field in ranks that were two arrow shots long and one long stone throw deep. This leads one to assume that the formation was not wholly composed of crossbowmen since only the first ranks, in such a formation, could make use of the weapons to shoot accurately.[90] The open field in question could be that area situated between the Mosscher, Groeninge and Grote Beek streams. However, Guiart nowhere mentions the Grote Beek in the context of their advance since he did not mention any ditch in front of the French vanguard. If one assumes that the long ditch which the author mentioned included the Groeninge and the Grote Beek, taken as one single stream or waterway, then the aforementioned objection is still valid: the Flemings would not have allowed the French to cross over without engaging in battle.

Thus, we see that the turning movement cannot be accepted without significant objections being given to it. What is more serious, however, is the fact that Guiart was alone in detailing this manoeuvre.[91] Moreover, he did not mention the countermeasures taken by the Flemings, nor the change in the front-line positions from the Groeninge to the Grote Beek stream. All this makes it difficult to accept that the turning movement took place from the Groeninge to the Grote Beek. And it makes it even more difficult to 'force' Guiart's account upon other sources, as has been done by various historians: Moke, Köhler, Frederichs and Fris.

In depicting the battle between the crossbowmen, it is evident that Guiart was speaking as a crossbowman. Still, for the period 1302–4, there is no sign of French crossbowmen being so numerically superior. At Pont-à-Vendin, battle was engaged for a whole day between the French and Flemish crossbowmen without any conclusive result.[92] The same happened at the Battle of Mons-en-Pévèle (18 August 1304), where the French were certainly in a superior position as the Ghentenaars, Yprois and other Flemish crossbowmen had thrown away their bows at the beginning of the battle, excluding, however, the men of Bruges and the Bruges Franc. Nevertheless, the French were not able to achieve any obvious advance against the deep phalanx that their opponents formed.[93]

---

[90] Indeed, this is the case for the Battle of Mons-en-Pévèle. The French crossbowmen advanced in the first ranks. See Guiart, 291, vv. 20,535–6: 'Bidauz targiez, les dars levant / Et arbalestriers sont devant' (The *bidauts* carrying their *targes* [large shields] and the dards in their hands and the crossbowmen are in front). See also chapter II on the numerical strength of the French forces.

[91] This movement was also not accepted by Wodsak, 46; Delbrück, 442–3; Oman, II:118 n. I; de Maere d'Aertrycke, *La Bataille des éperons d'or*, 52, 62; Lot, *L'Art militaire*, I:263 n. 4; and F. L. Ganshof, 'Staatkundige geschiedenis, XIIe, XIIIe, XIVe eeuw', in *Geschiedenis van Vlaanderen*, 2 (Antwerp and Brussels, 1937), 52. Nowé, *La Bataille des éperons d'or*, 76, accepts it with reservations.

[92] Guiart, 266, vv. 17,932–48: 'Li soudoier aus cotes noires, / Et plusieurs autres qui là ièrent, / Outre le fosse se lancièrent; / Devant les Flamens s'estendirent. / D'une part et d'autre tendirent / Arbalestriers leurs arbalestes; / . . . / A servir s'entrecommencièrent / . . . / Toute la journée dura / Le bruit des quarriaus qu'entreus traistre / François au vespre se retraitrent.'

[93] *Annales Gandenses*, 66; and *Chronique artésienne*, 85–6.

That many foot-soldiers were trampled under foot by the knights is also certainly exaggerated. It is possible that a certain number of them were trampled under foot although the number is certainly not as high as Guiart would have us believe. There is also a dearth of examples of this in the same period.

Finally, a naive explanation given for the Flemish victory has been arrived at. Where did Guiart get the idea of the especially cunning plan? Funck-Brentano was of the opinion that he did not invent this, even though he misinterpreted a Flemish account.[94] An account of the same nature given by Lodewijk might have misled him, since it depicted an attack by Jan van Renesse, commander of the Flemish reserve force, carried out (allegedly) behind the French knights.[95] Wagner did not exclude the possibility of intentional falsification on the part of Guiart.[96] It is certainly possible that Guiart was influenced by the Flemish account which was known to him and against which he sought to react. The attack by Jan van Renesse was echoed in various French sources, usually becoming wholly distorted.[97]

Finally, in tracing the sources for Guiart's depiction of the Battle of the Spurs, consideration must still be made of the possibility that he gained information from crossbowmen who had taken part in the battle. A careful reading of his text shows immediately, however, that this was not the case. In fact, in contrast to almost all other depictions of battles given by Guiart, and even for the period when he was not present on the battlefield, this depiction did not provide any accurate details about the Flemings.[98] Apart from mentioning the ditch, nothing is learned about their position.[99] From Guiart's account of the battle, it cannot even be determined whether only the Flemish crossbowmen were driven back or whether the general battle array was forced to give way.

During the account of the attack, made by de Lens, Guiart made no mention of the Flemish forces and claimed that the garrison took up positions facing Courtrai. This is incorrect since the position must have been facing away from Courtrai.

However, Guiart could have gained the information from the French light rear-guard foot-soldiers. This would explain the vagueness of his account since the light foot-soldiers had, perhaps, not taken note of the battle positions of the enemy. Nevertheless, one should be aware of the possibility of exaggeration in this regard.

---

[94] Funck-Brentano, 'Mémoire', 260–1.
[95] For further details see the discussion of this passage in the examination of Lodewijk's account below.
[96] Wagner, 397–8.
[97] *Chronographia*, I:109, had Jan van Renesse attacking the French camp with 400 Dutchmen (200 according to the *Istore et croniques*, I:235). *Récits d'un bourgeois de Valenciennes*, ed. Kervyn de Lettenhove (Louvain, 1877), 114–15; and Jean des Preis d'Outremeuse, *Ly Myreur des histors*, ed. St Bormans, CRH (Brussels, 1880), VI:18, described another plan of Jan van Renesse to have the French infantry retreat.
[98] Thus Guiart gave a beautiful desciption of the *goedendag* and the use of this weapon based on what he had witnessed. Still, his description of the Battle of the Spurs was during the period of his chronicle when he was not present on the battlefield (Guiart, 233, vv. 14,407–37).
[99] Compare the vagueness of the depiction with the detailed description of the Flemish battle positions at Arques (Guiart, 248, vv. 16,050–80) where Guiart was not present.

A person taking part in the battle could very easily, for example when fleeing, have gained information about the battle first-hand from soldiers who actually fought themselves, or who were positioned closer to the actual battlefield. To claim that they 'understood nothing of the movements and various attacks' appears very much exaggerated.[100] If Guiart had actually consulted such persons then he would, in my opinion, have given more details about the rearguard. His account of the events is too general to allow us to accept that he was given the information by men from the *batailles* under Gui de St Pol, Louis de Clermont and the Count of Boulogne. Furthermore, he also made no mention of the pursuit by the Flemings. All this supports the assumption that Guiart, for the Battle of Courtrai, only made use of documents from the abbey of St Denis, reworking and adapting them quite liberally for the crossbow battle and the treacherous Flemish attack.

Wagner explained Guiart's account in the following manner: as a soldier he took the dishonour occasioned by the battle at Courtrai as a personal disgrace and thus gave an explanation of the defeat as a treacherous plan. Nevertheless, as a participant in the battle he felt compelled to criticise the conduct of the commander in a severe manner,[101] as well as emphasising that of the crossbowmen. His account thus gives another aspect of the French version: the defeat is attributed to the rashness, imprudence and incompetence of the commander and the knights.

As a result, Guiart's account is very close to that of Geoffroy de Paris. The latter also exaggerated the role of the crossbowmen and of the lightly armed foot-soldiers, who attacked the Flemish foot-soldiers so ferociously that they drove them back despite the Flemish soldiers being so much better equipped for combat at close quarters. He also found an explanation of the French defeat in terms of tempestuousness and carelessness, or even in terms of stupidity on the part of the knights who had a mistaken concept of honour, leading them, in the end, to commit suicide in the marshes. Geoffroy de Paris's version consequently differed from that of Guiart who, ridiculously, attributed the knights' defeat to a cunning plan.

Geoffroy de Paris

This author was a burgher of Paris who wrote his rhymed chronicle at the beginning of the fourteenth century detailing the period from 1300 to 1316. He wrote between 1313 and 1317, and clearly took careful notes for these years detailing the most significant events since this section of his chronicle is of much value. Concerning the first years of the fourteenth century, the author declared that they were drawn up from memory,[102] and it is here that very serious errors are committed.[103]

---

[100] Fris, *De slag bij Kortrijk*, 27. However, Fris had little reason to claim the above. This was even less so since he positioned the rearguard, in his general map of the battle (370), so close to the battle area that many of the soldiers would have been able to observe it.
[101] Wagner, 399.
[102] Geoffroy de Paris, 89, vv. 6–8. See also Geoffroy de Paris's verses on Pieter de Coninc noted below.
[103] Pirenne, 'La Version flamande', 26–31; and Fris, *De slag bij Kortrijk*, 47, mentioned a typical mistake: Geoffrey had the Battle of Furnes (20 August 1297) taking place on Whit

Geoffroy de Paris was a typical representative of that form of history conceived for the common people. Thus, he rather regularly presented and interpreted events in a manner peculiar to Parisian burghers of that period.

On account of the numerous mistakes that he made in dealing with the first years of the fourteenth century, Geoffroy de Paris's account has not hitherto been highly regarded. Pirenne heavily criticised it on account of the ridiculous verses on Pieter de Coninc. Due to his misunderstanding of the name of the popular Bruges leader the chronicler claimed that the Flemings had chosen a new king on account of their hatred of the rightful prince, Philip the Fair.[104] Still there was no mention of how Geoffroy de Paris made such a serious mistake. The author certainly used a Latin text, translating it incorrectly. The same mistake, although without the preposterous elaboration of the original, is to be found in the manuscript of the *Istore et croniques de Flandres*,[105] where the following appears: 'li roys Pierre Connins, tisserans de linge', with this being the translation of 'nomine Petrus, cognomento Conin, alias Regis'. This is the name of the famous man of Bruges that appears in the *Chronographia Regum Francorum*.[106] The fantasy with which Geoffroy transformed his subject shows how he wrote his chronicle in a rather light manner thus justifying a sceptical approach to those passages drawn up solely on the basis of his own memory. His account of the Battle of the Spurs will be summarised:

The flower of French knighthood, accompanied by numerous mercenaries from France and from foreign countries, advanced towards the Flemings.[107] The crossbowmen marched first and engaged in battle with their enemies. The adversaries shot all the arrows in their quivers. Following this, the remaining French foot-soldiers advanced, closely ranked, attacking the Flemings who fought back vigorously even though they were driven back forcefully.[108]

As soon as the French knights noticed that their enemy had been weakened they wanted to gain the honour of the battle and recalled the foot-soldiers. Artois himself suggested this. Pierre Flote was of the opinion that this was not necessary and that the foot-soldiers must be allowed to continue fighting. The knights could observe the battle at a distance and, in the event of difficulty, rush to their aid immediately. In this way the foot-soldiers would act boldly, seeking to fight well and gain courage from the presence of the knights. This wise piece of advice was,

---

Thursday 1301, having confused the date with that of Whit Thursday, or *Jeudi absolu*, on which day the battle fought between Arques and St Omer took place in 1303.

[104] Geoffroy de Paris, 95, vv. 653–71. See also Pirenne, 'La Version flamande', 27; and Fris, *De slag bij Kortrijk*, 46. Also, the picture of Pieter de Coninc is fully erroneous: *Chronique artésienne*, 37–8, 38 n. 1.

[105] *Istore et croniques*, I:229 n. See also Moranvillé, in *Chronographia*, I:97 n. 4. He quoted the same conclusion drawn by A. and E. Molinier in their preface to the *Chronique normande*, xxix and n. 4.

[106] *Chronographia*, I:97: 'tunc eligentes quemdem textorem pannorum, nomine Petrum, cognomento Regis, ipsum super se elevaverunt in dominum'; I:106: 'Petrus cognomento Conin alias Regis'; I:117: 'Petri Conin, alias Regis.'

[107] Geoffroy de Paris, 99, vv. 1111–23.

[108] Ibid., 99–100, vv. 1124–39.

however, rejected and Artois answered very sharply: 'Pierre, among you men of Languedoc there is always a traitor.' Pierre Flote retorted classically that if the Count were to advance as far into the enemy's ranks as he himself would, then he might be called brave![109]

Artois gave the order: 'Soldiers, retreat!' Great clouds of dust rose up while the horses made a hellish noise. The French foot-soldiers were astonished and the men thought that something serious had happened, that the Flemings had appeared from another side and had attacked.[110] The proud French knights let their foot-soldiers be trampled down by the horses or thrown to the ground.[111] The Flemings retreated quickly to a passage in the direction of the Lys. They knew the passage and positioned themselves as soon as the knights approached. In a short period of time they rallied together again behind a marsh, on account of their treachery and malice,[112] and were ready to engage in combat once again with their *goedendags* held high.[113]

Stupidly, the French knights rode towards the marsh. They fell into the mud and could not get out again.[114] The will of God demanded their defeat, and, on account of their recklessness, they ran to their destruction.[115] The Flemings advanced into the marsh and killed their enemy there since no prisoners were taken.[116] In the end, the French knights defeated themselves as they killed each other without a battle.[117] No man wanted to flee for fear of being accused of cowardice.[118] Artois had defeat on his conscience, as did his father for Mansurah (8 February 1250) during the first crusade of St Louis in Egypt.[119] St Benedict's day had finally become a curse for the French, not a benediction.[120] The counts of St Pol, Boulogne, Burgundy and Champagne as well as other noblemen who fled did not act stupidly but, on the contrary, intelligently.[121]

This is the somewhat confused account given by Geoffroy from the which the various repeated passages, and the digressions, have been removed. Concerning military matters, the account is of no value. Only Wagner attached importance to it and employed it in his account of the battle. He praised the attempt made by the Parisian to write without bias. However, this does not alter the fact that Geoffroy

---

[109] Ibid., 100, vv. 1151–205.
[110] Ibid., 100, vv. 1206–15.
[111] Ibid., 100, vv. 1222–5.
[112] Ibid., 100–1, vv. 1227–33, 1239–41.
[113] Ibid., 101, vv. 1242–3.
[114] Ibid., 101, vv. 1261–2, 1269–70. For vv. 1265–6: 'Se férirent dedans la fange, / Aussi le privé com l'estrange.' See also Guiart, 238, vv. 15,009–10: 'Et vindrent privez et estranges / Sur l lonc fossé plain de fanges.'
[115] Geoffroy de Paris, 101, vv. 1278–82, 1283–4.
[116] Ibid., 101, vv. 1289–300.
[117] Ibid., 101, vv. 1310–11: 'Bien se mirent au col la hart, / Quant il s'ocirent sanz bataille'; v. 1352: 'A mort sanz cop férir se mirent.'
[118] Ibid., 101, vv. 1330–3.
[119] Ibid., 102, vv. 1357–60.
[120] Ibid., 102, vv. 1386–91. For Lodewijk van Velthem, the Flemish victory was a benediction: Lodewijk, II.1.IV:347, c. 41, vv. 2939–40.
[121] Geoffroy de Paris, 102, vv. 1421–5.

was very badly informed. The case of Pieter de Coninc also shows the fantasy with which he expanded his sources. Contrary to all other sources, he did not mention a council of war *before* the battle, but during it. His presentation of the French foot-soldiers' attack was even more biased than that of Guiart. It is clear from the account that the Parisian grossly exaggerated the French feats of arms. Geoffroy was certainly very biased with respect to the knights: their alleged stupidity and suicide in the marsh ought to be enough to prove this. In his account of the Battle of Mons-en-Pévèle he accused them, moreover, of treason.[122] The quick victory of the French light soldiers was practically impossible: the insufficiently protected soldiers must have dreaded close combat with the better-equipped Flemish pikemen. The Flemish retreat to a passage close to the Lys does not correspond with the terrain, of which much is known. It would be impossible for the passage of thousands of Flemish soldiers, along a narrow path, to have taken place in the space of several minutes, between the foot-soldiers' attack and the charge by the knights. The Flemish troops were alleged, in addition to this, to have taken up closely ranked battle positions. All of this was impossible for a militia that had not practised such movements in peace time. Finally, all the knights threw themselves, in a single movement, into the marsh. This is, once again, contrary to the accounts given by other sources as well as to all that is known about knights' battle techniques.

Geoffroy de Paris presents, in the end, an account that is of even less value than that given by Guiart, if we do not consider the naïvely treacherous plan that the latter detailed. Neither Guiart nor Geoffroy de Paris succeeded in giving an unbiased presentation of the events. We, therefore, consider it to be a methodological error to accept the improbable account of a victory by French foot-soldiers since only they presented such an event in this manner. Their heavy criticism of the French knights is, at the same time, to be considered invalid, at least to a significant extent. The same applies, however, to Geoffroy's account concerning the importance of the stream, or brook, instead of the marsh as well as to the explanation given by the *Chronographia Regum Francorum*, of the *Anciennes chroniques de Flandre*, and of the Florentine, Giovanni Villani, despite important mutual differences which these sources show. The account given by the Italian must now be examined.

Giovanni Villani
Giovanni Villani was a Florentine shareholder in the Peruzzi banking company, who began his historical work from the year 1300. It was a world chronicle with the history of his town, Florence, at the centre. Villani wrote until shortly before he fell victim, as did innumerable others, to the Black Plague in 1348.[123]

It is obvious that he was less accurately informed about events that took place far away from his native country. Nevertheless, the man of Florence succeeded in giving the most detailed account of the Battle of the Spurs, that is, the most

---
[122] Ibid., vv. 2815–24.
[123] For Villani see Funck-Brentano, 'Mémoire', 276–81; and Fris, *De slag bij Kortrijk*, 32–9.

detailed of the sources that adopt the French version of events. At first sight this appears to be a very remarkable phenomenon, but when we inspect the activities of this historian more closely, then all becomes clear. Villani himself stated that he explained the events in a detailed manner as it represented something new. The victory was 'an almost impossible event', such a surprising feat of arms that it merited full explanation.[124] Furthermore, he was able to speak with authority as regards the events in Flanders since he had visited the country. Villani did, indeed, claim to have seen the battlefield at Mons-en-Pévèle at a moment when the corpses of the fallen had not yet been buried.[125] The statement was disputed by L. Muratori, who published his work, as well as by Henri Pirenne.[126] This was until irrefutable documents, as well as an excerpt from the Bruges town accounts, confirmed Villani's presence in Bruges in 1306.[127] He came to Bruges as a banker of the King of France to receive the first payments of the indemnity imposed on the Flemings by the Treaty of Athis-sur-Orge (1305). In all events, it is remarkable that the Florentine devoted so much space to the Flemish struggle against the King of France, and that he did such justice to the magnificent victory beneath the town walls of Courtrai by calling it an almost impossible event. This brings out all the more clearly the fact that Villani, as an Italian, was very much acquainted with the art of warfare as practised by the townsmen of the north of Italy. The north Italian townsmen had already achieved an astonishing victory in 1176, at Legnano, against German knights, although with the help of their own knights. They had developed strong tactics for their foot-soldiers which were especially effective in defence and even, on occasions, leading to counterattacks.[128]

On account of Villani's visit to Flanders one might think that he had gained his information in Flanders. This reveals itself, however, as only partly true. He used some information from Bruges. But both for the Battle of Courtrai and for historical events in Flanders, Villani followed the French version and explanation of what took place.[129] He made use of the term *goedendag* for the famous weapon of the Flemish townsmen while Flemish sources never made use of this term, but *gepinde staf* or stave. In Villani's account Pieter de Coninc became Piero le Roy. This clearly indicates that he took this name from a French source. Certain mistakes made by the author also prove that he followed the French version: he erroneously placed the Flemish camp at the Battle of the Spurs on the other bank of the River Lys;[130] this also occurred in describing the aligned wagons allegedly employed by

---

[124] Villani, 388, 391. See also Delfos, *1302 door tijdgenooten verteld*, 95.
[125] Villani, 398, 415.
[126] Muratori, in Villani, 4; and Pirenne, 'La Version flamande', 43.
[127] Funck-Brentano, *Philippe le Bel*, 523 n. 1, 524 n. 5; and V. Fris, 'L'Historien Jean Villani en Flandre', *BCRH*, 5th ser., vol. 10 (1900), 1–7.
[128] Concerning the above see especially P. Pieri, 'Alcune quistione sopra la fanteria in Italia nel periodo comunale', *Rivista storica italiana*, 4th ser., 4 (1933), also reprint, 1–54. It is a most useful overview, being based on the best works.
[129] Pirenne, 'La Version flamande', 40; and Pirenne, 'Note supplementaire', 101 n. 3.
[130] Villani, 385. See also *Chronographia*, I:104–5; and *Anciennes chroniques*, 377.

the Flemings to protect their positions at the Battle of Mons-en-Pévèle;[131] the information given about both battles is also erroneous.[132] This all proves that the Italian's account of the Battle of Courtrai did not profit much from his stay in Flanders. It is possible that he picked up certain details in Flanders, but the fact remains that he could have gained such information from French sources.

It is not difficult to prove that he followed a French version. The terms used for the *goedendags* and for Pieter de Coninc as well as reference to the events in Bruges point to this. The Flemings owe their victory to 'the treachery of the ditch', of which the French were not aware, and which proved so fatal to them, above all following the second attack launched when the first formation of knights had been driven back towards the stream after crossing over it. In his account of the battle there are so many details identical to information given in French sources that it becomes irrefutable that he followed such sources. Villani also drew upon French sources for his account of the actions of Charles of Valois in 1300[133] and of the retreat by King Philip the Fair in September 1302.[134]

At this point one could make the objection that Villani was not a supporter of King Philip the Fair and that he was not favourable to the Count, Robert d'Artois.[135] The Florentine banker despised the King for his frequent debasing of coinage which had such negative consequences for Italian bankers.[136] Villani was against the Count of Artois as he suspected the Count of having burnt a papal bull.[137] This presented him with the perfect opportunity to speak of the punishment of God that mercilessly strikes down sinful evildoers. Of course, the disgraceful defeat of the most excellent knights in the whole world at the hands of a pitiful army of Flemish artisans and peasants, who were only half so numerous, could only be seen as a judgement of God. How could it have possibly been otherwise? The Italian drew clear pleasure from the sharp contrast between both armies and was most pleased at the bloody defeat of the arrogant French knights. Yet, despite this, one cannot conclude that he was favourable to the Flemings. According to him, they only thought of eating and drinking; the artisans were of the lowest sort in the entire world and let themselves be carried away by the most vulgar passions.[138] One might think for a moment that Villani would give an unbiased description of events. Perhaps this was his intention. However, in reality he completely followed the French version as we noted above and will show below.

Still, it is also possible that the Florentine had other Italian informants. He was

---

[131] Villani, 413; and *Chronographia*, I:156. See also *Les Grandes Chroniques*, VIII:239; and *Chroniques de St Denis*, in RHF, 20, ed. Daunou and Naudet (Paris, 1840), 678.
[132] Villani, 388, 415.
[133] *Istore et croniques*, I:223 n. 2; *Chronographia*, I:87–8; *Chronique normande*, 15; and Villani, 363.
[134] Villani, 391; *Istore et croniques*, I:256; *Chronique normande*, 20–3; and *Chronographia*, I:117.
[135] Lot, *L'Art militaire*, I:259.
[136] Villani, 384–95.
[137] Villani, 387. See also *Chronographia*, I:79.
[138] Villani, 386–8.

the only author who spoke of the Italian commanders of the Lombardian crossbowmen as well as of the *bidauts*, lightly armed soldiers from France, Provence and Navarre. Nevertheless, he was strangely silent about their battle against the Flemish crossbowmen, in contrast to most sources, although not the *Anciennes chroniques* that he also followed for the description of the battle.[139] Villani could also have gained information from compatriots such as the mercenaries of the famous Castruccio-Castracani company, whom he spoke of in 1303 when they fought for the French against the Flemings after being hired on the advice of Villani's fellow townsman, Musciatto Guidi di Francesi.[140] Still, all the information gained could only have been based on hearsay and does not provide much assistance. Such persons would certainly have given a French account of events to Villani and he might have added several details himself that he picked up in Flanders. Furthermore, he might have made the acquaintance of Thomas Fini who was, at that time, the general tax collector in Flanders. Moreover, Villani lent money to Philip of Chieti.[141]

Villani actually added very little new information. What he did add by way of new information, for instance on the foreign mercenaries' commanders, does not prove that he knew more than other chroniclers since he did not even mention the crossbow battle. His explanation for the French defeat is also to be found in the *Anciennes chroniques*. He very often digressed, giving general and rather vague pieces of information as, for instance, in his reproducing the speeches of the Flemish commanders and his depiction of the arrival of a priest, an event that is not confirmed by the Flemish sources. Attendance of a mass was certainly a common habit before a battle and it was reported for the French at Courtrai, although not for the Flemings. Villani's account is thus suspect on this point.

Let us turn to what he reported concerning the Battle of the Spurs. Following this we will make further comparison between his account and the French sources to which his account is so similar as to lead one to think that he followed such sources, albeit revising, expanding upon and, in some sense, adapting them.

Villani's account[142]

The King of France sent the Count of Artois with an army of seven and a half thousand knights and forty thousand foot-soldiers, including ten thousand crossbowmen. They arrived at a hill facing the road to Tournai and set up camp there at a distance of half a mile from Courtrai. Guy of Flanders understood that he could not avoid engaging in battle and could not retreat to Bruges since he would be destroyed on the way. For this reason he called for Willem van Jülich, who, at that time, was still before the castle of Cassel,[143] and together they had twenty thou-

---

[139] *Anciennes chroniques*, 377–8.
[140] Ibid., 391; Villani, 410–11; *Chronique artésienne*, 68; *Annales Gandenses*, 49; and *Chronographia*, I:143.
[141] Fris, *De slag bij Kortrijk*, 34.
[142] Villani, 384–8.
[143] In fact, Willem was already at Courtrai by this time.

sand foot-soldiers. After calling upon the help of God and of St George, they left the lands surrounding Courtrai, breaking up their camp on the other side of the River Lys,[144] and marched through the small open field just outside Courtrai on the road to Ghent. It was there that they had their troops take up battle positions while taking very good advantage of a stream that ran through the fields there. The stream carried water in that area to the River Lys. At most, it was five arms (*bracciae*) wide and three arms (*bracciae*) deep.[145] No banks of the stream were visible from afar, so that someone would be standing right in front of it before knowing it. Behind the stream, to their side, the commanders had their troops positioned in a (half) moon formation following the course of the stream. No one remained on horseback: lords and knights were to defend themselves on foot against the French knights' assault, as were the common people. One soldier, armed with a lance handled as a spear used in hunting boars, stood next to another bearing an enormous club with a heavy head; a stout steel pin was fastened to the thick wooden handle with an iron ring. This savage and crude weapon was used to thrust and hit, and was called a *godendac*, that is 'good day' in the Italian account. They were positioned close to each other, men who must defend themselves with the same weapon and attack as poor devils unused to combat, desperate men who saw no chance of being saved. They chose to engage in battle rather than to flee and be captured. Full of dread and fear they had a priest move round the battlefield with the body of Christ so that all could see, and instead of receiving Holy Communion they took up some soil and put it in their mouths. Guy de Namur and Willem van Jülich gave encouragement to the soldiers. They referred to the arrogance of the Frenchmen, to the injustice they had already done to their lords and themselves. They referred to what awaited them if the French were to prove themselves victorious, especially taking into account what had already happened (during the rebellion). They showed them that they were fighting for a just cause, to save their own lives and those of their children. Above all, they were seeking to kill or injure the horses. Following this, Guy, by his own hand, knighted Pieter de Coninc as well as more than forty commoners, promising them, in the event of victory, a knight's income.

When Artois realised that the Flemings had left their camp he had his own camp taken down and approached the enemy, ordering his troops, in the mean time, in ten formations in the following manner:

1. Jean Burlats   1,400 knights
2. Renaut de Trie   500 knights
3. Raoul de Nesle, the constable   700 knights
4. Louis de Clermont   800 knights
5. Robert d'Artois   1,000 knights

---

[144] The same mistake was also made by the *Chronographia*, I:104, and by the *Anciennes chroniques*, 377.
[145] The *braccia* (arm) was an Italian measurement shorter than 70 cm. Generally, historians assume that the stream, according to Villani, was three metres wide and approximately two metres deep.

6. The Count of St Pol[146]	700	knights
7. The Counts of Aumale, Eu and the chamberlain of Tancarville	1,000	knights
8. Ferri, son of the Duke of Lorraine and the Count of Sancerre	800	knights
9. Geoffrey de Brabant	500	knights
10. Jacques de St Pol, Simone di Piemonte and Bonifatio da Mantova	200	knights
	10,000	crossbowmen
	30,000	foot-soldiers

It was the most splendid army a King of France had ever mustered, with the flower of knighthood in the kingdom: barons and knights supported by noblemen from Brabant, Hainault and the Rhine valley. As soon as the formations were positioned for battle on the other side, the commanders of the foreign soldiers and crossbowmen, Jean de Burlats, Simone di Piemonte and Bonifatio da Mantova, very ingenious commanders, went to the constable and said to him:

> Lord, let this desperate people of Flanders attack without endangering the flower of knighthood of France and of the whole world. We know the customs of the Flemings: they stand there as desperately and most determined men: they have left behind their food and possessions. Let the knights remain in battle formations: we shall attack with our soldiers who are used to skirmishes and to attacking. With them and our crossbowmen, and other foot-soldiers, twice as many as the Flemings, we shall cross to the other side, to the lands of Courtrai,[147] and we shall attack them from different sides at the same time. Thus, for the greater part of the day we shall undertake skirmishes. The Flemings, who are used to eating and drinking much, will then have to remain on an empty stomach and will be forced to leave the battlefield without being able to maintain their good battle array. At that moment you ought to attack them from behind with the knights and without any danger you shall gain victory.

However, God was to punish Artois for the sins he had committed. When the Lord of Nesle had given the counsel to the commander-in-chief, the latter chided him with the following words: 'By the devil, this is the counsel of a man of Lombardy and you, constable, have traitors among your company!' To this Raoul de Nesle gave the answer typical of a knight whose courage was being doubted: 'Lord, if you move as far into the ranks of the enemy as I, then you will have advanced far indeed!' And, filled with indignation at the reproach as a man who sees death before his eyes, he had his standard bearers advance. He spurred on his horse, recklessly and unaware of the stream which he had to cross and behind which the Flemings were positioned. They reached the Flemings on the other side

---

[146] A mistake was made on Jacques de St Pol. The Count of St Pol was part of the rearguard. See also Guiart, 239, vv. 15,074–80.

[147] Villani appeared here to be forgetting that he claimed that the French did not know of the stream: 'e entreremo tra loro, e terra di Coltrai' (Villani, 386). See 'nè sapiendo del fosso' and 'la proda del fosso' (Villani, 387).

of the stream who hit at the French horses with their *goedendags*. The animals reared up and moved back towards the stream. The Count of Artois then threw himself into the battle with the other knights, behind the constable, in the hope that a powerful attack with the horses would enable the Flemish ranks to be penetrated and dispersed. But exactly the opposite occurred, since due to the attack of these knights, the men of the constable's and Artois's formations fell upon each other in the above-mentioned stream. The dust rose so high that knights in the last ranks could not see anything in front; the noise of the weapons and of cries prevented them hearing the fall. Still thinking that they were doing good, they were pushed forward with the horses running into those of the ranks in front. They reared up and threw their knights down, causing many to die, most of them without being wounded. The Flemings stood there full of confidence and courage on account of this 'treachery of the stream'. When the French and their horses faltered, the Flemings struck dead the warhorses and knights so that the stream lay full of knights and horses after a few hours. The will of God ruled that the French were not able to reach their enemies, and that they killed each other in their attempt to approach the Flemings and to break through their battle positions. The French as it were pushed their formations of knights against each other; they were so tightly gathered together that they could not move, either forwards or backwards. The Flemings, however, were completely fresh, hardly wearied and under orders of the commanders on their wings, Guy of Flanders and Willem van Jülich, who both performed great feats of arms that day. They advanced on foot across the stream and attacked the Frenchmen. That day lowly peasants had the privilege of being able to grasp noblemen by the throat. Of all the French noblemen, only Louis de Clermont, the Count of St Pol, and the Count of Burgundy with a few others were able to escape. As they did not attempt to enter into the midst of the battle, they were to be continually disgraced in France. All other dukes, counts, barons and knights were killed on the battlefield, some of them while fleeing in the ditches and marshes, in total more than six thousand men on horseback and innumerable foot-soldiers. Not a single prisoner was taken.

This defeat of the French took place on St Benedict's day, 21 March 1302.[148] It was certainly a judgement of God, since the Flemings were less numerous. The honour, fame and glory of the old French nobility has been disparaged as the defeat had been at the hands of their own subjects, the most common people of all, weavers, fullers and other lowly artisans, men who had absolutely no experience of warfare. By their victory, however, they became so inflamed and so daring that a single Flemish man on foot, armed with a *goedendag*, would have dared attack two French knights on horseback.

---

[148] Villani made a mistake here. He took as St Benedict's day the day on which it was celebrated in Italy and elsewhere in Europe, except in France where it is celebrated on 11 July. See Funck-Brentano, 'Mémoire', 278 and n. 3. This proves that Villani used a source that only mentioned St Benedict's day.

Since Villani attributes the same role to the stream as other French sources, and appears to follow them, the accounts of such chronicles must first be discussed and later a general comparison be made.

The *Chronographia Regum Francorum* and the *Anciennes chroniques de Flandre*

For the period from 1276 until 1342, and thus also for their account of the Battle of the Spurs, the *Anciennes chroniques* and *Chronographia* represent summaries of a chronicle written in French that is now lost.[149] Concerning the *Anciennes chroniques*, there are various versions of the Battle of Courtrai, the most complete of which was registered in the *Recueil des historiens de la Gaule et de la France*, while Kervyn de Lettenhove, in his *Istore et croniques de Flandres*, included more concise accounts.[150] The *Anciennes chroniques* was written in St Omer between 1337 and 1342.[151] The *Chronographia* is a later compilation that dates from 1415 to 1422 and was written in the abbey of St Denis near Paris. It is based on the same source or same documents as the *Anciennes chroniques*, although it is more extensive. The author appears to have possessed more detailed information than that now available in the short summaries of the French chronicles.[152] Other chronicles were also inspired by the lost source; they are, however, of lesser importance here.[153]

There was much difficulty in determining the origins of the most prominent of the chronicles: the *Anciennes chroniques*, the *Chronique normande* and the *Chronographia*. The editor of the *Chronographia*, H. Moranvillé, was of the opinion that the first two chronicles were actually translations from the Latin source later used by the *Chronographia*. However, Pirenne, as well as A. and E. Molinier, proved that all the sources were based on a more extensive source, now lost, of which the *Chronographia* gave the most detailed reproduction despite it also being merely a summary.[154] This explains why the later source in the end represents the most complete description of the Battle of Courtrai. Certain documents used by the author at the abbey of St Denis were also employed in other chronicles written at that important centre of medieval historiography.[155]

For the period which concerns this battle, the author of the *Chronographia*, a Benedictine monk, simply reproduced those documents available to him in a form

---

[149] H. Pirenne, 'L'*Ancienne chronique de Flandre* et la *Chronographia Regum Francorum*', *BCRH* 5th ser., 8 (1898), 208.
[150] *Recueil des historiens de la Gaule et de la France*, 22:377–9; and *Istore et croniques de Flandres*, I:234–5.
[151] *Istore et croniques de Flandres*, I:iii–v, xxi; and Fris, *De slag bij Kortrijk*, 80.
[152] Pirenne, 'L'*Ancienne chronique de Flandre* et la *Chronographia Regum Francorum*', 208; and *Chronographia*, III:xlvii.
[153] *Chronique normande*; *Chronique de St Denis*; and *Chronique des Pays-Bas, de France, d'Angleterre et de Tournai*, in *Corpus Chronicorum Flandriae*, iii, ed. J. J. De Smet (Brussels, 1856), 123.
[154] Pirenne, 'L'*Ancienne chronique de Flandre* et la *Chronographia Regum Francorum*', 208. See also *Revue historique* (1898), 90 ff.
[155] *Les Grandes Chroniques*, VIII:xiii–xiv.

very similar to the original, albeit generally in a more concise fashion.[156] He did not, however, restrict himself to a single source and appears to have used more than one version of the summary of the lost French chronicle. At certain points he seems to be following the *Chronique normande*.[157] The author introduced the excerpts, which often contradict his previous account, with the expression 'quidam vero dicunt', 'sicut quidam dicunt' ('according to other accounts').

The value of the *Chronographia*, as well as the versions of the *Anciennes chroniques*, varies tremendously. Some events are reproduced excellently. The detail given on the siege of Lille and the Battle of Furnes in 1297 is most interesting and valuable.[158] The author of the *Chronographia* was also very well informed about the number of French knights in the garrison defending the Courtrai castle in June and July 1302.[159] Elsewhere there is more important information that has been confirmed by other good sources.[160] The author also gave an excellent explanation of the long march that Philip the Fair undertook in 1304 in order to enter Flanders before the Battle of Mons-en-Pévèle.[161] Furthermore, he gave very significant information pertaining to the talks of the French and Flemish envoys during the negotiations at Vitry in September 1302.[162]

Yet, despite such excellent passages one notes some rather serious errors. Very prudent use therefore ought to be made of the *Chronographia* and *Anciennes chroniques*. In general, the information given should only be used when confirmed by a reliable source. The account of the Battle of Courtrai, however, requires careful attention, as it contains more information than the account presented by those French sources written immediately after the event under the influence of the bloody defeat.

The account of the Chronographia Regum Francorum[163]

Robert d'Artois left Lille with his troops and arrived at a place two miles from Courtrai where he remained for two days. He then sent the two marshals, with their formations, to the town. Following this, the Count arrived at the town of Courtrai himself. The Flemings were prepared for battle, but Artois was not intent upon engaging in battle that day since he wished, first of all, to let his troops set up camp. When the Flemings realised this they withdrew across the River Lys and the French thought that they were fleeing.[164] The following day, at dawn, the marshals left to seek the enemy and take note of their battle array. They saw the Flemish

---

[156] Moranvillé, in *Chronographia*, III:xlvii.
[157] Pirenne, 'L'*Ancienne chronique de Flandre* et la *Chronographia Regum Francorum*', 206.
[158] *Chronographia*, I:64–6, 68.
[159] Ibid., I:100–1.
[160] See Funck-Brentano, *Philippe le Bel*, 23 n. 2.
[161] *Chronographia*, I:150–5. On this point the source corresponds completely with that of Guiart, who was an eyewitness, at least until being wounded. See Moranvillé, *Chronographia*, I:153 n. 6.
[162] *Chronographia*, I:119.
[163] Ibid., I:104–12.
[164] This is the same mistake concerning the French camp made by Villani, as seen above.

formations in battle positions behind a ditch that was not very deep, but most slippery. The Flemish troops were on the higher bank of the stream or waterway.[165] They were being placed in battle array by the knight of Zeeland, Jan van Renesse, whose help they had called upon, and by Hendrik van Lontzen, two very able commanders.[166] The troops of both noblemen had formed a single unit, positioned as a shield with the point facing the French, as some recounted.[167] Wisely they were teaching the Flemings what each man should do and how they were to attack and defend themselves. Guy de Namur knighted some of his men: his nephew, Willem van Jülich, some other noblemen and Pieter de Coninc with several other burghers. All the Flemings were to fight on foot; even the noblemen sent away their horses in order to await the fight for life or death together with the common people. However, Jan van Renesse and Lonchy, having positioned the Flemings, remained on horseback together with several noblemen from their entourage.[168]

As soon as the marshals had taken note of the Flemish positions they reported what they had seen. At this moment there was a terrible feeling of premonition in the hearts of many of the French soldiers. Although there were more than 40,000 horses in their army, not one animal had neighed for over ten days, which, of course, astounded many men.[169] Artois then held a council of war after attending mass. Many noblemen gave the counsel that they should not enjoin in battle at that time, but the majority in the council accepted the battle, and Artois ordered the trumpets to be blown. All of the men prepared themselves for battle. Clothed in his full coat of arms, the Count mounted his horse, and all the French noblemen left for the battlefield. When the French commander saw the Flemings' position, he was enraged. At that moment, six formations had already been formed with more than 3000 horses, not counting the rearguard.

Jan van Renesse and Lonchy positioned the Flemings slightly more to the side and had the townsmen move closer together so that no one would be able to penctrate their ranks. They gave very strict orders that nobody was to think of booty or spoil, but only of defence.[170]

In the mean time, the crossbowmen of the first French division had been shooting at the Flemings for a while to move the Flemings aside. At this moment, the great lords, who were very keen to begin the battle, assumed that the Flemings would flee and declared to the Count of Artois: 'Our foot-soldiers will cross over to the other side to take victory and we shall not receive any honours in this battle. Let

---

[165] The passage on the ditch is a translation of MS 1006 of the *Anciennes chroniques* (377 n. 6). In this manuscript mention is made of grass having grown over the ditch.

[166] The name 'Lonchy' clearly has been mistranslated. Neither this piece of information, nor that following it, is in the *Anciennes chroniques*.

[167] See, for example, Villani.

[168] None of this information, following the description of the waterway, is found in the *Anciennes chroniques*.

[169] See *Chronique normande*, 18; and *Istore et croniques*, I:252.

[170] A comparison should be made with Lodewijk, II.1.IV:297, c. 25, vv. 1711–13: 'Die Vlaminge lagen tesen tiden / Op i. plaetse daer besiden, / Vaste in een ende al te voet'; II.1.IV:303, c. 26, vv. 1839–43. This line is also missing in the *Anciennes chroniques*.

the standard bearers take their places, each one to the front of his formation, and let us attack.' Artois agreed to this and gave the order for the banners to be carried to the front and for the charge to begin. The noblemen launched themselves forward on their warhorses in a rapid charge, but they fell, all together, into the ditch with such power that most of them died or were suffocated. When the Flemings realised this, they suddenly attacked, all at the same time, with their lances, their bludgeons and their swords. They killed the noblemen who could not defend themselves. This terrible slaughter lasted the whole day until the night. It took place on a Wednesday before St Benedict's day, in the year 1302.[171]

The chronicler then developed several episodes from the battle. Artois fought against butchers from Bruges. He shouted: 'Take me captive, take me captive. I am the Count of Artois!'[172] Despite this, he was killed. In the mean time, Jan van Renesse attacked the French camp with four hundred Dutchmen, thus causing all of them to flee. Several Dutchmen pursued and killed the French soldiers.[173]

The rearguard commanders, Louis de Clermont, Robert de Boulogne and Gui de St Pol, also fled. Raoul de Nesle fought stubbornly against the men of Ghent, not wishing to surrender as he had seen too many noblemen, the flower of all Christianity, fall. He too was killed.[174]

The author had not read anywhere else of an army being hit with such misfortune and being vanquished in such a battle. Some of the French said that the Flemings were less numerous, although they did not fear their enemies. They wished to negotiate with them, proposing to Artois that a chapel be erected in Bruges for all the men who fell there, to return all prisoners, to send five hundred men of Bruges across the sea without any hope of return and to pay all the costs of the army and of the Count following their departure from Paris. Artois replied, however, that the Flemings must subject themselves fully to his will.[175]

The author then gave a list of fifty-two noblemen who fell during the battle, adding the following words: 'Some say that the Flemings who searched the battlefield found nine counts, six eldest sons of counts, sixty noblemen who were bannerets and eleven hundred noblemen with a single shield, all knights, and not speaking of the others, whose number only God knows.'[176]

Finally, information was given about those men who escaped, such as the counts of St Pol and of Boulogne, Louis de Clermont, who led the rearguard, and Renaut,

---

[171] There is a mistake concerning Wednesday being St Benedict's day. Villani had a text in front of him with an indication of the date, but without a mention of the month. This explains his mistake in having St Benedict's day on 21 March. See the discussion of this above.
[172] See also Lodewijk, II.1.IV:324–5, c. 33, vv. 2367–9.
[173] The same version as in MS 1006, although the *Anciennes chroniques*, 378, only spoke of heroic feats.
[174] Lodewijk, II.1.IV:333–4, c. 36, v. 2584 ff., described the same actions by other knights.
[175] The author was confusing the negotiations which occurred in September 1302. See Lodewijk, II.1.IV:375–6, c. 50.
[176] These two paragraphs that form an addition to the account of the *Chronographia* were introduced with the classical words: 'quidam vero dicunt' taken from the *Chronique normande* (19). They differ slightly from the *Chronique normande* on the tallies: eight counts, two eldest sons. The author also repeated his text concerning the rearguard.

the son of the Count of Dammartin, who brought the news with several other men to the King. The Flemings collected the booty and hung the conquered banners of the noblemen in front of the castle of Courtrai so as to bring fear to the garrison.

The importance of the ditch according to the Chronographia and the Anciennes chroniques de Flandre

In the manuscripts of the *Anciennes chroniques de Flandre* and the *Istore et croniques de Flandres*, there are at times some significant differences in the account of the Battle of Courtrai. On occasions they differ considerably from the detailed text of the *Chronographia*. One of the differences is of much importance since it concerns the ditch. As to the importance of the waterway or stream the authors were indeed of different opinions and from their description one may deduce how each of them changed the source. Without doubt, the changes show bias. It is not difficult to prove this based on the *Anciennes chroniques* which presented the most logical and detailed account in this respect. It is reproduced here alongside the *Istore et croniques*:

Anciennes chroniques de Flandre[177]	*Istore et croniques*[178]
Adont aulcuns des haulz hommes lui vindrent dire, comme ceulz qui tendoient à honneur: 'Sire, que attendez vous plus? Noz gens de pié, quy de près nous sieuent, s'avanceront tellement, que ilz en auront la victoire, et nous ne y acquerrons point d'honneur.'	Si luy dirent: 'Sire, qu'attendés-vous? Nos gens de piet s'avanceront, si qu'il aront la victore; et nous n'y arons point d'honneur.'
Quant le conte Robert entendi ce que dit est, il fit marchier avant ses banières jusques dedens le parc des Flamens: et lorsque les Franchois et leurs banières et pennons furent passez le fossé, les Flamens, qui estoient à pié, armez et embastonnez, se férirent tous à ung fais sur eulx, tellement qu'ils n'eurent mie espace de ordonner leur gens. Et si ne povoient retourner hors pour la sieute de leurs gens; et tant furent illec reculez vers la rive du fossé, que, incontinent que les premiers cuidoient poindre d'esperons tresbuchoient en ce fossé (qui moult estoit large et parfont) l'un sur l'aultre.	Quant li contes les entendi, si fist passer ses bannières; et, tantost qu'elles furent passées, li Flamenc se férirent tout à un fais sur eulx, et chil, qui premier poingnoient, chéirent tout en ce fossé, l'un sur l'autre, à si grant randon que tout y furent mort et estaint.

[177] *Anciennes chroniques de Flandre*, 378 and n. 2.
[178] *Istore et croniques*, I:234.

Et les Flamens, qui véoient leurs ennemis en tel péril et dangier les oppressèrent tellement, que tous les firent renverser par si grant randon que tous y furent estains et mors.	
Et quant iceulz Flamens les veirent ainsi perdre place et tresbuchier, hommes et chevaulz sans nombre, si que relever ne aidier ne se povoient, ainchois craventoient et estaindoient l'un l'aultre en piteuz cris et regrets, ilz coururent sur eulz à hache et à macques, à lances et espées, et mirent illec tout à mort.	Quant li Flamenc, les veirent ainsi tresbuchier, si coururent à eux, à haches et à maches et à espées, et mirent tout à mort.

It is clear that the text given in the collection, *Istore et croniques*, is a summary of the first one. The summary has, however, been compiled in a most able manner: if the person summarising had not continually used the same words as the original one might think that it was an independent account based on some other version. However, it is evident that the author followed the account given in the *Anciennes chroniques* and reproduced here. An examination of how he completely changed the previous account demonstrates how very able he was in his work. In the *Anciennes chroniques*, the French crossed the stream without any difficulty but were attacked before the formations were able to deploy themselves: the French were then driven back to the waterway and, lacking room to move, they fell into the stream. From the account in the *Istore et croniques*, however, one could say that the French never reached the other side of the stream. If one studies the text carefully, however, it becomes clear that the French did not fall into the stream during the charge since the Flemings attacked them first before they were killed in this perilous adventure. If the *Anciennes chroniques* did not exist, then doubts would still remain about this event. However, the matter is now clear. It is therefore necessary to mention that this accomplished author avoided noting that the standard bearers reached the other side of the stream, that the French had no room there to move back, that they had to retreat under the pressure of a Flemish attack and that they fell or were thrown into the stream due to the Flemings pushing forward. After keeping silent on all this, he then summarised to a lesser extent, although he still omitted to note that the French had to give ground. Finally, the Flemings simply slew their enemies as soon as they were lying in the ditch.

Comparison is necessary since the *Chronographia* presents the same text as the summary of *Istore et croniques*.[179]

Straight away, this version of the *Chronographia* may be dismissed when it reports that all the knights had already fallen into the stream during the charge,

---

[179] The *Chronographia* at several points follows MS 1006 (*Anciennes chroniques de Flandre*, 378 n. 3) which reads: 'et ceulz qui premier poingoient, chéirent en cas rasques et trébuchèrent l'un sur l'autre de si grant radeur que ilz furent tous estains!'

since it is based on a tendentious summary. Certainly, on this point the Latin source has no merit: the Flemings were placed on the higher bank of the ditch which is not very deep nor very wide: the marshals after the reconnoitring mission note that the rebels were positioned behind an impediment: advice was taken in Artois's council of war on the above point; and finally, following this, everyone was to launch themselves towards the stream, falling head over heels into it! This brings us back to the absurdities presented by Geoffroy de Paris according to whom the knights committed suicide by charging into the marshes.

Gilles le Muisit
Among the French sources the account of the abbot from the abbey of St Martin, in Tournai, Gilles le Muisit, deserves examination. Concerning the battle itself, he did not add anything new, although having seen the desperate flight of the vanquished from the towers of his abbey he was able to give an excellent account of it. He also confirmed the attacks against Courtrai before 11 July.

Gilles le Muisit was born in January 1272, probably in Tournai.[180] It was there that he became a monk in the abbey of St Martin on 2 November 1289.[181] Le Muisit studied at the University of Paris, probably from 1297 until the summer of 1301.[182] In 1300 he visited Rome during the great jubilee. On 30 April 1331, he was elected abbot, although he was only able to take this function on on 25 May, since the financial position of the abbey appears to have been far from brilliant.[183] On 25 October, he was anointed abbot in Bruges in the Eekhout.[184]

It was first around the year 1345 that the abbot began to edit his comprehensive work: poetry, a chronicle and annals.[185] At that time he could no longer read, write or differentiate coins since he suffered from eye cataracts. On 15 August 1348, he became fully blind until 18 and 22 September 1351 when his eyes were cured and he saw again; as one might expect from an old man of eighty years, he saw the skies, stars, sun and moon, but recognised people with much difficulty and could no longer read or write.[186] The abbot passed away on 15 October 1352.

Gilles le Muisit was not a superficial chronicler: he had a critical spirit, evaluated the accounts that came to him, attempted to gain additional information and had a preference for interviewing eyewitnesses about incidents or those who took part in certain events. He took notes that he used at the end of his life when editing his chronicle. It is only this work that interests us here; it was begun in 1347 and completed around Easter 1349.[187] Gilles dictated his text but was not able to put the final touches to it. He was naturally well informed about events that took place in and around Tournai, as well as the Hundred Years War. For 1302 only two orig-

---

[180] Le Muisit, 11 and n. 2.
[181] Ibid., v.
[182] Ibid., vii and n. 3.
[183] Ibid., viii–ix.
[184] Ibid., ix.
[185] Ibid., x.
[186] Ibid., x, 306–7.
[187] Ibid., xxii.

inal pieces of information can be found: Gilles was aware of the fact that news of the Flemish victory reached Rome (through Michiel as Clokettes, Guy de Dampierre's envoy to the Pope), and he describes the flight of the French to which he was an eyewitness.[188]

As a man of Tournai, the abbot of St Martin was a supporter of the King since the town then was loyal to the French. This is very clear in one of his noteworthy and critical observations of the account given by his informants. Gilles gained a wide variety of information about the bloody French defeat at Crécy (1346), and one senses very clearly that he did not wish to accept the implications of the French defeat. It is well worth reproducing his text on this point since the passage shows a chronicler's ideas as well as how Gilles surpassed other more superficial chroniclers:

> Since the outcome of a battle is not certain, and each soldier puts greater effort during the battle into conquering than into being conquered, and since all those taking part cannot regard all the soldiers at the same time, nor give good judgement on the events that are taking place; in view of the above, it is the actual outcome of the battle that proves all. Numerous persons now report many things about the conflict; some make claims favourable to the King of France and his men, the truth of which cannot be ascertained. Others make mention of circumstances favourable to the King of England and his men, the truth of such not being known. Therefore, I shall not, in view of the different versions, report to those who come after me that which I cannot confirm with certainty. I have, then, only reported here that which I came to know from trustworthy men so as to still the thirst for knowledge on the part of future readers. Still I do not confirm that events took place exactly as reported.[189]

Following his account he gives the number of the fallen, according to what he had been told: four thousand foot-soldiers and seven hundred knights and cavalrymen of the French army were killed. The figures for the English losses reported to Gilles were apparently too meagre in his opinion, since he did not wish to give them. Rumour had it that many fell, 'since it is impossible to accept that such a great number of brave, noble men and so many foot-soldiers fell without causing many of their opponents to fall'.[190] 'Many indeed report so many things about the aforementioned battle which I do not believe that I shall end my account here.'[191]

When he gave an anecdote concerning the role played in September 1302 by the English King who let a false message be sent via his wife, the sister of the French King, he then added that he would not venture to confirm its truth; this version of events was generally given at that time and various trustworthy persons had confirmed it.[192] As to the siege of Tournai, in 1340, he did not wish to report it in full detail so as to remain concise, but also because certain things happen in such

---

[188] Ibid., 67–8.
[189] Ibid., 160–1.
[190] Ibid., 163.
[191] Ibid., 164.
[192] Ibid., 70, 72.

circumstances so that one cannot describe nor report the truth thereof.[193] The author continually drew attention to how untrustworthy are accounts spread by word of mouth among the common people, even though some truth may be at the bottom of such accounts.[194] He was also cautious about accepting various rumours too readily as well as fearing that he might lose the confidence of his reader for the more reliable sections of his work.[195]

Thus, Gilles le Muisit gave such an excellent example of the role of a historian that it is most unfortunate the abbot was not able to finish his work in the manner appropriate to proper historical accounts. In general, he attempted to remain completely neutral, although this is not to say that he was. No true neutrality in the work of a chronicler of that time can be found.

Of course, the abbot of St Martin was not favourable to the Flemish rebels. As a subject of the King of France he did not understand their struggle. The Flemish attack on Tournai, the destruction, plundering and malice with which the war was waged caused considerable damage to his abbey.[196] As a very God-fearing man he could not understand the indifference with which the Flemings reacted to the numerous excommunications and curses that rained down upon them. Their continual rebellion against the King or the Count, the proud and indomitable nature of the townsmen, the differences between the Flemish towns among themselves; all this led him to attack them very sharply.[197]

However, the immense difference in the account of the Battle of the Spurs between the rather concise, vague and dry account of the battle and the much more lively description of the desperate flight of the Frenchmen must be pointed out. Even forty-five years after the battle the eyewitness had kept a fresh and colourful picture of the event. This indicates, at the same time, that the impossibility for an eyewitness to see and to understand much about a battle is only to be accepted with reservation. For the battle of 11 July 1302 itself, Gilles le Muisit presented a French version of events. The claim that the abbot considered his account as complete and satisfactory cannot be ventured.

Gilles le Muisit's account of the Battle of the Spurs
Robert d'Artois, a renowned general, advanced with a large army that was composed above all of barons and noblemen, but also with a relatively large corps of townsmen and foot-soldiers. He wanted to enter Flanders by Courtrai where he arrived at this side of the River Lys. Against him stood the men of Bruges, of the coast and of Courtrai, although no men of Ypres or of Ghent were there. Artois had the lands surrounding the town laid waste, burning the villages as well as the dwellings near the town of Courtrai. He had many attacks carried out against the town.

[193] Ibid., 134.
[194] Ibid., 278–9.
[195] Ibid., xv. See also 275.
[196] Ibid., 71–2.
[197] Ibid., 212–15.

The Sources

On Wednesday 11 July he gathered together his whole army before the monastery of Groeninge. There the formations of knights were deployed. The Flemings left Courtrai and took up positions facing away from the town, that served as a wall for them, and towards the enemy. They all fought on foot; nobody remained on horseback; the cavalrymen were indeed few in number, even in comparison with the others. The Count gave his troops the command to advance. The battle began and Artois's foot-soldiers took the upper hand almost reaching the point of victory. As the Count noticed this he did not want to allow the honour of victory to be taken by the foot-soldiers. He had his formations of knights advance through the midst of the foot-soldiers. They did not know that there were ditches there and fell into them heavily. The Flemings trembled and shuddered: 'but, I do not know by means of which dark decision of God, the so noble French knights began to defy and provoke each other and the first knights fell in the ditches, one on top of another, and those following fell down in the same manner'. When the Flemings had seen this they recovered their courage and resisted bravely.

In this way, due to the arrogance of the Count, his units and those of other noblemen were destroyed by their fall and that of their horses. When the rest of the army, the cavalrymen and foot-soldiers, saw that the course of the battle was unfavourable to them they retreated. The majority of them fled, while the Flemings stayed in their positions and remained cautious. Since their enemy had fled they were victorious.

The men fled to various places: some to Lille, others to Tournai. From the towers of the Church of Our Lady in Tournai, of the abbey of St Martin and of the town, it was possible to see them fleeing along the roads, through hedges and fields in such numbers that it was incredible to those who did not see it. Their tents and baggage were left behind, and so they largely lost their possessions. In various villages, from Courtrai to the border at Dottenijs, several of them were robbed and killed. That same evening and the following day the Flemings searched the battlefield, killing those they found still alive. They enriched themselves with the booty found in the camp, in the tents and the baggage.

When the magistrate of Tournai saw so many men fleeing towards them he decided, following counsel, to close the town gates for fear of treachery. Thus, the Count of St Pol who was among the men fleeing could not enter the town and rested that night in the abbey of St Nicholas. In the dwellings before the town and the surrounding villages there were so many cavalrymen and foot-soldiers who suffered from great hunger that it was terrible to see them. The whole night and the following day those who had entered the town had such great fear that many of them could not eat. This amazing and distressing event was reported to the Pope as soon as possible so that he received a letter reporting it only seven days later. The envoy of the Count of Flanders, Michiel as Clokettes, who was also a chaplain to the Pope, was called upon in the middle of the night to show him the letter. The present author learned, from this very Michiel as Clokettes, that the Pope was favourable to the Flemings.

The defeat caused much anger and great pain in France. Gilles le Muisit ended his account with a list of the noblemen who fell.

The abbot of Tournai was following here an explanation similar to that given by the French burghers: the crossbowmen were on the verge of winning: the proud Count of Artois sent his knights forward. The knights did not know that there were streams there. This explanation is not sufficient: the knights defied and provoked each other and all of them, those in front and those last, fell into the waterways. Gilles le Muisit recognised that his explanation was not satisfactory since he added the words 'I do not know by which dark decision of God this occurred'. Somewhat in contradiction to the account of the fall of the knights, the abbot wrote that the Flemings defended themselves boldly and courageously, while, further on, he claimed that very few Frenchmen were killed by the rebels.

The same illogical facts were present in his account as in that presented by Geoffroy de Paris: the initial success of the crossbowmen, the attack of the knights through the midst of the foot-soldiers, the fall into unknown ditches (instead of a marsh). Allegedly, the noblemen also defied and provoked each other; the Flemings merely defended themselves. In the end it becomes only too clear why Gilles felt obliged to employ a dark decision of God.

In other sources there was also talk of a similar fall into a stream or waterway during the attack. One of these can be dealt with concisely.

Willem Procurator

Willem Procurator, a monk in the abbey of Egmond, in Holland, also devoted several pages to the famous Battle of Courtrai. However, on the beginning of the fourteenth century he was not so well informed, and certainly not on events in Flanders.[198]

Nevertheless, Willem was rather well informed about the Flemish commanders: Guy de Namur, Willem van Jülich and Jan van Renesse. The latter is given the major role by the author, although he gives a speech that is not very similar to the succinct advice presented in Flemish sources of the same period. The speech as it stands has already become completely abstract: the fight for the fatherland, for one's children, a just cause; a humble defence shall bring victory against an arrogant attack. Jan van Renesse put commanders in each of the Flemish formations and ordered the rebels' battle array with a flank on an old ditch.

The French advanced arrogantly, convinced that the battle would merely be a game with the troops of peasants. They fell in the ditch, however, suffocating each other. Such a great massacre of noblemen has not been seen since Roland's time.[199]

As one sees from this summary of all the details given by the long-winded and obscure author, Willem Procurator follows a French version of events. But this should not be astonishing after the battles that the Flemings waged in Zeeland and Holland in 1303 and 1304.

In the account given by Willem of Egmond Abbey, there is mention of an old ditch about which there is not sufficient information to be able to ascertain whether

---

[198] Fris, *De slag bij Kortrijk*, 73. See also A. J. Vis, 'Willelmus Procurator en zijn chronicon', dissertation (Amsterdam, 1950), 42–4.
[199] Procurator, 63–5.

it was the town moat at Courtrai or the stream connecting the Groeninge to the town ramparts. Such information therefore cannot be used.[200]

Guillaume de Nangis's Sequel to the *Chronicon*

Guillaume de Nangis's sequel to the *Chronicon* takes a most distinct place among the French sources: it is the only source that does not present an excuse for the defeat of Artois's knights and does not even mention the stream or brook.

The Benedictine monk who wrote the sequel in the abbey of St Denis, near Paris, attributed the French defeat to the pride and over-confidence of noblemen who looked down upon their enemy, thinking that they would easily overcome the artisans and peasants. In addition to this, the knights attacked imprudently without order.

> The men of Bruges are evenly positioned in very close ranks desiring to resist bravely. They are almost all fighting on foot. Our knights have too much confidence in their own power and arrogantly look down upon their opponents. Very quickly they have the foot-soldiers at the front of their battle array return since they soon hope to gain the victory and avoid the honour falling to the foot-soldiers. They attack with pomp and not in good order. Still, the men of Bruges receive them with their excellent pikes, called *goedendags*, and fight bravely killing all their enemies. The famous leader, an excellent commander, Robert d'Artois, charges to their side and fights as a roaring lion in the midst of the enemy. He falls and the monks who later buried him counted certainly thirty or more wounds on his body.[201]

From the account it is clear that the St Denis monk did not allow himself to be carried away by national identity.[202] His impartiality in this respect can easily be explained by his position as a monk alien to the conflict. This also makes it much easier now to understand why Philip the Fair in his letter to the clergy of the Bourges bailiwick (29 August 1302) did not present the popular version of the defeat. What has been shown above concerning the version of events with the treacherously dug ditches is confirmed once again here: chroniclers with a critical mind did not accept the rumours then being spread. There was not even a mention of a stream. It is possible, though, that the author was not aware of the existence of a stream. However, this is highly unlikely since Guiart worked in St Denis and speaks of it and, moreover, the lost source was also kept at the abbey. It can, therefore, be assumed that the author attributed little significance to the existence of a ditch since he understood that one could not call upon it to summarise the reasons for the defeat. He rightly saw the bravery of the closely and firmly ranked men of

---

[200] Frederichs, 'De slag van Kortrijk', 26 n. 1. Frederichs made use of the information to confirm the turning movement described by Guiart.
[201] Nangis, 585–6.
[202] Wodsak, 18. Wodsak claimed that the chronicler was a supporter of Flanders although he was rather lacking in any proof of this.

Bruges as one of the reasons of the French defeat.²⁰³ Another reason was the arrogance of the knights who underestimated their enemy, and this was certainly the case. Whether or not the lack of order, which had more than once been a cause of defeat for knights, was also one of the reasons has to be determined on the basis of other sources. Moreover, this exceptionally military explanation can always be used by a monk who prefers to hold the knights responsible for the defeat. The lack of strict order became an element in explaining the outcome of the battle as well as numerical inferiority, and so forth.

However, more remarkable in this rejection of the normal French version is the fact that the abbey of St Denis was, in many respects, the centre of official historiography in the kingdom. Thus, after the cunning advisors to King Philip had a popular version spread about, embellished with the necessary amount of treachery on the part of the evil Flemings,²⁰⁴ another version praising the bravery of the enemy was drawn up by the monks in the official centre of historiography. And the account given was also subsequently adopted in Girard de Frachet's *Chronicon*.²⁰⁵ *Les Grandes Chroniques de France*, which intended to spread the official historiography to the vast majority of French subjects, followed the *Chronicon* of Guillaume de Nangis.²⁰⁶

The *Récits d'un bourgeois de Valenciennes*

This rather long account of the battle does not present any new information allowing for a complete explanation of the battle to be given. This Hainault chronicle was written around 1370 and, already at that date, it contained numerous inventions and legends. However, it is of significance, as it allows one to see the development from the original French sources.²⁰⁷

When both armies were positioned opposite each other, prepared for battle, Jan van Renesse rode towards the Count of Artois asking him for some room in order to be able to engage in battle. Artois agreed to this and had his knights withdraw somewhat. The noblemen, however, fell into fresh holes. When Jan van Renesse realised this, together with Willem van Jülich he attacked the French. The horses fell into the new deep ditches and the knights could not help each other nor stand up again. The foot-soldiers began to flee. Artois did not, however, surrender and attacked powerfully, followed by his standard bearers. A savage battle commenced with the Flemings defending themselves stubbornly with their *goedendags* and pikes. They killed many a sturdy knight and many horses. The Count of Artois was wounded; his horse fell beneath him dead. However, Tancarville and Walepaièle

---

²⁰³ In another manuscript (RHF, 586), the defeat was attributed to the thick mass of lances employed by the men of Bruges. See also *Les Grandes Chroniques*, VIII:205.
²⁰⁴ See above concerning the instructions for royal officers of the seneschal of Poitou.
²⁰⁵ Girard de Franchet, *Continuatio Chronici Girardi de Fracheto*, ed. Guigniaut and de Wailly, in RHF, 21 (Paris, 1855), 20.
²⁰⁶ *Les Grandes Chroniques*, VIII:204–8; and Nangis, 585–7. See also the *Chroniques de Saint-Denis*, ed. Daunou and Naudet, in RHF, 20 (Paris, 1840), 670–1.
²⁰⁷ *Récits d'un bourgeois de Valenciennes*, 114–16. See also V. Fris, 'Récits d'un bourgeois de Valenciennes', *BCRH*, 5th ser., 11 (1901), 9; Fris, *De slag bij Kortrijk*, 98–9, 100–1.

saved him, together with Jean de Hainault. The battle continued for a long time. It was a terrible massacre. Finally, Artois fell, as did many noblemen, whom the author lists.

In this legendary and dramatic account one sees the combination of ditches, from the *Chronique artésienne*, and the naïvely cunning plan reported by Guiart. The chroniclers, with time, gained all the information they could from their sources and made use of various types of explanation. The same phenomenon is to be observed when examining the Flemish version of the battle.

The Sources of the Flemish Version

The *Annales Gandenses*

An anonymous Friar Minor from Ghent left a most valuable source for the years 1297–1310. His annals form an excellent historical work, whose events the author experienced himself. What he recorded derives from his being an eyewitness or from others who took part in the events.[208] Thus, he was well acquainted with the knight, Geraard de Moor, one of the Flemish negotiators in 1304.[209] His history of the war against Philip the Fair is the best work of this whole period. As a true historian he excelled, not so much by virtue of his analytical attention to detail, which for example characterises the *Chronique artésienne*, but rather because of his powerful synthesis and broad outlook. He was very conscious of the need for an overview of events and for coherence, and knew how to weigh up the significance of events. Concerning military matters, he was also a good judge of the tactics and strategy of that time.[210] He took part in person in the defence of the county, the *landweer*, which in September 1302 rallied the priests and clerks to the Nieuwendijk to defend the Flemish borders. He gave an excellent description of the morale that reigned in the communal armies, pointing to the pugnacious spirit, the bravery and triumphal elation following the surprising victory of 11 July, the self-confidence that grew due to the hesitant actions of the enemy, the popularity of a commander such as Willem van Jülich who sought to attack the enemy at any price.[211] As a Friar Minor he was very close to the common people, probably serving in the army as chaplain in September 1302 as well as perhaps taking part in the Battle of Mons-en-Pévèle in 1304 where one of his acquaintances, a chaplain from Ghent, fell.[212] Thus he wrote with much sympathy for the brave townsmen, artisans and peasants who formed the powerful Flemish foot-soldiery: they were 'sturdy and well-nourished men with most excellent weapons' far superior to the French foot-soldiers;[213] and for the men of Hainault who fought almost without

---

[208] *Annales Gandenses*, 1.
[209] Ibid., 76.
[210] Verbruggen, 'De Gentse minderbroeder', 4 ff.
[211] *Annales Gandenses*, 36.
[212] Ibid., 75. His lively and detailed description of the Battle of Mons-en-Pévèle (66–76) supports the view that he was an eyewitness. However, this cannot be completely confirmed.
[213] *Annales Gandenses*, 20.

protection due to the lack of defensive equipment while the Flemings were much more numerous.[214]

He was thus a staunch advocate of the cause of the artisans from the towns as well as a supporter of the Count. This did not prevent him from recognising that Philip the Fair was a very God-fearing and humble man who had been pushed into many wars by his counsellors. He showed the bravery of the King during the Battle of Mons-en-Pévèle; Philip did not want to flee and later took care of the sons of the knights who saved his life.[215] Queen Johanna of Navarre was, for this friar, a great benefactor of the Franciscans, and when he noted that she hated the Flemings, he added a significant and critical *ut dicebatur*: as the common people say. Furthermore, her hatred was a consequence of the fact that many of the members of her house fell in Flanders.[216]

He also upheld his independent spirit towards the members of the Count's family and did not hesitate to criticise them. His indictment of Willem van Jülich is very strong and the Friar Minor may have exaggerated.[217] The other victor of Courtrai, Guy de Namur, was also criticised strongly for his reckless actions only too typical of a knight in the naval battle near Zierikzee.[218] Count Robert de Bethune was, according to the Friar Minor, a weak prince, an instrument in the hands of his counsellors who enriched themselves by accepting gifts.[219] Despite all his sympathy for the men of Bruges, and for Willem van Saaftinge, he still condemned the atrocities committed by the lay brother on the abbot and cellar master at Ter Doest in 1308.[220]

Naturally, all this does not detract from the fact that the Friar Minor supported the cause of the common people. As a Fleming giving the Flemish version of events, he was for his time undoubtedly the most able historian and presented the least partial source. Where there is reason to doubt, as, for instance, with the Bruges Matins that were considered treachery by the French, he undertook a thorough investigation so as to refute the allegations and to show how recklessly the French knights had acted in Bruges.[221] He wrote his work in 1308 after showing a constant appreciation of historical accounts.[222] The history of the years 1309–10 was written later, but before 1312.[223]

Although the only known informant is Geraard de Moor, it may still be assumed that the author received information from other noblemen. This is proved suffi-

---

[214] Ibid., 98. Funck-Brentano, in his edition of the *Annales Gandenses* (Paris, 1896), xxviii, naturally reacted against this judgement of the French foot-soldiers. He did not fully comprehend the implications of the two passages. French foot-soldiers, at that time, had little value on the battlefield.
[215] *Annales Gandenses*, 72.
[216] Ibid., 82–3.
[217] Ibid., 41.
[218] Ibid., 62–3. See also Verbruggen, 'De Gentse minderbroeder', 18–19.
[219] *Annales Gandenses*, 97.
[220] Ibid., 91–2.
[221] Ibid., 24.
[222] Ibid., 1.
[223] Fris, *De slag bij Kortrijk*, 124.

ciently by the author's knowledge of military matters. He also indicates how the French knights, following their defeat on 11 July 1302, immediately began to apply new tactics of which he gives an excellent description. The detailed French chronicle given by Guiart, who was an eyewitness in 1304, confirms the account presented by the Franciscan monk.[224] His criticism of the military operations in 1304 also points in the same direction.

Unfortunately, this excellent source gives only a very brief account of the actual Battle of the Spurs. The Friar Minor was certainly not an eyewitness and most probably considered the events of the battle to be well known, and so in his summary he dealt with it briefly. That he assumed the account of the battle to be well known can be taken from two extremely important references in his detailed account of the Battle of Mons-en-Pévèle. The description of the events of 11 July will be given first, and, following this, it will be supplemented with the aforementioned allusions.

The Friar Minor's account of the Battle of the Spurs
The French King called together all the knights of France, Champagne, Normandy and Poitou whom he could oblige to serve him and also hired many knights with military experience as well as noblemen from Lotharingia, Brabant and Hainault. At the head of this most powerful army he placed the Count of Artois, a brave and noble man who had, from his earliest youth, taken part in battles and tournaments; this able commander had five or six great victories to his name. His army was composed of ten thousand heavy cavalrymen and very many crossbowmen and foot-soldiers, so many that the author never heard their number given. Guy and Willem learned this by means of their scouts as well as learning of Artois's intention of advancing to Courtrai and forcing the Flemings to end their siege. The French garrison had, indeed, provisions for only two months. Willem van Jülich left sufficient troops before the castle of Cassel and advanced with a great army from West Flanders towards his uncle at Courtrai.[225]

At the beginning of July, Artois advanced with his army to Courtrai and set up his camp before the town at a distance of about four or five furlongs (740 m or 925 m). After entering the Flemish-speaking areas of Flanders the French sought to show the savageness of their hearts and to instil fear in the minds of the Flemings: they spared none – women, children or the elderly – killing all whom they found. Even statues of saints in the churches were beheaded or mutilated as if they were living persons.[226] The Flemings, however, were not frightened by this: on the

---

[224] See Verbruggen, 'De Gentse minderbroeder', 19.
[225] *Annales Gandenses*, 28 ff.
[226] This is perhaps reported in order to excuse the Flemings beforehand, since in 1303 they beheaded a statue of St Louis at Térouanne. See *Chronique artésienne*, 68.

contrary it enraged them and spurred them on to the merciless battle now that they had been challenged.

Guy and Willem assembled their army of sixty thousand foot-soldiers, brave, well-armoured men of war. With them were all men trustworthy and loyal to them. Not only from the parts of Flanders that were already with them, but also from Ghent there were around seven hundred well-armoured men who had left the town secretly and had thus immediately been banished by the Leliaarts (the pro-French Ghentenaars). All of the soldiers who were gathered there eagerly awaited the final battle with the French. There were, however, no more than ten knights in all the army among them, the most noble and experienced in warfare: Hendrik van Lontzen from the Duchy of Limburg, Jan van Renesse from the county of Zeeland, Goswin van Gossenhoven of the duchy of Brabant, Diederik van Hondschote, Robrecht van Leeuwergem and Boudewijn van Popperode of the county of Flanders. Together with Guy and Willem, they rallied the Flemish troops into their battle positions and gave encouragement to them. For three or four days various small attacks and skirmishes took place between both armies. On 11 July, Guy and Willem learned from their scouts that all the Frenchmen were preparing themselves in the early morning for battle. They took the same measures for the Flemish army and positioned the men of Ypres before the castle to prevent the French from making a sally. At around six, they formed long and deep ranks. At around nine, armed Frenchmen appeared on the battlefield. Their whole army, cavalrymen as well as foot-soldiers, was divided into nine corps. However, as soon as they saw that the Flemings were positioned in one single and deep corps, bravely prepared for the battle, they reformed their nine *bataelgen* into three formations of knights: one of which was to serve as the rearguard, the other two to attack. Somewhat before midday, the battle began with a terrible noise and the turmoil of war; many fell; the men fought mercilessly and bitterly, albeit not for long, since God took pity upon the Flemings and quickly gave them victory. God poured shame on the French since, had they won, they intended to be most cruel in Flanders, as would become clear later. When the battle began, the soldiers of the castle put fire to the town and turned a beautiful house to ashes in order to instil fear in the hearts of the Flemings. When the cavalrymen and foot-soldiers dared to leave the castle to attack the Flemings from behind, they were forced to retreat back into the castle by the brave resistance of the men of Ypres. The Count of St Pol, commander of the rearguard, saw his two half brothers fall with the two attacking lines of knights. He did not rush to their aid, but fled dishonourably from the battlefield. 'And so, by the disposition of God who orders all things, the art of war, the flower of knighthood with horses and chargers of the finest, fell before weavers, fullers and the common folk and foot-soldiers of Flanders, albeit strong, manly and well armed, courageous and under expert leaders. The beauty and strength of that great army was turned into a dung-pit, and the glory of the French made mud and worms.' On account of the atrocities that the French had committed from Lille to Courtrai, the Flemings were so bitter that they spared neither those injured in the battle nor their horses, and slew them all cruelly, until they were completely assured victory. All were killed so that it became a complete victory. Before the battle commenced, the commanders had proclaimed that whoever during the battle gathered up a precious object as booty, or took captive a noble, however great, was to be killed immediately by the men fighting at his side.[227]

The author then lists the fallen who were of high rank. There were approximately seventy five, besides more than a thousand ordinary knights, many squires and foot-soldiers. More than three thousand precious warhorses were killed. The number of the fallen, together with those who died from their wounds, was twenty thousand, although many more fled. The number of knights at the King's disposal following the battle was not to be compared with that of those who had fallen. After the battle the Flemings took several noblemen captive since they were wounded and could not flee. They found much booty on the battlefield: tents, weapons and much more.[228]

The Friar Minor actually tells us nothing about the course of the attack undertaken by the two larger formations of French knights. He attributed the victory to the hand of God, the bravery of the Flemings, their excellent armour and their experienced leaders.[229] The author did not even mention the stream. Still, there are two allusions to it given during the description of the Battle of Mons-en-Pévèle.

At the beginning of this battle, on 18 August 1304, the crossbowmen of both armies fought against each other. Then, the French knights attacked suddenly after giving their crossbowmen the command to clear the front. As soon as the French knights had begun their charge, the Ghentenaar crossbowmen and those from other towns threw their bows at the feet of the horses. However, the men of Bruges did not follow this example. All of them retreated towards the deep Flemish ranks where they took their place. As the French knights approached, the Flemings remained unyielding and brave in their position and expected a complete battle and profitable close combat as at Courtrai. The French knights approached so close to the Flemings that they could touch the lances of their enemy with their own. Still, they held their reins tight, remaining there practically motionless. The French knights had pretended to charge, although they did not dare attack powerfully since they had agreed among themselves to fight artfully as they feared the same course of events as at Courtrai.[230] From this allusion to what happened in Courtrai, which was not made use of in earlier accounts of the Battle of the Spurs,[231] it appears clearly that the two French formations of knights that led the charge at Courtrai were annihilated after a powerful charge against the Flemish position due to the excellent combination of pikes and *goedendags*. Since the knights were very aware that the foremost reason for their defeat was this very fact, they desisted from a frontal charge after Courtrai, not daring to repeat it at Mons-en-Pévèle.[232]

The second allusion will now illuminate the other point that the Friar Minor neglected in his account of the Battle of the Spurs: the role played by the streams.

---

[227] *Annales Gandenses*, 31.
[228] Ibid., 31–2.
[229] Ibid., 30. See also Verbruggen, 'De Gentse minderbroeder', 11.
[230] *Annales Gandenses*, 66; and Verbruggen, 'De Gentse minderbroeder', 6.
[231] Fris, *De slag bij Kortrijk*, 361 n. 1. Fris employed it incorrectly.
[232] See Verbruggen, 'De Gentse minderbroeder', 6–9, 13–14.

A major part of the Battle of Mons-en-Pévèle took place without complete combat. Until midday, the smaller bodies of soldiers fought each other. At around 5 pm there was even a short pause for negotiations. However, since the Flemings did not expect a pause in the battle to be favourable to them, a decision was taken to execute a general attack to determine the battle. This surprise attack met with overwhelming success, with the French fleeing in utter panic: the knights fled in groups with their formations, with the Flemings pursuing them. Many knights whose horses were exhausted fell into the numerous holes and ditches that crossed the field. They fell in so heavily and in such numbers that many cavalrymen perished. In Courtrai, too, many more Frenchmen died in such accidents than were killed by weapons. The Flemings also suffered losses when pursuing the French; but their losses were not so great.[233]

In this passage the Friar Minor confirms the account given in the most reliable pro-Flemish source for the Battle of Courtrai, that of Lodewijk van Veltem, by stating that more knights perished in the ditches on 11 July than were slain in battle. Still, the first allusion shows how heavily the French attacked at Courtrai, while the second allusion has the horses fall when they were already very tired at a moment when the knights were being pursued by the Flemings. It is thus clear that, at Courtrai, the French fell into the ditches after their attack had failed and during the Flemish counterattack.[234] The townsmen were much more familiar with the Groeninge field than the battlefield at Mons-en-Pévèle.

In such a manner the Friar Minor completely confirms the version of events given by Lodewijk van Veltem: the Flemings took a defensive position awaiting the knights' charge, they resisted successfully, and in counterattacking they forced the retreating or fleeing knights into the streams. As is known, the Flemings pursued their enemies on 11 July to Dottenijs, Zwevegem and St Denijs. During the flight more French knights died in ditches and streams.[235]

The clear correspondence of the Friar Minor, Lodewijk and the *Chronicon Comitum Flandrensium* concerning the defensive position of the Flemings at the beginning of the battle and their victorious resistance to the general charge leads to the assumption that the events occurred as detailed above. The most able historian of that time indicated this not only with his first allusion, but also with his excellent description of French and Flemish tactics from 1302 till 1304.[236]

Lodewijk van Veltem's *Spiegel historiael*
The most detailed account of the Battle of the Spurs is that given by the Brabantese priest, Lodewijk van Veltem. It is remarkable that a chronicler from a nearby principality devoted more than twelve hundred verses to the battle of 11 July 1302. However, when one reads the account presented by the poet then it becomes clear

---

[233] *Annales Gandenses*, 70.
[234] Funck-Brentano, 'Mémoire', 267–8. Funck-Brentano was of the opinion that he could conclude from the above passage that the Flemings did not pursue the French at Courtrai. This is erroneous, as will be seen below.
[235] Lodewijk, II.1.IV:336, c. 37, vv. 2645–55; II.1.IV:337, c. 37, vv. 2686–93; and le Muisit, 67.
[236] Verbruggen, 'De Gentse minderbroeder', 5–19.

how great his love was for the Flemings as well as his sympathy for the artisans. It was these sentiments that spurred him into describing the battle in all its details, elaborating it with the most mythical of omens that he could find in his extensive reading of knightly romances. He not only had the events recounted on numerous occasions by the Flemings whom he questioned, but he also consulted the French sources so that he became well informed about the enemy's army. Justifiably then his account is regarded and employed by all scholars who have dealt with the battle in detail as the most prominent source.[237]

The chronicler was born in Brabant,[238] where he was the parish priest at Zichem, near Diest, in 1304.[239] In 1313, he occupied the same position, this time in the village of Veltehm, whence he received his name.[240] The author was well travelled, visiting Paris around 1292–3, where he stayed for some time, perhaps studying.[241] In 1297 he was in Ghent;[242] in 1313 he had moved to Reen;[243] and in 1315 to the camp near Antwerp.[244]

Lodewijk was a member of the entourage of the Dukes of Brabant and was thus present during a most secret discussion between Jan I and the Lords of Valkenburg and Kuik around 1293–4.[245] In 1297, he was in Ghent as part of the retinue of Jan II when the Duke was meeting with Edward I and Guy de Dampierre.[246]

Lodewijk's *Spiegel historiael* is a sequel to Vincent de Beauvais's *Speculum* that had been translated by Jacob van Maerlant. The Brabantese priest certainly sought to write a sequel to the above work. The eight books of his rhymed chronicle deal with the period 1248–1316: each of the books is devoted to the government of a German emperor, from Willem van Holland to Ludwig of Bavaria, except for the last two that contain all forms of prophetic statements and observations about the end of the world. For the period up to 1300, he mainly used Latin sources as well as others; thus he shortens the account of the Battle of Worringen given by Jan van Heelu.[247] From this point on, he based his account predominantly on his own informants: eyewitnesses, participants or well-informed persons. Where Lodewijk was present, then he was most able to give an excellent description: this is the case with the secret discussions held between the Duke of Brabant and the Lords of Valkenburg and Kuik. This was one of the most splendid explanations of the politics of the princes of that time.[248] He also gave a most lively description of the

---

[237] See, for example, Goethals-Vercruysse, Moke, Köhler, Fredericks, Fris, Delfos, and de Maere d'Aertrycke.
[238] Lodewijk, II.1.IV:341, c. 38, v. 2765.
[239] Ibid., II.1.IV:392, c. 55, vv. 4075–84; III.1.V:17–18, c. 7.
[240] Ibid., III.1.VI:159, c. 4.
[241] Ibid., II.1.III:184, c. 39, vv. 2694–8; I.1.II:354, c. 32, vv. 2481–97; II.1.III:211, c. 48 (esp. v. 3301).
[242] Ibid., II.1.IV:229, c. 2, vv. 105–6.
[243] Ibid., III.1.VI:182, c. 10, v. 715.
[244] Ibid., III.1.VI:204, c. 18, vv. 1274–7.
[245] Ibid., II.1.IV:181–2, c. 38, vv. 2616–51.
[246] Ibid., II.1.IV:229, c. 2, vv. 104–6.
[247] Ibid., II.1.III:12–131, cc. 3–121.
[248] Funck-Brentano, 'Mémoire', 266.

mores and equipment of the Welsh soldiers serving under King Edward I who, in 1297, were stationed in Ghent.[249] Lodewijk, moreover, had very good informants in Ghent and was well informed about what took place there.[250] He also had very good contacts among the Flemings,[251] giving an accurate list of the noblemen who followed Guy de Dampierre and his sons into imprisonment in France in 1300.[252] For the Battle of the Spurs he provided the most accurate and complete list of noblemen who took part in the battle.[253] Lodewijk also gives a singularly lively, interesting and fair account of the negotiations in September 1302 between the Flemish and French envoys who attempted to achieve peace.[254] His account of the war between the Flemish Count and the King of France is, therefore, very detailed and, in general, correct. One single serious mistake mars the account, adding some confusion to the history of the events: Lodewijk has the visit of Philip the Fair to conquered Flanders take place in 1300, not in 1301, and thus before the surrender of Ghent to Charles of Valois (8 May 1300).[255] This mistake on the exact year is, perhaps, the consequence of his account being written much later, apparently somewhat before 1313.[256] Only seldom does the author detail events in France, and, when he does, he commits some serious errors.[257] This is not, however, the case when he describes the French army at Courtrai.

One serious difficulty encountered in the study of Lodewijk's account arises from the fact that there is only one manuscript which is in numerous places very corrupt.[258] This can be ascertained on the battle itself in verses which are of the utmost importance to understanding his account. In various places figures have been deleted,[259] and numerous corrections still have to be made to the text.

As a historian, Lodewijk van Velthem had the best intentions, seeking to reproduce the events as they truly took place,[260] as well as criticising credulous historians who included fabricated elements in their histories.[261] When faced with contradictory versions he goes as far as to examine himself the veracity of docu-

---

[249] Lodewijk, II.1.IV:229–30, c. 2, vv. 92–121.
[250] Fris, *De slag bij Kortrijk*, 133.
[251] Ibid., 134.
[252] Lodewijk, II.1.IV:243–9, c. 7; Fris, *De slag bij Kortrijk*, 133–4; and Funck-Brentano, 'Mémoire', 267.
[253] Fris, *De slag bij Kortrijk*, 134. On the numerical strength of the two armies, see chapter II.
[254] Lodewijk, II.1.IV:374–7, c. 50; and Funck-Brentano, *Philippe le Bel*, 434–5. The text of verses 3681–4 is corrupt. See F. L. Ganshof, 'Aantekening over Lodewijk van Velthem, *Spiegel historiael*, IV. L, vv. 3681–4', in *Album Professor Dr Frank Baur*, I (Antwerp, 1948), 265–75.
[255] Lodewijk, II.1.IV:249–50, c. 8, v. 531, 545–7; and Fris, *De slag bij Kortrijk*, 133.
[256] Fris, *De slag bij Kortrijk*, 133.
[257] Funck-Brentano, 'Mémoire', 268.
[258] Ganshof, 'Aantekening over Lodewijk van Velthem *Spiegel historiael*', 271, 275 n. 30; and H. Pirenne, 'Note sur un passage de van Velthem relatif à la bataille de Courtrai', *BCRH*, 5th ser., 9 (1899), 214.
[259] See below.
[260] Lodewijk, III.1.V:2, vv. 23–8.
[261] Ibid., III.1.V:3, vv. 35–43.

ments at the place of occurrence. Even though he reproduces popular rumours, he nevertheless adds that the best-informed persons do not attach much credulity to them.[262]

However, Lodewijk was a staunch defender of the cause of the common people. His work, written in the vernacular, is a perfect example of popular historiography, reproducing rumours circulating among the people and even romantic explanations. This is not to say that he knowingly and wittingly distorted the truth, since there is information to the contrary. Thus, for instance, the author showed very correctly that, when the aldermen of Ghent reintroduced the tax in 1302, it was not Jacques de St Pol who was responsible. This is despite his not being at all favourable to St Pol.[263]

As a champion of the Flemish people, Lodewijk rejoiced at their astonishing victory on 11 July. It is evident at that point that he did not wish to omit any detail: 'Very often have I heard', he writes, 'that the monk (Willem van Saaftinge) struck Artois from his horse.'[264] The author must, then, have interviewed eyewitnesses to the battle since minor details can actually be confirmed in other sources.[265]

He presents us with an excellent picture of the great fear in the hearts of the townsmen before the battle.[266] He does not hesitate to describe the flight of the frightened Flemish fighters.[267] When the men of the Bruges Franc have to retreat, he excused them by pointing to the useful effect of the movement thanks to the intervention of Jan van Renesse.[268] Thus, Lodewijk did not omit such events, even detailing very accurately the fatigue of the victors after the battle.[269]

His knowledge of the battlefield and of the surroundings of Courtrai is excellent. It is possible to reproduce all the details of the terrain solely on the basis of his account. To his accurate description one needs merely to add several details from French sources, although one could, to a certain extent, infer them from information given by Lodewijk.[270]

Furthermore, Lodewijk spared no effort in seeking to gain reliable information concerning the French army. The details he presents on this are in no manner inferior to those in the French sources themselves. Like Villani, he gave ten formations of knights, the *bataelgen*, giving practically the same numerical strength and commanders as the Italian chronicler. Concerning the deliberations of Artois's council of war, he detailed the same points as the Florentine chronicler: no imme-

---

[262] Ibid., III.1.V:3, vv. 55–60; II.1.IV:401, c. 58, vv. 4330–45; II.1.IV:409, c. 60, vv. 4538–58. See also Obreen, xlv and n.2 (Lodewijk, II.1.IV:197, c. 43, vv. 2976–86).
[263] Funck-Brentano in his edition of the *Annales Gandenses*, 18 n. 3; and Lodewijk, II.1.IV:251, c. 8, vv. 568–79.
[264] Lodewijk, II.1.IV:324, c. 33, vv. 2350–1.
[265] Concerning Willem van Saaftinge see *Annales Gandenses*, 91–2.
[266] Lodewijk, II.1.IV:302, c. 26, vv. 1809–12; II.1.IV:303, c. 26, vv. 1834–5; II.1.IV:305, c. 27, v. 1898; II.1.IV:311, c. 39, v. 2033.
[267] Ibid., II.1.IV:329–31, c. 35.
[268] Ibid., II.1.IV:313, c. 29, vv. 2091–4.
[269] Ibid., II.1.IV:338, c. 38, vv. 2700–17.
[270] See the section on terrain below.

diate attack, but harassing and tiring the Flemish troops.[271] At this point, Lodewijk placed Geoffrey de Brabant at the forefront since this nobleman was better known to his readers. Like Villani, Lodewijk also had the first French attack take place under the command of Raoul de Nesle. However, the Brabantese priest protested most strongly against the French claim, also found in Villani's account, that the French were not aware of the Groeninge stream across which the second attack took place. Lodewijk was thus seeking to refute a version of events that agrees with that given by the Florentine. Both authors, Villani and Lodewijk, note that the French were twice as numerous as the Flemings.

Lodewijk van Velthem names so many French knights that he must have received the information from a French source: Martel,[272] Raoul IV Flamens,[273] Gilles de Hailly,[274] de Créquy,[275] de Sailly,[276] Nicaise de Richefort,[277] Raoul de Grantcourt,[278] le Brun de Brunembert,[279] Henri de Ligny,[280] Guillaume de St Valery,[281] Surgens or Jean de Ville,[282] the Lords of Beaunes,[283] de Apremont,[284] de Mello,[285] Jacob van Dorne and his brother, Joffrois.[286] and the Flemish supporters of the King, de Haveskerke,[287] Pierre du Breucq,[288] the bailiff of Bruges, and the Viscount of Lille.[289] Then are added to the list the commanders of the ten *bataelgen* (formations): Jean de Burlats,[290] Gui de Nesle,[291] Raoul de Nesle,[292] Robert

---

[271] See below.
[272] Lodewijk, II.1.IV:286, c. 21, v. 1453: Mertelet. Jean and Guillaume Martel fell at Courtrai. See *Chronique artésienne*, 50.
[273] Lodewijk, II.1.IV:302, c. 26, v. 1819: Raveel die Vlaminc. See also *Chronique artésienne*, 50; and *Chronographia*, I:111.
[274] Lodewijk, II.1.IV:302, c. 26, v. 1823: Gilijs van Haelgi (Gilles de Haelgi).
[275] Ibid., II.1.IV:302, c. 26, v. 1825: die here van Kerki (Lord of Kerki). See also *Chronique artésienne*, 50.
[276] Lodewijk, II.1.IV:302, c. 26, v. 1827: Sailgi.
[277] Ibid., II.1.IV:303, c. 26, v. 1829.
[278] Ibid., II.1.IV:302, c. 34, v. 2406: Raveel de Gaucourt. See also *Chronique artésienne*, 51.
[279] Lodewijk, II.1.IV:333, c. 36, v. 2588. See also *Chronique artésienne*, 50.
[280] Lodewijk, II.1.IV:293, c. 23, v. 1623: Heinrijc van Lingi. See also *Chronique artésienne*, 49: Henris de Luxembourc (Henri de Luxembourg), and *Chronographia*, I:111: Henricus dominus de Lyneyo.
[281] Lodewijk, II.1.IV:293, c. 23, v. 1624.
[282] Ibid., II.1.IV:294, c. 23, v. 1626.
[283] Ibid., II.1.IV:294, c. 23, v. 1627.
[284] Ibid., II.1.IV:308, c. 28, v. 1959; II.1.IV:320, c. 32, v. 2255; II.1.IV:339, c. 38, v. 2738. See also *Chronique artésienne*, 50; and *Chronographia*, I:111.
[285] Lodewijk, II.1.IV:340, c. 38, v. 2754: Merlos. See also *Chronique artésienne*, 50; and *Chronographia*, I:111.
[286] Lodewijk, II.1.IV:339, c. 38, vv. 2740–1.
[287] Ibid., II.1.IV:294, c. 23, v. 1627.
[288] Ibid., II.1.IV:285, c. 21, v. 1422. See also *Chronique artésienne*, 45.
[289] Lodewijk, II.1.IV:294, c. 23, v. 1625. See also *Chronique artésienne*, 50.
[290] Lodewijk, II.1.IV:292, c. 23, v. 1599.
[291] Ibid., II.1.IV:293, c. 23, vv. 1606–7.
[292] Ibid., II.1.IV:293, c. 23, vv. 1612–13.

d'Artois and Jacques de St Pol, Louis de Clermont,[293] the Count of Eu,[294] Tancarville,[295] Renaud and Mathieu de Trie,[296] Gui de St Pol and the Count of Boulogne,[297] and important noblemen such as Godefrois de Boulogne,[298] and the Count of Aumale.[299]

On two occasions Lodewijk confirmed that he had read what he related in his account, first concerning a conversation between d'Apremont and the knight, Moreul,[300] and later when he reported 'as we have found written, from no one country, did so many knights fall as from Normandy'.[301]

The number of Frenchmen who fell was very similar to that given in the French sources.[302] Lodewijk followed the same chronicles in reproducing Artois's curse: 'Paterne Dieu'.[303] When the commander of the French troops sought to surrender he shouted: 'Ic ben die grave van Artoys, neemt mi op' (I am the Count of Artois, take me), this being the translation of 'Prendez, prendez, le conte d'Artois' (Take, take, the Count of Artois) or 'Accipe, accipe, comitem Arthesii'.[304]

Lodewijk is alone in giving a complete description of the peace negotiations between the Flemish and French envoys that followed the Battle of Courtrai in September 1302. The *Chronographia Regum Francorum*, which shows agreement with Lodewijk's work concerning certain details of earlier events, provides specific elements of information confirming Lodewijk's account.[305] Lodewijk read the account in a French source, or gained the information by means of an intermediary since, after the negotiations, he gives details of the deliberations of King Philip's war council. In this council he has the Duke of Brittany play the same role as he did in the *Chronographia*:[306] the Duke protested heavily that nothing was being done

---

[293] Ibid., II.1.IV:307, c. 28, v. 1927.
[294] Ibid., II.1.IV:307, c. 28, v. 1932.
[295] Ibid., II.1.IV:320, c. 32, v. 2255.
[296] Ibid., II.1.IV:307, c. 28, vv. 1934–5: 'Ferijn een tsampenoys ende Mathijs sijn broeder' (Ferijn, a *champagnois* and Mathias, his brother). See also Lodewijk, II.1.IV:321, c. 33, v. 2285; *Chronique artésienne*, 51, *Chronographia*, I:111: Ragnierus de Tria; and Villani, 386: Ferri . . . del Loreno. Lodewijk placed Renaud de Trie in the second *bataelge* with Gui de Nesle (II.1.IV:293, c. 23, v. 1608).
[297] Lodewijk, II.1.IV:337, c. 37, v. 2686, 2690–1.
[298] Ibid., II.1.IV:331, c. 35, v. 2529; II.1.IV:340, c. 38, v. 2750.
[299] Ibid., II.1.IV:340, c. 38, v. 2142.
[300] Ibid., II.1.IV:308, c. 28, vv. 1958–9. Moreul was most probably not Béraud X de Mercœur, or Marcoel in the *Chronique artésienne*, 22, 31, 81, but rather de Moreuil (Somme). See, among others, RHF, 23, ed. de Wailly, Delisle and Jourdain (Paris, n.d.), 805, 808, G. (Vermandois).
[301] Lodewijk, II.1.I:339, c. 38, vv. 2722–4.
[302] Ibid., II.1.IV:326, c. 34, vv. 2400–3: 63 bannerets and 1100 knights. The *Chronique normande*, 19; and *Chronographia*, I:112, number these forces at 60 bannerets (without the princes) and 1100 knights.
[303] Lodewijk, II.1.IV:321, c. 33, v. 2305; *Chronographia*, I:169; and *Istore et croniques*, I:235.
[304] Lodewijk, II.1.IV:324, c. 33, vv. 2367–8; *Chronographia*, I:109; and *Istore et croniques*, I:234.
[305] Lodewijk, II.1.IV:374–7, c. 50; and *Chronographia*, I:119. Compare with the incorrectly dated Flemish proposals at the end of the Battle of the Spurs noted in *Chronographia*, I:112.
[306] Lodewijk, II.1.IV:383–4, c. 52, vv. 3867–80; *Chronographia*, I:119–20; and *Anciennes chroniques de Flandre*, 383.

and threatened to leave the army. Lodewijk naturally had at his disposal information received from eyewitness to the negotiations and is, therefore, able to present an excellent description.[307]

However, the author was not only an avid gatherer of information that would allow him to describe the Flemish victory accurately. He was also a poet and sought, as did most chroniclers of that time, to clearly show the intervention of God. Indeed, he stated it plainly: 'Fleming! You have not done this. The Lord has.'[308] As in Villani's account, the French were punished for their sins.[309]

As a poet, Lodewijk draws upon his rich poetic ability. His predilection for miracles and prophecies is sufficiently clear in the last two books of the *Spiegel historiael*. Why should he not make use of them to add a mythical touch to this incredible victory by the common people? Was there a better means to prove the intervention of God and of St George? Dark screeching birds flew above the enemies' ranks while white birds flew above the Flemish troops.[310] For sceptics and so as to rhyme, the poet adds that 'it is true!' The stars turned strangely in the heavens.[311] Artois's tame wolf sought to remove the armour and weapons from his master. During the mass the sacred wafer that Robert wanted to eat disappeared suddenly. A grey toad crawled from out of the Flemish ranks towards the Frenchmen. Once there it spit out its poison in the direction of the enemy. Artois's splendid horse, Morel, when stretched while trotting was almost fourteen foot long, was of such great value that the King of France was willing to give one thousand pounds for it as well as an income of one hundred pounds. Yet, this beautiful horse faltered three times as Artois tried to mount it.[312] In the midst of the battle the banner of St George appeared with the saint himself taking part in the battle.[313]

An impressive list of miracles and signs was thus presented. Still, one is also aware that epic elements in histories of that period were common. Even the best chronicles of the Middle Ages described such signs and miracles. There were continual reports of them in the period of the First Crusade with sources repeatedly noting the intervention of St George and of other patron saints of soldiers.[314] The *Chronographia* even reports that the men of Bruges carried the image of St George with them on horseback during their military expeditions, imploring the saint to help them and to give confidence to the artisans serving in the militia. After the Battle of Mons-en-Pévèle such a horse fell into the hands of the French.[315] This same French source notes the negative premonition on the part of the French

---

[307] Funck-Brentano, *Philippe le Bel*, 434–5. The author was extremely critical of Lodewijk. However, here he followed his account fully.
[308] Lodewijk, II.1.IV:342, c. 39, vv. 2796–7; II.1.IV:320, c. 32, v. 2263.
[309] Ibid., II.1.IV:320, c. 32, vv. 2267–8.
[310] Ibid., II.1.IV.288, c. 22, v. 1501 ff.; II.1.IV:312, c. 29, vv. 2061–6.
[311] Ibid., II.1.IV·312, c. 29, vv. 2061–6.
[312] Ibid., II.1.IV:294–7, c. 24.
[313] Ibid., II.1.IV:311, c. 29, vv. 2035–6; II.1.IV:330–1, c. 35, vv. 2532–3.
[314] P. Rousset, *Les Origines et les caractères de la première croisade* (Neuchâtel, 1945), 29, 37–8, 90–1, 140.
[315] *Chronographia*, I:161.

soldiers whose horses had not neighed for over ten days prior to the Battle of Courtrai.[316] According to *Les Grandes Chroniques de France*, the terrible catastrophe for the French had been foretold by a comet and an eclipse.[317] Thus, one sees that such epic elements appear in both versions and above all in texts intended for the common people, who were very trusting. When, after the Battle of Mons-en-Pévèle, the corpse of the most popular Flemish commander, Willem van Jülich, was not found, artisans under his command during the attack claimed that he had disappeared by magical powers and would reappear once again when most required later,[318] as had happened in 1302 when he came from the east to support them at the beginning of the rebellion and to ensure their victory.[319] In 1308, they were still most earnestly hoping that he would return. At around the same time, certain lowly characters were assuming false personalities, such as that of Jan van Vierson, a Brabantese nobleman who had fallen at Courtrai.[320]

All such miracles and portents were thus used in proving that God's help or the intervention of a saint was decisive and granted victory to the intrepid and outnumbered soldiers. This is the conception shared by Villani and by Lodewijk concerning the Battle of the Spurs. Exactly the same phenomenon is seen with the Battle of the Steppes (1213).[321] However, such an interpretation does not lead to the misrepresentation of events and thus it is methodologically incorrect to question the veracity of Lodewijk's account on the basis of his having reported such portents. The same is also true as regards the tone in which the author described the battles. One should make a clear distinction between an enthusiastic judgement of heroic actions and the accurate and correct depiction of the general course of the battle. For certain French historians, Lodewijk is an author of an epos, the creator of a myth, a poet pushed to the threshold of insanity by his power of fantasy.[322] In fact they mistranslated, or did not consult his work at all since the initial criticism levelled was continually repeated with new elements.[323]

Lodewijk's tone is without a doubt very sharply anti-French. He was certainly on the side of those who were content with the Bruges Matins.[324] He wrote with visible pleasure following the bloody defeat of 11 July 1302 that 'French glory has

---

316 *Chronographia*, I:106; *Istore et croniques*, I:252; and *Chronique normande*, 18.
317 *Les Grandes Chroniques*, VIII:208.
318 *Annales Gandenses*, 74.
319 Lodewijk, II.1.IV:255, c. 10, vv. 665–7; III.1.V:61, c. 25, vv. 1648–53.
320 Ibid., III.1.V:60–4, c. 25; and le Muisit, 18.
321 *Triumphus S. Lamberti in Steppes*, ed. J. Heller, in MGH SS, 25 (Hanover, 1880), 169 ff. Victory was often predicted to prove that 'divine providence had willed that our men, a mere handful in number, accorded victory to the intervention of the holy martyr (St Lambert)'. On the basis of the *Annales S. Jacobi Leodiensis*, ed. G. Pertz, in MGH SS, 16 (Hanover, 1859), 668–9, it can be said that both sources stem from a single common source which presented the same events. However, the *Triumphus* is quite partial to appearance of the knights of Liège, for which he underestimates their number, for the above reasons.
322 Lot, *L'Art militaire*, I:257 and n. 6; I:258 and n. 1. See also Funck-Brentano, in *Chronique artésienne*, 46 n. 1, 47.
323 See the refutation of their critique below.
324 Lodewijk, II.1.IV:272–3, c. 16, vv. 1125–7.

been done away with'.³²⁵ Lodewijk, as a member of the entourage of the Dukes of Brabant, is very much aware of the danger that the whole of the Netherlands would face if the King of France were ever to become the complete master of Flanders. He reports that, following the outright defeat of the Flemish rebels, Geoffrey de Brabant wanted to move to Ghent which had been allocated to him.³²⁶ The *Annales Gandenses* confirmed that the Brabantese nobleman was intent upon dethroning his nephew, Jan II, and accepting Brabant as a fiefdom of France.³²⁷ Geoffrey provisioned the Rupelmonde castle so well that it could resist until the winter of 1302.³²⁸ There was thus some form of *communis opinio* that attributed a plot to the King of France aimed at seizing the territory. Lodewijk reacted once more in recounting the events of 1315. He apparently did not belong to those who encouraged Jan II to make an alliance with the King of France in order to completely encircle the Count, Robert de Bethune. Flanders was, then, to be completely overcome with a French army from the south, and by the Count of Hainault and Holland from the north, while an English fleet would block the Flemish coast.³²⁹ Once again it appeared as something marvellous that the county could resist this enormous menace; the ambitious project failed entirely and even provided the Flemings with a rich source of booty since the French had to retreat leaving behind their camp after torrential rain had made any military expedition along the southern border impossible.³³⁰ Once again Lodewijk was most happy: 'And thus Flanders has now been saved on both flanks. This is certainly God's doing!'³³¹

The poet was apparently against any form of French intervention in the South Netherlands. In his work one undoubtedly sees the expression of a national sentiment that not only includes Flanders, but also Brabant, and hence both Dutch-speaking principalities in the South Netherlands. He certainly shows a predilection for the Dutch language in which his master, Maerlant, wrote, since according to him St Pol had been given the following task by the French queen: 'That he should, throughout all the land of Flanders, / So charge and break through, / That no man speak Dutch there any more.'³³²

However, on 11 July, that 'hallowed' day, Flanders' honour was saved among others by Boudewijn van Popperode, Viscount of Alost, and by Guy de Namur.³³³ Those Flemish who fought in the French ranks, such as Pierre du Breucq, a former bailiff, had betrayed Flanders for money.³³⁴ Lodewijk let it be known that no mercy

---

325 Ibid., II.1.IV:320, c. 32, v. 2258.
326 Ibid., II.1.IV:290–1, c. 23, vv. 1564–80.
327 *Annales Gandenses*, 31. See also Lodewijk, II.1.III:193–4, c. 42, vv. 2894–907, concerning Geoffrey's jealousy of Jan II.
328 The *Annales Gandenses*, 35, incorrectly noted the castle as that of Dendermonde. See Fris, *De slag bij Kortrijk*, 289.
329 Lodewijk, III.1.VI:195, c. 15, vv. 1034–46.
330 Ibid., III.1.VI:205–7, c. 19.
331 Ibid., III.1.VI:210, c. 21, vv. 1445–6, 1456–7; and le Muisit, 88.
332 Lodewijk, II.1.IV:265, c. 14, vv. 924–6: 'dat hij zou heel Vlaanderland / Zó doorrijden en doorbreken / Dat men geen Diets er meer zou spreken.'
333 Ibid., II.1.IV:318, c. 32, v. 2217; II.1.IV:331, c. 35, v. 2525.
334 Ibid., II.1.IV:285, c. 21, vv. 1422–32.

was given to the supporters of France. One was rent asunder 'from top to toe as if he were an animal for slaughter'.[335] Willem van Mosscher was also not spared: 'he had merited it', according to the poet.[336] Lodewijk was not worried by the fate of the 'great lords' of Brabant. When they sing aloud the Flemish battle cry, shaking with fear while being pursued, Guy de Namur gave the following order: 'Kill all that . . . / Has put on spurs!'[337]

The indignation felt by Lodewijk caused him to be most objective in his protest against the enemy's claim that the French were not aware of the existence of the Groeninge stream and suffered defeat for this reason. Lies and nonsense is the poet's answer![338] The knights fell into the ditch because following their unsuccessful attack they were driven back by the Flemings.

Thus, Lodewijk's tone is certainly very cutting and passionate. For this reason, Funck-Brentano took great pains to point out where Lodewijk exaggerated in the reproduction of events and in this manner sought to discredit the poet's account. Hence, he criticised Lodewijk's description of the terrain: 'an empty field, without any marked difference in height from the highest to the lowest point of more than four metres, is transformed by the author into wooded mountains and valleys'.[339] In fact, the poet was detailing the Pottelberg hill and the *nederinge*, or low-lying area, that was full of *grachten*.[340] The hill and valley appeared to be full of French troops;[341] seven thousand knights advanced into the low-lying area,[342] and towards the end of the battle other soldiers take up positions at the foot of the mountain.[343] 'Ditches', a field, wood and hedges were only mentioned during the account of the pursuit; Gilles le Muisit who had seen the French flee in disorder to the gates of Tournai also mentioned them.[344] The difference in height between the mountain and the lowest point in the area was indeed twenty-five metres. Was it necessary to point out that local inhabitants did actually regard the Pottelberg as a real mountain? Was the word, *berg*, mountain, not clear enough?[345] In fact, one cannot deny that Lodewijk gave by far the best description of the terrain.[346]

---

[335] Ibid., II.1.IV:329, c. 34, vv. 2478–83.
[336] Ibid., II.1.IV:334, c. 36, vv. 2608–13.
[337] Ibid., II.1.IV:337, c. 37, vv. 2680–1: 'Slaat al doet . . . / Wat dat sporen heeft gespannen.'
[338] Ibid., II.1.IV:317, c. 31, vv. 2192–203.
[339] Funck-Brentano, 'Mémoire', 269–70. This criticism is also given by Lot, *L'Art militaire*, I:258 n. 1, and by Wagner, 386.
[340] The author used *nederinge*, signifying 'hollow', and *grachten*, signifying 'ditches' [translator's note].
[341] Lodewijk, II.1.IV:290, c. 22, vv. 1556–8; II.1.IV:292, c. 23, v. 1606.
[342] Ibid., II.1.IV:311, c. 29, v. 2020.
[343] Ibid., II.1.IV:333, c. 36, v. 2606.
[344] Ibid., II.1.IV:336, c. 37, v. 2647; and le Muisit, 67.
[345] See, for example, G. Espinas, *Une guerre sociale interurbaine dans la Flandre wallonne au XIIIe siècle: Douai et Lille, 1284–85* (Paris and Lille, 1930), 131. The inhabitants of the area were inclined to call a hill a mountain. For a description of the 1356 Battle of Malpertuis (also called the Battle of Poitiers) see Lot, *L'Art militaire*, I:355. The historian did not understand why the chroniclers spoke of a mountain.
[346] For this reason, in examining the terrain below, the details given by each chronicler are dealt with separately.

According to Lot, and also to Pirenne, the poet contradicted himself on the ditches.³⁴⁷ His arguments are based on a rational distinction made by Frederichs between the words *gracht* (ditch) and *grachten* (ditches), employed by Lodewijk. For Frederichs, the *gracht* is the Grote Beek, the Great Brook, and the *grachten* are the trenches running across the field.³⁴⁸

Fris accepted the distinction and speaks of four types of ditches:³⁴⁹ a series of ditches to the west of the Groeninge stream, between the stream and the monastery; second, the St Jan's stream or the Grote Beek; third, the Klakkaerts stream and the Bloedmeers; fourth, the Lange Mere and the ditches not on the battlefield. As Lodewijk explained, before the battle the castle garrison at Courtrai gave a signal for Artois's army to show which way it could reach the castle.³⁵⁰ By the signals given, the French soldiers indicated a *nederinge*, a hollow or a low-lying area full of ditches, that the French could not avoid since they had to pass through it to reach the garrison. Then, however, comes the following verse: 'Daer si hem niet jegen en wachten' or in translation 'which they did not expect'.³⁵¹ From this Lot concludes that the French knights were not aware of the ditches and that Lodewijk contradicted himself at this point since he later protested against a French claim about the ditch, the Groeninge stream, although not against the ditches mentioned here.³⁵² This translation is, however, linguistically incorrect since the expression is *zich wachten voor iets*, 'to be on one's guard'. Lodewijk expresses this once again in another verse: after two major French attacks had taken place Artois wanted to provide support to his retreating knights. One knight warned Artois, before the commander crossed the Groeninge to attack with the following words: 'Noble prince! The ditch is deep. Stop, my lord! Be on your guard!'³⁵³ Thus, the words, 'daer si hem niet jegen en wachten' ought to be translated as 'against which they did not take guard'. In fact, the French knights did not take any precautions in fighting with the stream at their rear. This piece of advice was also given by the Frenchman, Guiart: 'Lord, be certain that our men shall fight in a dangerous position on the other side since as soon as the horses, when retreating, fall into the ditch, then they will not be able to get out again.'³⁵⁴ Thus, there can be no talk of contradiction in Lodewijk's account unless one seeks to find a contradiction at any expense, this being obviously methodologically incorrect.

---

³⁴⁷ Lot, *L'Art militaire*, I:258; and Pirenne, 'Note sur un passage de van Velthem', 220 n. 1.
³⁴⁸ Frederichs, 'Les Derniers Travaux', 181; and Frederichs, 'De slag van Kortrijk', 34, n. 4.
³⁴⁹ Fris, *De slag bij Kortrijk*, 254–6.
³⁵⁰ Lodewijk, II.1.IV:290, c. 22, vv. 1556–60: 'Ende wijsden se daer se niet conden ontgaen / In .i. n(e)d(e)ringe vol van grachten, / Daer si hem niet jegen en wachten, / Daer si in haer doet oec varen, / Alst hierna sal openbaren.' (And they showed them where they could not avoid a low-lying area full of ditches for which they were not on their guard, where they went to their death, as will be shown below.)
³⁵¹ Pirenne, 'Note sur un passage de van Velthem', 217; Funck-Brentano, 'Mémoire', 271; Funck-Brentano, in *Chronique artésienne*, 46 n. 1; and Lot, *L'Art militaire*, I:258.
³⁵² Lot, *L'Art militaire*, I:258; and Pirenne, 'Note sur un passage de van Velthem', 220 n. 1.
³⁵³ Lodewijk, II.1.IV:321, c. 33, vv. 2290–1: 'Edel prinse! Die gracht es diep / Hout op, Heer! Hoet er u jegen.'
³⁵⁴ Guiart, 238, vv. 15,018–24.

Moreover, the distinction made by Frederichs and Fris between Lodewijk's use of the words *gracht* and *grachten* does not bear critical examination. Their interpretation of the words is actually wholly based on their conception of the battle. Frederichs and Fris saw the French knights as only having attacked across the Grote Beek (the Great Stream);[355] Lot saw the charge of the knights as only having taken place across the Groeninge stream.[356] All the above conceptions are erroneous, as will be proved below.

Frederichs and Fris assumed that the Flemings first took up battle positions behind the Groeninge stream. Subsequent to this, when it appeared impossible that the French knights could cross over and the French had turned towards the Grote Beek, the main stream, the Flemings executed a swerving movement to take up positions behind the Grote Beek. The turning movement of the French troops is taken from Guiart's work.[357] Still, as noted above, this is the only source that mentions such an important movement and it is rather remarkable that no other chronicler alluded to it. Furthermore, as seen, the description given by Guiart does not correspond with the actual battlefield terrain. On the basis of historical methodology, one can dismiss Guiart's account on this point.

Concerning the military aspects, it is not possible to accept the alleged position of the Flemish troops from the Lys or the monastery, behind the Groeninge stream, to the source of the Grote Beek, as in the works of Frederichs, Fris and Lot. In fact, in this case the crossing over of the Grote Beek would not have been resisted and the entire Flemish right flank would have been exposed to the French knights who had descended from the Pottelberg hill. The knights would then have been able, very easily, to establish their connection with the garrison across the Grote Beek. The Flemish position in its entirety would subsequently have been caught from behind.

The rapid swerving movement, not mentioned in any other sources, can also be questioned since Flemish militias had not practised it. Their compact position would thus have become thoroughly disordered and dispersed. Indeed, Lodewijk's account goes against Fris's and Frederichs's conception of the Flemings alone having taken up positions behind the Grote Beek. Furthermore, the poet noted that the second attack made by the French noblemen was directed against Guy de Namur, the commander of the Flemish troops on the left flank positioned beneath the nunnery. It was there that a *gracht* ran from the Lys to the road to Ghent.[358] This was undoubtedly the Groeninge stream,[359] and Lodewijk's verse completely refutes Frederichs's and Fris's conception.

The aforementioned passage, on the signals given by the French garrison in the

---

[355] Frederichs, 'Les Derniers Travaux', 179–81; Frederichs, 'De slag van Kortrijk', 27 and map; and Fris, *De slag bij Kortrijk*, 257–8, 358.
[356] Lot, *L'Art militaire*, I:263.
[357] Guiart, 239, vv. 15,045–9. See the examination of Guiart's work above.
[358] Lodewijk, II.1.IV:317, c. 31, vv. 2186–91.
[359] See Lot, *L'Art militaire*, I:258.

Courtrai castle, also contradicts the analyses of the two scholars. Fris placed the *grachten*, the ditches, between the monastery and the Groeninge stream,[360] even though, according to his account, the French never attacked at that point and could not have died there. Lodewijk was writing here of all the ditches in the low field: above all the Groeninge and the Grote Beek, perhaps also the Mosscher and other streams in which the French died while fleeing.

Lodewijk's account allows us to give another interpretation of the events. The poet details the succession of events during the first French attack against the Flemish right flank, the men of Bruges, and against the centre, the soldiers from the Bruges Franc.[361] Why did the French attack merely reach the centre of the Flemish positions? This is simply because the first *bataelge* (formation), attacked along the Grote Beek, and from there could not during the charge reach the majority of the Flemish troops who were positioned right before them. At the same time, or perhaps several moments later,[362] the second formation started its attack against the troops of Guy de Namur, and thus across the Groeninge stream.[363] The reason why the soldiers of the Bruges Franc were pushed back and the knights were able to penetrate deep into their ranks is also easily explained. The men were positioned at the greatest distance from the stream, thus providing the knights, after they had crossed over, with the longest run and allowing for the most powerful charge to be executed against them.[364] If one adopts Lot's assertion that the French only attacked across the Groeninge and the Flemings were only positioned behind the stream – this being extremely illogical – then the front of the charge would hardly have been three hundred metres long and there would have been no justification for two *bataelgen* to attack separately.[365] The logical conclusion that flows from Lodewijk's account is that the Flemings were positioned from the monastery to the walls of Courtrai, or the Hoge Vijver (the Upper Lake). Since the crossbowmen were lined up before the Flemish positions,[366] the army was slightly further back, probably a hundred or more metres from both streams. In this case the Flemish troops formed a half moon as detailed by Villani and in the *Chronographia*.[367]

This interpretation corresponds completely with Lodewijk's mention of the *grachten*. The first passage concerning the *nederinge*, the hollows or low-lying fields with streams from surrounding areas, has been dealt with above. Lodewijk's second mention of the term is at a point when the French knights, who had successfully penetrated the ranks of the soldiers of the Bruges Franc, were forced back by

---

[360] Fris, *De slag bij Kortrijk*, 255–6, 355.
[361] Lodewijk, II.1.IV:313–14, c. 29, v. 2079 ff.
[362] Ibid., II.1.IV:319–20, c. 32, vv. 2233–46: the author noted that the attacks actually took place simultaneously, although he detailed them separately. Unfortunately, the verses are corrupt.
[363] Ibid., II.1.IV:317, c. 31: 'Hoe dander bataelge inquam' (How the other *bataelge* came).
[364] Wodsak, 79–80; and Delbrück, 446.
[365] That Lodewijk first protested against the French version after the second *bataelge*"s attack indicates that the attack took place along two different streams.
[366] Lodewijk, II.1.IV:311–13, c. 29, vv. 2041–74.
[367] Villani, 385; and *Chronographia*, I:105.

the reserve formation under Jan van Renesse's command: 'Then an extraordinarily large number of men were left behind dead in the "ditches" in which they fell over each other.'[368]

Into which 'ditches' were they pushed? Into the Groeninge and the Grote Beek streams that joined each other in front of the centre of the Flemish position. The last example was given in the description of the massacre of the French knights after their charges had been overcome: the French met their end 'in deep ditches, here and there'.[369] In Lodewijk's account, the verses came just after those which detailed Raoul de Grantcourt's surrender to Willem van Jülich. This allows a simple explanation of the text to be given: the 'gracht her', or 'ditch here', represented the Grote Beek stream in front of the right flank and the centre of the Flemish troops. The term 'gens' (there) referred to a ditch 'there', i.e. the Groeninge in front of the left flank.

Thus, one sees how Lodewijk did not contradict himself at all on the streams. On the contrary, he was very accurate. The *grachten* did not then refer to any waterways on the side of the Flemish troops and behind the Groeninge and the Grote Beek. This explication was fully confirmed by the poet's protest against a French claim that the knights were not aware of the *gracht* across which the second attack took place (that is the Groeninge).[370]

In addition to this, a further passage has until now been completely incorrectly interpreted by almost all historians examining the battle. The verses in question relate to the attack of the reserve troops under the command of Jan van Renesse. The lines are of great importance as the events they deal with may lead to different perceptions of the battle according to the interpretations adopted. Lodewijk details Jan van Renesse's reserve troops at two points: first, before the battle, and second, at the point of the determinant and significant intervention that turned the course of the battle once again in favour of the Flemings.

Before the battle Jan van Renesse told the Flemings not to allow their battle array to be penetrated by the French knights.[371] If they made a charge against Guy de Namur's troops then 'we shall thrust upon them from behind' and anyone who penetrated into the Flemish ranks would be killed. Historians interpreted 'van

---

[368] Lodewijk, II.1.IV:314, c. 29, vv. 2104–5: 'Toen bleven er wonderveel in "grachten" dood, waarin de een over de ander viel.' See also Fris, *De slag bij Kortrijk*, 255–6. Fris was thinking of the Klakkaerts brook and the Bloedmeers. This is not possible as the streams, or waterways, were behind the Grote Beek (Great Brook), or St Jansbeek, and the Flemings had not yet crossed the stream at that point.

[369] Lodewijk, II.1.IV:328, c. 34, vv. 2473–4. Fris (*De slag bij Kortrijk*, 255–6), once again, had the Klakkaerts stream and the Bloedmeers in mind.

[370] Lodewijk, II.1.IV:317, c. 31, vv. 2192–203. For Frederichs and Fris, it is the Grote Beek or the St Jansbeek (Frederichs, 'Les Derniers Travaux', 181; and Fris, *De slag bij Kortrijk*, 255–6).

[371] Lodewijk, II.1.IV:305–6, c. 27, vv. 1894–903: 'Dat si hem niet lieten dorbreken, / Ende haer biechte souden spreken, / Ende sijt nu niet vervart, / Bodelt al man ende pard / Vlaendren ende Leu! es onse gecri. / Alsi slaen op mijn her Ghi, / Sele(n) wi van achter op hem dringen, / Het blijft al hier dat si bringen.' (That they do not let them break through and make their confession and not be fearful. Kill man and horse. "Flanders and the Lion!" is our cry. If they attack my lord Guy, we shall support him from behind. All that breaks in shall remain here.)

achteren dringen' (thrust upon [them] from behind) as if it actually happened to the French knights.[372] This was not the meaning of the phrase, but rather a *thrusting* towards Guy de Namur's men, whose section could be weakened or thinned out following a charge by the French knights.

Thus, Jan van Renesse put great store on preventing the French from penetrating into the ranks of the Flemish foot-soldiers. Such a penetration was a major concern for any commander of foot-soldiers in the Middle Ages. And in this case it was the most important concern since both wings of the Flemish troops were positioned up against an impassable impediment. Thus, the townsmen did not need to be concerned about their flanks. One should also add that, at the end, Jan van Renesse took command over all the Flemish troops since Guy de Namur and Willem van Jülich actually took part in the close combat. As soon as the battle had begun they were not able to bring in fresh troops, either to strengthen weak points, or to force a decisive outcome. This was a matter for Jan van Renesse, and one understands why he explained to soldiers placed in the deep and long ranks how he would support them during the French attack. If the French knights were successful in breaking through the Flemish phalanx, then the fate of the townsmen would be sealed, unless Jan van Renesse did appear rapidly with reserve troops. However, it may be assumed that the nobleman of Zeeland would not let things go so far and would intervene as early as the danger of the French troops actually breaking through the lines became apparent. This did indeed happen, not in Guy de Namur's ranks, but in those of the men of the Bruges Franc. Jan van Renesse rushed to provide support.[373] The reserve corps gave support to the retreating men, strengthening them, and once the immediate danger had been overcome, new force was given to the weakened troops, both physically and on their morale. Jan van Renesse's corps pushed the thinned ranks of the men of the Bruges Franc forward, and the French, who had penetrated far into their ranks, were then attacked from the front duc to the support of the reserve troops. On their flanks the French were being attacked by soldiers whose ranks they had pushed past. The consequence of the above was soon felt. The knights were promptly obliged to retreat, ending up in the Groeninge or the Grote Beek streams which joined together in front of the central positions.

This interpretation is not only logical and simple, it also corresponds fully with Lodewijk's text. It has been assumed then that Jan van Renesse had the intention of rushing to support weakened and collapsing sections of the Flemish position, to strengthen them and to exert pressure that would have to push back or kill the less numerous French knights who had penetrated the ranks. The second text explains how Jan van Renesse rushed to give support at the point where close combat was taking place, arriving there 'van achter welven met zijn schaar' (attacking from

---

[372] Funck-Brentano, 'Mémoire', 260–1; Pirenne, 'Note sur un passage de van Velthem', 219; Fris, *De slag bij Kortrijk*, 353; and Delfos, *1302 door tijdgenooten verteld*, 69.
[373] Lodewijk, II.1.IV:313–14, c. 29, vv. 2096–102: 'Doe trac hi over toter perssen, / Van achter welvende met siere scaren. / Die Fransoyse worden in varen, / Doen si dus belopen waren / Van haren vianden tusschen .ii. struken / En waren el niet dan clare (b)uken / Van desen lieden, daer si opliepen.' (Then he went to fight, coming from behind with his units. The French were afraid when they were attacked by their enemies along the entire battle line.)

behind with his men). *Welven* means 'attack' or 'push', as one can see in another verse.³⁷⁴ Any other explanation can only be accepted with much difficulty. For an attack by Jan van Renesse's reserve troops from behind, or on the flanks of the knights, to be possible the men of the Bruges Franc would have had to pull back so far that van Renesse's corps could get at the French through the gap between the men of Bruges and the centre ranks. Such a breach would necessarily have to be wide enough to let the troops through. However, if this were the case, the knights would have been the first to make use of the situation and would have exploited it to their favour more rapidly than the Flemings so that they could attack the whole position of the townsmen from behind.

Still, such a breakthrough did not occur. In fact, Jan van Renesse could rest assured that the danger had been overcome when, following their charge, the knights were brought to a standstill. From this moment on the Flemings possessed a considerable numerical superiority and were also superior in weaponry since their weapons were longer than the knights' swords. Furthermore, the knights would experience much difficulty if they were to make use of their lances in close combat. The Flemings then slew the horses and disarmed the knights.

Obviously, Jan van Renesse only intervened after the French attack upon the whole front had taken place: with the first *bataelge* across the Grote Beek, and with the second across the Groeninge. Only in the centre was there any danger of the French breaking through, and it was to this point that he rushed. Of the utmost importance for this interpretation are those verses in which Lodewijk related that he first detailed the attack of the first *bataelge* before the other attack, although they did in fact take place simultaneously.³⁷⁵ Once the French had attacked all along the Flemish front line, then Jan van Renesse could intervene without any major worries, since the enemy at that point only possessed a limited number of troops for a new attack. At that moment, his intervention had the greatest chance of complete success. And this is what happened: in strengthening the centre positions, the French knights were crushed, thus allowing for a general Flemish advance towards the two streams into which the retreating knights fell.

Two other passages in Lodewijk's account have also been interpreted erroneously. Even though they are of less importance we shall devote some attention to them since they could easily be used to discredit the poet's account. The first is as follows:

> The staff split and broke open,
> From the point to the handle since with them
> They slew the princes from their horses ³⁷⁶

---

³⁷⁴ Ibid., II.1.IV:303, c. 27, vv. 1853–4: The French 'selen op ons comen welven / Met enen vreseliken gemoete' (The French will attack us with a terrible clash).
³⁷⁵ Ibid., II.1.IV:319, c. 32, vv. 2233–40. However, these verses are corrupt. It seems that Lodewijk did not count the third attack, that undertaken by Artois. The Count did indeed attack after some knights had been thrown into both streams. Thus, with his attack, he aimed at halting the Flemings and turning the battle to his favour.
³⁷⁶ Ibid., II.1.IV:314, c. 30, vv. 2120–3: 'Die stave scorden entie borsten / Daer si de prinsen

Fris translated the verses as follows: '[the Flemings] rent asunder the soldiers from the head to the foot'.[377] De Maere d'Aertrycke committed the same error,[378] noting elsewhere that this was impossible even for a warrior with the physical force of Milo of Crotone.[379] The verse actually refers to the fact that the handle of some *goedendags* quite simply split. The weapons had been used so forcefully that the wooden staff split from the handle to the iron ring at the top.

Lot also made some points of criticism on the signals given by the garrison. Erroneously he was of the opinion that the signals were given in the afternoon instead of at dawn. Lot thus raises a question about how Artois was able to turn to the sun since the castle was to the west. Obviously, he immediately suspected Lodewijk of not being familiar with the terrain.[380] Lodewijk writes:

> Artois took note of the sign,
> And quickly he turned around with his back to the sun.[381]

The passage cannot be translated by 'Artois moved east' since this would ignore the word *omme* (around). The Count moved in the direction of the sun, but also turned around, with his back to the sun in order to see better and to look from near the Pottelberg towards the castle. In this example Lodewijk was not making an error.

Concise summary of Lodewijk van Velthem's account
L. IV, c. 21. Guy de Namur called Willem van Jülich to Courtrai, where the castle, situated beside the church of Our Lady was being defended by a French garrison. On Monday, 9 July, the French attacked at the Tournai gate.

In the evening of the following day an attack was undertaken against the Lille gate. Artois's army had, in the mean time, set up camp at Mossenborch, or the Berg van Weelden, at five bowshots from the town. The foot-soldiers carried out attacks while the lords stayed in their tents.

C. 22. The men of Ghent, of the Four Ambachten, that is, of Axel, Hulst, Assenede and Boechoute, and of the Land of Waas were not present in the Flemish army. However, Jan Borluut arrived from Ghent with artisans. The night passed, and at sunrise suddenly a fire was seen alighting on the castle. The castellan and his men were trying to show the French how they could best take the town. They

---

mede ontorsten, / Van den pinnen toter hant.' In modern Dutch: 'De staven, waarmee ze de prinsen van hun paard sloegen, spleten en barstten van aan de pin tot aan de hand.'
[377] Fris, *De slag bij Kortrijk*, 365.
[378] De Maere d'Aertrycke, *La Bataille des éperons d'or*, 63.
[379] De Maere d'Aertrycke, *Mémoire sur la guerre en Flandre de 1302 à 1304*, 2nd edn (Bruges, 1905), 18. Delfos, *1302 door tijdgenooten verteld*, 110 n. 47, had already refuted this absurd remark by pointing to the erroneous translation.
[380] Lot, *L'Art militaire*, I:258; Funck-Brentano, 'Mémoire', 271; and Pirenne, 'Note sur un passage de van Velthem', 217. They all translated the text in this way.
[381] Lodewijk, II.1.IV:290, c. 22, vv. 1550–1: 'Artois heeft dit teken vernomen, / Ende trac bat omme ter sonnenwaerd.' In modern Dutch: 'Artois heeft dit teken opgemerkt en keerde zich snel om, met zijn rug naar de zon.'

carried round the fire then threw it towards the Grey Nuns' nunnery, against the ramparts. This meant that they should move in that direction. Artois saw the signal and quickly turned his back to the sun. The French in the garrison were still carrying bare swords so as to show that they were in need of help. They believed they had done well, although in fact they had pointed to a low-lying field full of ditches that the French could not avoid. Against such ditches they did not take any precautions and it was there that they were to meet their deaths.

Cc. 23 and 24. The sun indicated that the first hours of the day had come (6 o'clock). Artois rode round to observe the Flemish troops. The French soldiers were divided into ten *bataelgen*.

1. Jean de Burlats with very many foot-soldiers and 400 cavalrymen, mercenaries.
2. Gui de Nesle and Renaud de Trie, 500 armoured cavalrymen.
3. Raoul de Nesle, constable of France, 600 armoured cavalrymen.
4. Artois.
5. Jacques de St Pol.[382]
6. Louis de Clermont.[383]
7. The Count of Eu, with 300 armoured cavalrymen.[384]
8. Renaud and Mathieu de Trie with 600 heavy cavalrymen.[385]
9. Geoffrey de Brabant with 300 armoured cavalrymen.[386]
10. Gui de St Pol and the Count of Boulogne, commanders of the rearguard.[387]

In total there were 7024 heavy cavalrymen. Elsewhere, the poet spoke of seven thousand cavalrymen.[388]

C. 25. The Flemings were on foot (on the side of the town). They were positioned close together and were very eager to begin combat. Artois sent a herald out to see whether there were any important noblemen in the Flemish army who could be spared in the battle by being captured. When the herald returned, he reported that he had only seen commoners, except for Willem van Jülich and Guy de Namur. The Flemings were standing on foot along the other side of a stream and could not be reached from behind. A banner was blowing in the wind with the black lion rampant (Liebaert) on a golden field.

Geoffrey de Brabant then said: 'The knight carrying the Liebaart is Lord Jan van Renesse. He is to be feared the most. In the whole world there are no six men better in war than he.' Geoffrey advised against fighting that day. On the following day,

---

[382] Ibid., II.1.IV:302, c. 26, v. 1813.
[383] Ibid., II.1.IV:307, c. 28, vv. 1927–9.
[384] Ibid., II.1.IV:307, c. 28, vv. 1930–3.
[385] Ibid., II.1.IV:307, c. 28, v. 1935. Lodewijk had already mentioned Renaud de Trie in the second *bataelge*.
[386] Ibid., II.1.IV:307, c. 28, vv. 1938–40.
[387] Ibid., II.1.IV:337, c. 37, v. 2686, 2690–1. Lodewijk first spoke of nine formations, although he actually listed ten.
[388] Ibid., II.1.IV:302, c. 26, v. 1811; and II.1.IV:311, c. 29, vv. 2020–1.

the Flemings, all poor men, would be worn down by having stood in battle array for so long. Artois reproached Geoffrey de Brabant very severely, saying arrogantly: 'We are on horse and they are on foot! One hundred heavy cavalrymen are of the same value as one thousand foot-soldiers! Take a look at our brave warriors. I would not want the enemy to lie bound before us!'

C. 26. Geoffrey promised that he would, that very day, share the fate of the Count, who was satisfied with his response.

Vv. 1844–54. The Flemings were fearful of the battle. They could not retreat backwards, and the enemy was approaching in front of them. They made their confession and then drew close together against each other. They formed a wall of stone, as it were, to overcome the terrible event.

C. 27. *How the battle began*. Guy told his troops not to have fear: 'Brace yourselves. The sun has just been covered by a cloud. I see already the victory being gained. Flemings, be on your guard, for they will charge with great power. Stand strong in your place. Pray to the Lord that he will help us in our need.' Willem van Jülich unfolded his banner and encouraged his men. Jan van Renesse told the troops: 'Do not let the formation break. Make your confession now and do not be fearful. Slay both man and horse to the ground. Flanders, the Lion, is our battle cry. If they attack our Lord Guy de Namur, then we shall come to his rescue from behind. Any man who penetrates our ranks will be killed.'[389] Following this, the order was given throughout the Flemish army that no man was to look for booty. No man was to pick up anything, even if it lay under his feet. Whoever dared to do so would be slain by his fellow soldiers. Willem van Jülich and Guy knighted the brave men under them, both poor and rich. Pieter de Coninc and his two sons were knighted so that they would become even bolder. The men tensely awaited the battle.

C. 28. *The bataelgen and Jean de Namur*.[390] Jean de Namur sent six hundred armoured cavalrymen to his brother. He would have liked to take part in person with all his soldiers. However, he was informed late since the battle took place too quickly.

The men of Ypres continued the siege of the castle with a large number of their troops in the town. They numbered twelve hundred, and all of them wore black tunics. Whatever the French tried they could not leave the castle while the battle was taking place on the battlefield.

C. 29. *The first battle*. 7024 French cavalrymen advanced to the valley. The number of men on foot could not be counted. Guy and Willem van Jülich rode around the Flemish troops, putting them into their battle array: 'The enemy is coming. Do not be frightened. The Lord will send us help from heaven.' And this came true, since that day many saw the banner of St George. After posting the troops both men took to their positions on foot, each with a staff in his hand between the other soldiers and prepared to share the fate of their men.

---

[389] One should point to the practical nature of the advice given here by the commanders to their troops. The poet, Lodewijk, is certainly the best source on this point.
[390] Following this, Lodewijk listed the French *bataelgen* noted above.

The bow strings were drawn. Never had a battle begun so terribly. The arrows flew through the air so thickly that one could hardly see the sky. Still the Flemish army did not give way, even though the neckpieces, tunics, bucklers, targes, helmets and shields which they used to protect themselves were full of arrows. From their heads to their feet there were arrows, in their equipment and in their clothing. This was how the battle began. It was an unequal contest with two knights attacking each Flemish soldier. But whoever approached them did not leave alive!

When the Flemings, in large ranks, had shot their arrows, they cut the strings and threw the bows at the feet of the horses. Then they retreated towards their friends, who praised their action.

Willem van Jülich was attacked by many men on horseback, while Artois and St Pol called out in French. The battle raged fiercely. The men of the Bruges Franc resisted bravely, but the French advanced and the soldiers of the Bruges Franc were driven back. However, they recovered quickly, and it was actually good that the troops had retreated since whoever penetrated into their ranks would not leave alive. Indeed, when Jan van Renesse learned this, he advanced to where the close combat was taking place and strengthened the troops with his men. The French then took fright since they were being attacked on both sides by their enemy. The Flemings gave their battle cry, 'Flanders, the Lion', and an astonishing number of Frenchmen were killed in the ditches where they fell upon each other.

C. 30. *How the battle was stabilised.* Geoffrey de Brabant rode so hard into the Flemings that he knocked over Willem van Jülich, throwing his banner to the ground. However, his battle horse with its rider fell so hard head over heels that both horse and horseman were killed. The Lord of Nesle also fell quickly. Neither at Alisant nor at Roncevalles, where Roland fought, had so many noblemen been killed as at Courtrai.[391] In vain the noblest princes offered their swords in surrender.

Jan van Renesse also fought excellently there. At a certain moment, Willem van Jülich was exhausted from the blows suffered at the hands of the enemy and had to be carried from the battlefield. His standard bearer, Jan Ferrant, was thrown to his knees four times. Jan Vlaminc, one of Willem van Jülich's servants,[392] put on the coat of arms of his master while he was absent from the ranks.

C. 31. *How the other bataelge rode into the battle.* Then the other *bataelge* rode up and pushed into Guy's troops with a terrible force. This was the most powerful charge ever heard of. Many speak of that of Roncevalles, but this charge was much more powerful. In the midst of his army Guy was prepared for the defence, beneath the nunnery where a *gracht* ran from the Lys to the road to Ghent. Listen now to these lies. The French say of the ditch that they did not know of it and due to this met with disaster. This is pure fiction since they were all well aware of the ditch and had crossed over it. But as soon as they retreated with their horses, since the

---

[391] This is an allusion to the two very heavy defeats suffered by Christian knights in their battle against the Saracens according to the *Chansons de geste*: Roncevalles in the *Chanson de Roland* and Alisant in the *Chanson de Guillaume*, or in a related epic poem, *Aliscans*.
[392] See Gilliodts-van Severen, I:83, no. 159.

animals retreated on account of the blows they received, they all fell in the ditch and suffocated there.

C. 32. *More about the Flemings*. Bouden van Popperode was there with his companions. In the midst of the charge he resisted with a strong staff. He was one of the best men on the battlefield and may be mentioned alongside Jan van Renesse. With Guy, he helped determine the battle. Wherever knights come together may his name be praised. For Flanders' honour he was prepared to throw himself into the battle both day and night. Also Zeger Lonke, the Ghentenaar standard bearer, was thrown to his knees four times. There were also several men from the Four Ambachten. And Willem van Boenhem appeared unflinching.

Although he spoke thus of the first *bataelge*, of their failure and also of their courage before speaking of the other two, they all attacked together. They did not wait for each other. Each *bataelge* chose their enemy, but they were crushed more quickly than the time needed to say the Pater Noster fully. The flower of Christianity lay there dead in front of the common people.

C. 33. *How Count Artois fell and the deeds of the monk*. Renaud, a knight from Champagne, stayed back with Artois and called out in a loud voice: 'Noble prince, the *gracht* is deep. Stop, master! Beware of it. Our friends lie there vanquished.' Around Artois the trumpets were being sounded. The Count had his horse take its run up and, followed by his men, he charged forward. On account of the great strength of his horse, he reached the other side of the *gracht*, where he found his soldiers in a difficult position and many dead. Guy approached him intrepidly with the men of Ghent. However, Artois rode so deep into those men that he reached the banner, wrenching and ripping a piece from it. Before he could be brought down much time passed. He advanced, retreated and charged through his enemy once again. Many a pike was broken on him. However, a monk from Ter Doest[393] had rushed to the battlefield and changed his mare for a staff. Together with a Carmelite monk who had left his order he did wonders there. Both were very strong men, capable of 'binding a bear'. They came to fight for the Count. Often I have heard recounted that the monk slew the Count of Artois. He felled Artois's horse, Morel. The Count then wanted to surrender to Willem van Jülich. But the Flemings replied to him: 'There is no nobleman here who can understand your language.' The French commander was then killed.

C. 34. *The Count of Eu*. The Count of Eu fell. In total, sixty-three bannerets and eleven hundred knights fell. Raoul de Grantcourt was, however, taken captive after resisting bravely and was brought to Willem van Jülich, who gave him to Borluut. The Flemings went to attack the French in sizeable groups and found them near the two streams.

C. 35. *How the Flemings retreated and were sent back*. Many among the Flemings were very fearful. They left the battlefield; some fled towards the town, others to the banks of the Lys, where they wanted to swim across. Guy called out to them: 'Stop, Flemings! New enemies are arriving!' Barely five hundred men had stayed with him. His formation of men had become so weak and thin that it stood

---

[393] Willem van Saaftinge, a lay brother of Ter Doest. See also *Annales Gandenses*, 91–2.

completely open. However, Borluut, Gossenhoven, Jan van Renesse, Boenhem, Bangelijn, Ferrant and Popperode brought the Flemings back to their positions.

C. 36. *How the Flemings gained the upper hand*. As soon as their fear had been overcome, the Flemings fared well once again. After Guy, Willem van Jülich and Jan van Renesse, the following performed best of all: Popperode, Bangelijn, Borluut and Ferrant. The knights of West Flanders, of Bruges and the Bruges Franc and of Ghent cannot be praised enough. They lost fewer than twenty men. Of the French, many hundreds remained in the Lange Mere in the stream. So many men had not fallen in one single day, even when Darius fought against Alexander.

Several French knights who had escaped came back. After Artois had fallen, they did not want to live any longer. Among them was Jean le Brunembert, who was in the service of the Count of St Pol and reproached his lord since he had fled with the rearguard. These noblemen fell into the Lange Mere. At tSiexmans, another group of men as well as a third group had taken up positions below the hill where Willem van Mosscher lived. This Flemish supporter of France was killed, even though he wanted to be taken captive.

C. 37. *The flight of the French and the death of the men of Brabant*. Then the sound of trumpets was heard in the east by the Lange Mere. There the counts of St Pol and of Boulogne approached, with their troops, as if they wanted to undertake a charge. The Flemings quickly rallied back together into their battle position. A section of men of Hainault was also ready for battle, although in the mean time they had their equipment taken away. When the Flemings advanced towards them, the men fled. The Flemings pursued them up to Dottenijs, Zwevegem and St Denijs. The enemy fled to Tournai and Moen. The men of Brabant ran among the Flemings shouting the battle cry, 'Flanders, the Lion'. This was noticed and Guy gave the order to kill all men who wore spurs. St Pol and the Count of Boulogne fled without looking back to Tournai, where the gates of the town remained closed for them. Many of those fleeing were killed between the Lys and the Scheldt Rivers.

C. 38. *How the Flemings remained on the battlefield*. The Flemings were completely exhausted. They did not talk to each other. Their arms were completely wet. Their hands were stiff; they could not close them since they had held their staffs too tightly during the battle. Many had such thirst that their tongues and mouths hurt and blood ran from their noses. They had nothing to drink and stood there, worn out, leaning on their staffs. At night they still guarded the fallen.

C. 39, vv. 2795 ff. The battle had taken place between midday and nones (3 pm). After the battle, the soldiers were very hungry since they had not eaten or drunk all day, aside, that is, from some who had taken bread dipped in wine. The first bread came from Ename. While Guy and Willem van Jülich went to sleep, the others watched over the battlefield, since the taking of booty had not yet been allowed. That was the law of a battle: they who had gained mastery of the battlefield were to watch over the dead with unfurled banner, and if no man came to take revenge for the defeat by break of the next day, then they might say that they had gained victory. After this, the booty and spoils might be gathered. The dead were stripped and remained completely naked on the battlefield.

Synopsis

When summarising, in a few short lines, this long account of the Battle of the Spurs, it can be seen that the battle, begun between the crossbowmen, did not, however, prove conclusive. The first French *bataelge* attacked across the Grote Beek, the second across the Groeninge stream. The threat of a breakthrough was present in the centre, but Jan van Renesse restored the positions there. The French were then driven back and fell into the two streams. Artois vainly attempted to push the Flemings back. The rearguard of the French troops fled, after a fake manoeuvre, carried out so as to clear the army's train.

Like most chroniclers of his time, Lodewijk exaggerated, above all since he sought to dismiss a French lie. What constitutes the exaggerated element in his account? The numerical strength stated for the French army? Certainly not; in this respect he follows Villani. Still, his account allows this to be altered somewhat. When Artois told Geoffrey de Brabant that a hundred knights were worth a thousand foot-soldiers, this meant that the French knights, albeit inferior in number, were qualitatively much superior to the Flemings. Guiart expressed this same point before the Battle of Mons-en-Pévèle when declaring that ten thousand French noblemen, on horseback, could certainly take on a hundred thousand Flemish foot-soldiers.[394]

His description of the terrain is also not far-fetched. The tone of his account is admittedly somewhat pompous, and individual descriptions of the feats of arms of the soldiers may certainly be excessive, but, given the general tactical course of the battle this is of less significance.

Those elements in Lodewijk's account that are far-fetched occur, naturally, when reacting against the French version of events familiar to him. By emphasising that the French fell into the streams after their charge had been resisted by the robust Flemish defence, the author completely avoided mentioning the significance of the streams as frontal hindrances. In this sense, he exaggerated as much as those French sources that have all the knights falling into the streams, although in Lodewijk's account no knight fell into them, since he remained silent on this point. However, it is indisputable that both streams played a role in this respect. Most probably, knights fell into the streams during the attack. Moreover, the streams provided, above all, a hindrance to the French charge that was then limited to a small distance on the other side. Furthermore, the good order of the French formations was greatly weakened by the crossing of the hindrance. Consideration of this fact should be made when examining the account of the battle.

Chronicon Comitum Flandrensium or
Genealogiae Comitum Flandriae Continuatio Clarismariscensis

In the sequel to the chronicles of the counts of Flanders from 1214 to 1329, one notes the most simple and excessive Flemish version of the Battle of the Spurs. In this version the streams are of no significance: they are not even mentioned. And, since the common people prefer splendid triumph, the victory was obtained by a

---

[394] Lodewijk, II.1.IV:300, c. 25, v. 1771; and Guiart, 290, vv. 20,454–6.

poor and numerically insignificant group of Flemings against the much more numerous Frenchmen, Frenchmen, who, moreover, were knights and whose attacking troops were all crushed.

The chronicle was written in 1329 by the monk, Bernard of Ypres, in the abbey of Clairmarais near St Omer.[395] The author wrote the account during the rebellion in maritime Flanders (1323–8) and was very hostile to the rebels. The fact that he reproduced such a version of events clearly indicates that it was a generally accepted opinion in his time. His account of the happenings of 1302 to 1304 and of the Battle of Mons-en-Pévèle, on 18 August 1304, allows much insight into the views of Flemish townsmen and the military events of the period. The chronicle is, therefore, a valuable document that enables us to determine how much self-confidence the Flemish townsmen had gained on account of their great victory on 11 July 1302 and their courageous resistance against the French armies in 1303 and 1304. It also to a large extent explains their intrepid actions during the rebellion of 1323–8. Despite the fact that the Flemings were in the end defeated at Mons-en-Pévèle the common people never perceived the battle as a defeat since a section of the townsmen had gained a splendid victory and had left the battlefield as victors. They were also not pursued by the enemy[396] who, however, remained master of the battlefield and thus justly claimed victory. The account of the Battle of the Spurs given by Bernard of Ypres was not so accurate as that given by Lodewijk. Furthermore, it lacks the immediacy of the more contemporary *Annales Gandenses*, although it still contains interesting points that confirm and add to information given in other sources. Like the other two sources that follow the Flemish version of events, the chronicle indicates that the Flemings were in defensive positions when they stopped the charge of the French knights. A report of the account is given below.

The battle according to the Chronicon

Guy and Willem arrived in Courtrai with few soldiers to resist the Count of Artois and his powerful army. The French had confidence in their numbers; the Flemings knew that God grants victory both to the powerful and to the weak and they hoped for the assistance of God. They gave encouragement to each other and marched out of the town. Willem van Jülich and Guy of Flanders put the army in battle array before the monastery at Groeninge. Guy and Jan van Renesse ordered the troops and sent the men of Ypres, who were all wearing red tunics, to watch over the castle. With the rest of the soldiers a single corps was formed with the crossbowmen in front and, following them in alternating order, soldiers with pikes and *goedendags*. The horses were brought back to Courtrai. The leaders spoke to their troops, saying the following:

---

[395] Published in E. Martène and U. Durand, *Thesaurus Anecdotorum*, 3:402–35; and in J. J. De Smet, *Corpus Chronicorum Flandriae*, 1:168–71. However, De Smet included two later insertions in his edition: one concerning the heroic deeds of Willem van Saaftinge, and the second presenting a list of those who had fallen.
[396] See *Annales Gandenses*, 73.

Men, be brave and fight as true men for your wives and children and for the laws and freedoms of your fatherland. If you do not gain victory no one of you or your family will remain alive since all will be killed. Whoever flees or retreats or bends down to pick up booty before the end of the battle must be killed immediately. Attack first the horses with the pikes and *goedendags* since once the horse has been pierced then the knight is easily overcome.

Artois underestimated these foot-soldiers and formed four *bataelgen*: the first under his own command, the second led by the Count of Hainault, the third by Jacques de St Pol, and the fourth by the Count of St Pol. In each of them there were five thousand excellent heavy cavalry.

When the Flemish foot-soldiers, who for the most part had never seen such a spectacle, saw this wild mass approaching with the sound of trumpets, battle cries, the neighing of horses and the clash of weapons, then they would have fled immediately if Guy and Willem had not given them fresh courage. Nevertheless, several of the men of the Bruges Franc fled but they were sent back by force by the men of Ypres after some had been killed beside and in the River Lys. When the Count of Artois saw this, he said: 'Look, the Flemings are fleeing; the victory will be attributed to our village crossbowmen; let us follow them and carry out a rapid attack.'

The crossbowmen were placed behind the knights who carried out a terrible attack against the Flemings, first with their lances. However, the Flemings resisted boldly; they set their pikes against the lances of the Frenchmen and, following the advice given to them, they killed all the horses in the first attack. The pierced animals fell over with their masters who died. When the Flemings realised the success of their tactic, they became bolder and killed the horses with their pikes while attacking the knights with their *goedendags*. They killed all of them without giving mercy or taking prisoners. The Lord of Lens left the castle with his men to attack the Flemings from behind, since he thought that the Flemish troops would not be able to resist after the first attack by such powerful knights. The men of Ypres, however, killed all those who had left the castle.

In this manner, the victorious Flemings crushed the first, second and third *bataelge*, and no single man of the enemy escaped even though the Count of Artois and other barons eagerly sought to be taken captive as soon as they saw that fate was turning against them. More than fifteen thousand counts, dukes, barons, knights and other noblemen fell there. The Count of St Pol fled with the fourth *bataelge*. The Flemings pursued those who fled almost as far as Lille and, following their return as victors, took the booty.

Later Flemish chronicles

The Flemish chronicles exhibit the same characteristics as those following the French version. Their authors did not have access to any account of the battle that was based on an oral report. They examined French and Flemish sources, reworking the information and thus the different versions into one single entity. This ought not surprise us: it was still being done at the end of the last century by historians of merit who did not take into consideration the fact that certain explanations excluded information given in other sources.

In the translation and, at the same time, in the sequel of the *Chronicon Comitum Flandrensium*, the chronicle written at the beginning of the fifteenth century by Jan van Dixmude, it is already to be noted that the Flemings had dug holes between the monastery and the town of Courtrai. The holes were covered with grass and patchwork. A thick mist prevented the French from seeing the obstacles. The Flemings retreated agilely and quickly, pretending to be fleeing, and the French fell into the obstacles. Approximately four thousand noblemen fell there.[397]

The Flemish author presents the same version of events as that followed by the *Chronique artésienne* or Ottokar von Stiermarken. Since, however, it appears illogical that the enemy would let themselves be caught so easily, he added that the Flemings pretended to flee and that a thick mist prevented the holes from being seen. Such additions to the original sources clearly show that many chroniclers sought to explain the result of the battle and make it appear a logical occurrence. One should not, therefore, be astonished that there are so many different versions. The more stupid the account, the more the author has to add in order to make it acceptable, providing that the author is intelligent enough to see the absurdity in his version while not being critical enough to reject the nonsense.

In other Flemish chronicles, written at a later date, such details about the mist and the feigned flight can also be found.[398] However, it is unnecessary to consider them here.

Conclusion: the Flemish and French Versions

In examining the French version of the events of 11 July 1302, it can be ascertained that there were at least three different explanations. The first was probably already held by common people before being officially propagated by the royal entourage. The version, adopted by the *Chronique artésienne*, was, however, developed by Ottokar von Stiermarken and Jean de Winterthur. It attributes the defeat to the ditches and holes that were dug in a cunning and treacherous manner by the Flemings. Nevertheless, the sources that follow this version were not at all unanimous. The royal version differed according to the public for which it was intended: an unfortunate event for the clergy at Bourges, and ditches and holes dug treacherously for the burghers and commoners of Poitou. The *Chronique artésienne* was already silent about the betrayal and that it was a question of a stratagem. This chronicle, otherwise so excellent, is at this point brief and incomplete when dealing with the battle of the 11 July. Important events which the author ought to have known were not mentioned, despite his knowing so much about the Viscount of Lens. The account is also silent about the date of the arrival of the French army before the town of Courtrai. Therefore it would certainly be erroneous, methodologically, to attach the greatest value to such a work. Ottokar had practically no

---

[397] Fris, *De slag bij Kortrijk*, 182.
[398] Fris, 194; and *Kronijk van Vlaenderen van 580 tot 1467*, ed. P. Blommaert and C. P. Serrure (Ghent, 1839), I:154–62.

knowledge of the events of 11 July and did not provide any interesting information. Only on the ditches did he provide information that cannot be found elsewhere. But he simply invented this and elaborated the legend. The account given by Jean de Winterthur is too ridiculous and too far-fetched to be considered seriously.

The employment of some cunning battle plan, as detailed in the French sources, must, then, be rejected. This is all the more so as no single Flemish source of that period mentions such a stratagem. These Flemish chronicles were written by a Friar Minor, a clergyman from Brabant and a monk from Clairmarais. There is no reason why such persons would have remained silent concerning a stratagem. One could object that they remained silent on account of their national sentiments. But why? National feelings do not prevent a person from mentioning a cunning stratagem employed against the enemy. On the contrary, one can rest assured that the chroniclers in this case would have mocked the arrogant noblemen who had so easily let themselves fall into the trap. The use of a cunning battle plan was, furthermore, not dishonourable and certainly not when employed by a people fighting desperately for survival. Knights could possibly view its use as dishonourable and disloyal; soldiers from the communes had no reason for doing so. The Scots never hid the fact that they dug ditches on the battlefield of Bannockburn where they defeated the English knights in 1314.[399] And the English did not hide the fact that they used such means during the Hundred Years War.[400] Most importantly, not one single Flemish source hides the fact that the French knights were not taken captive and that this took place following the advice of the commanders. This action went completely against all customs of the time and above all against the knightly code of warfare. It is much more serious when one takes account of the fact that during the attack by night in Bruges relatively many prisoners were taken, despite the burning passions let loose in such popular revolts.[401] Chroniclers and other sources did not hide the fact that the event was referred to as 'Good Friday' in all Bruges.[402] Concerning Courtrai, the authors praised the excellent orders given by the Flemish leaders that included the order not to take the enemy noblemen captive. Thus, cold-bloodedly and intentionally, an inhuman and savage strategy of war was ordered. It was not passed over in silence but, quite to the contrary, was praised. It is certain that the same authors would also have praised the skilful digging and covering up of ditches and holes; if, that is, it had actually happened. Those Flemish authors writing at a later date and finding such information in the French sources accepted it and had no objections to reporting it. Since it appeared rather illogical to them that the enemy would allow themselves to be overcome so easily, the authors stated in addition that a very thick mist prevented the covered holes from being seen.

One already sees in the French sources themselves sufficient proofs against the

---

[399] Oman, II:86 n. 2.
[400] Ibid., II:137, at the Battle of Crécy (1346). A further example is provided by T. F. Tout, 'The Tactics of the Battles of Boroughbridge and Morlaix', in *The Collected Papers of T. F Tout* (Manchester, 1934), II:224.
[401] Wyffels and Vandewalle, 56–8.
[402] Ibid., 12, 56; and Lodewijk, II.1.IV:272, c. 16, vv. 1108–9.

version of the cunningly dug ditches. Guiart actually lived along the border in 1304 where he came to know many soldiers in the army, as well as remaining some time in the town of Arras. Although reacting against the Flemish version of events, he still did not report any obstacles dug intentionally in his work, which was dedicated to the French King. This is sufficient proof that the above version was not accepted in France and quickly disappeared. The same observation is true concerning Geoffroy de Paris who would have certainly noted the version of events with much pleasure if he had heard or had believed it. Furthermore, this is the case for the lost source of the *Chronographia*, for the *Anciennes chroniques de Flandre*, as well as the sequel to the chronicle by Guillaume de Nangis and *Les Grandes Chroniques de France*.

Guiart and Geoffroy de Paris gave a second version: the victorious attack by the French crossbowmen was stopped prematurely by the proud Count, Artois, and his overly confident knights. This explanation was then followed by the naive account of treachery on the part of the Flemings in Guiart's work, and, according to Geoffroy de Paris, a form of collective suicide of the knights in the marshes.

Two types of argument speak against such a conception of the events. Firstly, all sources and chronicles, derived from the lost source of the *Chronographia* and *Anciennes chroniques de Flandre*, indicate that the skirmishes between the crossbowmen did not have any determinant influence. This is confirmed by Lodewijk. These French sources talk of the possibility of success by the crossbowmen. Villani did not even report their actions in the battle. Sources, following both versions, disprove the far-fetched conceptions presented in the work of Guiart and Geoffroy, who as burghers themselves must be suspect in this regard. They described feats of arms that are impossible, considering the actual context in the period 1302–4. The French foot-soldiers and crossbowmen never showed so great a superiority. And what indication is there of a claim that the French crossbowmen were much more numerous than the Flemings? Merely the fact that some sources, exaggerating wildly, speak of ten thousand crossbowmen.[403] But how many would there have been, in this case, in the Flemish army if a numerical strength of sixty thousand for the Flemings can be assumed, as reported in one reliable source?[404]

Other arguments of a military nature also speak against a decisive intervention of the crossbowmen. In virtue of the terrain, it would have been very dangerous for them to cross the streams and to enjoin in battle with this obstacle behind them. A successful counterattack by the Flemings would have thrown them into the stream without any hope of assistance from the knights.[405]

---

[403] *Chronique artésienne*, 47; and Villani, 384.
[404] *Annales Gandenses*, 29. See also chapter II on the numerical strength of the two armies.
[405] This was noted in the field of military science by German researchers, Wodsak (59–60) and Delbrück (443). They were misled by the assumed superiority of the crossbowmen in Artois's army. On this basis they assumed that the Flemish crossbowmen were driven back but that the French commander then called back his light infantry before they crossed the stream. The order for the crossbowmen to retreat was, according to them, a logical and intelligent measure.

The sequel to the account is closely linked to the third version: the fact that the French were, or were not, aware of the streams; and that they fell into them after they had been surprised on the other side by the Flemish attack at a moment when the knights had not fully developed their array. Significant areas of agreement are arrived at, on the one hand, in the accounts given by Lodewijk, Villani, the *Chronographia Regum Francorum* and, on the other, the *Anciennes chroniques de Flandre*, as well as to a reconciliation of the French and Flemish versions.

Lodewijk, Villani, the *Chronographia* and the *Anciennes chroniques*
Both Lodewijk and Villani provided the same information concerning the French camp being situated opposite the road to Tournai. However, Villani, as well as the *Chronographia* and the *Anciennes chroniques*, was incorrect in situating the Flemish camp on the other side of the River Lys. While Lodewijk detailed the attacks against the Tournai and Lille gates, on which there is brief confirmation in the *Annales Gandenses* and in Gilles le Muisit's work, both the *Chronographia* and the *Anciennes chroniques* claim that the Count of Artois refused to enjoin in battle. Villani did not mention this. According to Lodewijk, on the morning of 11 July, Artois sent a herald to reconnoitre the Flemish positions. In the *Chronographia* and the *Anciennes chroniques* the two marshals were sent to reconnoitre. All three sources state that Artois attended a mass and, once again, Villani was less detailed. As a result of the reconnoitring mission, a council of war was held since the Flemings were posted behind a stream.

In Villani's account, the stream did not have any banks that were visible from afar. The *Chronographia* claimed that the bank on the Flemish side was higher. Furthermore, manuscript 1006 of the *Anciennes chroniques*, that is more detailed on this matter, added that grass had grown over the ditch. Lodewijk gave more detailed and complete information on the terrain and the streams, and to a large extent his account here corresponds with the preceding information. Like Villani, Lodewijk noted the road to Ghent and described the Groeninge stream, although he also spoke of the Grote Beek and Lange Mere.

Both Lodewijk and Villani developed the same aspects of the council of war: not to attack with the knights, to harass and exhaust the Flemish troops by skirmishes. Guiart had a constable, as did Villani, argue against engaging in battle with a deep stream behind the army. This proposal is actually the best and most appropriate given the tactical situation. While Guiart worked in the abbey of St Denis and most probably drew his account of the Battle of the Spurs from documents there, he may also have used the same sources as the *Chronographia* and the *Anciennes chroniques* in their most detailed form. These two sources indicate that the council of war was held because of the ditch as well as reporting that some lords advised against engaging in battle. The majority, however, insisted on the battle.

Lodewijk, Villani and the *Chronographia* present an excellent explanation of the measures taken by the Flemish commanders. The Flemings were positioned so close to each other that they formed a wall of spiked rods (Lodewijk): soldiers with *goedendags* were standing next to others with pikes (Villani); Jan van Renesse and Hendrik van Lontzen taught the Flemings how they were to attack and defend themselves (*Chronographia*); their weapons were also to be used both defensively and offensively (Villani).

The accounts given in Lodewijk's work and in the *Chronographia* correspond well with each other on the advice given and speeches held by the commanders. Lodewijk was obviously able to provide additional information. The two sources also agree with each other on the role played by Jan van Renesse in positioning the troops. However, the *Chronographia* exaggerated the actions of Hendrik van Lontzen. Villani was more vague in this respect: his account of the speech was too general, the practical advice given being replaced by general considerations. But like Lodewijk and the other Flemish sources, Villani also reported the counsel given on first hitting at the horses.

Our three sources confirm that all the Flemings, both the noblemen and the artisans and peasants, fought on foot. The *Chronographia* made an exception for both commanders who posted and ordered the troops. The *Chronique artésienne* also noted the above for Jan van Renesse. Still, one may pose the question of whether the commanders fought on foot. Lodewijk actually reported that Guy de Namur and Willem van Jülich ordered the troops on horseback and following this they fought on foot – this is also confirmed by the depiction of the battle on the carved Flemish chest at New College, Oxford.[406] However, since Jan van Renesse was in command of the reserve troops, it is also possible that he remained on horseback in order to select the most appropriate moment to intervene.

The three sources also report that Guy de Namur knighted artisans, among them Pieter de Coninc. It is here that Villani appears to have been at his most accurate since he gave the number of new knights as forty. Still, this figure was exaggerated since the Bruges accounts noted only thirty-one new knights.[407]

Lodewijk and Villani agreed in their reporting ten *bataelgen* of cavalry. The *Chronographia* reported only six *bataelgen* that had already been formed, without counting the rearguard. The *Chronographia* also named the commanders of the rearguard as Clermont and the counts of St Pol and of Boulogne, thus two or three *bataelgen*. Both the *Chronographia* and the *Anciennes chroniques* gave a summary account of their source. As with the advice given by the constable, one finds the missing link in Guiart's account that was drawn up in the abbey of St Denis. Guiart named the commanders: Jean de Burlats led the attack of the crossbowmen, and Artois was situated to the right of the battle array (as in Lodewijk's account). Following this he noted Jean de Hainault, Geoffrey de Brabant, the counts of Eu and Aumale, the two brothers de Nesle, Jacques de St Pol, Louis de Clermont, the Count of St Pol and the Count of Boulogne; the last three formed the rearguard as reported in the *Chronographia*. In comparing the lists of Lodewijk and Villani, there are also ten formations in Guiart's account, if the formations of the counts of St Pol and of Boulogne are counted as one *bataelge*. There is a difference on one formation: that of Renaud and Mathieu de Lorraine (Lodewijk) or of Ferri de

---

[406] See illustration V below.
[407] Wyffels and Vandewalle, 84.

Lorraine, and the Count of Sancerre (Villani) is not mentioned here although Jean de Hainault is.

While Villani and the *Anciennes chroniques* do not have the crossbowmen intervene, both Lodewijk and the *Chronographia* indicate that the skirmishes between the foot-soldiers and crossbowmen did not lead to a conclusive result.

In both Lodewijk's and Villani's accounts, the first attack was carried out under the command of Raoul de Nesle. The French knights crossed the ditch. According to the *Anciennes chroniques*, all formations of knights crossed to the other side and then (according to Villani) attacked the Flemings, and the French did not possess sufficient space to develop their position. The knights were driven back towards the stream and fell over each other into it. For Villani, the stream was important during the second attack and Lodewijk's reaction to this has been noted above. Here one should point once again out that Villani states the French were not aware of the stream, even though the *Anciennes chroniques* and the *Chronographia* state they were.

After the general attack, carried out by the two Flemish *bataelgen*, Lodewijk describes the conclusive intervention of Jan van Renesse with the reserve corps. The French chroniclers did not receive a clear picture of the intervention by those who escaped from the battle. The *Chronographia* turned it into an attack against the French camp. Villani did not mention Jan van Renesse, perhaps since the nobleman was only mentioned in the *Anciennes chroniques* for feats of arms during the battle itself. This was possibly also the consequence of the Florentine banker's stay in Flanders where Guy de Namur and Willem van Jülich were obviously better known.

Lodewijk and Villani show how the Flemings crossed the ditches and continued their pursuit. In the *Chronographia* the pursuit already began after the attack made by Jan van Renesse against the French camp. Here, once again, Lodewijk is much more accurate and detailed than the other sources: the pursuit was continued to Dottenijs, St Denijs and Zwevegem. This is confirmed by Gilles le Muisit who witnessed the flight at Tournai.

However, despite these large areas of agreement over the general course of events there are very many details that can only be found in two sources and were ignored by the third source.

In Lodewijk's and Villani's account emphasis was given to the help of God and of St George. Villani had a mass held on the battlefield among the Flemish ranks; Lodewijk spoke of confession. In the answers given by Artois in the council of war, both chroniclers emphasised that the courage of the nobleman who advised against the battle was questioned. It should be added that Villani quoted in French and that this corresponded very well with expressions used by Geoffroy de Paris in detailing the same events. Villani's account also agreed with that of the Parisian chronicler regarding the actions of the Flemings in the battle and the clouds of dust during the charge. Finally, Lodewijk and Villani both attributed twice as many soldiers to the French as to the Flemings.

Lodewijk, the *Chronographia* and the *Anciennes chroniques* agreed with each other on the French losses. They also agreed on the following details: Artois's curse (Paterne Dieu); the appearance of St George in the battle and the saint's figure being carried on horseback; the information given on Artois's horse and the fearful premonition of the French whose horses had not neighed. Finally, there was the agreement between the sources about the negotiations of September 1302.

It seems also certain that Lodewijk was acquainted with a version that bore strong resemblance to that of Villani. Villani could have drawn upon one or more versions of the *Anciennes chroniques* and Lodewijk may have read that account in a similar source or been informed of it by an intermediary. The Florentine banker was probably informed by Italian merchants in France; Lodewijk may have gained similar information from the Duke of Brabant or his entourage. Such a picture of events is probable since both chroniclers agreed on other points with the *Chronographia* and the *Anciennes chroniques*. Proving this, however, is hindered by the fact that the *Chronographia* and the *Anciennes chroniques* are summaries of the original source that was used by both Lodewijk and Villani. For this reason, certain elements of this source are noticeable in the works of Guiart and Geoffroy de Paris.

Consideration must also be given to the fact that Lodewijk and Villani may have gained their information from the French version of events held by the common people, which to a great extent was transmitted orally. Still, as both sources correspond so well in their lists of the ten formations of knights, this leads to some degree of doubt about their having gained information from oral accounts. In this case, the popular accounts would be presenting more accurate and precise information on this matter than the written accounts and the oral account would be more complete than the written account. It is rather difficult to accept this; it appears more logical that each chronicler became acquainted with the battle via intermediaries. That this account presents the same version of events has been sufficiently proven by Lodewijk's reaction against the French account that largely corresponds with the account given by Villani.

Obviously, both Lodewijk and Villani gained information from other sources and both were in Flanders, which would explain the source of certain details found in Villani's account. Other details may have been omitted, following information received from Italians serving in the French army which contradicts his French account. The same is even more true for Lodewijk, who drew above all from Flemish sources as well as consulting eyewitnesses, participants and well-informed persons. Both of these chroniclers undertook independent research on their sources.

The study presented here of the agreements between Lodewijk, Villani, the *Chronographia* and the *Anciennes chroniques* leads to more important conclusions than the fact that Lodewijk and Villani used the same source as the two French chronicles. One may consider the agreement between them as insufficient for any conclusion that they consulted a single source, or one may be of the opinion that the single source was not one of the versions used by the *Chronographia* and the *Anciennes chroniques*. However, an important element arising from the study remains: the possibility of reconciling the Flemish and French versions. The lost source of the *Chronographia* and the *Anciennes chroniques* was certainly as immediate to the events as the account given by Villani. At all points where the information in the account is confirmed by Lodewijk they may be accepted, since if they were not true Lodewijk would have responded vigorously. Villani may also have had reason to confirm certain details and deny others. Still, this comparison has determined that most details can easily be reconciled. There is one important difference: the role of the streams during the battle. A reconciliation of the different sources must now be attempted.

Were the French aware of the streams?
It has been shown above that one French version can actually be retained: that of the *Anciennes chroniques*, with a light variation in Villani's account that has the first *bataelge* cross the stream unhindered, although it has the disaster occur after the other formations of knights rushed to aid the constable who had come into difficulty. The defeat was, then, the result of the knights being pushed together too closely on the other side where they were attacked by the Flemings while in addition a number of noblemen had immediately fallen into the stream during the second attack. The latter did not see what had happened due to the dust. However, this interpretation of the events given by the Italian was based on the fact that the French were allegedly not aware of the stream. According to the *Anciennes chroniques*, they were indeed aware of this obstacle and it was discussed during the council of war.

Might it now be accepted that the French noblemen were not aware of the stream? Information given by various sources does not allow for this. In fact, not only the *Anciennes chroniques*, but also Guiart and Lodewijk indicated that they carried out reconnaissance missions and that the discussion in the council of war took place because of the stream. One must also take into account the arrival of the French before the gates of Courtrai from 8 July onwards, and the fact that the attacks on 9 and 10 July against the gates of the town had failed. Logically it can therefore not be maintained that the French did not consider other means of reaching the garrison. From the Pottelberg hill they could certainly see the castle. It also appears improbable that the French commander first sent men to reconnoitre the Flemish camp on the Groeninge on the morning of 11 July. It is more probable that he first sought by other means to relieve the garrison before taking the decision to engage in battle on an unfavourable terrain. Furthermore, there were enough Flemings in his army who knew that in Flanders account always had to be taken of the streams or waterways. The French army had already experienced difficulties because of this during the advance.[408] Moreover, Willem van Mosscher was in the army, and this nobleman had his possessions and house in the area around the Pottelberg. He would, then, certainly have known the terrain; why would he not inform the French commanders of this? In addition to this, the crossbowmen first engaged in battle, and it is even more illogical to assume that they would not have seen the stream and not have warned the knights. Indeed, it is already known that

---

[408] See the accounts of Robert d'Artois in Funck-Brentano, 'Mémoire', 311–17; and Funck-Brentano, *Philippe le Bel*, 408.

the sources reported a reconnaissance mission and that Guiart also reported the advice given, pointing out how dangerous it would be to engage in battle with the stream behind the soldiers.

From amongst the French sources, the version of events presented by the *Anciennes chroniques* must be maintained: the crossing of the streams or waterways by the formations of knights followed by an unexpected Flemish attack surprising the noblemen at a moment when they had not fully developed their formations. Before the Frenchmen were able to charge properly, they were driven back by the Flemings and fell in the streams.

Against this there is the Flemish version: the Friar Minor with his allusions to this in the description of the Battle of Mons-en-Pévèle, Lodewijk and the *Chronicon Comitum Flandrensium*: all related how the Flemings awaited the impact of the French charge in a defensive position.

German military historians, such as Delbrück and Daniels, relying on the defective study of the sources by Wodsak, accepted that the Flemings attacked the French.[409] However, this opinion is based on weak foundations; against it, the unanimous evidence given by the Flemish sources may be invoked, including Lodewijk's and the Friar Minor's excellent accounts of the history of their period that are, in any event, much more reliable than the *Anciennes chroniques de Flandre* and its source, the lost French chronicle. In addition to this, the opinion of the German historians is based on insufficient knowledge of foot-soldier tactics of that period, and particularly on the battle techniques used by the Flemish townsmen in 1302–4. They were erroneously of the opinion that the foot-soldiers could not resist charges made by the knights. When the foot-soldiers were provided with good weapons and were aware of their power, then they could beat back attacks made by knights by taking up a very tightly packed position with pikes and lances or with shields and other weapons. Here it is noted that the first charges of the Norman knights failed at Hastings (1066) in England.[410] At Legnano (1176) and at Cortenuova (1237) in Italy, the foot-soldiers also resisted very vigorously.[411] At Bouvines the foot-soldiers, who were only two ranks deep, kept the attacking knights outside their positions due to their long lances.[412] At Falkirk (1298), the Scottish foot-soldiers also successfully resisted the repeated attacks made by the Anglo-Norman knights.[413] There are further examples of this kind.

Moreover, one notes that the Flemings constantly engaged in battle in a defensive position in the period 1302–4. It was here that their power lay, and also their

---

[409] Delbrück, 443; and E. Daniels, *Geschichte des Kriegswesens*, vol. II: *Das mittelalterliche Kriegswesen*, Sammlung Göschen, no. 498, 2nd edition (Berlin and Leipzig, 1927), 112.
[410] Delbrück, 155; Oman, I:161–2; and Lot, *L'Art militaire*, I:284.
[411] Delbrück, 357, 361; Oman, I:448, 495; Lot, *L'Art militaire*, II:166, 169; and P. Pieri, 'Alcune quistione sopra la fanteria in Italia nel periodo comunale', *Rivista storica italiana*, 5th ser., 4 (1933), 19, 27–8.
[412] Verbruggen, *The Art of Warfare in Western Europe during the Middle Ages*, 239–60; and Verbruggen, 'Le Problème des effectifs et de la tactique à la bataille de Bouvines en 1214', *Revue du nord*, 31 (1949), 191 n. 44.
[413] Delbrück, 407; Oman, II:80; and Lot, *L'Art militaire*, I:323.

weakness. This can be seen at the Battle of Mons-en-Pévèle where they initially took up a defensive position. Afterwards, they attacked, but were unable to attain any conclusive advantage and suffered defeat. When the Flemings attacked right from the beginning of battle, they suffered a decisive defeat: this is the case at Cassel (1328) and Westrozebeke (1382).[414]

From 1302 to 1304, it is also to be noted that the French knights did not undertake any more frontal charges. This was a consequence of their failure at Courtrai and shows, once again, that the Flemings took up a defensive position in waiting for the enemy.

Thus, it is sufficiently clear that at the Battle of the Spurs the Flemings first repelled the enemy onslaught. The mistake made by the *Anciennes chroniques* in this respect now becomes easier to explain. What is presented as a Flemish attack may very well have been an active defence. In Villani's account, indeed, it is most difficult to determine whether the Flemings simply defended themselves or also advanced and attacked. His text points rather to a very active defence.

The explanation given by Villani and the *Anciennes chroniques* for such an attack by the Flemings cannot be accepted: their mistake is the consequence of not having detailed the crossbow battle. For this reason, both chroniclers were of the opinion that the Flemings were posted very close to the stream. This was not possible, as the Flemish crossbowmen would not have had any room for action and in this event the French crossbowmen would have inflicted much damage on the long, drawn-out Flemish position.

In this manner, one is able to reconcile the pro-Flemish and pro-French versions without distorting the sources and by consistently relying upon a series of accounts. One should, however, not forget to point to the great value of Lodewijk's account in the light of the general comparison of the sources. Lodewijk was in general superbly informed about the battle from beginning to end, and his account always survives comparison with the other accounts in matters of small detail. This all points to the complete veracity of his chronicle when he alone speaks of certain events or other sources contradict him, such as with the streams.

The value of Lodewijk's account of the Battle of the Spurs
Lodewijk's account appears excellent in its description of the battle on 9 July where he is alone in giving the correct position of the French attack against the Tournai gate. This is also the case for the skirmish on 10 July: the storming of the Lille gate. The information given on this by Lodewijk is confirmed vaguely in the *Annales Gandenses* and by Gilles le Muisit.[415]

Concerning 11 July, Lodewijk was alone in describing the signals given by the garrison in the Courtrai castle. He knew the subject matter of Artois's council of war after the reconnaissance mission to the Flemish positions. Here his account

---

[414] H. Pirenne, *Le Soulèvement de la Flandre maritime de 1323–1328* (Brussels, 1900), xxix–xxx; Pirenne, *Histoire de Belgique*, I:360; and Lot, *L'Art militaire*, I:276, 451–2.
[415] Funck-Brentano followed Lodewijk's account here. See Funck-Brentano, *Philippe le Bel*, 408.

can be improved by adding the advice in Guiart's account. He was as accurate as Villani in his description of the French formations. Lodewijk is the best source on the Flemish position and the measures taken by the commanders.

Lodewijk's description of the terrain has been fully confirmed by later documents as well as cartographic sources. Only for one detail can an additional point be added to his account by the French sources, the half-moon formation.

As in another Flemish source, the *Chronicon Comitum Flandrensium*, his account shows how afraid the Flemings were before the battle and how much they wanted to be rid of the tension by battle.

Lodewijk's account of the battle between the crossbowmen corresponds well with French sources that do not exaggerate as well as with what is now known on the intervention of light foot-soldiers in that period.

Like Villani and the Ghentenaar Friar Minor, Lodewijk spoke of two significant attacks; the third, led by Artois, does indeed appear to be of lesser significance. The intervention on the part of Jan van Renesse with the reserve corps fits perfectly well into the general picture of the battle.

Lodewijk is the best source for the feats of arms performed by the Flemish soldiers. For several details his account can be verified using other good sources: both Lodewijk and the Ghentenaar Friar Minor spoke in the same manner of the lay brother, Willem van Saaftinge. Boudewijn van Popperode, who held high 'the honour of Flanders', was rewarded for so doing by Jean de Namur.[416]

Moreover, very many of the Flemish knights that he mentioned, and who took part in the battle, are confirmed by the Bruges town accounts and by other Flemish and French sources. This is the case among others for one of the soldiers of Willem van Jülich, Jan Vlaminc.

Lodewijk did not obscure the significant role played by the stream after the charge had been stopped. While he did not mention the ditches during the charge itself, then this was an exaggerated reaction against the French attack that attached too much importance to them.

His account of the pursuit is also correct, being confirmed by the eyewitness, Gilles le Muisit. In addition, Lodewijk was more accurate in his listing of the villages. He was also aware of the fact that the French knights were not let into Tournai. That he knew of such details, as if actually an eyewitness, shows how carefully he gathered his information.

In addition to this, he also gained information from the French side, as is clear from his description of the French army. For the rest of the campaign of 1302, he constantly had access to good information: he knew the high morale of the Flemings as well as the Ghentenaar Friar Minor.[417] He was superbly informed about the

---

[416] Algemeen Rijksarchief Brussels, Trésor de Flandre, series I, no. 1050. On 4 February 1303, Boudewijn van Popperode was rewarded with an annual income of 300 pounds per year on rents and income in the land of Ninove: 'pour le grant leautei et le bon serviche' (for great loyalty and good service).

[417] Lodewijk, II.1.IV:373–4, c. 49, vv. 3606–12; II.1.IV:379, c. 51, vv. 3765–75. Lodewijk provided interesting information in this chapter drawn from the entourage of the Duke of Brabant: Lodewijk, II.1.IV:380–1, c. 51, vv. 3798–823.

negotiations in September 1302, as well as being able to present interesting details about the French council of war. Like the *Chronique artésienne*, Lodewijk reported details about the difficulties in Arras and the retreat of the French army.[418]

The account of the battle itself forms an excellent tactical whole that allows us to resolve all difficulties and may be accepted fully. In the account, Lodewijk described the general French attack with two separate *bataelgen*, the danger of a breakthrough in the centre and the intervention of Jan van Renesse.

Lodewijk van Velthem therefore presents us with the most complete and detailed account, and the account is, for most points, confirmed by Flemish and French sources. From a methodological standpoint, its veracity may be accepted in those places where it is alone in giving specific details about the battle. Even there, one still finds much agreement with the French sources and the differences can easily be explained. Thanks to more than twelve hundred verses that he devoted to the events, we are finally in a position to sketch a picture of the battlefield and to place the battle spatially. This is very rare for battles of that time even when in possession of accounts given by eyewitnesses.

---

[418] Ibid., II.1.IV:385, c. 53, vv. 3921–2; II.1.IV:386, c. 53, vv. 3940–4; and *Chronique artésienne*, 56.

Part Two

HISTORICAL OVERVIEW OF THE 1302 CAMPAIGN

3

The Terrain at Courtrai

There has been no complete and critical study of the terrain that deals with all problems arising from a reconstruction of the Battle of Courtrai. Almost all the material required was nevertheless gathered and examined in the valuable contributions presented by Sevens.[1] However, the studies, which complement and correct each other, are not very well known. It thus comes as no surprise that several historians working after Sevens completely ignored his work.[2]

Researchers who have examined the Battle of the Spurs were naturally very concise in dealing with the terrain. There were several solutions proffered on it that differ markedly from each other. For this reason there are now four viable reconstructions of the battlefield.[3] The best known and most generally accepted reconstruction is that provided by Sevens and Fris, which is in reality a slight improvement on the map given by Moke, Köhler and Frederichs.[4] Funck-Brentano established another version that was first accepted in 1892 by Sevens although he rejected it definitively in 1902. In 1931 the solution presented by Funck-Brentano was still seen as possible by Delfos.[5]

Delfos did, however, propose another map.[6] The most recent reconstruction of the battlefield has been proffered by Baron M. de Maere d'Aertrycke who did not follow his earlier opinions based on Sevens's studies.[7] In order to avoid having to

---

[1] T. Sevens, *De slag van Kortrijk in 1302*, 1st edn (Ghent, 1892), 2nd edn (Ghent, 1902); Sevens, 'Hoeken en kanten op Groeninge', *Bulletijn van den geschied- en oudheidkundigen kring te Kortrijk*, 4 (1906–7), 35–48; and 'De Groeningebeek', *Bulletijn van den geschied- en oudheidkundigen kring te Kortrijk*, 6 (1908–9), 261–76.

[2] This was the case with Delfos, *1302 door tijdgenooten verteld*, 105–7, who was aware only of the 1902 work.

[3] The reconstruction provided by Wodsak, 33, and also by his professor, Delbrück, 441, corresponds, to a large extent, with the representation given by Funck-Brentano.

[4] Sevens, *De slag van Kortrijk*, 2nd edn, 27–43, 87; Fris, *De slag bij Kortrijk*, 340–3; Moke, 1–63; Köhler, *Die Entwickelung des Kriegswesens*, II:216–49; Frederichs, 'De Slag van Kortrijk', 257–95; and Frederichs, 'Les Derniers Travaux', 163–81.

[5] Funck-Brentano, 'Mémoire', 235–27, see map; and Delfos, *1302 door tijdgenooten verteld*, 105–6.

[6] Delfos, *1302 door tijdgenooten verteld*, 49, 105 n. 30, 106–7.

[7] M. de Maere d'Aertrycke, *De slag der gulden sporen* (Ghent, 1899); de Maere d'Aertrycke, *Campagnes flamandes de 1302 et de 1304, ou gloire militaire de Bruges au XIVe siècle* (Ghent, 1901); and de Maere d'Aertrycke, *Mémoire sur la guerre de Flandre*, all of which follow the traditional solution. In the *Guerre de Flandre de 1302 et de 1304*, 2nd edn (Bruges, 1913), the above solution was not followed on account of the objection arising from the increasing contour

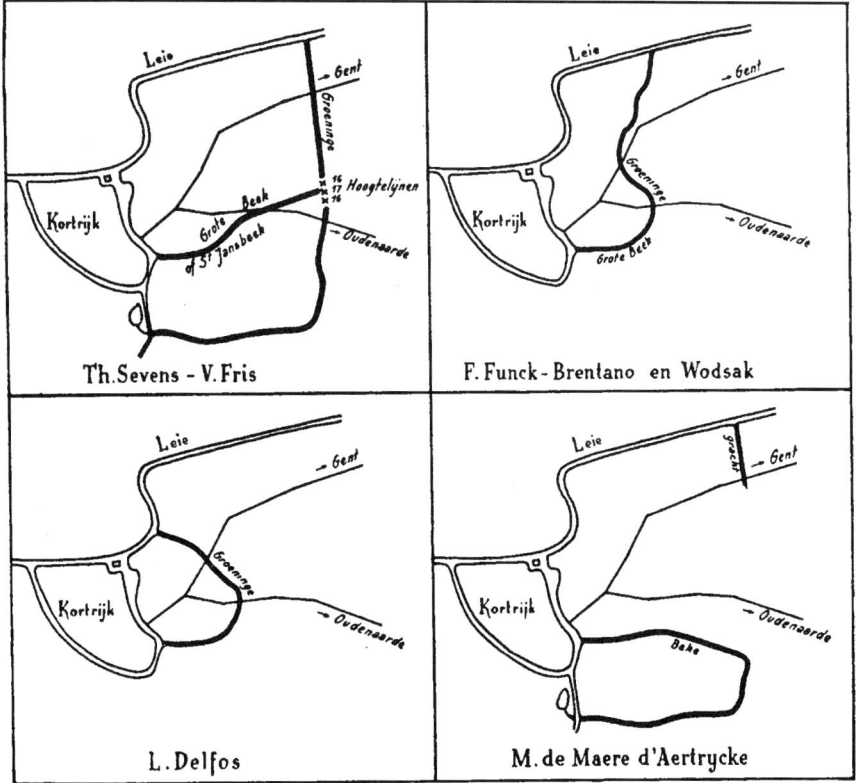

1. The four solutions proposed for the streams

continually refer back to the four proposed solutions, they have been reproduced here in simple sketch form.[8] In a concise summary of the versions, which sources the above historians relied upon will also be shown.

Sevens and Fris based their system on an important text of 1444 concerning the connecting stream, the Groeninge–Hoge Vijver, which they refer to as St Jan's stream, or the Grote Beek (Great Brook) according to Funck-Brentano and Frederichs.[9] The course of the Groeninge is reproduced following a map of Courtrai drawn up by Jacob Roelofs van Deventer, the ordnance survey map at a scale of 1:20,000 as well as the course of the Groeninge at the moment that Sevens

---

value for the Groeninge stream (from 16 to 17 meters). The author fully developed and presented his own opinion in *La Bataille des éperons d'or* and in *De la Colme au Boulenrieu* (Namur, 1935). His conception was accepted completely in a study that is rather more a translation of de Maere's works: R. Wittenberg, 'De waarheid over den guldensporenslag', *Handelingen van den koninklijke geschied- en oudheidkundigen kring van Kortrijk*, n.s. 15 (1936), 317–54.

[8] See also Delfos, *1302 door tijdgenooten verteld*, 107.
[9] Sevens, *De slag van Kortrijk*, 2nd edn, 41; Fris, *De slag bij Kortrijk*, 255–6, 181; and Funck-Brentano, 'Mémoire', map.

was writing (1902).¹⁰ However, Funck-Brentano, on the basis of the map provided by Jacob van Deventer, suggested that there was a stream situated more to the west than the Groeninge, part of the drawing of which was prolonged by him as a section of the town moat as it was in 1453.¹¹ Delfos criticised this solution, although regarding it as possible. He nevertheless proffered his own reconstruction that actually identified the Groeninge with the town moat which, after 1453, was used for the new town ramparts running across the battlefield of 1302.¹² He rejected the solution proffered by Moke, Köhler, Frederichs, Sevens and Fris since, in their sketches, the Groeninge stream rises for part of its course from the sixteenth to the seventeenth contour line.¹³ According to de Maere d'Aertrycke, there was no stream in front of the Flemish front line. There was, however, the *gracht* (the ditch or moat) to the north and the *beke* (stream) to the south. Both of the waterways were referred to thus by Lodewijk, but between the two waterways there was an open space that was closed off by the ranks of the Flemish townsmen. Later, in 1442 and 1444, a connection between the *gracht* and the *beke* was dug, partly underground, with the whole waterway then being called the Groeninge stream.¹⁴

The existence of these four different solutions that follow each other almost chronologically¹⁵ makes a new and thorough study necessary in order to determine which reconstruction is most reliable in terms of historical methodology. For this the problem needs to be examined in all its aspects, not only to come to an objective and acceptable solution, but also in order to collect the most important documents and make them accessible for future historians. This would certainly allow the question to be examined without any difficulty and thereby use to be made of results already attained so that the past work will not have to be tackled once again.

The historians mentioned above employed different methods. Some only emphasised the historical aspects of the problem they sought to solve, and in so doing they did not discuss possible geographical objections to their system. Thus de Maere and Delfos criticised the solution presented by Sevens and Fris on account of the Groeninge rising along a section of its course from the sixteenth to seventeenth contour line, which does not appear to be acceptable for a natural stream.¹⁶ Neither Sevens or Fris informed their readers of this difficulty. However, de Maere and Delfos relied too much in their own solutions on the present state of the contour lines without taking into consideration changes that were brought about over time, above all due to the building of a fortress. Delfos's documentation was moreover incomplete and the historian made a mistake in the interpretation of his

---

¹⁰ Sevens, *De slag van Kortrijk*, 2nd edn, 40–1; Fris, *De slag bij Kortrijk*, 341 n. 2; and *Atlas des villes de Belgique au XVIe siècle: Plans du géographe Jacques de Deventer*, ed. by C. Ruelens, E. Ouverleaux and E. P. van den Gheyn, SJ (Brussels, 1884–1924).
¹¹ Funck-Brentano, 'Mémoire', map.
¹² Delfos, *1302 door tijdgenooten verteld*, 49, 105 n. 30, 106–7.
¹³ Ibid., 105.
¹⁴ De Maere d'Aertrycke, *La Bataille de éperons d'or*, 4.
¹⁵ The solution proferred by Funck-Brentano is an exception to this, although Delfos still considered it possible in 1931.
¹⁶ Delfos, *1302 door tijdgenooten verteld*, 105 n. 30.

sources.17 After following the traditional approach of Sevens for many years, de Maere finally came up with his own completely new plan of Courtrai. He based it on the contemporary state of the terrain, although completely misinterpreting the information given in accounts as well as documents held in the Courtrai town archives.18

For these reasons this new study has been made, taking account of the advantages and disadvantages of each solution proposed. The accounts of those living at the time will first be examined and following this information about the surrounding areas of Courtrai gained from documents, texts and maps that are chronologically as close to the events as possible will be discussed. This will allow information given by those living in the period in question to be clearly separated from information given by later sources, thus opening the way for reconstruction.

The Battlefield According to Accounts of the Period

Lodewijk presented here, as well as for the other aspects of the battle, the most numerous and accurate details. However, it is unfortunate that the author appears to have written for a public that had already heard much about the battle and thus gave certain details merely in passing as if it were assumed that the topographical features of the surrounding areas of Courtrai were known. However, no chronicler of that period knew the battlefield and the town as well as he did.

Lodewijk mentioned the Tournai and Lille gate,[19] and there are no doubts about its correct position. This is due to its being on the roads to both the above towns, along which the French army camp was situated, that is along the Mossenborch, or on the *berg*, obviously the Pottelberg, then also known as the 'berg der Weelden'.[20] It was there that the house of Willem van Mosscher was situated.[21] In the vicinity, along the road to Lille, the tSiexmans was still situated, this certainly being the lepers' house, which according to custom in the Middle Ages was located outside the town.[22]

As for Courtrai itself, Lodewijk was very accurate in placing the castle next to the church of Our Lady,[23] and close to the market.[24] The moat was situated next to

---

[17] He was not aware of Sevens's two later studies and therefore erroneously interpreted the manuscript 1444.
[18] His definitive reconstruction can be found in *La Bataille des éperons d'or*, and in *De la Colme au Boulenrieu*.
[19] Lodewijk, II.1.IV:286, c. 21, vv. 1450–1, 1466–7.
[20] Ibid., II.1.IV:287, c. 21, vv. 1485–7. A literal translation of *berg der Weelden* is 'mountain of wealth or luxury' [translator's note].
[21] Ibid., II.1.IV:334, c. 36, vv. 2602–9. Today a farmhouse, *Hoog Mosscher* (High Mosscher), lies just to the east of the Pottelberg. See Ordnance Survey map, 1:20,000. Sevens, *De slag van Kortrijk*, 2nd edn, 35.
[22] See previous note, Sevens, *De slag van Kortrijk*, 2nd edn, 35. In March 1233, a *terra leprozorum* was mentioned. See also Sevens, 'Hoeken en kanten op Groeninge', 47.
[23] Lodewijk, II.1.IV:284, c. 21, vv. 1406–8.
[24] Ibid., II.1.IV:284, c. 21, vv. 1414–17.

the fortress, and the monastery of the Grey Nuns was outside the town ramparts opposite the castle.[25] From the fortress it was possible not only to enter the town, but also to leave it.[26]

The battlefield lay in the *dal* (valley) as opposed to the French camp which was situated on the (Pottel)berg, mountain.[27] The *dal* formed a *nederinge*, a hollow or low-lying area, full of ditches.[28] The Flemings were first situated in a 'plaetse daer besiden' (a place there besides), with the word 'besiden' (besides), certainly being considered in relation to the town of Courtrai itself.[29] This is so since some of the Flemings wanted to flee 'in die port' (into the (town) gate).[30] The militias were situated with the River Lys behind them so that they could not be attacked from behind and some of those fleeing attempted to swim across the river.[31] As soon as the French had advanced, the Flemings no longer had any means of escape, either from behind due to the waterway, or to the front due to the enemy's position.[32]

The road to Ghent ran through the battlefield, with a hedge on both sides.[33] Besides the monastery of the Grey Nuns, a *gracht* (ditch, moat or canal) ran from the Lys to the road. Guy de Namur's men were positioned behind this waterway.[34] This was the Groeninge stream. The French claimed that they were not aware of the impediment. For Lodewijk this was untrue since they had already crossed it and were then thrown back into it.[35] The *gracht*, that is the Groeninge stream, was deep and, already following the first attacks and before Artois's charge, many knights lay there vanquished.[36] Artois, however, was to reach the other side thanks to the powerful charge of his horse.[37]

Willem van Jülich, the commander of the other Flemish formations, of the men of Bruges and the Bruges Franc,[38] had positioned himself more to the south, closer to the town ramparts.

The Flemings did not suffer at around midday from the sun, since this was

---

[25] Ibid., II.1.IV:289, c. 22, vv. 1544–5. The *hagedochten* (aquaduct) is the town moat. See also Jean des Preis d'Outremeuse, *Ly Myreur des histors*, ed. St Bormans, CRH (Brussels, 1880), VI:17: 'Li castelain de Lens . . . prit un wamalle de strain espriese, et alat tout altour de la fortereche et puis le gettat en fons del fosseit.' (The castellan of Lens . . . took a torch of straw and went around the castle and then threw it down into the moat.)
[26] Lodewijk, II.1.IV:310, c. 28, vv. 1997–8; and *Annales Gandenses*, 27, 29, 30. See also the Oxford Chest, illustration VI: the soldiers in the front of the exit of the castle bore the coat of arms of the town of Ypres on their tunics.
[27] Lodewijk, II.1.IV:292, c. 23, v. 1606; II.1.IV:311, c. 29, v. 2020; II.1.IV:333, c. 36, v. 2606.
[28] Ibid., II.1.IV:290, c. 22, vv. 1556–8.
[29] Ibid., II.1.IV:297, c. 25, vv. 1711–12.
[30] Ibid., II.1.IV:329, c. 35, vv. 2484–90.
[31] Ibid., II.1.IV:329, c. 35, vv. 2489–90; II.1.IV:298, c. 25, vv. 1736–7.
[32] Ibid., II.1.IV:303, c. 26, vv. 1836–7.
[33] Ibid., II.1.IV:296, c. 24, vv. 1687–8.
[34] Ibid., II.1.IV:317, c. 31, vv. 2186–91.
[35] Ibid., II.1.IV:317, c. 31, vv. 2192–203.
[36] Ibid., II.1.IV:321, c. 33, vv. 2288–90.
[37] Ibid., II.1.IV:322, c. 33, vv. 2308–12.
[38] Ibid., II.1.IV:313, c. 29, vv. 2079–90.

covered by a cloud at just that time.³⁹ This would correspond to the position taken: a bow-like formation running from the north to the south-west.⁴⁰ When Jan van Renesse rushed to help the centre positions he pushed back the French into the ditches.⁴¹ This was into the Groeninge and the second stream, which connected the Groeninge and the town ramparts, the Hoge Vijver, with the two certainly coming together in front of the Flemish centre positions. Here the deep ditches provided protection for Willem van Jülich's troops as well as for Guy's troops further down.⁴² The *beke*, or connecting stream, also referred to as the Grote Beek or St Jansbeek, ran through the Lange Mere where hundreds of French soldiers lost their lives.⁴³

The last French knights advanced through the Lange Mere for a desperate attack while the eastern section of the rearguard carried out a feigned manoeuvre.⁴⁴ Furthermore, another body of soldiers was situated near the tSiexmans and a further formation at the foot of the hill where Willem van Mosscher lived.⁴⁵

The French fled along the roads towards Zwevegem, St Denijs and Dottenijs.⁴⁶ The French rearguard fled rapidly to Tournai, Antoing and Moen.⁴⁷ The numerous stragglers were killed in the ditches, fields, woods and hedges and along the roads.⁴⁸ This meant that in the end the battlefield outside Courtrai and the area between the Rivers Lys and the Scheldt was strewn with the fallen soldiers.⁴⁹

Villani, the *Chronographia* and the *Anciennes chroniques de Flandre* present a few more details. Thus, the Flemings were in a hollow, low-lying area, through which the road to Ghent ran.⁵⁰ The townsmen were situated behind a stream in the form of a half-moon with the curve facing the French.⁵¹ The three sources wrongly place the Flemish camp on the other side of the Lys.⁵² Villani did, however, correctly situate the French camp⁵³ and, what is more, reported ditches and marsh outside the actual battlefield.⁵⁴

As for the stream itself, the authors contradicted each other. According to Villani, the stream had no banks, while the *Chronographia* and manuscript 1006 of

---

³⁹ Ibid., II.1.IV:303, c. 27, vv. 1847–8.
⁴⁰ See map.
⁴¹ Lodewijk, II.1.IV:314, c. 29, vv. 2104–5.
⁴² Ibid., II.1.IV:328, c. 34, vv. 2473–4.
⁴³ Ibid., II.1.IV:333, c. 35, vv. 2576–80; II.1.IV:334, c. 36, v. 2602; II.1.IV:334–5, c. 37, vv. 2615–18.
⁴⁴ Ibid., II.1.IV:334–5, c. 37, vv. 2615–21.
⁴⁵ Ibid., II.1.IV:334, c. 36, vv. 2602–9.
⁴⁶ Ibid., II.1.IV:336, c. 37, vv. 2650–5.
⁴⁷ Ibid., II.1.IV:337, c. 37, vv. 2686–93.
⁴⁸ Ibid., II.1.IV:336, c. 37, vv. 2647–9.
⁴⁹ Ibid., II.1.IV:338, c. 37, vv. 2694–8.
⁵⁰ Villani, 385.
⁵¹ Ibid., 385, the stream carried water in the area to the River Lys. See also Lodewijk, II.1.IV:317, c. 31, vv. 2188–90; and *Chronographia*, I:105–6.
⁵² Villani, 385; *Chronographia*, I:104–5; and *Anciennes chroniques*, 377.
⁵³ Villani, 384.
⁵⁴ Ibid., 388.

the *Anciennes chroniques* placed the Flemish troops on the higher bank of the stream. Manuscript 1006 not only reported, as did the *Chronographia*, that the ditch was muddy and marshy, but also that grass had grown over it.[55] This information may be correct, although it is still curious that the *Chronographia* neglected this detail even though it usually followed the text of manuscript 1006. It is thus possible that the detail was not in the lost source, but was added by the author of manuscript 1006. According to the *Anciennes chroniques*, published in the *Recueil des historiens de France*,[56] the stream was very deep and wide, while manuscript 1006 and the *Chronographia* state that it was *not* wide.

Here, as in the account of the battle, it appears as if Villani reconciled the two versions in his work. Indeed, before the battle, according to Villani, one formation of French knights crossed the stream unimpeded, as in the *Anciennes chroniques*, but the second formation experienced difficulties, and horsemen fell into it already when charging, and this agrees with the account in the *Chronographia*. For the stream, the Florentine banker reproduced the normal measurements: a sort of average between the non-wide ditch in the *Chronographia* and the very wide and very deep waterway in the *Anciennes chroniques*.

The contradiction is evident. The *Chronographia* and manuscript 1006, according to which the stream would have to be very wide and very deep for all knights to die in it during the charge, both explicitly stated that the stream was not deep. In the *Anciennes chroniques*, which first noted the impediment after the French had crossed it, the claim was made that the stream was very deep and very wide, although this was actually not necessary in view of the presentation of the events given. The latter source did not describe the ditch/stream so that the claim made at the end of the account may simply be an addition on the part of the author. Since the sources do not give any measurements, it may be provisionally concluded that the ditch/stream was relatively wide and deep.

The contributions made by other chroniclers about the description of the terrain is rather insignificant. However, they will be presented, thus completing the examination.

The Friar Minor, author of the *Annales Gandenses*, noted in passing in his description of the Battle of Mons-en-Pévèle that there were also ditches and holes on the battlefield at Courtrai. He also indicated the position of the French camp and was aware that the men of Ypres were positioned before the castle.[57]

The *Chronique artésienne* and Gilles le Muisit confirmed the fact that the battle took place near the Groeninge monastery and both were informed about there being ditches that cut across the battlefield. The author of the *Chronique artésienne* claimed, however, that they were dug and hidden by the Flemings while Gilles le Muisit merely spoke of unknown waterways.[58]

It is certain that Guiart described a long, marshy ditch that was situated approxi-

---

[55] *Anciennes chroniques*, 377 n. 6.
[56] Ibid., 378.
[57] *Annales Gandenses*, 70, 73, 29, 30.
[58] *Chronique artésienne*, 47; and le Muisit, 66–7.

mately at a distance of two bow shots from the Flemish positions. The French, however, found an area that they could wade through and then crossed the stream with the greater part of their knights – with the stream being of no significance as a frontal obstacle.[59]

Geoffroy de Paris spoke of a passage near the Lys and a marsh,[60] while Willem Procurator reported an old ditch beside the Flemish positions.[61]

Ottokar von Stiermarken and Jean de Winterthur actually presented no real information about the battlefield. They did, though, present us with many details concerning the conditions in which the Flemings dug either wide and deep ditches putting iron spikes in them,[62] or underground holes into which water from a nearby stream was redirected.[63]

Conclusion concerning the narrative sources
All detailed sources reported ditches, or one stream, on the battlefield except for the *Chronicon Comitum Flandrensium*, the sequel to the chronicle of Guillaume de Nangis, as well as those sources that drew upon that account: that is the sequel to the chronicle by Girard de Frachet and *Les Grandes Chroniques de France*. It is evident that the omission made by these sources cannot influence the conclusions reached here on the terrain and surroundings of the town of Courtrai. The authors were either uninformed about the waterways or did not feel it necessary to mention them. The detailed information given by Lodewijk, Villani and the *Chronographia*, as well as the less accurate information provided by other sources, indicates, clearly and incontestably, that the front of the Flemish ranks was protected by relatively wide and deep obstacles. From the expressions used by Lodewijk, *grachten* (ditches, moats, streams), *gracht* (ditch, moat, stream) and *beek* (brook, stream) it may be conjectured that there were at least two waterways. Villani, the author of the *Chronographia*, as well as the authors of the various copies of the *Anciennes chroniques de Flandre*, merely spoke of *one* stream. Still, on account of the half-moon position, which the first two sources mentioned, the conclusions drawn from Lodewijk's text are not at all weakened since the other authors came from far-away countries and did not know the terrain well. Therefore, they could not make any differentiation between the two ditches of which one flowed out of the other. The position in the form of a half moon fits excellently with the conjuncture of the Groeninge and the connecting stream, as will be seen below in examining the cartographic sources as well as other documents of that period.

Thus, it has been proved beyond question that the Flemings skilfully profited from the course of the streams and were positioned behind them. The conception of Baron Maurice de Maere d'Aertrycke, according to whom there was no waterway in front of the Flemish position, may then be completely dismissed.

---

[59] Guiart, 238, vv. 15,008–13, 15,019–24; 239, vv. 15,047–9; 239, vv. 15,074–7, 15,167–9.
[60] Geoffroy de Paris, 100, vv. 1227–32; 101, vv. 1261–2, 1303–4.
[61] Procurator, 64–5.
[62] Ottokar von Stiermarken, 852, vv. 64,305–21.
[63] Jean de Winterthur, 32.

How are the surrounding areas of Courtrai in 1302 to be reconstructed? Where are the streams to be placed on the map? How deep and how wide were the waterways?

These questions can only be answered following a thorough examination of the evidence given by the documents and a study of old maps that depict the streams.

The Terrain According to Deeds, Records and Old Maps

Despite the information provided by the most detailed chronicles, there are certain specific features of the battlefield which are still unknown. The accounts of the battle are vague and, at times, contradict each other. This is above all noticeable on the description of the waterways. Except for the Rivers Lys and the Scheldt, none of them are referred to by name. Despite the fact that the Groeninge monastery was mentioned by various chroniclers,[64] not a single author referred to the Groeninge stream even though it must have flowed through the grounds of the abbey or just beside it. Fortunately, the battlefield can be clearly located from the mention of the monastery, the road to Ghent and the Lange Mere. This information is of the utmost importance, since the layout of the town of Courtrai is known in great detail thanks to the excellent maps provided by Jacob Roelofs van Deventer in around 1555, by Louis de Bersaques in 1634 and by Ferraris – to give only the best-known and most accurate cartographic sources. The town ramparts of 1302, as well as the River Lys, the road to Ghent and the Groeninge monastery, can be mapped out without any difficulty on the basis of these maps.

The greatest difficulties for the historian are presented by the reconstruction of the waterways of that period. First, the connecting stream between the Groeninge and the Hoge Vijver should be examined. This will enable us to dismiss immediately certain solutions proposed by current researchers; following this, it is important to determine the course of the Groeninge, then to examine the Lange Mere and finally to turn to the Mosscherbeek stream and the Neveldries.

The connecting stream,
also referred to as the St Jansbeek or the Grote Beek

This stream was briefly mentioned as early as 1406 when a house stood on one of its banks.[65] On 15 December 1444, an important agreement was concluded with the town authorities concerning the waterway. A request was made by Zegher

---

[64] Lodewijk, II.1.IV:289, c. 22, v. 1544; II.1.IV:317, c. 31, v. 2188; *Chronique artésienne*, 48; le Muisit, 66; and *Chronographia*, I:114.
[65] Courtrai Town Archives, Weeserieboek den Lupaert, f. 77; and Sevens, 'Hoeken en kanten op Groeninge', 37: 'Eerst deen heeilt van eenen huuse ende erve gheleghen ende ghestaen buten Steenpoerte up sente Jans brugghe. Item deen heeilt van eenen huuse ende erve buten der vorseiden poerten dat broedere Jan Bets was, staende op de beke.' (First one half of a house and garden lying outside of the Steen gate near St Jan's bridge. Item: one half of a house and garden outside the same gate that belongs to brother Jan Bets, situated on the same stream.)

Tanghe, who was the hereditary owner of a water mill at the Canonic gate.[66] In this same request he was joined by those persons living outside the Steen gate, in the Harelbeke street (which was the road to Ghent), and whose farmsteads bordered the stream[67] that proceeded from the Groeninge stream flowing under the St Jan's bridge and ending in the Hoge Vijver.[68] The town authorities ruled, allowing the stream to be filled from the bridge 'in the Lange Meersch street, before Roger of Maldeghem's house, continuing along the Haerlebeke street until the front of the St Jan's bridge'.[69] Those persons whose land bordered the stream and thus gained additional land[70] were, on Christmas eve, to pay the yearly sum of twenty-four shillings *parisis* from the Flemish mint as a hereditary payment to the town starting on Christmas Eve, 1444.[71] So that the Hoge Vijver would have more water flowing into it and that Zegher Tanghe's water mills would mill better, the town authorities allowed Zegher Tanghe to forgo his rights to the old stream in the Harelbekestraat and to lay a new waterway. This waterway would run from the aforementioned Groenincbeke, 'commende uter voorseide Groenincbeke', and run under the street by the Lange Mere, along the town fortress to the Vannekine.[72] From here it would run under the street to the Hoge Vijver. The stream would have to be fourteen feet wide, from the Lange Mere to the Hoge Vijver, and as deep in the ground of the fortress as would be necessary. Zegher Tanghe and his heirs were always to maintain the waterway as well as all wooden or brick conduits that were necessary and were to construct two bridges or conduits, one in the Lange Mere street, of the same width as the street itself, and the other bridge, three foot wide, along the road that runs from the fortress to the Clessenare estate.[73] Zegher Tanghe then renounced all rights that he had as the owner of the water mill on the old stream

[66] The gate of the castle of 1302 that led to the Groeninge monastery. Sevens, *De slag van Kortrijk*, 87.
[67] Courtrai Town Archives, Perkamenten Priviligieboek, f. 406r, and Sevens, *De slag van Kortrijk*, 2nd edn, 87: 'ende ghelandt up de beke, commende uuter Groenincbeke, ende hueren loop hebbende in den hooghen vijver onder sent Jansbrugghe' (And located on a stream, coming out of the Groenincbeke, and having its own course to the Hoge Vijver under the bridge of St Jan).
[68] Sevens, *De slag van Kortrijk*, 28. Hoge Vijver (Upper Lake), as opposed to the Lage Vijver (Lower Lake), since a sluice kept back the water and connected it to the lower lake. The Lange Meerschstraat is the road to Oudenaarde.
[69] In the Dutch of the period, this was from the 'Lange Meerschstraete voor . . . Rogier van Maldeghems huuse, voort lanx der Haerlebekestraete totter voorseide sent Jansbrugghe' (Lange Meerschstraat, in front of Rogier van Maeldeghem's house, onwards along the Harelbeke street to the bridge of St Jan).
[70] 'de welcke rente de voornoemde ghelanden vander voorseyde brugghe voort tot svoorseyde Roeger van Saerseghems huuse besedt, bewyst ende verbonden hebben up den grondt van der zelver beke hemlieden uut ghegheven ende daer toe mede elc up zynen huusen ende erven.' See also the ban on building on ground above the former stream: Courtrai Town Archives, Perkamenten Privilegieboek, ff. 406v–407r.
[71] '24 schellingen parisis Vlaamse munt.'
[72] Sevens, *De slag van Kortrijk*, 40; and Sevens, 'Hoeken en kanten op Groeninge', 37. This was a mill built at the top of a small rising. 'A part of the hill upon which the Vanneken was built is still clearly visible along the small St Jan's street opposite the *Le général Boulanger*.'
[73] To the south of the Mosscherbeek, opposite the Akker land to the north of the stream.

that ran alongside the Harelbeke street underneath the St Jan's bridge. The same is reported for the 'neighbours on the aforementioned filled stream from the aforementioned bridge in the aforementioned Langhemeer street beside the aforementioned house of Roeger van Maldeghem until the aforementioned house of Roegers van Saerseghem',[74] as well as for the town of Courtrai.

This document, so significant for the topographical details about the battlefield, requires careful consideration since it has led to two or even three different interpretations.[75]

The filling in of the stream took place at the request of Zegher Tanghe and of persons living in the Harelbeke street whose farmsteads bordered the waterway that had its source in the Groeninge stream and ran across the Lange Mere street, where a bridge covered it. Following this, it ran to the Hoge Vijver where it came out under the St Jan's bridge. The stream was to be filled from Roeger van Maldeghem's house, in the Lange Mere street, to the St Jan's bridge.

Why was all this necessary? At first sight, it appears that Zegher Tanghe had no reason for his request since he would have to lay a new stream at his own cost. However, older texts indicate that the old stream was costly in terms of maintenance, needing to be dredged regularly for it to remain deep enough and for the water to flow properly.[76] It is possible that people whose properties bordered the stream threw waste into it or did not maintain the banks. Thus, Zegher Tanghe considered a new stream, perhaps underground, an advantage which would allow the water to flow freely. The Hoge Vijver would thereby continue to contain enough water, thus allowing, by means of a sluice, both the Lage Vijver and the water mills to be supplied with water.

The owners of properties bordering the stream would see their properties extended as well as the value of the land rise due to the removal of the stream. For this reason, the nine persons who possessed the ten houses and five farmyards made the annual payment of twenty-four shillings. However, they were not allowed to build on the filled stream or to plant gardens without the permission of the town authorities.

According to the classical interpretation, most developed in the works of Sevens

---

[74] '. . . ghelanden ande voorseide ghevulde beke van der voorseide brugghe in de voorseide Langhemeerstraete bij svoornoemden Roeger van Maldeghems huuse tote svoorseiden Roegers van Saerseghems huuse.'

[75] Moke, Köhler, and Frederichs, corrected by Sevens, who was followed by Fris, gave the first interpretation. A second interpretation was presented by Delfos who proposed a stream running along the Harelbeke street and rejected the Funck-Brentano solution. See plan below. A third interpretation was provided by de Maere d'Aertrycke in 1913, and affirmed in 1933 and 1935.

[76] Courtrai Town Accounts, 1412/13, Algemeen Rijksarchief, Brussels, f. 19; and Sevens, 'Hoeken en kanten op Groeninge', 37: 'Item besteedt te rumene de beke onder zente Jansbrugghe . . . ende die te diepene alsoet heescht omme twater zinen loop te hebbene, dewelke versluust ende ghevult was' (Item: paid to clean the stream under the bridge of St Jan . . . and deepen it as was necessary to let the water run. It was filled and silted up).

and Fris, and dealt with by Funck-Brentano, the stream at hand, a waterway joining the Groeninge and the Hoge Vijver, was intended to fill the Vijver.[77] Delfos, misled by part of the text of the document, was of the opinion that the stream actually ran alongside the Harelbeke street and therefore objected to Funck-Brentano's proposed solution, having already rejected the solution given by Sevens.[78]

The explanation provided by Delfos is, however, incorrect. The stream did not flow straight along the Harelbeke street, but along the back side of the gardens and farmyards in the street. It cut across the Lange Mere street, that is the road to Oudenaarde, thus flowing out from the Groeninge to the north thereof. Nevertheless, the Lange Mere was, as early as 1302, situated around and to the east of the stream.[79] Since the connecting stream ran from the Groeninge through the Lange Mere street in the direction of the St Jan's bridge, it was situated at a certain distance from the Harelbeke street, as was seen for other reasons. Finally the stream supplied the Hoge Vijver with water, and thus the town moat, and for this reason it could not disappear completely. Moreover, the stream also had to supply the water mills with the necessary quantity of water.

A section of the connecting stream (Grote Beek or St Jansbeek) was thus filled in by 1444, since the document already mentioned the stream that had been filled in. However, until now, it has been assumed that the stream disappeared fully following the expansion of the town enclosure in 1453 to include the terrain of the battlefield in 1302.[80] This is incorrect since Louis de Bersaques's map, drawn in 1634 and still kept today in the town hall at Courtrai, allows the course of the stream to be followed to the St Jan's gate that was then the town rampart.[81] The waterway that is presented there from the Groeninge to the town moat corresponds fully with the connecting stream that can be drawn on the basis of the information given in the document of 1444.[82]

---

[77] Sevens, *De slag van Kortrijk*, 2nd edn, 41; Sevens, 'Hoeken en kanten op Groeninge', 39–40; and Fris, *De slag bij Kortrijk*, 342.
[78] Delfos, *1302 door tijdgenooten verteld*, 106, for the connecting stream; 105, for the course of the Groeninge.
[79] Lodewijk, II.1.IV:334–5, c. 37, vv. 2615–18.
[80] Sevens, *De slag van Kortrijk*, 41; and Fris, *De slag bij Kortrijk*, 342 n. 1.
[81] See below. Jacob van Deventer also still indicated the stream.
[82] De Maere d'Aertrycke, *La Bataille des éperons d'or*, 4, defends the following solution: the stream which Lodewijk mentions, the Mosscherbeek was connected, in 1444, to Lodewijk's *gracht*, the Groeninge stream, that lay more to the north: 'Toutefois, un tracé artificiel fut créé, vers le nord, là, où venant d'en dessous de la route de Gand, un aqueduc joint, en siphon, les eaux de la *beke* prémentionnée de la propriété Lauwers [the St Athonius hospital], à celles du *gracht* en propriété Vercruysse . . . le cours des deux eaux fut dénommé de 1442, puis vers 1444, *Groeninghebeek*, nom étendu ensuite à l'amont des eaux appelées *Lange Mere* ou *Lange Mare*.' It is clear that this categorical claim is, in fact, unfounded. The document of 1444 shows that the Groeninge stream existed and that another stream flowed from it to the Hoge Vijver. There is no talk of a new connection, that would have formed a new waterway. Baron de Maere d'Aertrycke felt obliged to add the date 1442 as the Groeninge was already mentioned in that year. He actually based his theory on the layout of the terrain in 1932–3, whereby the remains of a stream still in existence today in front of the St Antonius buildings and the property of the Vercruysse family suggested to him quite simply that these two remaining sections were part of the

During excavations in Courtrai in 1880, remnants of the connecting stream were discovered when the bed of the stream was found several metres north of the entrance to the Stompaerds corner.[83] It was around three metres wide. Further remains were discovered in the Groeningelaan in 1903.[84]

In order to map out the stream correctly, which is made much easier by the map drawn up by Louis de Bersaques, account must be taken of the fact that until 1570, and certainly also in 1302, the road to Oudenaarde ran more to the south, as can partially be verified using Jacob van Deventer's map of the town.[85]

The Lange Mere
It has already been shown that the Lange Mere ran, for the greater part, to the east of the Groeninge. The toponym indicates a marshy terrain that was originally very swampy, which appears to have been the case at the time of the battle since the pro-French sources clearly emphasised this aspect of the battlefield. It is, then, not astonishing to find a stream there, the Groeninge, which carried the water of the area to the River Lys, and the Grote Beek or St Jan's stream that was dug to supply the northern part of the town moat, above all the Hoge Vijver, with water.

The name 'Lange Mere' was later used in the fifteenth century to indicate the street that led to the meadow and thence on to Oudenaarde. A new bridge across the Groeninge was constructed in the street in 1412–13.[86] The town fishing rights

Mosscherbeek stream (property of the Lauwers) and of the Groeninge (property of the Vercruysse family). This position fully contradicts the text of the document of 15 December 1444. Still, there is an even earlier mentioning of the Groeninge that cut across the Lange Meerschstraat. However, since Sevens was incorrectly of the opinion that it was a question of the St Jan's stream, and not the Groeninge, he did not consider the text any further. See also the note on the Lange Mere.

[83] Number 10 on the plan below.
[84] Sevens, 'Hoeken en kanten op Groeninge', 40–1.
[85] F. van de Putte, *Chronique et cartulaire de l'abbaye de Groeninghe à Courtrai*, Société d'emulation (Bruges, 1872), 101–2: 19 September 1570, an agreement between the mayor and the aldermen of Courtrai and the abbess of Groeninge nunnery concerning the transfer and straightening of the old road to Oudenaarde: 'dat men de voornoemde passaigie ende Oudenaertsche strate legghen ende maken zoude up de zudwest cant vanden coutere der voornoemde abdesse ende tconvent toebehoorende, ligghende neffens den ouden voetwech, die over denzelven coutere gheleghen es, beghinnende ande Harelbeeckstrate, ende uutcommende zuutoost in de voornoemde Oudenaertsche strate' (That the aforementioned path and the Oudenaarde street be constructed on the south-west side of the field belonging to the aforementioned abbess and convent situated along the old foot-path which goes across the field, starting at the Harelbeek street and coming out south-east in the aforementioned Oudenaarde street). Sevens, 'Hoeken en kanten op Groeninge', 38. The old road had fallen into a state of disrepair.
[86] Courtrai Town Accounts, 1412/13, Algemeen Rijksarchief, Brussels, f. 19: 'al nieuwe van houte ... dweers der straete also men gaet ter Langhe Meere wart ... up de vors. Groenincbeke' (A bridge, all new made of wood ... across the street going in the direction of the Langhe Meere ... upon the aforementioned Groenincbeek). Sevens, 'Hoeken en kanten op Groeninge', 40, was of the opinion that it was a question of the St Jan's stream or connecting stream. However, it is difficult to comprehend why this accurate text must be changed and this all the more so since the Groeninghe cut across the street as appears from the content of the document of 1444. See also the document concerning the mentioning of the Lange Merestraat.

in the Hoge Vijver and in the Lange Mere were also reported.[87] This indicates either that the meadow was still partially under water, or, more probably, that the name 'Lange Mere' was also used to indicate the St Jan's, or the connecting, stream in which the town authorities conferred the fishing rights in 1444 on Zegher Tanghe.[88] The assumption that the St Jan's stream joined the Groeninge in the Lange Mere could already be made on the basis of both Lodewijk's text and now the document of 1444. But how can the correct course of the other important stream be determined?

The Groeninge stream
The name given to this waterway, first mentioned in the Courtrai town accounts of 1412–13, naturally indicated its crossing of the 'Groeninc', a meadow which originally had so much water flowing into it that it was continually covered with green. On the basis of what is known about the Lange Mere, it may be assumed that it was initially a very watery terrain since the name continued long after the terrain had largely or even completely lost its original characteristic. Historians also differ over this stream and one is once again confronted with the four reconstructions presented above. First, the primary sources for the stream will be discussed, and its course traced, and, following this, in passing, the incorrect solutions will be noted.

The oldest source for the reconstruction of the battlefield, on the basis of a map of the town, is Jacob van Deventer's superb chart.[89] After careful examination of this map, one notes, however, that merely two fragments of the stream are depicted. Moreover, the map presents sections of two waterways, so that historians are faced with two possibilities.[90] Funck-Brentano presented the stream situated farthest to the west as the Groeninge; Sevens and Fris, as well as Moke, Köhler and Frederichs, chose the stream to the east.[91] A historian such as Sevens could test his choice against his knowledge of local topography. At the turn of this century, Sevens could still fully trace and depict the stream.[92] In a later contribution, he was better able to justify his choice due to information more closely linked to the period

---

[87] Courtrai Town Accounts, 1416/17, Algemeen Rijksarchief, Brussels, f. 4v: 'Ontfaen van Jhanne van Durmeys van dat hi in pachte heift de visscherie van den Hoghen Vivere met der Langhe Meere' (Received from Jhanne van Durmeys, on account of him having a lease of the fishery in the Hogen Vivere with the Langhe Meere). See also Courtrai Town Accounts, 1417/18, Algemeen Rijksarchief, Brussels, f. 5v: 'de visscherie van den Hoeghe Vivere met der Langhe Meere, der stede toebehorende' (the fishing rights in the Hoeghe Vivere (Upper Lake) and the Langhe Meere, belonging to the town). See also Sevens, 'Hoeken en kanten op Groeninge', 37.
[88] Courtrai Town Archives, Perkamenten Privilegieboek, ff. 406v–407r: 15 December 1444: 'Emmer wel verstaende dat de zelve stede te haerwaerts behout de visscherie van den zelven waterloope ende van al den anderen watere, ende ooc bezuydt van de zelver veste.'
[89] Published by Baron de Bethune in the aforementioned *Atlas des villes de Belgique au XVIe siècle*.
[90] Neither of the two streams was fully depicted on the map. This is easily understood since the aim was to reproduce the town layout, and the surroundings of the town were therefore certainly not drawn so accurately.
[91] The eastern *gracht* (stream/ditch) is depicted on the Ferraris map.
[92] Sevens, *De slag van Kortrijk*, 2nd edn, 40–1.

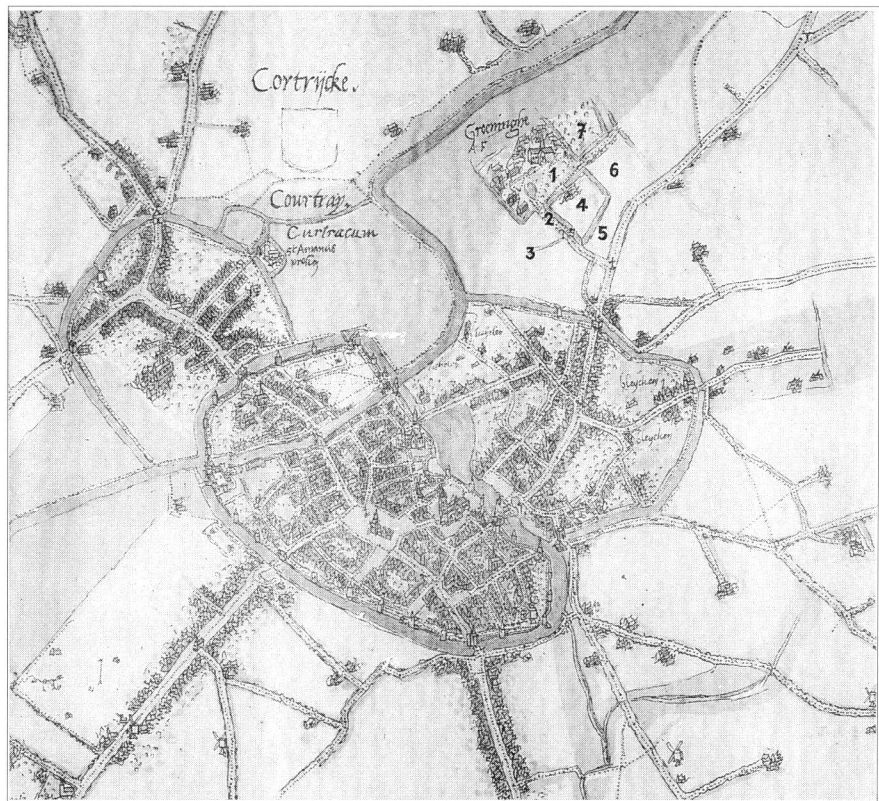

2. Jacob van Deventer's map. For points 1 to 7 see text on next page. Note the northern section of the Groeninge, to the east of points 6 and 7, stretching southwards

around 1302.[93] Finally, in a subsequent study, he drew upon another important source as evidence, although he did not fully exploit the source. The source, drawn by Louis de Bersaques in 1634, carefully reproduced the layout of the town and surrounding areas.[94]

Funck-Brentano's conception can be dismissed straight away. The Groeninge monastery's cartularium does indeed contain a very significant document: a measurement, carried out in March 1601 by the surveyor, Pierre de Bersaques, on the grounds of the monastery.[95] Thus, a description of the situation of the 1302

---

[93] Sevens, 'Hoeken en kanten op Groeninge', 47–8.
[94] Sevens, 'De Groeningebeek', 265. The map now hangs in the Council Chamber of the Courtrai Town Hall. See the map below.
[95] Van de Putte, 110. In number 4, the description of the 'hooghen lochtinck' (upper gardens), the erroneous statement is made that this parcel of land bordered the lane to the *east*. One should read *west* instead of *east* as is seen from the description given by number 5, a parcel of land situated to the south of number 4.

battlefield at that time may be gained. The survey and description enables a mapping out of the various parcels of land, roads, meadows, etc. This has been undertaken on the basis of the Deventer map and of Louis de Bersaques's map. By so doing, one arrives at the following:

1. The ruins of the monastery with the stalls.
2. The lane that ran southwards as far as the cross, noted by both van Deventer and Bersaques as well as Sanderus.
3. A footpath or track that ran from the lane westwards towards the town fortifications.
4. The upper 'lochtinck' or gardens.
5. A plot of land, bordering the 'nieuwe ghedelf vande beecke' (the newly dug canal of the stream) to the east.
6. A plot of land between the new 'bedelf' (canal) to the west, and the 'doude beecke' (old stream) in the east.
7. The upper orchard.
8. A field through which the footpath to Harelbeke ran and that bordered the 'doude beecke' to the west.

This accurate description can easily be mapped out on the basis of the two maps, from Deventer (in around 1555) and Louis de Bersaques (1634), which respectively precede and follow the measurements. They prove beyond any doubt that the waterway to the west, given by Deventer, was a 'nieuw ghedelf', a new channel of the stream, while the 'doude beecke' (old stream), was situated more to the east. It is now clear that only the old stream fits the description of the course of the Groeninge.

The solutions proffered by Funck-Brentano, and partially that presented by Delfos, can thus be refuted. The reconstruction given by Delfos presents the Groeninge stream as following almost completely the town moat that was dug in 1453 around the new ramparts of the town in that area. However, there is not one single document that can be used in support of such a contention.

Delfos made further objections to the classical presentation of the course of the Groeninge since the stream rose from the sixteenth to the seventeenth contour line in its course.[96] This objection, made on the basis of the 1:20,000 ordnance survey map, has no conclusive value whatsoever. It would have value as evidence if there were an ordnance survey map with the contour lines as present in the fourteenth century, since, despite any claims to the contrary, from a geological point of view it is possible that a change in the height of the terrain could have taken place.[97] However, such a process is not necessary in indicating the veracity of the classical

---

[96] Delfos, *1302 door tijdgenooten verteld*, 105.
[97] See, in this respect, among others, C. Stevens, 'Les Déformations naturelles et récentes du sol belge', *Bulletin de la société royale belge de géographie* 59 (1935); Stevens, 'Les Élements directeurs de la géomorphologie de la Belgique', *Bulletin belge des sciences militaires* (July/August 1938); and General Seligman, *Les Nivellements en Belgique*, Congrès natonal des sciences (Liège, 1931).

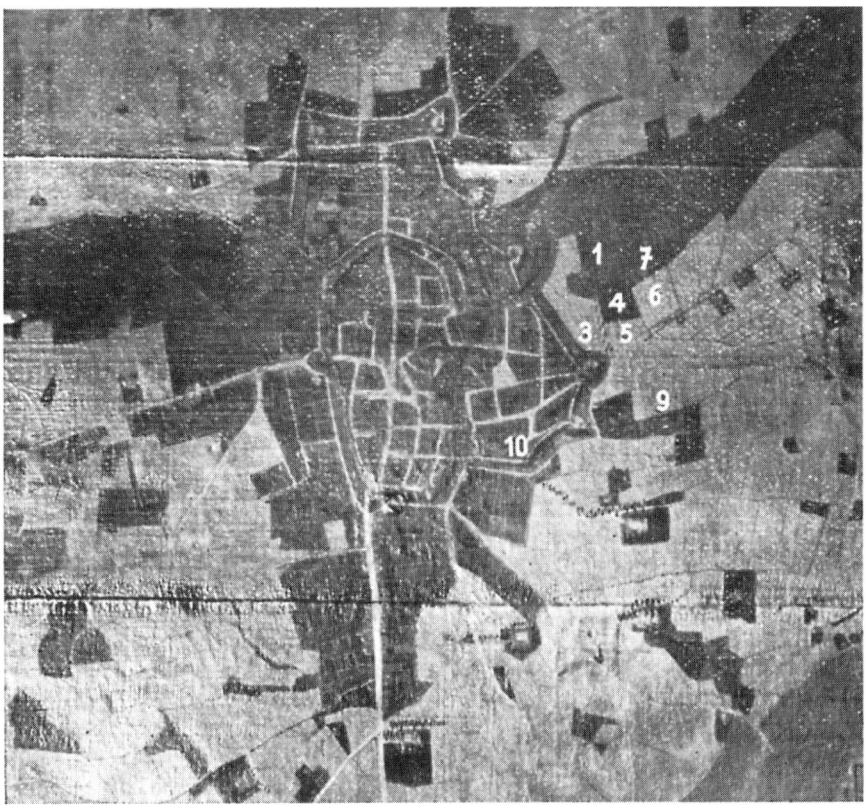

3. Louis de Bersaques' map. The connecting stream (9) along the Lange Merestraat that ran north, to the right of point 10, on the old road to Ghet.

version since the missing sections of the Groeninge can be mapped out using the Deventer map and on the basis of the painting by Louis de Bersaques in which the new stream was separated from the old stream, following the survey taken by Pierre de Bersaques in 1601. Moreover, one should add the following piece of information: Deventer reproduced sections of the Groeninge, and Louis de Bersaques reproduced the stream almost completely in his map, together with the St Jan's stream, right up to the fortifications; the stream is reproduced fully in his painting of the Courtrai castellany (1641).[98] Ferraris also mapped out the Groeninge along its whole course. In 1902 Sevens gave a complete description of the stream which at that time passed through various underground passages that had been laid partly to lead them under the railway and the Bossuit canal as well as under the streets of the expanding town. For this reason, the course of the Groeninge is outlined as it was in January 1950: at that time sections of the stream

[98] Also kept in the Courtrai Town Hall.

4 & 5. Two maps of the town of Courtrai from the Petit Beaulieu, a series of plates published by Chevalier de Beaulieu in 1647 in Paris. (See J.G. de Brouwere, 'Iconographische bronnen van onze militaire geschiedenis', *Het leger. de natie* 4 (1949), p. 66)

4. The terrain before 1646.

Key: G = Lille Gate, H = Tournai gate, I = St Jan's gate, K = Former Steenport (Stone Gate)

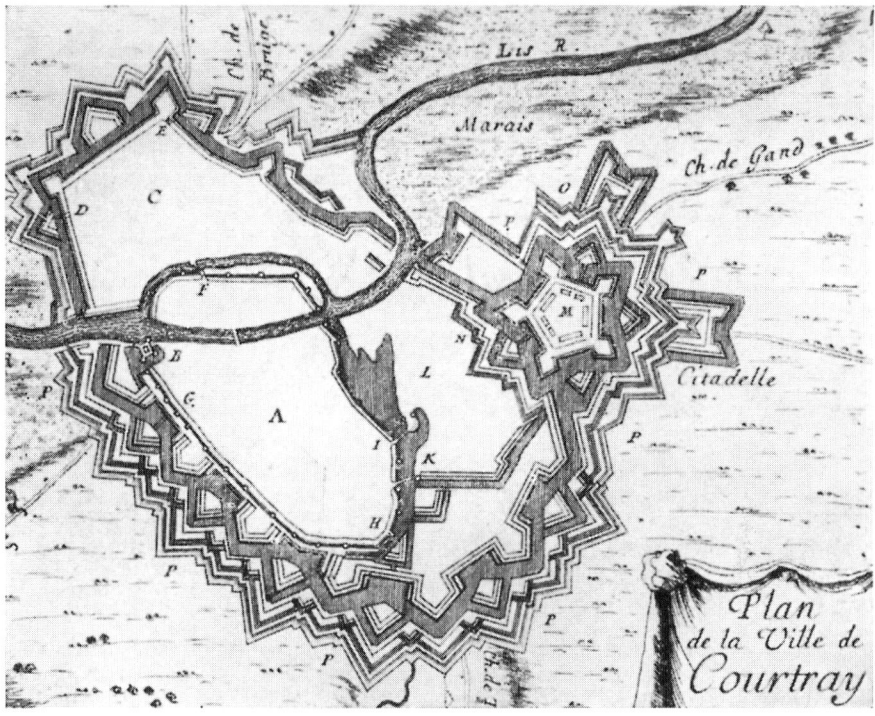

5. Plan showing all the changes that occurred after the seizure of the town in 1646. The letter P refers to the new fortifications. The letter M indicates the citadel built at that time upon the battlefield of 1302.

Key: G = Lille Gate, H = Tournai gate, I = Former Steenport (Stone Gate), K = St Jan's gate

were once again made to flow underneath the streets by means of sewer pipes so that almost no visible remains of it could be detected. The course of the water still ran along one section that did not differ much from the course deduced from reconstructions from the Deventer, de Bersaques and Ferraris maps. For this reason, it is difficult to understand why a difference in contour height should be invoked today. The contour lines could have changed completely as a result of the construction of the citadel in 1647,[99] or of the Ghent–Brussels railway, the Bossuit canal or other unknown factors. Delfos claimed that almost nothing remained of the stream. In this respect, he was insufficiently informed and appeared not to have had confidence in the description given by Sevens that noted the number of underground passages beneath the railway, streets, etc.[100]

[99] See map. See also M. van Hemelrijck, *De vlaamse krijgsbouwkunde* (Tielt, 1950), 213.
[100] The proposition made by de Maere d'Aertrycke concerning a connecting stream between the Mosscherbeek and the Groeninge after 1444 has already been refuted above. De Maere d'Aertrycke made the mistake of seeking to proceed from the present topographical data of the

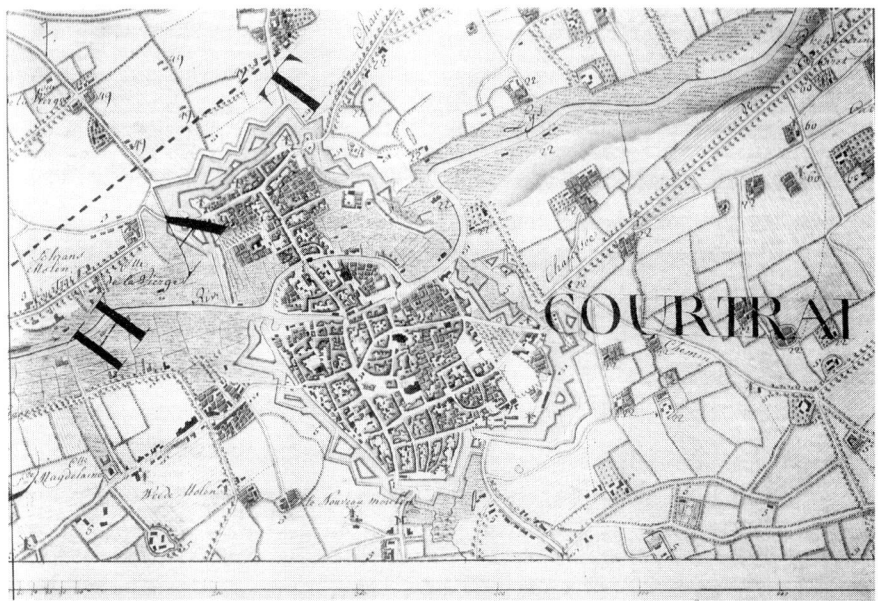

6. Ferraris' map.

Since the maps referred to used different scales it is very difficult to map out the course of the Groeninge in great detail. It is also possible that limited changes in its course had been effected. Nevertheless, the various characteristics: the farmstead where the Groeninge begins, the large curve, and so forth, do not essentially differ in the Deventer, de Bersaques (1634 and 1641) and Ferraris maps, nor in Sevens's description and in the map drawn up for us by J. M. L. Demeyere, the Courtrai town engineer in 1950. On the basis of sound historical methodology, the stream is to be considered as the Groeninge stream of 1302.

In January 1950, the stream could be followed from the wall at the Vierschaar ten Akker farmstead. It flowed south to north, being led through underground passages underneath the Renaix, Ghent and Brussels railways. The stream was visible in the St Antonius gardens. Between these buildings and the Lys–Scheldt canal (Bossuit canal) the stream was covered and passed underneath the canal by means of an underground channel. Further on a section of the stream was still visible almost up to the point where the roads leading to Ghent and Harelbeke separated. Once again the stream passed under the roads by means of an underground passage. The stream was then visible almost up to the River Lys.[101]

---

town. He made assumptions on an outlying area of the town which had undergone more significant change in the past fifty years than in the six hundred years from 1302 to 1902. Delfos also partially made the same mistake in his attempt to construct a logical system that is in other respects worthy of merit.

[101] This corresponds exactly with the description given by Sevens, *De slag van Kortrijk*, 2nd edn, 40–1.

Since January 1950, however, changes have taken place, as can be seen from the map that has also been provided by J. M. L. Demeyere.[102] The southern section of the stream runs now almost wholly through channels and past the statue of Groeninge to the River Lys. There is also an interruption at the St Jan's church. The lake to the north of the church now forms the source of that separate section that flows downstream from the Groeninge bridge, under the canal and the road to Ghent into the River Lys.

On Louis de Bersaques's map one can see a large curve in the stream between the roads to Oudenaarde and Ghent. This indicates that the battlefield was to some extent on higher ground. The connecting stream, or St Jan's stream, had its source at a distance of approximately nine hundred metres from the mouth of the Groeninge.

There is an additional very significant problem that arises from both Louis de Bersaques's map, and above all the map of the castellany, and from Ferraris's: the Groeninge had its source alongside the embankment at the farmstead, Vierschaar ten Akker. In this case, however, the stream would not have a long course and doubts would arise about whether its measurements actually corresponded to those given by Villani, three metres wide and approximately two metres deep. Such doubts arise primarily due to the state of the terrain at the turn of the century. In fact, for 1302, it must be taken into account that the Lange Mere certainly still formed a watery terrain and that this was perhaps also the case for the Groeninge field. This clearly appears from information given by the French sources and by Lodewijk: 'a low-lying area full of ditches'. The banks of the streams also appear to have been marshy. Moreover, the sources state that ditches were relatively deep and wide. Furthermore, the town's fishing rights also indicate that the waterways contained much water.

Thus, it may be accepted that the Groeninge stream had more water flowing through it in 1302 than at the end of the nineteenth century. If the opposite were true, there would not have been any reason to lay another connecting stream to the Hoge Vijver.

Still, one other solution remains, leaving aside the possibility that the stream in 1302 had its source solely in the Lange Mere and perhaps in the still watery Groeninge field as well. Was there at that time no connecting stream between the Groeninge and another larger stream, the Mosscher, now referred to as the Klakkaerts stream? This interesting problem will be examined below.

The Mosscher stream
This waterway has its source in the chain of hills between St Anna and the main Courtrai–Tournai road and flows alongside the Nedermosscher stream towards the Tournai gate. It is an important stream drawing water off an extensive area of land.

The stream is almost fully depicted on Deventer's map. At that time a branch of the stream flowed into the town moat to the west of the road to St Denijs. Another

---

[102] See the map below. For this and the following discussion, the reader is indebted to Demeyere.

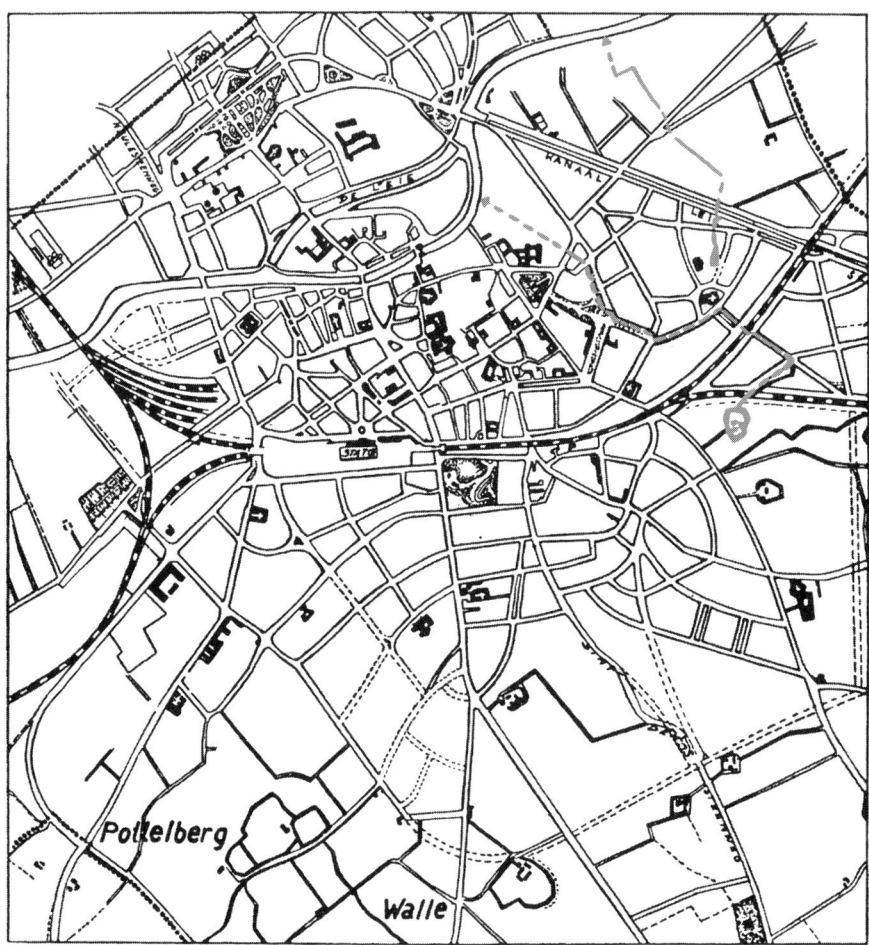

7. Map of Courtrai as it is today showing the Groeninge stream.
The southern section of the stream, between the farmstead and the St Jan's church, that is now directed through a channel system to the Lys river, is indicated by a grey dotted line. A small section, to the north of the railroad leading to Renaix and indicated by a grey line still exists.

The northern sections, from the lake to north of the St Jan's church, have also been indicated by a grey line: the section that has remained open is shown in a solid line, while dotted lines indicate those sections in the channel system.

The farmstead, where the stream has its source, is the Vierschaar ten Akker. The Mosscher or Klakkaerts stream runs to the south of the farmstead and is indicated by a grey line.

branch went east towards the farmstead, Vierschaar ten Akker, and therefore towards the Groeninge. This leads to the assumption that the Mosscher stream was connected to the Groeninge.[103] Much water thus ought to have flowed into the stream and it would have had the depth and width noted by Villani. Some old maps, among them that of La Royère, of which a copy has been kept at Courtrai, show the connection.[104] Still, it is very difficult to determine the value of such maps.

Sevens was of the opinion that the ditch drew water from the Mosscher stream alongside the wall of the Vierschaar ten Akker, carrying it therefore to the Groeninge stream. Several years before the above work was published, he had written that the ditch was still visible.[105] Additional proof of the first assumption (on the basis of the Deventer map) and Sevens's observations is the fact that on 20 August 1678 the decision was taken to retain the town fortifications and the Courtrai citadel and 'to divert a certain Groeninge stream, coming from the north of Courtrai, and to direct it to the Gaver'.[106] The Groeninge would double the amount of water in the Gaver stream. The redirecting of the stream took place because of the fear of floods being caused by impediments in the streams.

Since the Groeninge had its source to the north of Courtrai, according to the document from the Harelbeke Cartularium, one ought then to be dealing with the Mosscher or Klakkaerts stream. This stream ought to have had and to have kept the name 'Groeninge' for that section that ran to the south of the farmstead, Vierschaar ten Akker, flowing northwards towards the River Lys. It is indeed possible in this case that they would have doubled the waters flowing in the Gaver stream. This danger of flooding corresponds well with what is now known about the Klakkaerts stream.[107] It is not very logical that the stream in question was the Groeninge between the Vierschaar ten Akker and the River Lys. However, the text is not clear enough to allow us to draw indisputable conclusions.

If, however, the Mosscher stream, or merely one branch of it, flowed first eastwards and then northwards, then the Groeninge stream would have formed a significant impediment that was certainly three metres wide and approximately two metres deep. It would have been easier to lead water from the Groeninge to the Hoge Vijver by means of a connecting stream. In all events, the Mosscher was at a later stage completely redirected to the east, since the stream is now connected to the Gaver stream, and it is only in the Courtrai area that it has the name Klakkaerts, being referred to as the Gaver stream elsewhere.

---

[103] Sevens, *De slag van Kortrijk*, 2nd edn, 28, 40, 54 (maps); Fris, *De slag bij Kortrijk*, 341; and Delfos, *1302 door tijdgenooten verteld*, 106. Delfos was doubtful about the possibility of there being a connection due to the present contours. They are obviously not determinant.
[104] La Royère, *Corte anotatien ende beschrijvinghe van de stadt Cortrijck*, Courtrai Town Archives, Codex 504, Box 52, ff. 102–3, 202, 203.
[105] Sevens, *De slag van Kortrijk*, 40.
[106] Sevens, 'De Groeningebeek', 267–9: 'te diverteren sekere Groeningebeke, commende van boven Cortrycke, ende die te leeden in den Gavere'.
[107] *Stad Kortrijk. Stedebouw. Survey* (Courtrai, 1948), 8.

One problem that remains to be solved concerns the branch of the Mosscher stream that according to the Deventer map flows into the southern sections of the town moat.

The Neveldries and the Bloedmeers

The Neveldries is situated between the Tournai gate and the connecting stream, Groeninge–Hoge Vijver, outside the town ramparts. Until 1358, the land belonged to the family of the Lords of Nevele.[108]

When Sevens wrote his work in 1902, there was a branch leading from the Mosscher stream, near the road to St Denijs, through an elevation towards the St George park and the old town ramparts. The stream was referred to as the Bloedbeek by inhabitants probably on account of its flowing through the Bloedmeers to the Neveldries.[109]

The branch was depicted on other maps by Jacob van Deventer, Louis de Bersaques and Ferraris. It is possible that the branch already existed in 1302[110] so as to provide water for the southern sections of the moat, although there is no certainty in this respect since the waterway could also have been dug later.[111]

General Conclusion on the Terrain

Although a full century separates the information given by both the narrative accounts and the official documents, one can still accept the identity of the waterways noted in the archival documents as being the same as those reported by Lodewijk, Villani, and in the lost source of the *Anciennes chroniques de Flandre*, as well as the *Chronographia Regum Francorum*: sufficient elements are found in common, allowing us to situate components in both sets of information, above all in the 1444 document. These components are the Groeninge monastery, the stream that flowed alongside it towards the Ghent road (Groeninge stream), Lodewijk's Lange Mere with the stream flowing there and the Lange Mere both as a stream and road or, in official documents, as the road to Oudenaarde.

For the size of the Groeninge stream and the flow of water to it we are faced with two possibilities. First, if the stream had its source to the south at the farmstead, Vierschaar ten Akker, then the Lange Mere must still have been in parts a meadow – something that is not contradicted by the sources. Second, if there had been a connection between the Mosscher and Groeninge, or these streams formed merely *one* stream, then there is certainly no difficulty in explaining the size of the stream and accepting the measurements given by Villani.

---

[108] Sevens, *De slag van Kortrijk*, 36.
[109] Ibid., 37.
[110] This is Fris's opinion. See Fris, *De slag bij Kortrijk*, 341.
[111] Sevens was not of this opinion (*De slag van Kortrijk*, 37). Still, it appears logical that a connection with the town moat was also dug at that point.

The northern section of the battlefield, between the monastery and the Lys, was certainly a meadow in 1302, since it is still reported as being so even as late as 1601. For this reason the Flemings would not have had to fear an attack from that side, between the river and the monastery.

4

The Two Armies

The Numerical Strength of the Two Armies

The Flemish forces
On 11 July 1302, three major divisions were grouped together under the Flemish flag. The right wing was formed of militias from Bruges, the centre of men of the Bruges Franc. The left wing was formed of men of East Flanders, joined by the men of Ghent who had come together with Jan Borluut. Jan van Renesse took his post behind their ranks with the reserve corps. The men of Ypres were positioned before the castle of Courtrai.

Soldiers from the Waas country were fully occupied with the siege of the Rupelmonde castle and with surrounding Ghent. This was also the case for the men of the Four Ambachten,[1] where perhaps several of those fighting belonged to the entourage of certain noblemen present.[2] In Ghent the Flemish supporters of the King of France were still in power, so that no militia was sent from the town.[3]

The rebel army consisted predominantly of artisans and peasants supported by foreign mercenaries and Flemish nobles. What was the numerical strength of each of these contingents?

The town militias
Two special contingents from the Flemish towns are known to have taken part since they were only represented by a few of their soldiers: the men of Ypres and Ghent. In Ypres, those favourable to the French cause were still in power, although the guildsmen rallied behind the insurgents. The town council, however, limited the number of the town contingent to five hundred men and a number of crossbowmen.[4] This number, given by the Ghentenaar Friar Minor, is wholly credible since the numerical strength of the militia drawn up was known to the town council, who needed the information for the payment of the crossbowmen, and wagon men for the hire of wagons and horses. The chances are that a smaller rather

---

[1] The Vier Ambachten (four shires) were Axel, Hulst, Assenede and Boechoute.
[2] Lodewijk, II.1.IV:319, c. 32, v. 2225: 'Uten Vier Ambachten wasser .i. deel'. Perhaps they belonged to Willem van Boenhem's entourage (Lodewijk, II.1.IV:319, c. 32, vv. 2227–8). See also Lodewijk, II.1.IV:288–9, c. 22, vv. 1521–3, for Ghent, the Waas country and the Vier Ambachten, for which there is no list of those soldiers who took part.
[3] Ibid., II.1.IV:319, c. 32, v. 2225; and *Annales Gandenses*, 27.
[4] *Annales Gandenses*, 26–7.

than a greater number is accurate. The numerical strength of the men of Ypres, twelve hundred according to Lodewijk,[5] is in fact too high for the task with which the militia was charged: keeping the French garrison in the Courtrai castle under control. The garrison merely contained thirteen knights, forty-nine squires, two hundred and twenty crossbowmen and fifty-two other persons.[6] Obviously, only a certain number of the men would have been able to take part in an outbreak, and they would also have had to leave the castle through a narrow gate.

The Ghentenaar Friar Minor also gives the number of the men of Ghent as approximately seven hundred.[7] Some of these troops were most certainly relatives of Jan Borluut who, on account of a feud with other burghers, was in exile with followers in Tournai.[8] As a man of Ghent, the Friar Minor would have been well informed about the matter. It also appears from the above source that men of Ghent, aside from those exiled, also left the town.[9] The numbers given there also seem to be acceptable since they are based on a sound local tradition, and the Friar Minor did not appear to be biased in that respect.[10] However, the possibility that it is exaggerated should constantly be borne in mind.

In addition to the information about these two contingents there is a whole range of material on the Bruges militia. Thus, the numerical strength of a section of the forces can be determined while the remaining forces can be approximately calculated.

A Brugeois communal army was composed of:

1. Special units: in 1302, these were only the crossbowmen.
2. The burghers.
3. The guildsmen.[11]

To this the aldermen and council, with entourage, ought to be added, as well as the commando of the communal army, which was often aided militarily by a marshal, a nobleman with military experience in tactical command of the troops.

In July 1302, the above army was probably under the command of Hendrik van Lontzen, a knight from the duchy of Limburg who had been appointed marshal of Bruges by Willem van Jülich.[12] The militia was accompanied by the new Bruges council with its entourage and minstrels. The town banner was carried on a wagon. Masons and other workmen were sent to undermine the Courtrai castle. Springalds and other projectile machines were also taken along.[13]

There are no figures from the council and its entourage. Nevertheless, its

---

[5] Lodewijk, II.1.IV:310, c. 28, v. 1999.
[6] *Chronique artésienne*, 44–5.
[7] *Annales Gandenses*, 29.
[8] F. Blockmans, 'Een patricische veete te Gent', *BCRH*, 99 (1935), 607–8, 630.
[9] *Annales Gandenses*, 29; and Lodewijk, II.1.IV:289, c. 22, vv. 1524–7.
[10] Elsewhere he did not avoid mentioning events that were not favourable to the honour of the men of Ghent. See, for example, his account of the Battle of Mons-en-Pévèle: *Annales Gandenses*, 66, 70 (see also 53).
[11] Verbruggen, 'De organisatie van de militie te Brugge', 163.
[12] Funck-Brentano, *Philippe le Bel*, 403 n. 1.
[13] Wyffels and Vandewalle, 94–5.

expenses amounted to 482 pounds and nearly 7 shillings[14] with the aldermen and members of the council always receiving a higher payment than normal soldiers.[15] For three bodies of crossbowmen who travelled to Wijnendaal and Courtrai, the sum of 492 pounds was paid.[16] This would make a total of ninety men, including at least thirty helpers who did not necessarily take part in the fighting. Furthermore, a doctor and two or three trumpeters accompanied the militia.[17]

The crossbowmen left in two groups: the first with Willem van Jülich in the direction of Cassel and from there towards Courtrai. The second left with Guy de Namur in the direction of Wijnendaal and Courtrai. The first formation included the following constables: Veys van der Biest, Jan Sailge, Geraard de Ketelboetre, Jacob de Vos, Meus Dullekin, together with their companions, a hundred crossbowmen and fifty *garsoenen* (pavisers, who carried the large shields, the crossbowmen's *targen*, providing protection for the crossbowmen while they spanned their bows and shot the arrows), who took part in the expedition for a period of forty-six days.[18] This probably took place from 31 May till 15 July 1302, since Willem van Jülich left on 31 May to liberate the coastal regions and entered Ghent on 15 July.[19]

It is certain that the following constables were present in Wijnendaal and Courtrai: Diederik Lauward, Colard de Garter, Willem Wederick, Gilles Rommel, Bouden de Vos, Ghisel Hanscoewerker, Jan Busard and Jan Volcard. The latter, Colard de Jonghe, Jacob van den Beckine and Clais van Oudenburch, also served for twenty-five days and were therefore present in this expedition from Wijnendaal onwards.

It is only for the first group of five constables that an explicit mention of crossbowmen being under their command can be found. However, the following three constables were also commanders of crossbowmen, since they had thirty pavisers with them. For the last two entries the information is less extensive although the same bodies of soldiers are actually being dealt with. Nevertheless, it is sufficient to draw a comparison with the Douai expedition on 30 August 1302. Here thirty-six pieces of cloth were mentioned being used for the *frocken* (tunics) of the two hundred crossbowmen.[20] Following this, there is a list of ten constabularies, each consisting of a constable, nineteen crossbowmen (*serianten*), ten pavisers (*garsoenen*) and two wagons, as at Courtrai.[21] By comparison, the same commanders are seen. And for the years 1302, 1303 and 1304, almost all the

---

[14] Ibid., 95: 482 pounds, 6 shillings and 8 pence.
[15] Ibid., 173: each alderman and member of the Council received 10 pounds. Also in 1281–2 and 1292: see Wyffels and De Smet, 38, 344. For Douai see Funck-Brentano, *Philippe le Bel*, 311; each alderman received one pound per day.
[16] Wyffels and Vandewalle, 95.
[17] Ibid., 95: Master Jan Raepsaed and the minstrels.
[18] Ibid., 95.
[19] Ibid., 808–16.
[20] Ibid., 97. In an unpublished thesis C. Didier came to this same conclusion.
[21] Wyffels and Vandewalle, 97.

constables present on 11 July 1302 are once again in command of crossbowmen in other expeditions.[22]

This leads to the conclusion that in Courtrai there were sixteen constables who took part in the battle, all with nineteen crossbowmen, ten pavisers and two wagons. This implies a total number of 320 crossbowmen and 160 pavisers.

Contrary to an earlier opinion[23] expressed before more about the classical organisation of the communal army was learned,[24] the crossbowmen did not belong to the burghers. They formed a special corps, as noted for other Flemish towns.[25] For this reason they were paid by the town and the cost of replacing lost bows or other pieces of equipment was carried by the town. Not one of the constables from Bruges mentioned above was a burgher.[26] The professions of some of them are known. Thus Veys van der Biest was a brewer,[27] Meus Dullekin was a weaver,[28] Colard de Garter was a clothmaker,[29] Jan Volcard belonged to the carpenters', masons' and tilers' trade,[30] Clais van Oudenburch was a grocer or sock maker[31] (all of these were taken as hostages by Jacques de St Pol, being held captive at Tournai in 1301);[32] Willem Wederick was a purse maker, and Jacob van den Beckine was an broker.[33]

The crossbowmen formed an elite corps which was comprised of all classes from the town's inhabitants with the corps' commanders not belonging to the rich burghers.[34] For this reason the contingent cannot be considered as a body of burgher soldiers.

The crossbowmen all received a decent payment – the same sum as squires who had not yet been knighted, that is four shillings.[35] After them came the guilds, with their expenses of hiring their wagons being paid by the town treasury.[36]

---

[22] Ibid., 99. On 1297 see Wyffels and De Smet, 558; on 1303 see Wyffels and Vandewalle, 174, 186; on 1304 see Wyffels and Vandewalle, 359, 362, 487, 494–5, 500–1.
[23] J. F. Verbruggen, 'De Brugse effectieven in de slag bij Kortrijk', *Bijdragen voor de geschiedenis der Nederlanden*, 2 (1948), 242–3; and De Smet, 'Les Effectifs brugeois à la bataille de Courtrai', 868.
[24] Verbruggen, 'De organisatie van de militie te Brugge', 163.
[25] For Ghent see van Werveke, 'Het bevolkingscijfer van de stad Gent', 346; and A. van Werveke, 'Het godshuis van St Jan en St Pauwel', *Maatschappij der vlaamsche bibliophilen*, 4th ser., 15 (1909), 102. Ghent's St George guild was comprised of three 'members' of the town: burghers, small tradesmen and weavers.
[26] See list in De Smet, 'De inrichting', 499–505.
[27] L. Verriest, 'Le Registre de la "loi" de Tournai, de 1302 et listes des otages de Bruges (1301) et de Courtrai', *BCRH*, 80 (1911), 486.
[28] Verriest, 487.
[29] Ibid., 498.
[30] Ibid., 494.
[31] Ibid., 495, 498.
[32] Ibid., 495, 498.
[33] Bruges Town Accounts, 1304, 3 (October–February), Kladrekening, f. i (draft of the account).
[34] That is: inhabitants of Bruges with possessions of a value of more than 300 pounds.
[35] Wyffels and Vandewalle, 97. For the squires see ibid., 93.
[36] Ibid., 95–6. For the Douai expedition see also ibid., 98–9.

In 1302, there were thirty-one guilds during the Courtrai expedition. Certainly, some of them were composed of smaller guilds which later, in the fourteenth century, provided separate bodies of soldiers in the communal army. In 1302, however, they provided a contingent together. The following guilds took part in the Courtrai expedition: 1. Fishermen; 2. Glove makers; 3. Fullers; 4. Weavers; 5. Carpet weavers and ticking weavers; 6. The lambskin makers; 7. Smiths; 8. Brokers; 9. House decorators; 10. Greengrocers; 11. Hay merchants; 12. Barbers; 13. Mattress makers; 14. Masons; 15. Carpenters; 16. Purse makers; 17. Shippers; 18. Wine carriers; 19. Old fur merchants; 20. Fruit merchants; 21. Millers; 22. Candle makers; 23. Wool shearers; 24. Tailors; 25. Wine merchants; 26. Tilers; 27. Shoemakers; 28. Sawyers; 29. Dyers; 30. Tanners; and 31. Butchers.

We can now proceed to the calculation of the number of horses used by the guilds, and it is already known how much was paid to hire a horse. It is also known how long the expedition lasted: twenty-five days. The bodies of crossbowmen had at their disposal six horses for two wagons. The number of horses used can be determined on the basis of this piece of information, as well as how much each guild was paid for hiring horses. The calculation leads to a sum of 619 horses used by the above guilds. Since each constable with twenty soldiers needed six horses, a figure of 103 bodies of twenty soldiers or 2060 soldiers sent by the guilds is arrived at.[37]

However, it is possible that the six horses were used by the guilds for thirty soldiers since the constabulary of crossbowmen was composed of twenty crossbowmen and ten pavisers. The wagons would have been used to carry their equipment (shields or pavises, tents, pavilions) and provisions. If this were so, the Bruges guilds then sent 103 × 30, that is 3090 soldiers, to Courtrai. This is a maximum figure, since these calculations have been made on the basis of only six horses for two wagons, which is a minimum, since during the journey to Douai eight, nine or ten horses were used for two wagons.[38] If one takes the number of horses used per wagon as being higher, then the number of bodies of soldiers will be less. It can also be calculated on the basis of the shortest duration of the expedition: twenty-five days. If the figure of forty-six days for part of the forces can be accepted, then the number of soldiers could also have been less.

A definitive conclusion can be reached on the crossbowmen, and for the guilds a satisfactory approximation can be given. However, it becomes clear that one corps is missing from the communal army: the burghers. The rich inhabitants of Bruges did not have to march alongside their fellow guild members once they possessed more than three hundred pounds, if they were craftsmen; they joined the ranks of the burghers.[39] In 1292, the burghers were subdivided according to their posses-

---

[37] For this calculation see Verbruggen, 'De Brugse effectieven in de slag bij Kortrijk', 242–3. See also De Smet, 'Les Effectifs brugeois à la bataille de Courtrai', 868.

[38] Verbruggen, 'De Brugse effectieven in de slag bij Kortrijk', 242 n. 4. See also Wyffels and Vandewalle, 97.

[39] De Smet, 'De inrichting', 505: 'ende so wat manne die ghegoedt es boven 300 lb. die sal moeten varen als porter ende niet als seriant van sinen hambochte' (and that man who possesses more than 300 pounds will have to travel as a burgher and not as a servant of his guild). See also

sions into five classes. According to the class to which they belonged, they were obliged to possess a horse of a certain value.[40] They had therefore to serve in the militia on horseback following this order.

One cannot, however, assume that they took part in the Courtrai expedition, since they were not mentioned in the town accounts of 1302. If the Brugeois burghers had taken part in the expedition, they would actually have been mentioned in the accounts. The town made high payments to foreign knights and their entourage, it paid the crossbowmen, compensated the costs incurred by the guilds for their wagons, or horses and wagon drivers. The town maintained Willem van Jülich and his entourage of Flemish noblemen, as well as the son of the Count, Guy de Namur. Why would the town not have recompensed its burghers for costs incurred if they had really taken part in the military expedition?

In addition to the above evidence, there is no explicit mention of a burgher corps in the military expeditions of 1302, 1303 and 1304 until they took part in the Zierikzee expedition of 11 May 1304.[41] It is only for the latter expedition that the participation of the burghers can be certain.

Moreover, there is a further indication. The *pointinghe* (burghers' tax), collected for the military expedition to Cassel, Wijnendaal and Courtrai, raised the high sum of 3022 pounds.[42] The returns of the tax came at least partially from payments made by burghers who did not take part in the expeditions.[43] The high sum raised indicates that many burghers did not leave for Courtrai.

However, the organisation of the burghers as a cavalry unit in 1292 clearly indicates that the burghers formed, prior to 1302, a separate group in Bruges. As such, they served separately from the units formed by the guilds. Among the 468 Bruges hostages sent to Tournai in 1301, one notes that a first group consisted of

---

De Smet, 'Rond een Brugs poortersgeslacht', 10. In Ypres, one was required to possess the sum of 500 pounds in order to join the burgher class.

[40] De Smet, 'De inrichting', 498, 505.

[41] The participation of the burghers in the expedition is based on a list of debts incurred, since there is only information concerning this very hastily prepared expedition *after* the return of the troops. Burghers and members of the guilds lent sums of money to their shippers. See Wyffels and Vandewalle, 567–8. There is more information in the draft of the account (Bruges Town Accounts, Kladrekening, f. i) with comments in the margin on the guilds and burghers. See also Wyffels and Vandewalle, 451. Concerning the 1303 Zeeland expedition (ibid., 367–9), it is not certain that the burghers of Bruges took part.

[42] Wyffels and Vandewalle, 58: 3022 pounds, 15 shillings and 3 pence. For the two other expeditions, to Douai and Gravelines in 1302, the *pointinghe* tax raised the sum of 1456 pounds, 13 shillings and 1037 pounds and 10 shillings respectively (ibid., 59).

[43] Ibid., 59: 'Meuse Arnekine, den vischere, van sier pointinghe van der herevard te Duay, 10 lb.' (Meuse Arnekine, the fisher, from his *pointinghe* of the Douai expedition, 10 pounds). Soldiers from Cadsand made a payment thereby freeing themselves from their participation in the expeditions (ibid., 59). For 1303, see also ibid., 147, 151, 205. For 1304 see ibid., 308–16. For Ypres see G. des Marez and E. de Sagher, *Comptes de la ville d'Ypres de 1267 à 1329*, CRH (Brussels, 1909), I:178: 'recheut delle "pointinghe" faite sur cheus qui ne furent mie en l'ost devant Lille' (received from the *pointinghe* that was from those who were not sent in the army to Lille).

twenty-eight burghers.[44] The same occurred in 1309 with sixty-nine burghers included in the list of hostages.[45]

Therefore, the conclusion is that the burghers of Bruges did not take part in the Battle of the Spurs. They preferred to give financial support in the form of a voluntary or obligatory loan, or a *pointinghe* tax. They were obliged to pay such a tax on each occasion that an expedition took place, and in Bruges the tax was only paid by burghers.[46]

Several wealthy burghers lent very large sums to the town. Joris van der Matte advanced the highest sum of 1245 pounds, an immense fortune for a burgher with moderate possessions.[47] This example is very instructive: in 1297, Joris van der Matte was actually arrested by the Count, only being freed following the payment of one thousand pounds to Guy de Dampierre.[48] Joris van der Matte was one of the richest burghers, possessing more than three thousand pounds and having to maintain a horse with a value greater than forty pounds for military service.[49] It is difficult to explain why he was taken captive, if he were actually a loyal supporter of the Count. This leads rather to the conclusion that he belonged to the opponents of the Count who at the beginning of the war in 1297 were taken captive.[50] The loan in 1302 was therefore an obligatory loan, as also occurred in 1303 and 1304. This is all the more convincing in the case of Joris van der Matte since he loaned a sum of 2400 pounds in 1294–5.[51] This was certainly the case for those noblemen, such as Ghildolf van Gruuthuus and Jan Mast, who were taken captive during the Bruges Matins.[52] One ought therefore to be careful in

---

[44] Verriest, 485.

[45] L. A. Warnkoenig, *Flandrische Staats- und Rechtsgeschichte bis zum Jahre 1305* (Tübingen, 1835–42), I.2:145, Urkunden no. lxx; and de Limburg-Stirum, I:405, no. 180; I:406–12, no. 181.

[46] Wyffels and Vandewalle, 226: 'Willekin van Ghent ypoint over portere ende makelare vonden, van wederkeringhen van pointingh'; ibid., 181: 'Lamsin Balden den bakre van dat hie ghepoint was ende betaelt hadde als portre, 3 lb.'; ibid., 190: 'Wouter Vinnen van siere pointinghe van siere herevaert'; and ibid., 432: 'Willem Rijnvisch van dat hie thuus bleef'.

[47] Ibid., 67. Around 243 inhabitants of Bruges had possessions in excess of 1000 pounds. See De Smet, 'De inrichting', 487–8.

[48] Gilliodts-van Severen, I:56, no. 105. There were two burghers with this name, and Joris van der Matte, junior, was also a Liebaart, supporter of the rebellion, in 1302. See Wyffels and Vandewalle, 75, 77.

[49] De Smet, 'De inrichting', 502.

[50] See therefore the entry in Wyffels and De Smet, 561: 'Item, clericis scribentibus querelas opidi super bonis ipsorum sub Comite arrestatis.' See also Gilliodts-van Severen, I:55 n., and *Memoriaal der Schulden*, f. 15v.

[51] Wyffels and De Smet, 254, 282, 318, 341.

[52] Wyffels and Vandewalle, 56. The list of loans is reproduced by Gilliodts-van Severen, I:110–11, no. 169. Delfos, *Verkenningen door onze geschiedenis*, 31, based his example of Ghildolf van Gruuthuus on the above list. See Wyffels and Vandewalle, 374–5 and 921–2. In 1303 the men of Bruges had apparently learned that Ghildolf still had money hidden in the Ter Doest abbey. He then had to lend 1000 pounds, of which only 700 pounds would be repaid within a year following the war. See ibid., 130: 'Item van minen here Ghildolve yleent der stede van sinen ghelde dat cam van der Does, 1000 lb., van den welken men hem es sculdech te gheldenen bi der stede lettren binden jare na desen orloghe, 700 lb.' (The same being true for my lord, Ghildolve, who lent the town 1000 pounds of his own money that came from Ter Doest and

making judgements about the sentiments of Brugeois burghers who lent money to the rebels.

It is known that of 134 wealthy burghers – whose political persuasion can be ascertained in 1302 – fifty-nine were supporters of the King of France, while seventy-five burghers were still active in public life and supported the rebels.[53] However, as the example of Joris van der Matte indicates, we cannot consider all of the seventy-five remaining burghers as strong supporters of the Count. In fact, there is a further case similar to the above: that of burghers who before 1302 received a yearly income of twenty pounds from the King of France and were therefore supporters of the King. Among them one sees the following Flemish partisans of the King in 1302: Wouter f. Adelisen Calkre,[54] Jacob Groenendijc,[55] Jan van Hertsberghe,[56] Jan f. ser Pieters,[57] Jacob Lam,[58] Jan Wandelard.[59] The political opinion in 1302 of one wealthy burgher who did receive payments is not known: Robert or Roblot Cant.[60] Nicholas Alverdoe did not belong to the burghers' cavalry in 1292. His son Colard did, however, and also received the payment for his father as a supporter of the King in 1302.[61] Gerald Cant died before 11 November 1301, the date on which his brother, Philip Cant, a supporter of the King, received the payment.[62] Among them there was nevertheless a supporter of the Count in 1302, Willem Rijnvisch.[63] While Roblot Cant is to be seen as a supporter of the King, Willem Rijnvisch had perhaps been a supporter of the King and had been converted to the Count's cause following the Bruges Matins.

It is indeed self-evident that one cannot differentiate too clearly between them. Some wealthy burghers were perhaps very moderate supporters of the King; others had taken no position, although they followed those in power at that time. Certain burghers did not dare show their support of the Count in public. After the events of

---

of which the town is to pay him within a year following this war, 700 pounds.) In 1304, he lent a sum of 400 pounds: ibid., 374. Jan Mast's possessions were administered by the town: ibid., 175. In 1303, the town also received a further compulsory loan: ibid., 130: 'Item van Reinvarde f. Wouters ende Brande sinen neve van Jan Masts goede der stede yleent up der stede lettren, te gheldene sinen kindren binden jaren der naer dat dit orloghe sal sijn ghepaist, 566 lb.'

[53] De Smet, 'De inrichting', 488. Joris van der Matte, junior, has been counted as one of the supporters of the Count. Herman Bradenhee, or Hybradenheicle, must be considered as one of the supporters of the King of France. See V. Gaillard, *Inventaire analytique des chartes des comtes de Flandre* (Ghent, 1857), 143, no. 933. Bradenhee asked for compensation for losses incurred while supporting the King.

[54] *Journaux du trésor*, c. 1895; and De Smet, 'De inrichting', 501.

[55] *Journaux du trésor*, 771, c. 5305; and De Smet, 'De inrichting', 504.

[56] *Journaux du trésor*, 790, c. 5427; and De Smet, 'De inrichting', 502.

[57] *Journaux du trésor*, 226–7, 581, 790, c. 1398, 3956, 5427; and De Smet, 'De inrichting', 500.

[58] *Journaux du trésor*, 745, c. 5141; and De Smet, 'De inrichting', 499.

[59] *Journaux du trésor*, 790, c. 5427; and De Smet, 'De inrichting', 499.

[60] *Journaux du trésor*, 291, 546, 740, 772, c. 1837, 3678, 5105, 5308; and De Smet, 'De inrichting', 502.

[61] *Journaux du trésor*, 291, 584, 772, c. 1836, 3986, 5017, 5308; and De Smet, 'De inrichting', 502.

[62] *Journaux du trésor*, 645, 796, c. 4425, 5480; and De Smet, 'De inrichting', 503.

[63] *Journaux du trésor*, 790, c. 5427; and De Smet, 'De inrichting', 502.

Bruges Friday, they were faced with a clear choice: either they could join the artisans or not and be seen as a supporter of the King, this bringing with it the confiscation of their possessions. Should it be surprising that they chose to lend money, rather than have their possessions confiscated?

Perhaps there were fewer supporters of the King in 1297 than in 1302. In all events, they were able to impose their political decisions, since they transferred Bruges to Philip the Fair even though it had not been attacked. However, the events of 1301 and 1302 opened the eyes of a number of wealthy burghers, and they came to the conclusion that the situation had changed completely. During the government of Guy de Dampierre, they strove to maintain and even to extend their power in Bruges. At the same time, they sought to increase the town's power vis-à-vis that of the Count or at least to exercise powers of co- decision in the administration of the county. In order to attain this goal, they drew upon the support of the King of France. Now, however, they were suddenly faced with a much more powerful prince, Philip the Fair, who henceforth supported his representative in Flanders, Jacques de St Pol, against the men of Bruges. Their appeal to parliament also failed during the winter of 1301–2.

We note, then, that following the Bruges Matins the majority of the wealthy burghers supported the Count. Those sixty supporters of the King who were still to be found had certainly gone too far in the period 1297–1302. Other supporters of the King, who had not compromised themselves too much, would most probably have been left alone. Nevertheless, the consequence of all this was that the common people, the *gemeente* (townspeople), did not trust such burghers nor did they trust certain noblemen. This distrust is still to be noted after two years of war, on 18 August 1304, just before Battle of Mons-en-Pévèle was to begin.[64] This is clearly sufficient to explain why there was no mention of a separate burghers' corps in the rebels' army at Courtrai. The burghers' corps was not mentioned in the three military expeditions in 1302, that is Courtrai, Douai, Gravelines. It was not explicitly mentioned before the Zierikzee expedition on 11 May 1304. For these reasons, it may be assumed that it did not take part in the Battle of the Spurs. Obviously, individual burghers took part in the battle as supporters of the Count, whether in their guilds, or as crossbowmen, if members of that corps.

Conclusion. It has been seen above that the Bruges communal army present at Courtrai consisted of the following:

Council and entourage	60	soldiers	30	auxilaries
Crossbowmen	320	soldiers	160	auxilaries
Guildsmen	2060 or 3090	soldiers		

This gives a total of 2440 or 3470 heavily armed soldiers and 190 helpers carrying lighter weapons. It is known that the men of Bruges formed one of the three major corps in the battle array. This all points to their contingent having been

---

[64] *Annales Gandenses*, 65.

the greatest in numbers, as well as the most eminent. One can now proceed to an approximate calculation of the numerical strength of the whole army:

Bruges	2440 soldiers	190 helpers
Bruges Franc	2300 soldiers	160 helpers
East Flanders	2300 soldiers	160 helpers

The three major corps were composed therefore of a little over seven thousand soldiers with five hundred more lightly armed helpers. To this, the five hundred men of Ypres must be added, as well as the reserve corps, also composed of probably five hundred men, under the command of Jan van Renesse.

In total this makes eight thousand heavily armed soldiers and five hundred others, who were mostly helpers for the crossbowmen.

If the maximum numerical strength of the Bruges militia, with 3470 soldiers, can be assumed, the following is arrived at:

Bruges	3470
Bruges Franc	3000
East Flanders	3000

That is 9470 soldiers, or rounded off, 9500. A figure of 10,500 heavily armed soldiers is arrived at once the men of Ypres and Jan van Renesse's reserve corps are added. With the helpers this brings the figure to a maximum of 11,000 men. The Flemish army probably consisted of 8000 heavily armed soldiers, at maximum 10,500. If the helpers are included, a figure of 8500 to 11,000 men is arrived at.

If this information is compared with information from the period 1302–4, the conclusion is arrived at that Bruges had at that point not raised and sent large militias. For the first military expedition to Zeeland in 1303, the communal army consisted of aldermen and their entourage, 43 men, 200 crossbowmen, their 100 helpers, 190 mercenaries, and 830 guildsmen, a total of 1363 men.[65] The expedition began on 22 or 23 April. This first contigent was partially relieved or received replacements on 15 May and on 11 June. No other major expedition in which the men of Bruges participated had taken place in the intervening period.[66]

It is noted therefore that the lowest figure calculated for the Brugeois militia (2440 soldiers and 190 helpers) is still rather large, in comparison with the numerical strength of militias raised for the Zeeland expeditions in 1303 and 1304, and above all at the beginning of the campaign. In fact we see this original contingent being strengthened. Most probably the Battle of Courtrai was over earlier than expected, and thus troops could no longer be sent from the communal army to the battlefield. The Courtrai expedition was actually a *herevaart*, a count's expedition undertaken by part of the contingents in the county. If the army then raised was insufficient to carry out the task given it was strengthened with a *retrobannum*

---

[65] Wyffels and Vandewalle, 186–8; and Verbruggen, *Vlaanderen na de guldensporenslag*, 42.
[66] *Annales Gandenses*, 44; and Verbruggen, *Vlaanderen na de guldensporenslag*, 42, 46–7.

(reserve troops), and as a final resort the local militias comprised of all men, even priests, were called upon to take up arms.[67]

For the above reasons, it can be concluded that the lowest figure calculated for the rebels' army, that is eight thousand well-armed soldiers with around five hundred helpers, is the most probable. One should bear in mind that this was actually an army hurriedly drawn up at a time of revolution. Even Jean de Namur, the instigator of the rebellion, did not arrive on time. During this campaign, the fearful and indifferent, as well as those who had chosen a 'wait-and-see' approach, could all stay behind, since the authorities had not yet been fully established and were not able to make any investigations.

The forces included a contingent of Flemish and foreign noblemen, knights and squires. A determination of their numerical strength will now be attempted.

The noblemen

The most reliable sources, drawn up by those living at that time, give strong confirmation that only very few Flemish knights took part in the Battle of the Spurs. The Ghentenaar Friar Minor observed that there were barely ten knights in the army of Guy de Namur and Willem van Jülich.[68] He noted the following as the most prominent: Hendrik van Lontzen of the duchy of Limburg, Jan van Renesse of the county of Zeeland, Goswin van Gossenhoven of the duchy of Brabant, and Diederik van Hondschote, Robrecht van Leeuwergem and Boudewijn van Popperode, all three from the county of Flanders.[69] The *Chronique artésienne* noted, aside from Guy and Willem, Hendrik van Lontzen, Jan van Renesse, Diederik van Hondschote, Rogier de Lille, Robrecht van Leeuwergem, Otto van Steenhuize, and others from the guilds who had been knighted by Guy de Namur on 11 July.[70] Therefore, not many knights were present, and this is the general view given by the chroniclers. Villani also stated that there were no men on horseback aside from the commanders.[71] Gilles le Muisit explicitly confirmed the fact that, in comparison with troops on foot, there were few or very few men on horseback.[72]

One element is certain: those living at that time were of the opinion that the

---

[67] Lodewijk, II.1.IV:280, c. 19, vv. 1323–4: Guy de Namur, representing the Count, called together the *herevaart*, military expedition: 'Doen dedi gebieden herevard / Dapperlike te Cortrikeward' (called together an army to go bravely towards Courtrai). This can be seen when comparing the Lille and Douai military expeditions, *heervarten* (Lodewijk, II.1.IV:357, c. 44, vv. 3195–6; and *Annales Gandenses*, 33). In addition to *heervaart*, there was the *landweer*, national or local militia, formed to protect the country when a new French army advanced under the command of Philip the Fair: 'Het was in Vlaenderen uutgeboden / Om te werne dese noden, / Papen ende clerken, wat dat was, / Om lantwere te doen opten pas.' (In Flanders were summoned to defend against such dangers that priests and clerics all who were to have come forth as a *landweer*) (Lodewijk, II.1.IV:370, c. 48, vv. 3530–3). The Ghentenaar Friar Minor was actually in the army at that date: *Annales Gandenses*, 36.
[68] *Annales Gandenses*, 29.
[69] Ibid., 29.
[70] *Chronique artésienne*, 51: 'mais petit en y eut' (but few there were of them).
[71] Villani, 385.
[72] Le Muisit, 66.

knights and squires were scarce in comparison with the commoners fighting on foot. Since they were all fighting on foot, one was suddenly confronted with a wholly new army, the body of which was comprised of artisans and peasants rather than an elite corps of knights and squires. During the war, from 1302 to 1304, such foot-soldiers formed the only weapon for the rebel army, as well as later during the rebellion in the coastal areas of Flanders (1323–8). Noblemen, however, consistently played the most significant role in the French army; they formed the central force while the foot-soldiers were merely used as light foot-soldiers or counted for so little that they were not even mentioned in the sources. A revolution had thus taken place in the army of the county of Flanders on recruitment and, on account of this, tactics. From the texts cited, it is clear that those living at that time were very much aware of this fact. Since the chroniclers emphasised the fact that few noblemen were present a cautious approach must be adopted in determining their actual numerical strength.

The number of noblemen on horseback in the Flemish army is in fact very difficult to determine. The chroniclers did not know all the knights and, above all, the squires. The best source, the Bruges town accounts of the year 1302, do not for the most part give any dates for when noblemen were enlisted. For this reason, it cannot be ascertained whether they were already in the army before 11 July, whether they arrived with Jean de Namur or whether they were supporters of the King who joined the rebels following the great victory.[73]

In fact, the position of the noblemen in the period 1297 to 1304 has never been subjected to an exhaustive study.[74] In this respect, a significant amount of information from the sources on the approximately five hundred Flemish noblemen and around fifty foreigners has been gathered together. This research is still not complete, although it will nevertheless be useful to present some of the results at this stage. A separate study will develop the findings further.

(a) The position taken by the Flemish nobility in the period 1297–1302
It is generally assumed that the rupture of feudal ties between the Count, Guy de Dampierre, and his feudal lord, Philip the Fair, presented the Flemish nobility with a difficult problem. In the event of a rebellion, they were obliged, according to the Treaty of Melun, to support the King against their prince. However, since Philip IV had refused recourse to a judgement by the peers, they were no longer obliged to fulfil the treaty.

The Count's termination of allegiance naturally led to the rupture of the feudal ties between him and certain French noblemen. Thus, the following French or foreign noblemen, having previously received fiefs from Count Guy, then terminated their feudal ties with the Count. They were the Count of Dreux, Raoul

---

[73] *Annales Gandenses*, 33.
[74] Delfos, *1302 door tijdgenooten verteld*, 98–9, made a first attempt with a study of the supporters of the Count, although he also included foreign noblemen and did not take account of the defections among the future supporters of the King. W. Prevenier, 'Motieven voor leliaardsgezindheid in Vlaanderen in de periode 1297–1305', *De Leiegouw*, 19 (1977), 275–7; several of the nobles in his list were French and not Flemish.

Flamens,[75] Jean de Harcourt and Baudouin de Fontaine.[76] Only one Flemish nobleman acted likewise: Eustaes van Neuville.[77] In addition to this, there was also Gilbert, the Viscount of St Winoksbergen, who in 1297 fought with the French army in Gascony and following this fought against his compatriots with the French knights.[78] Finally, there is the special case of Jan van Oudenaarde, Lord of Rosoit. In 1296, he was living in the centre of France at Berry.[79] Moreover, he had, prior to this, been in constant conflict with the Count and supported Jean d'Avesnes during the dispute about the properties, Lessen and Flobecq.[80] His brother, Arnulf, was alleged to have hesitated so much about which party he ought to choose that he entrusted to Walram van Valkenburg and Willem van Mortagne the solution to this matter of conscience.[81] In fact this is not wholly true and the choice of adjudicators indicates how erroneous the above conception is. Walram van Valkenburg was a nobleman of the Rhine area who served in Guy de Dampierre's army in 1297 in return for a fief or as a mercenary. Willem van Mortagne was one of the Count's most loyal vassals.[82] Clearly, the judgement given by the two noblemen would, at the outset, have been favourable to the Flemish Count.

In fact, there is another reason for the animosity of Jan van Oudenaarde and the actions of his brother, Arnulf. Their brother, Robrecht, committed several murders at a time that is difficult to determine, and was subsequently murdered himself probably at the instigation of the Count.[83] On account of this, a dispute arose, certainly as early as 1295, when legal proceedings were initiated by the Count against Arnulf. The dispute was only settled by Walram van Valkenburg and Willem van Mortagne on 25 June 1297 in Lille, which at that time was already encircled. For this reason, Arnulf joined the Count's army. Furthermore, the judgement pronounced mentioned the murder of Robrecht van Oudenaarde.[84]

The political persuasion of another nobleman is just as arbitrary. On 2 June

---

[75] Funck-Brentano, *Philippe le Bel*, 216. Fris, *De slag bij Kortrijk*, 300, erroneously considered Raoul Flamens to be a supporter of the King.
[76] Funck-Brentano, *Philippe le Bel*, 216 n. 1.
[77] Ibid., 216–17. The author saw such an action as general without any proof thereof.
[78] *Journaux du trésor*, 99 and n. 1, c. 622; and *Chronique artésienne*, 15.
[79] Funck-Brentano, *Philippe le Bel*, 221 n. 1. The text proves that he was living in Berry at that time. Following this, he received a fiefdom from Philip the Fair.
[80] C. Dehaisnes and J. Finot, *Inventaire sommaire des archives départementales antérieures à 1790, Nord, Archives départementales, Série B* (Paris, 1872–1931), I.2:250–1 (22 January 1296).
[81] According to Funck-Brentano, *Philippe le Bel*, 220–1. Brentano referred very cleverly to the work of L. Devillers, 'Notice sur un cartulaire concernant les terres dites de débat (Hainaut et Flandre)', *BCRH*, 4th ser., 3 (1875–6), 480, no. 15. However, the analysis of the document was so summarized that it permits any conclusion to be drawn. The document can be found in the Lille Archives départementales, B. 244, 3870. See Godefroy, V, no. 3970.
[82] He accompanied the Count when he was taken captive. See below.
[83] De St Genois, 230, no. 784.
[84] Godefroy, V, no. 3970. A sound analysis was given by Dehaisnes and Finot, I.1:190. Two documents, erroneously dated to around 1260, still exist which concern crimes committed by Robrecht van Oudenaarde: Godefroy, I, nos. 1271, 1272 (B 1543, 1271, 1272). See also Dehaisnes and Finot, I.2:497, also dated incorrectly.

1297, Robert de Bethune temporarily removed the Lille bailiff, Pieter van Sainghin, until the arrival of his father, as Pieter had taken several clerics captive, contrary to orders given by the Count and by Robrecht.[85] However, this was judged not to have been the real reason, which allegedly had to do with the fact that Pieter was a supporter of the King. As bailiff, Pieter would have been in command of the troops in that area.[86] The above reasoning is complete fiction: in Lille the Viscount was in command of the troops.[87] Furthermore, Pieter van Sainghin was not a supporter of the King, but of the Count, as evidenced by another document. Charges had actually been brought against Pieter who was subsequently excommunicated by the Tournai official for holding captive Piat de Seclin, priest and chaplain at the church of Seclin. The bailiff appealed to the Pope since he had not been able to attend the proceedings in Tournai because of the war and furthermore had not been able to send a representative.[88] If Pieter had been a supporter of the King, he would have been able to travel to Tournai or to send a representative. As a supporter of the Count, he was not able to do so. This is certainly not an example of clear reasoning on the two tests: the name of Pieter van Sainghin clearly figured in the list of Flemish noblemen who accompanied Guy and his sons in 1300 when taken captive.[89]

Thus, the great majority of Flemish noblemen rallied to the Count's cause at the beginning of the war. This appears from the following list of knights who took part in the defence of Lille:

Willem van Mortagne, Lord of Dossemer
Raas of Liedekerke
Wouter, Viscount of Courtrai, Lord of Nevele
Geraard, Lord of Zottegem, Viscount of Ghent
Wouter van Hondschote
Robert, Lord of Montigni
Geraard de Moor, Lord of Wessegem
Olivier, Lord of Aishove
Jan, Lord of Gistel
Goswin, Lord of Erpe
Geraard, Lord of Vertbois
Diederik van Hondschote
Baudouin, Lord of Auberchicourt
Willem van Gistel
Jan, Lord of Praat

---

[85] Dehaisnes and Finot, I.2:261.
[86] Funck-Brentano, *Philippe le Bel*, 244.
[87] R. Monier, *Le Livre Roisin*, in *Documents et travaux publiés par la société d'histoire du droit des pays flamands, picards et wallons* (Paris and Lille, 1932), II:125, c. 195.
[88] See de St Genois, 276–7, no. 953. Funck-Brentano also cited the same document. De St Genois gave further examples of such appeals made to the Pope as Flemish knights were not able to make appeals at Tournai (Robert de Bethune, Willem van Nevele, etc.). See de St Genois, 265–6, no. 910; and 275, no. 948.
[89] See the list of those taken captive below.

Hellin, Lord of Armentières
Willem van Nevele
Wouter van Halewijn
Geraard, Lord of Rode
Jan van Rode, Lord of Ingelmunster[90]

Thus, noblemen who were later to support the King were still fighting for the Count: Jan and Willem van Gistel, Jan van Praat, Wouter van Halewijn, and Robert de Montigni were to receive a fief-rente or to be compensated or to join the King's army later, as did Wouter van Hondschote and Baudouin van Auberchicourt.

The defections began at the time of the negotiations of the surrender of Lille. Supporters of the King still in the Count's army chose that moment to secure their future. Or was it rather a skilful move on the part of royal counsellors? In any case, knights and their squires were able, for a period of fifteen days following the capitulation of Lille, to join the King's men or to stay with the Count. These were the conditions, reached by the negotiations led by the above noblemen, by which the capitulation of the town was effected. Due to the above conditions of capitulation, the supporters of the King now had a legal basis on which they could join the King following their fulfilment of their feudal obligations towards the Count.[91] It is known that the retreating Flemings attempted to take with them one of the defectors, Robrecht van Archises.[92] It was at that stage that Robrecht van Wavrin, Lord of St Venant, Jan, Lord of Gistel, and Wouter van Hondschote defected to the King's side.[93] According to Lodewijk, Jan van Gistel and the Viscount of Furnes defected during the Battle of Furnes.[94] However, Jan van Gistel was then in the Count's army at Lille, and the Viscount of Furnes continued in his support of the Count.[95]

There is also another very interesting list of knights and squires showing goods delivered at Damme and Aardenburg. The list has hitherto been dated to 1300, although this appears rather improbable since a number of supporters of the King still figure in the list. They included the Lord of St Venant, the Lord of Hazebrouck and other supporters of the King in 1302, such as the Lord of Sijsele. The document more probably relates to the military operations that took place in 1297,

---

[90] De Limburg-Stirum, I:199–200, no. 58.
[91] Ibid., I:199–200, no. 58; and Funck-Brentano, *Philippe le Bel*, 258.
[92] *Chronique artésienne*, 17: Robrecht van Attiches?
[93] *Annales Gandenses*, 3–4.
[94] Lodewijk, II.1.IV:241, c. 6, vv. 389–91.
[95] Ibid., II.1.IV:241 n. The Viscount of Furnes, at that time, was presumed to have been Christiaan de Brabantre whose possessions were given to Boudewijn van Zeggherscappel. See Godefroy, V, no. 4095; and de Coussemaker, 108. According to Nowé, Jan van Stavele was the Viscount of Furnes at that time, and his possessions were given to the Flemish supporter of the King, Wouter Ronne. See H. Nowé, 'Fonctionnaires flamands passés au service royal durant la guerre de Flandre', *Revue du nord*, 10 (1924), 270.

although it is also possible that it is to be associated with an earlier campaign such as, for example, the Zeeland expedition.[96]

It is of more importance in studying the Battle of Courtrai to ascertain who was a supporter of the King, since such noblemen obviously did not take part in the battle, unless, that is, they changed sides. This is perhaps the case for several knights and squires. The names of those noblemen who supported the King and received possessions confiscated from the Count's followers are known. There is also an interesting list of supporters of the King from the bailiwick of Cassel on which there is full information. There is a list of knights serving the King of France in 1303, although the list omitted to mention the squires. Finally, one can add several individual noblemen who were known to have been supporters of the King, as well as those Flemish knights who were taken captive during the famous events of Bruges Friday.

(b) Flemish supporters of the King who received payments or other compensation for damages suffered

	Date	Godefroy, V, no. 427[97]
Hendrik van Zoutenaaie, knight	April 1298	4062
Jan Lauwaerd, knight	April 1298	4063, 4064
Simon Lauwaerd, knight	April 1298	4065
Jan van Zoutenaaie, knight	April 1298	4066
Willem van Zoutenaaie	April 1298	4068
Wouter Ronne, knight[98]	April 1298	4069
Michel Renier (possibly not a nobleman)	April 1298	4070
Baudouin de le Planke, Lord of Thiennes, of Steenbecque and of Heuchin	15 July 1298	4088
Boudewijn van Zeggherscappel	28 July 1298	4095
Boudewijn Stier	28 July 1298	4096
Jean du Bois	28 July 1298	4097
Jan Plateil, knight	28 July 1298	4100
Hugues li Flamencs	21 October 1298	4120
Jan, Lord of Haveskerke	30 November 1298	4129
Gillis van Haveskerke, knight	30 November 1298	4130
Lonis van Moerkerke, knight	3 December 1298	4131
Jan van Praet, knight	28 January 1299	4143
Rogier van Lichtervelde, knight	28 January 1299	4144
Hendrik van Rosebeke	29 January 1299	4145
Boudewijn van Assebroek, knight	29 January 1299	4146
Boudewijn Prijm, squire	29 January 1299	4147
Boudewijn van Wendin, knight	29 January 1299	4148

[96] De Limburg-Stirum, I:300–2, no. 118. See also Funck-Brentano, *Philippe le Bel*, 335, who also incorrectly dated it to 1300.
[97] Part of the documents has been published by de Coussemaker, 104–66.
[98] For further information on Wouter Ronne, Jan and Simon Lauwaerd, see Nowé, 'Fonctionnaires flamands passés au service royal', 265.

Jan van Hangest, knight	29 January 1299	4149
Wouter, son of Wertin (or Wetin?)	11 February 1299	4151
Jan van Cadzand	11 February 1299	4152
Wouter van Halewijn, knight	11 February 1299	4153
Hues dele Court, creek-keeper	20 February 1299	4158
Anselm van Aigremont, knight	23 February 1299	4159
Willem van Boulinghiem, squire	19 March 1299	4167
Philips du Breucq, knight	20 March 1299	4168
Wouter van Broekburg, knight	20 March 1299	4169
Daniel van Ghuines, squire	23 March 1299	4171
Willem van Mosscher, squire	2 April 1299	4179
Boudewijn van Haveskerke, knight	16 July 1299	4225
Jean de le Planke, knight	25 July 1299	4246
Robrecht Broiart van Maldegem, squire	February 1300	4276
Pierre du Breucq, knight	February 1300	4277
Robert de Montigni, knight[99] Jacob van Lokeren, knight[100]	15 June 1301	4359

(c) Flemish supporters of the King in the bailiwick of Cassel[101]

Henri du Briard	Cassel town and the parish of Our Lady
Gilles Baras	Cassel town and the parish of Our Lady
Jean du Cornus	Cassel town and the parish of Our Lady
Guillaume du Breucq	Cassel town and the parish of Our Lady
Colard du Breucq	Cassel town and the parish of Our Lady
Jan van Landas	Hardifort and Zermezeele
Jacob Hardifort	Hardifort and Zermezeele
Simon van Cornus	Hildeward-Cappel
Willem van Cappel	Hildeward-Cappel
Raoul van Eecke	Eecke
Geraard Ghiselbrecht	Eecke
Gerard de le Borre	Borre
Lord Cordewans de le Borre	Borre
Pieter Boudens	Borre
Lord Capelains de le Borre	Borre
Hendrik Lonis	Strazele[102]
Lord Walter de l'Escaghe	Vieux-Berquin
Jean, son of the above	Vieux-Berquin

---

[99] *Chronique artésienne*, 32 n. 2.
[100] Jacob van Lokeren was perhaps not a supporter of the King. He received confirmation of his previous fief that was increased slightly.
[101] De Coussemaker, 162–6. The list was apparently drawn up by the Count of Flanders since it indicated who was a vassal of the Count. Only the knights and vassals have been listed and, it is probable, although not certain for all of them, that the vassals were squires. In total, the list contains the names of 20 lords and 55 vassals as well as common subjects of the Count. It was probably drawn up after the war, and certainly after 11 July 1302, since it noted that two noblemen fell at Courtrai.
[102] Also Boudewijn van Wendin (see above).

Lord Alelm of Berquin	Vieux-Berquin
Walter de Lespesse	Vieux-Berquin
Jean de Lespesse	Vieux-Berquin
Jean f. Jean de l'Escaghe	Vieux-Berquin
Lord Hugo of Tannay	Thiennes[103]
Lord Gilbert Dorey (or Dorez)	Thiennes
Lord Jean Dorey (or Dorez)	Thiennes
Didier des Preis	Thiennes
Gilbert, son of the above	Thiennes
Jean de Morbecque[104]	Morbecque
Jean de le Gumiele	Morbecque[105]
Mathieu de le Couture	Blaringhem
Lord Pasteis van Mussem	Blaringhem
Jean li Grans	Blaringhem
Pieter Reymons	Blaringhem
Robert Barisiaus	Blaringhem
Baudouin de le Valée	Blaringhem
Gerald Montreul	Merville
Jean de Koysiancourt	Merville
Kamus de Lescaghe	Merville
Walter du Sart	Merville
Jacob Warmisel	Merville
Frans, son of John of Haveskerke	Haverskerque[106]
Guillaume de Eske	Haverskerque
Lord Hendrik van Hazebrouck	Hazebrouck[107]
Hendrik, son of the above	Hazebrouck
Boudewijn van Hazebrouck	Hazebrouck
Henri of Castres (Caestre)	Hazebrouck
Maes Chavet	Hazebrouck
Jean du Biest	Hazebrouck
Laurens du Werf	Hazebrouck
Lord Jan van Hazebrouck	Hazebrouck
Jan van Walloncappel	Walloncappel
Jean del Ekout	Walloncappel
Lord Maelins van Kaudescure	Kienvile = Hondeghem
Raas van Kienville	Kienvile = Hondeghem
Gillis Mervelle	Kienvile = Hondeghem
Jean du Gardin	Kienvile = Hondeghem
Guillaume du Briard	Kienvile = Hondeghem
Lambert du Briard	Kienvile = Hondeghem[108]
Jean du Cornhus	Our Lady of Cassel and Oxelaere[109]

[103] Also the Lord of Heuchin (Baudouin de le Planke).
[104] Also 'medame de Morbieke'.
[105] At Sercus: Lord Jean de le Planke (see above).
[106] Lord Jan van Haveskerke (see above).
[107] Lord Jan van Hangest (see above).
[108] And 'medame de Wiske'.
[109] In Oudezeele: Lord Jan van Zoutenaaie and Willem van Zoutenaaie. See also above.

Lord Rogier van Oxelaere[110]	Our Lady of Cassel and Oxelaere
Oste van Oxelaere	Our Lady of Cassel and Oxelaere[111]
Bertelmeus de le Mote	Our Lady of Cassel and Oxelaere
Lord Geraard Mauwer	Pene
Jan Mauwer	Pene
Lord Jan van Pene	Pene
Lord Isoret van Pene	Pene
Gilbert van Pene	Pene
Wouter van Bolc	

(d) Flemish supporters of the King serving in France in 1303[112]

Hellin de Vaisières (or Waisiers)	Wouter van Woumen
Jan van Gistel	Otto Bruni (?)
Bernard de Colompna (?)	Hugo Guillart (Gaillart?)
The Lord of Hondschote	Hellin de Cysoing
Gui du Bois (de Bosco)	Karreu de Brolio (Colard du Breucq?)
Pierre du Mès (Moys?)	
Rogier de Pesques	Jan van Sijsele
Ro. van Halewijn (Wouter?)	Jan van Woumen
Boudewijn Ruffin	Jan van Poele
Philips van Gistel	Gislijn Kief
The Lord of Izegem	Nicholas de le Borre
Rogier van Izegem, the younger	Meslin de Beausart
Boudewijn van Dudzele	Jean de Brueil
Aimer de Neuville	Walter, Viscount of Douai
Willem, brother of Jan van Pene	Robrecht van Bambele, having recently become a knight
Jan van Esen	
Wouter van Gistel	Baudouin de Mote
Bernard de Auberbus (?)	Gerald Maine, having recently become a knight
Jean de Courts (Jan van den Hove?)	
Goswin de St Aubin	Jan Drincham

---

[110] Prior to this, the possessions of Rogier van Oxelaere and his wife, Beatrice, had been given to Willem van Zoutenaaie. See de Coussemaker, 146–7.

[111] Concerning Boudewijn van Zeggherscappel (see above).

[112] This list was given by du Cange who, however, did not copy the names of the squires. See RHF, 22:765–6. It gives the names of the Flemish knights and the sums paid for the period of Ascension 1303. There are 67 names, although two people are mentioned twice: Hellin de Vaisières (Waisiers) and Anselm de Aigremont, keeper of Tournai. Furthermore, there are five noblewomen included in the list: the wife of Landas; the widow of Hendrik van Hazebrouck, Aelipdis; the sister of Lord Hazebrouck, Ydo; Wistachia, Lady of Morbecque and a widow; and, in addition to this, Maria, Lady of Cussell. However, the names given are at times corrupt. From the list of noblemen already mentioned, the list notes: Jan van Zoutenaaie, Jan van Hangest, Wouter Ronne, Jan van Haveskerke, Hendrik van Zoutenaaie, Baudouin and Jean de la Planke, Jan and Isoret van Pene, Simon and Jan Lauwaerd, Anselm de Aigremont, Willem van Zoutenaaie, having at that point become a knight, Alelm de Berquin, Jan Plateel, Gilbert Dorez, Jan van Hazebrouck, recently knighted, and Daniel de Ghuines, who had also been knighted.

Gislijn van Poele
Michel le Maucre
Willem Platiau

Wouter van Teteghem
Robert of St Venant

(e) Flemish, French and other noblemen taken captive on Bruges Friday[113]

Flemish noblemen	French, Hainaulter and other noblemen
Riquard van der Beerst	Lord Gillis Dousard
Wouter van Heule	Lord Jean Warchiniel
Jan Mast	Hughe le Poure
Lord Rogier van Lichtervelde	Jean de Dareniau
Lord Ghildolf van Gruuthuus	Jean de Molenbays
Lord Willem van Clerken, the younger	Gerald de Molenbays
Lord Jan Casekin van Beerst	Jean dele Carnoye
Lord Lonis van Moerkerke	Lambrecht Dousard
Lord Willem van Straten	Pierre Pottreans
Gillis Brunele van Stavele	Guyon Cretoene
Wouter Randolf van Seclin	Lord Robert Ferteele
Lord Gillis van Bavikhove	Lord Renoud dou Sens
Pieter de Deurwaerder	Lord Jean de Mons
The Lord of Broukerke	Lawrence den Clerc
Diederik van der Gracht	Guillaume de Moermay
Jacob van der Capelle	Jean de Maugrei
The Lord of Pene[114]	Jean de Hamelincourt
The Lord of Halewijn	Jean de Walebeke
Jan van der Haghe	Bouden de Beauche
Wouter van der Muelne	Jean de Moyenvile
Jan de Clerc van Risele	Colard dou Puuts
Willem van den Hove	and his son
Bouden van den Bussche	Gillis de Lens du Casteler
The Lord of Poeke	Bredon de Bethune
The Lord of Aishove and his entourage	and his brother
Jan van Harelbeke	Jean de la Faleche
Lord Gilbert Dorez	Lord Mathieu du Vail (or de le Val)[115]
Wouter, Lord of Hondschote	Gontelette of Mauden
Lord Willem van Gistel	Gillis Maugrete
Bouden van Langelede	Gillis de la Hemme
The Lord of Praet	Jean de Nueville (Neufville)
Lord Willem van Zeggherscappel	Jean dele Fosse[116]
Daniel Scake	Rogier de Corbinangiel

---

[113] Wyffels and Vandewalle, 56–8; and J. De Smet, 'De gezindheid van de Vlaamse ridders in 1302', *Biekorf*, 51 (1950), 145–7.

[114] Wyffels and Vandewalle, 126, n. g: Jan van Pene and his brothers, Willem and Isoret, were warrants for Venant van Teteghem.

[115] On 17 October 1297, Philip the Fair gave the fiefs of Mathieu de le Val, Hugo and Robert de Maude, and Gerald de Potes to the Count of Hainault, all previously being held in fief from Guy de Dampierre. See Godefroy, V, nos. 4005, 4209.

[116] It is possible that Jean de Neuville and Jean dele Fosse (vander Gracht) were Flemish.

Bouden van der Vichte
Philip, his brother
Pieter van der Ameyde
Jan de Valkenare
Rogier van den Bussche
Willem van Wulskerke
Jan van Wulskerke
Lord Diederik van der Hasselt
Jan van Coeyenghem
Lord Venant van Teteghem[118]
Bossart of Roebaais

Colard de Beaumont
Alard de Frennoyt
The Lord of Fosseus
Lord Hastiau de Noele
and his brother
Machette de Brittany
Havet de Fermin[117]
Le borgne de Merchays

The list includes the names of several supporters of the King mentioned earlier, such as Rogier van Lichtervelde, Lonis van Moerkerke, the Lord of Pene, the Lord of Halewijn, Wouter van Hondschote, Gilbert Dorez and the Lord of Praet. However, it cannot be assumed that all those noblemen whose names were not listed were supporters of the King. The difference became clear immediately upon their release, with some noblemen entering the service of the King, where they were to be found in 1303, and the others knights who stayed in Flanders. It is possible that the latter continued to be supporters of the King, although they did not undertake any action against the followers of the Count. Among them, however, there were men who quickly joined the Flemish army, such as Wouter van Broukerke and the squire, Riquard van der Beerst.[119]

Finally, there are still several supporters of the King whose names were not given in the lists:

Gilbert, Viscount of St Winoksbergen (who had already died by 15 June 1299)
Jan van Oudenaarde
Eustaes van Neuville
Jan V, Viscount of Lille
Robrecht van Archises (Attiches?)[120]
Hugo van Hondschote
Alart van Berdelaar[121]
Michel, Lord of Wendin,[122] all knights

---

[117] For this nobleman see Wyffels and Vandewalle, 126.
[118] For this nobleman see ibid., 126.
[119] Gilliodts-van Severen, I:162–3, no. 185. Bouffart van Roebaais fought on the side of the Flemings in 1304. See de Limburg-Stirum, I:316, no. 316.
[120] See above for the noblemen.
[121] For Hugo van Hondschote and Alart van Berdelaar see Lodewijk, II.1.IV:361, c. 45, v. 3284, 3305. Alart van Berdelaar was a supporter of the Count in 1300. See de Limburg-Stirum, I:299, no. 117.
[122] *Journaux du trésor*, 745, c. 5142.

The list of the Flemish supporters of the King is obviously not complete, with some individuals certainly having been overlooked, and the list omits the squires for 1303. However, some form of an estimate can be provided since the number of squires from the bailiwick of Cassel is known. It is sufficient to calculate the percentage that knights from the Cassel bailiwick formed in the 1303 list. Following this, the figure can be used to calculate a theoretical number of squires for the whole of Flanders.

In 1303, the list of Flemish noblemen included the following persons from Cassel: Jan, Hendrik and Willem van Zoutenaaie, Jan van Hangest, Jan van Haveskerke, Boudewijn Ruffin, Boudewijn and Jan dele Planke, Jan, Willem and Isoret van Pene, Alelm van Berquin, the lady of Landas, Gilbert Dorez, Nicolaas de le Borre, Jan van Hazebrouck, the widow of Hendrik van Hazebrouck and his sister, Boudewijn van Mote, Wouter van Teteghem, Robrecht van St Venant, Wistachia, widow of the Lord of Morbecque. This makes a total of twenty-two persons out of sixty-seven. Now it is still possible that noblemen, such as Pieter van Mès, Gislijn Kief and others, also came from that area. Thus, it seems that Flemish supporters of the King from the Cassel area made up approximately one third of the total in 1303. This would give a total for those squires supporting the King throughout the county of 3 × 55 or 165. To this, one can add the knights listed above: approximately one hundred. This then gives a provisional total of 265 noblemen who were Flemish supporters of the King, certainly not a majority in the county.

Concerning the knights, however, the lists of names might be considered almost complete since, in particular, the lists for Cassel for 1303 and for the Bruges Matins are confirmed by other reliable sources. These other sources are, for example, the Bruges town accounts for 1302 which also noted the confiscated goods of noblemen in the Bruges Franc. Thus, against the hundred or so knights listed above who supported the King may be set an equal number of prisoners in France, for the year 1300, as well as for 1302 (according to the Brugeois documents).[123] If an account of the period 1297–1300 and the period 1302–4 is taken, there are at least a hundred and fifty knights supporting the Count and probably many more once a more complete examination has been undertaken.

It is also certainly possible that, among the noblemen, there were more Flemish supporters of the King than of the Count in the Cassel area, since it was situated on the border. This certainly appears to have been the case for the knights, although it can still be doubted for the fifty-five squires from that area.

Obviously, the Flemish supporters of the King did not fight on the side of the common people at Courtrai. Other noblemen were still being held prisoner in France. Originally, in 1300, the following Flemish prisoners, most of whom belonged to the nobility, were being held prisoner there.

---

[123] See below.

(f) Flemish supporters of the Count held prisoner in France

(a) *Codex Diplomaticus*, I:303–5, no. 120

Lord Jan Boie Pieter de le Foresterie
Jan dele Hongherie
Lord Wouter van Broukerke (see also Bruges Matins, the Lord of Broukerke)
Lord Geraard van Massemen
Jan Sporart
Robrecht de Biaurepair
Eustaas Scemekart
Conrad de le Heille
Boudewijn Phelippe
Lord Rogier van Clarout
Adam van Dierdonc, and several others
Olivier van Voroud
Jacob Dorchies (of Orchies?)
Tassins de le Langerie
Jacob Meurins
Rogaus de Herignies
Bouden van Bantingni
Bouden van Gorgenies and several others
Lord Jan Bondues
Lord Jan van Menen
Lord Jan van Lembeke
Lord Michiel van Lembeke
Lord Willem van Huise
Jan van Kemmel, son of the Lord of Kemmel
Lord Godfried van Ranzières (or Rozières)
Lord Philips van Axel
Lord Boudewijn van Mooregem
Lord Jan de la Pontenerie
Lord Jan Hernust[124]
Philips van Glenne
Arnout li Alemans
Libert van Fero
Defraines van Kevalcamp
Jan Heem
Wouter van der Gracht (dou Fossé)
Olivier van Clarout
Diederik, son of Wouter van der Gracht (see also Bruges Matins, prisoner)
Geraard van Hoorne
Caudrons, and others
Tassins de Rustine
Lord Arnout Barnage
Lord Wouter van Lauwe
The Lord of Clarout
Lord Jan Brisepot
Lord Jan van Oostkerke
Lord Hendrik Evelbaren
Lord Thomas van Vaernewijck
Lord Jan van Vimi
Lord Jan Tick (Tisike, le Muisit, p. 59; de Tileque, *Codex Diplomaticus*, II:9)
Lord Boudewijn van Passchendale
Lord Boudewijn van Heyle
Lord Ywein van Beukemare
Lord Pieter van Senghien
Lord Jacob van Mounes
Lord Jan van Annetières, chaplain to the Count
Jan de Tollenare

(b) Kervyn de Lettenhove, *Histoire de Flandre*, II:618–19

Lord Geraard de Moor
Lord Geraard van Vertbois
Lord Willem van Mortagne
Lord Jan van Rode
Lord Willem van Clanlers
Lord Ywein van Vaernewijck
Lord Willem van Nevele
Lord J. Chapis
Lord Rijkaard Standaart
Lord Philips van Axpoel

---

[124] Also Jean de Juede of Oostburg and Jan van Homberke, *keukemaistre* (cook or kitchen master). Willem, squire of the Lord Jan Hernust and all the squires of Libert van Fero have also been omitted.

Lord Zeger van Kortrijk
Lord Arnulf van Oudenaarde
Lord Wouter van Nevele
Lord Alard van Roubaix (Roebaais)
Lord Raas Mulaert
Lord Willem van Steenhuize
Lord Jan Barnage
Lord Jan van Poele
Lord Valentijn van Nieperkerke
Lord Gwij van Torhout
Lord Wouter van Lovendegem
Lord Jan Wevel (or van Wevel)
Lord Jan van Heyle

Lord Boudewijn, the younger (also known as Boudewijn van Kwaadieper)
Lord Rogier van Gistel (ibid., p. 615)
Lord Philips van Maldegem
Lord Pieter van Uitkerke
Lord Diederik de Vos
Lord Jan van Gent (Jan van Aalst, bailiff of Ghent?)
Lord Jan van Belle
Lord Willem van Knesselare
Lord Godschalk van Volmarbeke[125]

In this list have been included all those names gained from the diplomatic sources – confirmed, on the whole, by the narrative sources even if such sources are not so exhaustive – and finally several other persons found in the chronicles. Any person who could have been a squire has been included, since there is not, in fact, very secure knowledge in this matter. The list thus contains many more names than previous works, since it was usual practice only to note the better-known and more powerful noblemen. Such a practice was obviously incorrect, as the squires also must be counted. It is of the utmost importance to know who was being held captive, as members of their family, as well as those supporters of the Count who had possessions confiscated, rushed to Courtrai in July 1302. If it cannot be ascertained which noblemen were held prisoner, then important details of events remain out of our grasp. Several examples indicate this. Jan van Menen was being held prisoner in France and his son, Jan, was already fighting in the siege of Cassel in June 1302.[126] In addition to Jan van Menen, the documents from the end of July 1302 also mention Pieter van Menen.[127] This all indicates that both knights took part in the Battle of Courtrai.[128] Geraard de Moor was still being held captive in France. His brother, Philips de Moor was mentioned in the July 1302 Bruges town accounts, and this is also the case for squires who had belonged to Geraard's entourage, such as Gheylinc[129] and Geraard van Uitkerke. who in the mean time had become a knight. A member of his family, Pieter van Uitkerke, was still being held captive in France.[130] Michiel and Jan van Lembeke were also still being held in France. One squire, Jakemin van Lembeke, however, was mentioned in the Bruges town account.[131] Thomas and Iwein van Vaernewijck were also being held in

---

[125] Philips van Maldegem was taken prisoner in 1300 (*Annales Gandenses*, 10). From Philips van Maldegem onwards, Lodewijk (II.1.IV:248, c. 7, vv. 510–19) and the *Chronicon Comitum Flandrensium* (164–5) have been followed. See also le Muisit, 59.
[126] Lodewijk, II.1.IV:282, c. 20, vv. 1355–6.
[127] Gilliodts-van Severen, I:77, no. 155.
[128] Neither of the two was mentioned in the list of participants given by Fris, *De slag bij Kortrijk*, 303–12.
[129] Wyffels and Vandewalle, 76. See also de St Genois, 263, no. 902.
[130] Wyffels and Vandewalle, 74. See also de St Genois, 263, no. 902.
[131] Wyffels and Vandewalle, 75.

France; Simon van Vaernewijck was one of the first followers of Willem van Jülich.[132] Jan Wevel and Jan van Belle were still being held captive; Hugo Wevel, Zeger and Pieter van Belle were mentioned in the same place in the town accounts.[133] Alard van Roebaais was also being held prisoner in France; Geraard van Roebaais took part in the Battle of Courtrai.[134] Philips van Axel had managed to escape and fought on 11 July in the Flemish ranks.[135] Willem van Steenhuize was also being held captive in a French castle, although Otto van Steenhuize fought at Courtrai.[136]

Others, such as Thomas de Lille, had lost their possessions in 1298.[137] However, Thomas was mentioned as being one of those who fought on the Flemish side from the earliest moment. At a later time, he ensured the defence of the Carembaut area with the Pont-à-Vendin passage.[138] Is it possible to claim that a person such as the above knight did not take part in the Battle of Courtrai since he was not mentioned by a chronicler?[139]

After drawing up the list of Flemish supporters of the King and those of the Count who had been taken prisoner, those who fought at Courtrai probably cannot be ascertained. Nevertheless, some noblemen had meanwhile escaped and others had stopped supporting the King. Here certain exceptions will be briefly indicated.

It is now possible to turn back to the main problem: who took part in the battle on 11 July 1302? In drawing up the list of Flemish noblemen who took part, there are some very difficult problems. One may take the point of view that there is only complete certainty about those noblemen mentioned in the narrative sources.[140] However, it should not be forgotten that such an opinion is not only based on the exaggerated claims made by the *Annales Gandenses*, but also on an erroneous perception that the great majority of noblemen belonged to the King's party. Since this argument is not tenable, only the former remains. It is certain that the Ghentenaar Friar Minor very much underestimated the number of noblemen, giving a figure of ten or so knights, since more are to be found in the narrative sources.

There is one very important source that remains to be examined concerning the noblemen who took part in the battle: the Bruges town accounts. Two types of documents are available here: the hotel accounts of Willem van Jülich and the general town accounts of 1302, now published by C. Wyffels and A. Vandewalle.[141] However, the hotel accounts (with the list of noblemen) were only dated to 6

---

[132] Ibid., 75. See also Fris, *De slag bij Kortrijk*, 309.
[133] Wyffels and Vandewalle, 77.
[134] *Chronique artésienne*, 53.
[135] Ibid., 53.
[136] Ibid., 51, 53.
[137] Godefroy, V, no. 4088.
[138] Wyffels and Vandewalle, 78; Gilliodts-van Severen, I:133–4, no. 173; and Kervyn de Lettenhove, *Histoire de Flandre*, II:622.
[139] Fris, *De slag bij Kortrijk*, 309, did not mention Thomas de Lille although he accepted the presence of several noblemen at the battle without citing any narrative source.
[140] Ibid., 301–12.
[141] Wyffels and Vandewalle, 69–86, 821–6, 828–31, 848–52, 856–7.

August and give information that is certain only from 22 July 1302 onwards. There is a further document of 10 August and a final document of 29 August 1302 for a period of a fortnight. Thus there is a complete account, except for five days, for the period of 22 July to 29 August. Following this, the documents end most certainly as a new expedition, that against Douai, began on 30 August.[142]

Careful comparison of the hotel accounts with the general town accounts leads to the conclusion that the expenses given in the hotel accounts were transferred to the town accounts and were at times copied. The expenses of noblemen in the Bruges hotels were listed in the accounts under the entry *wedden*, salaries or payments. Different sums were entered for most of the noblemen, either according to the landlord in whose hotel they were staying or according to the date of the hotel bill. The last sum entered is usually that for 29 August. Entries before this are certainly for expenses incurred prior to this date. There is information concerning the expenses from 22 July to 10 August. Careful comparison indicates that the sums given in the town accounts exceed, for the most part, those in the hotel accounts. On account of this, it seems that the expenses were for the period prior to 22 July, thus most probably prior to 11 July. This is important since there is now a criterion to ascertain, for a whole group of knights, whether they were already participating in the rebellion before the Battle of the Spurs. The fact that the additional expenses given in the town accounts do not refer to the period following 29 August is proven by the lack of hotel bills for that period, since the noblemen were, once again, on a military expedition. Furthermore, the payments effected on 29 August appear last in the town accounts. Thus, the following conclusion is justifiable: those noblemen who received more in the town accounts than in the hotel accounts may be considered as having taken part in the Battle of the Spurs.

However, the town and hotel accounts are not exhaustive, very often only giving expenses incurred in Bruges if the noblemen lost horses. Several examples make this clear: Diederik van Hondschote and Robrecht van Leeuwergem were not mentioned, even though they took part in the battle. Boudewijn van Popperode was only mentioned after the battle.[143] Philips van Axel was only mentioned due to his having lost a horse.[144] Bangelijn van Aardenburg was solely mentioned for the period from 22 July to 10 August.[145] Jan Borluut was only mentioned, together with his brother, in the hotel expenses, for the period from 22 July to 10 August.[146] Thomas de Lille was only mentioned, on hotel expenses, for the period from 22 July to 6 August.[147]

An explanation for this is the fact that the noblemen served at their own cost until that date, since it is known that they all, except for Thomas de Lille, took part in the battle.

---

[142] Ibid., 96, 843–7.
[143] Gilliodts-van Severen, I:155, no. 173.
[144] Wyffels and Vandewalle, 91.
[145] Ibid., 831.
[146] Ibid., 831, 80: 25 pounds in both sources.
[147] Ibid., 78, 825: 10 pounds.

Another document from the Gilliodts-van Severen inventory, no. 155, also lists the names of many noblemen, of whom a high number were present at Courtrai. However, the document appears to have been drawn up after the battle. This is arrived at as the marshal, Hendrik van Lontzen, was mentioned, together with fifty squires. This was obviously not the case in his own personal accounts for the expedition to Cassel, Ypres and Courtrai.[148] In addition to this, the titles of the documents point in the same direction.[149] This was a new enrolment of the noblemen each with their own entourage, since the list contains a total of 494 noblemen for 31 knights and 47 squires.[150] It was probably for one of the following expeditions in 1302.

One question that arises is whether the knights from Zeeland should be added to the noblemen mentioned in the hotel and town accounts: Floris, Raas and Wolfert van Borselen, Hendrik Buffel, Hendrik and Wolfert van Zoetenlande, Niklaas van Cats, Jan Mulard and their squires.[151] They probably did not take part in the battle. The Ghentenaar Friar Minor actually stated that a group of men from Zeeland did not take part in the expedition.[152] Moreover, we note, first, that two journeys were made to Hulst to persuade the men from Zeeland,[153] and, second, that Jan van Renesse was only enrolled on 8 July.[154] Furthermore, we should take into account the fact that all the above noblemen, excluding Jan van Renesse and his entourage, were mentioned in connection with expenses incurred to defend the Zwin. At a later point, they were explicitly mentioned due to their participation in the Douai expedition.[155] If they had fought at Courtrai, they would have been noted in an entry, as was Jan van Renesse. Also, we should not forget that Jan van Renesse and the Borsele family were enemies.[156]

It is also possible that noblemen from the east, usually assumed to have taken part in the battle, were not present.[157] They were in fact mentioned in an entry headed by Jean de Namur,[158] who arrived after the battle. Furthermore, it is suspicious that an important nobleman such as the Count of Katzenellenboghe was not mentioned in the narrative sources. Other German noblemen were present in the entourage of Willem van Jülich. However, it is possible that they were commanding the auxiliary troops sent by Jean de Namur.

---

[148] Ibid., 800–2, 82, 870. Lontzen was accompanied by 25 squires.
[149] 'Dit sin de rudders die sin ghenomen uten brief van den livrisone onder van Allemalgen ende van Vlaendre die men wille sien' and elsewhere 'Dit sin de sciltknapen die men wille sien die waren ghenomen uten brieve van den livrisone, onder van Almangen ende van Alst ende van Vlandre'.
[150] Wyffels and Vandewalle, 800–2. Perhaps these were the 484 noblemen mentioned in Gilliodts-van Severen, I:155, no. 180, who served for half a year.
[151] Wyffels and Vandewalle, 92–3.
[152] *Annales Gandenses*, 47: 'multi ipsorum, non omnes'.
[153] Wyffels and Vandewalle, 116.
[154] Gilliodts-van Severen, I:98, no. 165.
[155] Wyffels and Vandewalle, 98, 846.
[156] See the introduction above on events in Holland and Zeeland.
[157] Fris, *De slag bij Kortrijk*, 316; and Delfos, *1302 door tijdgenooten verteld*, 104.
[158] Wyffels and Vandewalle, 90, 889.

Generally, the first and third lists presented by Delfos[159] give the most probable participants in the battle with the exceptions of Jean de Lange, Simon van Neuville, Wouter van Boelare, Willem van Nevele, Geraard van Zottegem and the Lord of Kuik. The above forces reinforced the army after the battle, as they were mentioned in the town accounts at such a late date.[160] Walter de Grote, head of the White Templars, must also be omitted: the White Templars were explicitly mentioned in the accounts of the Douai expedition, although not for Courtrai.[161] Therefore, there is no reason to assume that they were present on 11 July.

(g) Those who took part in the Battle of the Spurs
According to the narrative sources and dated documents pertaining to the Bruges town accounts, it is certain that the following noblemen took part in the battle:

Hendrik van Lontzen, from Limburg	Jan van Renesse, from Zeeland
Goswin van Gossenhoven, from Brabant	Diederik van Hondschote
Robrecht van Leeuwergem	Boudewijn van Popperode[162]
Rogier de Lille	Otto van Steenhuize
Geraard van Roebaais	Philips van Axel[163]
Willem van Boenhem	Jan van der Maerct
Geraard Ferrant	Jan Borluut
Bangelijn van Aardenburg	Hendrik van Pietersheim, from Loon
Jacob Cortals[164]	Jan van Menen, losing two horses[165]
Willem de Visch[166]	Zeger van Gent, the elder
Zeger van Gent, the younger	Vranke van Zomergem, losing one horse[167]

Bruges town and hotel accounts[168]
The following noblemen most probably did take part in the battle:

Knights

Daniel van Bellegem, losing two horses	Geraard van Uitkerke
Wouter van Roden	Boudewijn van Hondschote
Olivier van Bellegem, losing one horse	Jan van Hondschote, his brother

---

[159] Delfos, *1302 door tijdgenooten verteld*, 103–4 n. 29.
[160] Wyffels and Vandewalle, 88–90.
[161] Ibid., 99.
[162] *Annales Gandenses*, 29.
[163] *Chronique artésienne*, 51, 53.
[164] Lodewijk, II.1.IV:319, c. 32, vv. 2227–8; II.1.IV:325, c. 33, v. 2391; II.1.IV:321, c. 32, v. 2275; II.1.IV:328, c. 34, v. 2464; II.1.IV:320, c. 32, v. 2269; II.1.IV:305, c. 27, 1890; II.1.IV: 321, c. 32, v. 2278.
[165] Wyffels and Vandewalle, 83, 74; and Lodewijk, II.1.IV:282, c. 20, vv. 1355–6.
[166] Wyffels and Vandewalle, 82; and Fris, *De slag bij Kortrijk*, 306.
[167] Wyffels and Vandewalle, 74, 83.
[168] Ibid., 74–84.

Jan Plateel[169]
Eustaes van Meilegem
Michiel van Coudekerke
Jacob Abboud
Alexis van Assenede
Bernard van den Abele, losing one horse
Zeger van Belle
Jan Tornoye
Thomas de Lille
Bouden de Vos
Gillis van Mullem
Bouden van Crumbeke
Wouter van der Hauwe
Pieter de Backer, losing one horse
Pieter van Menen[170]

Willem van der Haghe, losing two horses
Willem van der Bredermersch
Eustaes Lauwaerd
Philips de Moor
Jan de Calewe
Arnoud Casekin van Beerst
Gillis van Moorslede
Everard van Calken, the elder
Everard van Calken, the younger
Gilbert van Berlingen
Godfried van Meerhem
Everard, son of Gillis
Philips uten Hove
Hellin van Steenland, losing one horse
Wouter van Vinct, losing one horse
Lord of Massemen[171]

Squires

Simon van Vaernewijck
Coerlebacke
Wouter Ketele
Boiden Prijs
Amelricke
Gosin van Lauwe
Arnout van Affelgem
Jan van Aalst
Koukelare
Jan van der Mersch
Clais Bertheloet
Jan Wandelard
Jan van Poelvoorde f. Wouters
Richard van den Castele
Clais Springhe
Wouter van Poesele

Jakemin van Lembeke
Jan den Aleman
Gillis van Geraardsbergen
Gillis van Mesnil
Jan of Berlare
Gheylinc
Jan Tichelt
Simon van Poelgen
Jan van Sloten
Pieter van Belle
Hugo Wevel
Hannekin van Pierweys
Pieter van der Mersch
Jan van Oudenburg
Hellin van Calken
Boidin Braem

Foreign knights

(Hendrik van Lontzen)
(Goswin van Gossenhoven)

(Jan van Renesse)
(Hendrik van Pietersheim)

---

[169] Possibly a former Flemish supporter of the King, although it is more probable that there were two noblemen of that name since there was still a certain Jan Plateel who was a supporter of the King in 1303.
[170] Wyffels and Vandewalle, 821.
[171] Ibid., 85.

Arnout of Los (Loon?)
Willem van Julermont, losing one horse[172]
Hendrik van Lontzen, nephew of the marshal, with 8 squires

Hendrik van Cruninghe, monk, losing one horse
Hendrik van Brabant, losing one horse[173]

Squires

Willem van Rossemaer Geraard van Jülich
Jan van Pietersheim
Willem van Jülich
Reinaar de Inghelsche
Stalin Mandol and entourage
Gillis Duffel and entourage
Loeve van Berkensdorp and entourage
Jan Semale, with three squires

Librecht van Trecht
Herman van Bustein
Pieroot Suffraye and entourage
Willem f. Lowis Commensaille
Ywein van Cruninghe and entourage
Master Rogier of Jülich and entourage
Herman Dorp
Reineken van Harne, with five squires

In total, there could have been fifty-five knights and thirty-two squires from Flanders with, in addition to this, nine foreign knights and seventeen squires, several of whom attended with their entourage. Now, the question is whether all the knights and squires were there with noblemen under their command? An answer to this question is difficult and, although it appears logical that they had noblemen under their command, it is impossible to determine their exact number. Perhaps there were around two hundred Flemish noblemen and approximately a hundred foreign noblemen, since on several occasions there are references to the latter having an entourage.

One should also add the auxiliary troops that were sent by Jean de Namur and arrived at the very last moment. It is doubtful whether there actually were six hundred armoured horsemen.[174] It ought not to have been possible to draw up so many cavalry in such a short period of time. If three hundred armoured horsemen for the auxiliary troops can be assumed, then this already represents a considerable number.

All together there would, then, have certainly been four hundred Flemish and foreign noblemen who fought in the battle, perhaps six hundred in the most favourable of circumstances. Since this number is very small in comparison with the thousands of commoners fighting, it is possible that the narrative sources other than Lodewijk took very little notice of them, especially as the noblemen were fighting on foot.

Finally, it should be noted that the above Flemish noblemen, reported in the town and hotel accounts, all belonged to the entourage of Willem van Jülich. We may then ask whether Guy de Namur did not have an entourage? This was certainly the case for Jan van Renesse and also, perhaps, for Diederik van Hondschote, Boudewijn van Popperode, Robrecht van Leeuwergem and the other knights not

---

[172] Ibid., 83.
[173] Ibid., 83, 77.
[174] Lodewijk, II.1.IV:308, c. 28, v. 1946.

mentioned in the Bruges documents before the 11 July. The expenses of Guy de Namur entered in the town accounts began on the 22 or 23 July, excluding a few minor entries.[175] This is actually the date of the arrival of Jean de Namur in Bruges, and it is perhaps because Guy de Namur had not until that time incurred great expenses, or had paid for expenses himself. However, this tends to confirm that his entourage was small.

The French forces
Less than two months after the events of Bruges Friday, a powerful French army of knights was advancing to avenge the bloodshed of 18 May and to crush the rebellion. Those living at that time were unanimous in seeing the army as the most splendid that the King was able to draw up. It was seen as the flower of French nobility with the most magnificent knighthood in the whole world.[176] Due to the relative haste with which it had been drawn up, it was not possible to call upon noblemen from all the regions of France. Still, there were foreign mercenaries from the south, led by Jan of Burlats, seneschal of Guyenne and commander of the crossbowmen, and a division of knights and squires from Brabant commanded by Geoffrey de Brabant[177] and his son, Jean de Vierson.[178] Geoffroy had participated in the expeditions of 1297 and 1300 in Flanders, Jean in that of 1300. The son of the Count of Hainault was also present with a contingent of noblemen; Jean the Merciless had already fought against the Flemings in the French army in 1297.[179] Finally there was an unknown number of Flemish supporters of the King fighting in the French ranks.

How strong was this splendid army commanded by Robert d'Artois? The information given by the narrative sources does not, in general, merit much confidence. The *Annales Gandenses*[180] and the *Chronique artésienne*[181] both gave a figure of ten thousand noblemen on horseback. Villani converted this to 7600[182] and Lodewijk to 7024.[183] The Brabantese parson exaggerated the least of all, since the French kings had never been able to raise such a powerful army of knights in the thirteenth and the beginning of the fourteenth century. Only one source gives a low figure that is close to the real number: the *Chronographia Regum Francorum*, which noted that the constable of the French army, Raoul de Nesle, was sent by Philip the Fair to St Omer with 1500 men on horseback in order to free the besieged

---

[175] Wyffels and Vandewalle, 71: *Paneterie* (bread/food) from 23 July; Ibid., 73: *Camere* (rooms/accommodation) from 24 July; ibid., 73, *Marscalkerie* (stables/upkeep of horses) from 22 July on.
[176] Geoffrey de Paris, 99, v. 1122; Villani, 388; le Muisit, 69; *Anciennes chroniques de Flandre*, 378; *Annales Gandenses*, 27–8; and Lodewijk, II.1.IV:320, c. 32, v. 2261.
[177] *Chronique artésienne*, 22; and *Journaux du trésor*, 51, c. 287.
[178] *Journaux du trésor*, 630, c. 4295.
[179] Le Muisit, 52–3; and *Chronique artésienne*, 22.
[180] *Annales Gandenses*, 27–8.
[181] *Chronique artésienne*, 47.
[182] Villani, 384.
[183] Lodewijk, II.1.IV:311, c. 29, vv. 2020–1.

castle of Cassel.[184] There he was told that he had too few knights to engage in battle with the Flemings. The French army was then strengthened and placed under the command of Count of Artois. How strong this army was is not said by the chronicler who gives the greatly exaggerated figure of 40,000 horses. This exaggeration also casts much doubt upon the what at first sight was interesting information.

Concerning the Battle of Courtrai, there are several letters calling knights up for military service. Yet it is not known to what extent such calls were actually answered.[185] In addition, there are the chroniclers' lists of the most prominent noblemen who fell, which most probably made use of official documents, although even the most detailed list is not complete.[186] However, they can be employed in making calculations about the numerical strength of the army.

On the military expeditions in 1297, and above all in 1300, there is a range of extremely significant information that has never been used. For 1297, there is a list of prominent noblemen who took part in the expedition.[187] For 1300, there are two sources. The first source is an official document, dating from 1299, giving the names of the knights enlisted for the Flanders expedition (in 1300), although not the names of knights then in Flanders under the command of St Pol.[188] The second source is the journals of the royal treasury (end of 1299 and beginning of 1300) that state how much noblemen were paid and how many soldiers accompanied them.[189] The two sources confirm each other for many noblemen, but are also complementary, since some noblemen were paid in their own regions and not directly by the royal treasury.[190] Unfortunately, no source gives information about the numerical strength of the Count of St Pol's army in Flanders.

Since the official document of 1299 has not been published, the full list of noblemen enrolled will be reproduced. On more than one occasion it has been necessary to transcribe names where identification was doubtful or impossible. Names will be added to the list of noblemen based on information given in the *Journaux du trésor* and at times the Latin name has been kept.

Commanders	*Bannerets*	*Knights*	*Cavalrymen*	*Journaux du trésor*
Charles de Valois			240	
Louis de France	4		200	
Louis de Clermont, The Count of Auxerre	3		60	

---

[184] *Chronographia*, I:103–4.
[185] Funck-Brentano, *Philippe le Bel*, 405 n. 1; and *Ordonnances des roys de France de la troisième race*, ed. M. de Laurière (Paris, 1723), I:345, 350.
[186] *Chronique artésienne*, 49–51; *Chronographia*, I:110–11; and le Muisit, 68–9.
[187] *Chronique artésienne*, 21–3.
[188] Archives nationales, Paris, J 543, no. 17.
[189] *Journaux du trésor*, 518–662.
[190] This is the case for, among others, the knights G. de St Just and G. d'Amblepui et Montaou given in the list.

Commanders	Bannerets	Knights	Cavalrymen	Journaux du trésor
The Count of Forez	3		60	p. 540, c. 3634
Béraud, Lord of Mercoeur	3		60	p. 541, c. 3635
Guichard, Lord of Beaujeu	3		60	p. 541, c. 3636
Gaucher, Lord of Châtillon	5		100	p. 560, c. 3802
Jean, Lord of Harcourt	5		100	p. 540, c. 3633
Jean, Count of Joigny	2		40	p. 552, c. 3727
Jean de Beaumont, Lord of Poncé	2		40	p. 545, c. 3675
Pierre and Guillaume de Villebéon			10	p. 540, c. 3627
Jean des Barres, Lord of Champrond			5	p. 539, c. 3626
Henri de Richebourc			5	p. 539, c. 3626
Jean Bourreau de Baigneaux			4	p. 540, c. 3628
Guillaume de Percigni and another nobleman			8	p. 545, c. 3674
Jean le Camus Payen			4	p. 540, c. 3629
G. de St Just (in Beaucaire) and another nobleman			10	
G. d'Amblepui and Montaou			10	
Gui de Brisay			8	p. 545, c. 3673
Hugues de Camberon			5	p. 541, c. 3637
Gui de Nesle, marshal of France		6	30	p. 530, c. 3527
Jean Pesloe			4	p. 536, c. 3598
Baudouin de Caumont			5	p. 541, c. 3637
Colart de Brimeu			5	p .541, c. 3637
Pierre de Franchieres			5	p. 550, c. 3716
Baudewijn van Mote (Flemish supporter of the King?) and another nobleman			8	p. 572, c. 3882
Philippe de Trie			4	
Guillaume Clingnet		2	10	p. 571, c. 3881
Oudart de Rippe Haute (Rebaust)	1		20	p. 571, c. 3880
All of the noblemen were knights				

(Total: Commanders 34 + 1118 cavalry = 1152 men in armour)[191]

Commanders	Bannerets	Knights	Cavalrymen	Journaux du trésor
Symon du Ménil-David squire			10	p. 543, c. 3657
Joc. d'Augeron, squire			10	
Moncassin de Galart, squire			10	p. 555, c. 3758

[191] This is the total given in the document. It is followed here since it is the same as that of the men on horseback and the commanders.

Commanders	Bannerets	Knights	Cavalrymen	Journaux du trésor
Béraud de Montaigu, squire			10	p. 555, c. 3758
Dargecon (d'Argecon?), squire			4	
Guillaume de Danonville (or Denovilla), squire			4	p. 582, c. 3964
Lord Pierre l'Orrible		2	10	p. 588, c. 4021
Guillaume de Rouvroy, banneret		4	15	p. 602, c. 4110
Lord Guillaume de Lens		2	10	p. 590, c. 4028
Gilec de Letries (de Letryers), squire			10	p. 591, c. 4029
Lord Jean de Beaumont			4	p. 593, c. 4045
Lord Pierre de Ressons			4	p. 592, c. 4042
The master of the crossbowmen		3	10	
Lord Jean de Noient			5	p. 595, c. 4062
Jean and Guillaume de Barres with another squire			3	p. 599, c. 4085

(Total: 11 + 119 = 130)

Commanders	Bannerets	Knights	Cavalrymen	Journaux du trésor
Lord of Waudripont			20	p. 519, c. 3454[192]
Lord of Walincourt			20	
Lord Mathieu de Freylaines			4	p. 529, c. 3525
Lord Guillaume de St Martin			4	p. 519, c. 3455
Lord Jacques de Toufflet			4	p. 518, c. 3451
Lord Jean de Mons			4	p. 518, c. 3449
Lord Pierre de Rechincher			4	
Lord Gautier de St Loht			5	p. 518, c. 3452[193]
Lord Robert de Launay			4	
Lord Aleaume de Monceaus			5	p. 540, c. 3630
Lord Jean de Molignehem or Mollanguehem			4	p. 518, c. 3450
Lord Dreu de Bachimont			4	p. 529, c. 3525
Lord Garnier de Forberi			5	
Lord Jean de Flaisseres			4	
Lord Hugues de Gaillart			4	p. 518, c. 3453
Lord Robert de Hamel			5	p. 529, c. 3526

(Total: 100 men in armour)

---

[192] The *Journaux du trésor* only gave a figure of eight soldiers for Egidius de Waudripont.
[193] The *Journaux du trésor* gives a figure of four men on horseback, but the payment actually corresponds to five soldiers.

Commanders	Bannerets	Knights	Cavalrymen	Journaux du trésor
Vermandois: knights:				
Anseau de Molincourt			4	
Giles de Markais			3	
Baudouin de Frincourt			4	
Darli sur Somme			20	
(Total: 31 men in armour)				

Commanders	Bannerets	Knights	Cavalrymen	Journaux du trésor
Berry, all knights:				
Jean Heigrins			4	
Pierre Chanlus			4	
Geoffroy le Bouteillier			4	
G. de Goury			4	
Jean de Noiers			4	
Ph. des Chasteliers			4	
J. de Gyry			4	
J. Mazon			4	
G. de Favencourt			4	
Gérard de Vernaps			5	
Dreu de Poray			4	
(Total: 45 men in armour)				

Commanders	Bannerets	Knights	Cavalrymen	Journaux du trésor
Artois, all knights:				
Anseau de Kayeau			5	p. 593, c. 4044
Enguerrand de Lens			4	
J. de Villers			8	
Baudouin de S. Nicholas			4	
Nicholes de Bailleul			4	
Gilbert Dorez (Flemish supporter of the King)			4	
Philipe de Criky (Créquy)			5	
Aleaume de Gimbersay			4	
Jean Roussel			4	
Jean de la Lake			4	
Guillaume de Gynenchi			4	
Gilles de Villers			4	
Guillaume de Blequin			4	
Jean de Berquain			3	
Enguerrand du Mesnil			4	
Pierre Corbel			4	
Lord of Mourqueque			5	
Jean Danlert			4	
Le Bastarz de la Frete			4	

Robert de Pucherwiller[194]	4
Jean du Bierz (= du Biest, Flemish supporter of the King?)	5
Anseau de Houdeinville	4
Denis de Grant Viller	4
Michel de Raencourt	4
Jean de Voudrignehen	5
Guillaume de Liere	20
Guillaume de Radinchan	4
Guillaume de Morregni	4
R. de Vignemont[195]	4
G. de Briieres	7
Baudouin de Vanlignchan (Verlinghem?)	5
Jean de Prouville	4
Jean de Beaufort	4
Gui Wavreaieul	4
Richard de Challetot	4
Anseau de Norain	5
Gilles Disques (d'Isques?)	4
Eguerrand de Framesetz	10

(Total: 187 men in armour)

To be added from the *Journaux du trésor de Philippe le Bel*:

Commanders	Cavalrymen	Journaux du trésor
Robert de 'Alneto', knight	4	p. 518, c. 3447
Pierre de Yerbelinguehem, knight	4	p. 518, c. 3448
Baudouin Buridan, knight, all three accompanying St Pol	20	p. 537, c. 3607
Guillaume 'de Ruppe', knight	10	p. 552, c. 3728
Jean 'de Angervillari', knight	4	p. 552, c. 3729
Jean, Lord of Averay, knight	4	p. 591, c. 4030
Mathieu de Kayeu, together with another knight	12	p. 592, c. 4043
Jean de Bullaz, together with 3 knights	13	p. 594, c. 4051
Guillaume Longue Epée	3	p. 599, c. 4089
Pierre de Boucli, together with 6 knights	30	p. 600, c. 4094
Bertrand de 'Turre', squire with	10	p. 606, c. 4140
Adam, Lord of Cardounoy, together with 4 knights	20	p. 608, c. 4150[196]
Amaury, Lord of Narbonne, together with 12 knights among whom 3 bannerets	60	p. 612, c. 4180
Pierre 'de Crisperiis', squire	3	p. 625. c. 4245

---

[194] Gilliodts-van Severen, I:62–5, nos. 114, 117, 120, 121.
[195] Ibid., I:62–5, nos. 114, 117, 120, 121.
[196] Ibid., I:63, no. 116. In 1299, Adam de Cardounoy was the guardian or keeper of the *establie* at Bruges (from 25 June 1298 to 22 March 1299).

Commanders	Cavalrymen	Journaux du trésor
Simon de Hamel, with another knight	10	p. 625, c. 4254
Otton de Montaut, banneret, with three knights	15	p. 655, c. 4492
Conrad Warner, with 5 knights	20	p. 662, c. 4539

(Total: 245 men in armour)
(Preliminary total: 1152 + 130 + 100 + 31 + 45 + 187 + 245 = 1890)

Other knights listed in the *Journaux du trésor*

	Payment	Numerical strength	Reference
Aymar de Poitiers	1500 pounds	(40)	p. 586, c. 3997
The Count of Eu	2000 pounds	(56)	p. 601, c. 4102
Jean of Vierson	2000 pounds	(56)	
The Count of Sancerre	3000 pounds	(80)	p. 536, c. 3593

(Total: 232 + 1890 = general total 2122 armoured cavalrymen)

These figures given for the numerical strength are, however, not final, since there are still no figures relating to the troops of the Count of St Pol and of the Count of Boulogne and Auvergne.[197] The troops would certainly bring the numerical strength to somewhat more than 2500 armoured cavalrymen. The *Chronique tournaisienne* gives the strength of about 2500 men-at-arms for the army of Jacques de St Pol at the moment of his nomination as governor of Flanders on 18 May 1300.[198]

In addition to the cavalrymen, the following should be mentioned:

Ymbert de Romans	500 foot-soldiers from Vienne	p. 586, c. 3998
Guillaume de Pezans	5 crossbowmen	p. 601, c. 4070
The Count of Forez	26 foot-soldiers	p. 601, c. 4104

If we compare those who took part in 1297, as listed in the *Chronique artésienne*, with those taking part in 1300, we arrive at the conclusion that there were certainly as many armoured cavalrymen in the army and probably many more in 1297.

Several elements indicate that there were fewer French noblemen in the army at Courtrai. The expedition had been carried out quickly, so that not all French regions were represented. According to the Ghentenaar Friar Minor, the noblemen were enlisted from the crown territories, from Champagne, Normandy, Picardy and Poitou, with reinforcements from Lorraine, Brabant and Hainault.[199] To these areas Geoffroy de Paris added Burgundy, Gascony, Anjou and Brittany.[200] An examination of the composition of the army can now be immediately undertaken on the basis of the list of those noblemen who fell in battle or were taken captive. The

---

[197] There is no information on how long the Count of Boulogne and Auvergne was paid.
[198] *Chronique tournaisienne*, in *Chronique artésienne*, 34–5.
[199] *Annales Gandenses*, 27.
[200] Geoffrey de Paris, 99, vv. 1119–21.

Chronique artésienne is the best source for this, even if it remains incomplete.[201] In addition to the noblemen mentioned, which families the most prominent barons and knights in 1304 belonged to is also mentioned.[202]

Noblemen

	1304
FRANCE (crown territories)	
Raoul de Nesle, constable	x
His brother, Gui de Nesle, marshal	x
Renaud de Trie, marshal	x
Pierre Flote, chancellor of the King	x
Pierre de le Tournele	
Richard de Milly	
Mahieu de Trie, the younger (taken captive)	x
Gui le Vidame	
CHAMPAGNE	
Jean, Count of Grandpré, or Jean, Count of Roucy[203]	x
The vidame of Chalons	x
Drieu de Molaines, Lord of Mello	x
The Lord of Hans	x
The Lord of Apremont	x
Mahieu de Lorraine, squire (taken captive)	
Henri de Ligny, from Bar[204]	
ARTOIS	
Robert, Count of Artois	x
Jacques de St Pol	x
The Lord of Fiennes	x
Jean de Neuville	x
Bidiaus de Neuville	x
Walepaièle	
Guillaume Deleau	
Enlart de Seninghem	
Guillaume de Bethune, of Locres, Lord of Hébuterne (taken captive)	
Raoul du Sart (taken captive)	
Baudouin d'Allennes (taken captive)	

---

[201] *Chronique artésienne*, 49–51. Another list is to be found in the *Chronographia*, I:110–12. See also le Muisit, 68–9.

[202] See the list of *Barons et grands chevaliers du roi* in the RHF, 23:802–6. The order given in this list is followed in classifying the noblemen although Vermandois and Ponthieu is listed together, since it is difficult to differentiate between the noblemen from these two areas.

[203] Funck-Brentano, in *Chronique artésienne*, 107. Funck-Brentano was of the opinion that the Count of Grandpré was not killed. The author of the *Chronique artésienne* perhaps made a mistake here, confusing the Count of Grandpré with Jean, Count of Roucy, who also came from Champagne and was listed among those who fell in battle by le Muisit (69). The *Chronographia* (I:111) also mentioned Grandpré. The Count of Dammartin, mentioned in the *Chronographia* (I:111) and by le Muisit (69), fell at the Battle of Mons-en-Pévèle (1304).

[204] *Chronographia*, I:111; and le Muisit, 69.

Ferrand, Lord of Arainnes and Achicourt
Jean, Lord of Créquy
Michel de Harnes
Raoul VI le Flamenc, Lord of Cauny and of Verpillière
Jean le Brun de Brunembert
Gérard de Boubers, Lord of Abbeville
Renaud de Boubers

PONTHIEU AND VERMANDOIS
The Count of Aumale   x
Jean de Hangest   x
Robert de Fins   x
Raoul de Soissons[205]
Gérard de Sorel
Jean de Bouchavesnes (and his two sons)
Raoul de Grantcourt (taken captive), or de Gaucourt, Berry

NORMANDY
The Count of Eu   x
Robert de Tancarville, chamberlain of Normandy
The Lord of Estouteville   x
Robert d'Esneval   x
The Viscount of Blosseville
Jean de Brillecourt
Jean Martel
Guillaume Matel (or Malet?)
The Lord of Préaux (Praias?)   x
Jean de St Martin

BRITTANY
Guillaume des Brieux
Aillelme, son of the Duke of Brittany[206]

ANJOU
The Viscount of Beaumont[207]

NEVERS
Jacques de Dornes
Geoffroi de Dornes, his brother

POITOU
Pauthonnes de Montendre (taken captive)
Gauchier de Metry (taken captive)

LANGUEDOC
Jean de Burlats, seneschal of Guyenne

AUVERGNE
Godefroid de Boulogne

---

[205] Le Muisit, 69, listed the Count of Soissons among those who fell.
[206] *Chronographia*, I:111.
[207] Ibid., I:111.

NOT FROM THE KINGDOM OF FRANCE
Geoffrey de Brabant
His son, Jean de Vierson, Viscount of Tournai
Jean de Hainault, son of the Count
The Marshal of Hainault, Mathieu de Ligne[208]
Baudouin d'Auberchicourt, guardian of Tournai[209]
Gilles d'Antoing (Hainault)[210]
The Viscount of Lille (Flemish supporter of the King)

NOBLEMEN WHOSE REGIONS ARE NOT KNOWN
Jourdain de Lin-de-boef
Jacques Loyre
Jean d'Urnas
The Lord of Cleves
The Lord of Séchelles

NOBLEMEN OF BRABANT WHO FELL
The banneret of Wezemael
The banneret of Boutersem
The banneret of Walhain
Arnout van den Eechove
His son, Jan
Laureins Volkaert
The son of the Lord of Walhain
Hendrik van Wilre
Arnout van der Hofstat (with three sons of his sister)
Gheldolf van Winghen
Willem van Redinghen[211]

The Count of Boulogne and of Auvergne, as well as the Count of St Pol and Louis de Clermont, can be added to the list as commanders – they escaped with the rearguard. As can be seen from the list, there were many noblemen from the north of France who fell on the Groeninge field. Normandy also suffered heavily, since the dozen or so prominent noblemen from the incomplete list provided by the anonymous Artesian author[212] clearly represent practically the full contingent of 180 men on horseback. This had been a normal contingent that the principality would send to the royal army.[213] Artois, Vermandois and Ponthieu were undoubtedly represented by a very strong contingent on the battlefield. This is understandable since the expedition took place in the border area of these regions.

---

[208] The *Chronique artésienne*, 50, noted the seneschal. However, this is a mistake. The marshal of Hainault fell. See *Chronique artésienne*, 108–9.
[209] From le Muisit, 69.
[210] From le Muisit, 69.
[211] From Jan Boendale, *Brabantsche yeesten*, ed. J. F. Willems, CRH (Brussels, 1836), I.V:421–2, vv. 225–55.
[212] *Chronique artésienne*, 51.
[213] See Lodewijk, II.1.IV:339, c. 38, vv. 2722–4. The Brabantese poet noted that Normandy suffered the greatest losses. This is possible in relation to the contingent it sent.

For the crown territories, Champagne and Normandy, one can assume a normal contingent of 180 armoured cavalry for both Champagne and for Normandy.

For other regions, such as Berry, Brittany, Anjou and Poitou, it is not possible to reach any conclusions on the basis of the text about the contingents they provided. However, it is important to be able to ascertain that there were troops from these regions.

From the list of those who fell, it appears that Hainault and Brabant sent relatively many noblemen, thus strengthening the French army with hired soldiers under Burlats, Geoffrey de Brabant and Jean de Hainault. This compensated for the absence of contingents from certain regions in France.

The numerical strength of the royal army can be calculated on the basis of the usual contingents sent by Champagne and Normandy. These contingents were certainly present at Courtrai, given the high numbers of noblemen who fell. One of the ten formations of knights certainly contained the contingent from Champagne and was probably that of Mathieu de Trie in which Lodewijk and Villani placed the noblemen of Champagne and Lorraine.[214] This formation of knights would then have comprised at least 180 men on horseback. It is, however, certain that the Norman contingent and a formation from Ponthieu belonged to the formation of knights under the command of the Count of Eu, of the Lord of Tancarville and the Count of Aumale, with a total strength of at least 240 noblemen. If we assume an average of 250 noblemen for each formation of knights, we arrive at a total of 2500 armoured horsemen for the ten formations into which the army was initially subdivided.

However, just before the battle the army was divided into three formations: two were to advance and attack, and one was to act as the rearguard and serve as the reserve force.[215] The two *bataelgen* that attacked were composed of eight formations of knights, the rearguard of two formations.

The above numerical strength of the attacking forces completely corresponds to the number of losses incurred (knights and squires). According to the chronicler giving the lowest number of losses, the Frenchman, Jean de Saint-Victor, there were fifty-four high lords and nine hundred knights from France who fell.[216] According to Lodewijk, sixty-three bannerets and eleven hundred knights fell.[217] The Ghentenaar Friar Minor spoke of seventy-five barons and more than a thousand knights being killed.[218]

However, more than fifty-four important noblemen died, as seen above in the incomplete list given in the *Chronique artésienne,* including the sixty well-known

---

[214] Ibid., II.1.IV:307, c. 28, vv. 1933–7; and Villani, 386.
[215] *Annales Gandenses*, 30.
[216] Jean de Saint-Victor, *Memoriale historiarum (excerpta)*, in RHF, 21, ed. Guigniaut and N. de Wailly (Paris, 1855), 638–9.
[217] Lodewijk, II.1.IV:326, c. 34, vv. 2400–2.
[218] *Annales Gandenses*, 30.

noblemen of whom one also lost his two sons.[219] Thus one comes quickly to a figure of seventy-five prominent noblemen.

More than sixty knights bannerets were killed according to the *Chronique artésienne*, sixty-three according to Lodewijk, seventy-five according to the *Chronographia Regum Francorum*, the *Chronique normande* and the *Annales Gandenses*. The names of these counts and knights bannerets were recorded. A banneret was the chief of twenty men at arms. Probably twelve hundred and sixty knights and squires were killed in the battle, perhaps fifteen hundred. The five hundred pairs of golden spurs confirm this number.

Most of the slain noblemen belonged to the eight formations that were attacking. However, it cannot be assumed that all knights in those formations died, since this would lead to the acceptance of the most biased Flemish version. It does, in fact, appear evident that the eight attacking formations were comprised of two thousand three hundred knights and squires. Perhaps the reserve or rearguard had seven hundred men at arms.

This calculation is made on the basis of the number of formations of knights and of the contingents provided by regions such as Normandy and Champagne, corroborated by the numbers of those who fell. This indicates that Artois's army was 3000 knights and squires. In fact, it can be ascertained that the armies of the kings of France at the beginning of the Hundred Years War were much stronger. For the beginning of the fourteenth century, there is no official and comprehensive information about the numerical strength of a strong royal army. The figure of three thousand men on horseback assumed for the year 1297 could well have been exceeded; for Courtrai, it could have been two and a half or three thousand.

Foot-soldiers

Even more problems arise when determining the numerical strength of the French foot-soldiers. Once again there is no single official document. In 1300, five hundred foot-soldiers from Vienne were reported in the army of the King's brother, Charles de Valois. It is also known that on occasions the French towns on the border certainly sent contingents of several hundred soldiers, often three hundred[220] and at times a thousand soldiers. Still, there were never very large numbers of soldiers sent.

Moreover, the foot-soldiers played almost no role in the battle. Although crossbowmen were employed in the preparatory stages of battle they did not take part in the determining phase of a battle. This was indeed also the case in Flanders before the Battle of Courtrai and although the foot-soldiers were superior there to those in France, they still played a subordinate or even insignificant role.

---

[219] In the *Chronique artésienne*, 49, Jean de Brabant (Jean de Vierson) and Renaud de Trie still have to be added here. See above.
[220] The town of Tournai sent three hundred townsmen in 1297 to join the army of Philip the Fair during the siege of Lille. See le Muisit, 53.

How numerous were the French crossbowmen? Where did they come from? Most studies of the Battle of the Spurs report that they were from Genoa, then famous throughout Western Europe for its crossbowmen, who thus were always employed as mercenaries by French kings. It must be admitted, however, that these crossbowmen were not to be found at the Battle of Courtrai nor elsewhere in French documents of the beginning of the fourteenth century. They were, however, deployed during the Hundred Years War at, among other places, Crécy in 1346.

Villani spoke of Lombardian commanders of the foot-soldiers with crossbowmen under their command. However, the Florentine chronicler did not portray the foot-soldiers as playing any role, and they were not even mentioned during the course of the battle. The possibility nevertheless still remains that crossbowmen from Lombardy were present. But we might ask where the King recruited them in the short period between the Bruges Matins and the Battle of the Spurs. If the King had such men constantly at his disposal, this could be determined from accounts and other documents. If crossbowmen from Lombardy were present, they would have been very few in number, perhaps a few hundred, supported by French crossbowmen sent by the towns.

However, one element speaks against the presence of crossbowmen from Genoa. They were not mentioned whatsoever by the French and Flemish sources, while on the contrary the Lombardian men with pikes, led by the famous captain Castruccio Castracani, were mentioned by all the sources. Even the quality of their weapons caught the attention of the chroniclers.[221] In 1303 they defended the town of Térouanne for the King of France.

Thus we arrive at the conclusion that the crossbowmen were from France, not Genoa, and that they were consequently no better trained than the Flemings. They were probably more numerous than the Flemish crossbowmen and were moreover continuously supported by other light foot-soldiers, among them the *bidauts*, mercenaries from the south of France and from Spain. Still, aside from these able crossbowmen and the *bidauts*, there were usually also ordinary foot-soldiers whose effectiveness in battle was insignificant. Guiart, who actually fought against the Flemings in 1304 in a contingent sent by the town of Orleans, reported that part of the foot-soldiers had to fetch weapons from the wagons of the King's *artillerie* before the Battle of Mons-en-Pévèle.

If these troops are estimated at a thousand crossbowmen accompanied by several hundred *bidauts*, this would obviously be sufficient to force the approximately nine hundred Flemish crossbowmen back, above all as the Flemish crossbowmen immediately noticed that the knights, who were to be feared the most, were advancing behind the French foot-soldiers.

The French army may have had a total of five to six thousand foot-soldiers. This would mean that it had about the same number of troops as the Flemish army. But the best part of the French forces was formed by knights and squires, and had a great qualitative advantage.

---

[221] *Istore et croniques*, I:270; *Anciennes chroniques*, 391; Villani, 410–11; *Annales Gandenses*, 49; and *Chronique artésienne*, 68.

The Carved Flemish Chest at New College, Oxford, and the equipment and arms of the Flemish troops

A most fortunate event secured possession of a very beautiful representation of Flemish militias in the fourteenth century. As a result of its discovery, the Ghent archaeologist, de Vigne, helped save the magnificent mural paintings in the Leugemeete chapel in Ghent.[222] This means that there is now a splendid illustration of the Ghent communal army. In around 1909, an English military historian, Sir Charles Oman, discovered a most beautiful depiction of the Battle of the Spurs on a wooden chest held at New College, Oxford. He showed his brilliant discovery to Henri Pirenne who accepted the identification of the illustrations as being of the Battle of the Spurs.[223]

This valuable depiction of the battle was, however, to remain long unknown in Belgium. Delfos noted the scenes from the Oman book, although he appeared to have been sceptical about identifying them with the battle.[224] Despite a small copy of the chest appearing in the *Geschiedenis van Vlaanderen*, there were still no studies of it in Belgium.[225] However, there was a study by a British archaeologist, Charles ffoulkes, which went unnoticed because it was published in 1914 in a foreign journal.[226] Only the beautifully illustrated edition of Pirenne's *Histoire de Belgique* discussed, and saw the significance of, the chest's depiction of the battle.[227] There has thus been no study devoted to the matter except for the commentary given by Schauwers and Paquet in their edition of the *Histoire de Belgique* by Pirenne. This gap will now be filled.

Despite its great merit, ffoulkes's study is somewhat flawed. The Oxford chest is an authentic source for the Flemish version of events, depicting various details including, among others, the failed outbreak undertaken by the French in the Courtrai castle and the defensive position of the Flemish phalanx. It is also such a rich source of information about the equipment and weapons that it will be examined in the chapter dealing with both armies. It also allows us to put an end to the ridiculous debate about the form of the *goedendag* and the legend of the *goedendag-coulter*, clearly qualifying such discussion as mere fiction. Studies by

---

[222] F. de Vigne, *Recherches historiques sur les costumes civils et militaires des gildes et des corporations de métiers* (Ghent, 1847). See sketches. See also van Werveke, *Het godshuis van St Jan en St Pauwel*, plates and studies of the whole problem. For an attempt at a reconstruction of the original, see H. Koechlin, *Chapelle de la Leugemeete à Gand: peintures murales, restitution* (Ghent, 1936).
[223] Oman, II:pl. xxv and 114 n. 1.
[224] Delfos, *1302 door tijdgenooten verteld*, 101 n. 20b.
[225] *Geschiedenis van Vlaanderen*, ed. R. van Roosbroeck (Antwerp and Brussels, 1937), II.
[226] C. ffoulkes, 'A Carved Flemish Chest at New College, Oxford', *Archaeologia*, 2nd ser., 65 (1914), 113–28.
[227] H. Pirenne, *Histoire de Belgique*, ed. F. Schauwers and J. Paquet (Brussels, 1948), I:245, 250.

The Courtrai Chest, by kind permission of New College, Oxford

van Duyse,[228] A. van Werveke[229] and ffoulkes[230] are, on the above, important and with a few little corrections merit full confidence.

The chest is now held at New College, Oxford. Prior to 1905, it belonged to William Harris, a tenant whose family had traditionally farmed college grounds. The chest had already been in their possession for at least sixty years, although it is not known how this came to be so.[231]

It is only the front side of the chest that has been sculpted, and it measures 100.3 cm by 71 cm. The sides are nailed to the front, which was originally wider, as it is clear that some figures have been cut off.[232]

Who was the maker of this depiction of the battle? The British archaeologist ffoulkes was of the opinion that it was a *scrinewerker*, a maker of chests or coffins, of Ypres. To support this, he employed the following argumentation: the men of Ypres were the only soldiers who bore the town's coat of arms on their clothes or on their doublets. Moreover, the only example of French heraldry correctly shown

---

[228] H. van Duyse, 'Le Goedendag, arme flamande: sa légende et son histoire', *Handelingen der Maatschappij voor Geschied- en Oudheidkunde te Gent*, 3 (1896).
[229] A. van Werveke.
[230] ffoulkes, 120–2.
[231] Ibid., 120–2.
[232] Ibid., 113.

is, ffoulkes argues, given on the Courtrai castle facing the men of Ypres, that is the banner of Jean de Lens, the commander of the fortress. As a soldier, the artist only saw that banner and would, therefore, have been able to depict it, although he did not know the other banners of the French commanders. He also clearly depicted the banner of the carpenters' guild in his presentation of the guilds' flags (see illustration V). This was taken by ffoulkes to indicate that the artist was a member of the above guild, which is obvious since the chest and carvings were made by someone from that guild.

The argument is, however, not plausible. There is certainly no doubt that the artist was a *scrinewerker*, a maker of coffins and chests. But was the carver from Ypres? This is doubtful, and the following is proposed. The men of Ypres were clearly differentiated from all the other soldiers and bore their town's coat of arms – which was perhaps the case or was at least presented as if it were so by the artist so as to differentiate between the men of Ypres and the men of other towns. This all goes to show that the maker of the chest, a member of a guild from another town, considered it necessary to show that they did not belong to that town of which the most banners were depicted, that is Bruges.

The most significant reason for attributing the work to a man of Bruges is the following. Among the ordinary guild members, only a person from Bruges would have been well informed about what had happened in his town. It is for this reason that the artist was able to depict the coat of arms of Hendrik van Lontzen, who had been appointed marshal of Bruges in 1302, before the Battle of the Spurs. This Limburg knight was certainly less well known to the common people in Ypres. Since ffoulkes did not identify the knight, this explanation escaped him. The reproduction of the banners of Pieter de Coninc and the Lord of Sijsele also points in this direction. On the other arguments: a man of Bruges who had spent several days in front of the Courtrai castle knew the banner of the French King and of Jean de Lens as well as someone from Ypres. On the other hand, a man of Ypres would be less familiar with the banners of Hendrik van Lontzen, Pieter de Coninc and the Lord of Sijsele. The Brugeois artist considered it necessary to differentiate the men of Ypres from his own townsmen and depicted them with their town's coat-of-arms on their garments.

Illustration I

To the far right there is a carving of a female figure in a little canopied shrine. This is a saint's figure placed near one of the town gates since, beneath it, there appears to be an offertory box. And there were, certainly from 1297 onwards, images of saints at some of the town gates at Bruges.[233] On the edge of the chest, to the right of the depiction, we also see a foot and hand of a figure that has been cut off from the sculpted section.

The centre section of the depiction presents the Bruges Friday and appears to show the attack against the French noblemen and the Flemish nobles who

---

[233] Wyffels and De Smet, 565: 'Item pro duabus ymaginibus positis ad portam Beate Marie, 14 lib.'

Illustration I: The Bruges Matins

supported them. One of them was caught by surprise, perhaps in bed. The soldier who is about to behead the person being attacked is holding his sword in his left hand. This possibly enabled persons living at that time to identify the person. It is, however, more probable that the artist depicted the scene in such a manner for reasons of symmetry.

Next to the above figure, we note an open town gate. To its left there is the Bruges town council where a member is kneeling and offering the keys to the town to knights arriving from the other side.

The lock is situated between illustrations I and II.

Illustration II

Guy de Namur and Willem van Jülich arrive in Bruges where the town council presents them with the keys to the town. Guy de Namur can be recognised by the coat of arms of the county of Flanders, with a bar over a rampant lion to show that he is the younger son of the prince. Only the bar is depicted on his ailette without the lion. Guy is wearing a small helmet and his face is unprotected. This is also true of Willem van Jülich, who is wearing a lion rampant and a lily on the shoulder of the lion.[234] On his ailette are five annulets or bezants, an error made by the carver. It is known that Willem actually went to fetch the armour and weapons of his grandfather, Guy de Dampierre, from the Lord of Moerzeke where the old Count had left them behind when he went into captivity in France under Charles de Valois.[235]

While both commanders were on horseback with their faces unprotected, most other noblemen wore the pointed helmets which were common at the beginning of the fourteenth century.

Now, it is possible that the two princes were not wearing the same helmet as the foot-soldiers, but a small cap that knights wore under their helmet. That it was a small cap, *bassinet*, can be assumed from the small helmet in illustration V showing an edge that is only depicted, in illustration II, on Guy's headgear.[236]

It is significant that the princes were wearing a helmet that was very similar to that of the soldiers from the communal armies. This indicates that for psychological reasons they were wearing part of the clothing of the common people.

To the left of Guy de Namur, there is a knight with a scalloped cross in the shield which is the coat of arms of the Marshal of Bruges, Hendrik van Lontzen.

To the right of the prince, there is a soldier of the Bruges communal army with a thick club. In the head of the club a stout steel pin is placed and fastened by an iron ring. This weapon is the *goedendag* of the French sources, the *gepinde staf* of the *Spiegel historiael* and the *staf* of the *Annales Gandenses*.[237]

The coat of arms of some of the knights accompanying Guy de Namur and

---

[234] The *Istore et croniques de Flandres* confirms this.
[235] *Istore et croniques*, I:280n, and Lodewijk, II.1.IV:275–6, c. 17, vv. 1175–205.
[236] Concerning the *bassinet* see E. van Vinkeroy, *Costumes militaires belges* (Braine- le-Comte, 1885), 22.
[237] *Annales Gandenses*, 72, 91–2.

Illustration II: The arrival of Guy de Namur and Willem van Jülich in Bruges

Willem van Jülich have not previously been identified. Their horses are fully covered, with two covers placed in front and behind the saddle. The illustration depicts both parts clearly. The knights are wearing a coat of mail strengthened by *ailettes* or plates on the shoulders and have *poleyns*, or knee-caps. On top of the coat of mail, they are wearing a *sorcoot*, a thin piece of clothing with their coat of arms.

The noblemen are sitting firmly in their saddles which have high pommels and cantles. Their legs are stretched in front of them with the feet as far as the horses' chests.

The two other knights whose shields carry coats of arms have proved impossible to identify. One, to the right of Willem van Jülich, has a cross between four annulets. The other, to the left of Willem van Jülich, bears on his shield a saltire between four annulets and a saltire upon the pennon of his lance.

In fact, Willem van Jülich and Guy de Namur did not arrive at the same time in Bruges. We know that they reached the centre of the rebellion on different dates. It is most probable that the artist intentionally reproduced these two events in one depiction, as this was common practice in work of that period, at which contemporaries took no offence.

Illustration III

The historical events portrayed in this depiction are more difficult to determine. We are already at the beginning of June 1302 since we have had the Bruges Matins (in illustration I) and the arrival of Willem van Jülich and Guy de Namur (illustration II). It is, then, more probable that the events depicted refer to the capture of the castle of Wijnendaal. It was there that the sheriff of Torhout, who was a supporter of the King of France, was decapitated.[238] The scene is on the right side of the depiction. The soldier who decapitated the prisoner is holding a sword in his left hand, and the crossbowman carrying his weapon on his shoulder is also about to shoot with his left hand. This is probably due, once again, to reasons of symmetry in the depiction. One can also see how short the crossbow bolt actually was. A soldier of the communal army is lying on the ground, dead.

It is difficult to ascertain who the knight being attacked by three soldiers actually is. Some have suggested that the knight was Geoffrey de Brabant, with the scene thus taking place during the Battle of Courtrai.[239] But Geoffrey de Brabant had a bend running through his lion, thus making any identification of the knight as Geoffrey unconvincing. Perhaps it is Jean the Merciless, son of the Count of Hainault, who was wearing the Flemish coat of arms and was killed in the battle at Courtrai.

The interesting illustration IV is to the left of the above illustration.

---

[238] Lodewijk, II.1.IV:279–80, c. 19, vv. 1299–304.
[239] ffoulkes, 124; and Oman, II:118, pl. xxv.

Illustration III: Taking the castle of Wijnendale

Illustration IV

Moving from left to right, a priest can be made out, perhaps a Friar Minor as was common in the Flemish militias.[240] The priest is blessing a soldier or perhaps absolving him from his sins following confession. In addition, there is a row of guild banners.

The first banner to the left is that of the fullers, the second is that of the weavers with a shuttle. The third is the shippers' banner with a ship, the fourth represents the wine measurers and the last banner is that of the wine carriers or loaders: there is a simple depiction of a barrow for carrying wine barrels on.

The soldiers are wearing open helmets, a neck-covering in mail, iron gloves and thick doublets. The soldier next to the priest appears to be wearing a short coat of mail. The banners are attached to pikes. In the centre of the depiction there is a soldier with a *goedendag*. To the far right the bearer of the wine carriers' banner can be seen armed with a special sword that is very wide and ends in a sharp point, a falchion. Such weapons were made following eastern examples and can also be seen in the mural paintings of the Ghent Leugemeete chapel.

Illustration V

Illustration V is by far the most significant. It is here that an authentic representation of the strong Flemish battle array is given, just as described respectfully and enthusiastically by Guillaume Guiart. At the same time, the charge of the French knights is depicted after the horses had already been struck down. It is, however, unfortunate that the depiction does not provide anything more. In any case, it can be seen that there was no ditch just in front of the battle positions, as well as that the Flemings stood still and awaited their enemy.

The packed ranks of Flemish townsmen stopped the French charge with their grounded pikes and lances. At the front, behind the protective barrier formed by the pikes, the crossbowmen can be seen, who in some battles shot from the first ranks.[241] Guy de Namur can be seen at the front carrying a large pike in his hand. His coat of arms can be seen on his shoulder plate. Willem van Jülich can be identified in the second row with a *goedendag* in his hand. The six following soldiers are all townsmen. Between both commanders there is a banner of Guy de Namur. The banners are flying in the wind above the heads of the soldiers portrayed here in depth and not from in front of the battle array. First, the banner of the crossbowmen with a scalloped cross is seen. However, this could also be the banner of the Lord of Lontzen. After this, a flag with a lion and a lily on the shoulder is seen, the banner of Willem van Jülich. There is then the banner of the guild of carpenters, to which the maker of the chest belonged. The banner also depicts two tools, an axe and an

---

[240] See *Annales Gandenses*, 36, for after the Battle of Courtrai in 1302; and *Annales Gandenses*, 75, for the Battle of Mons-en-Pévèle. For a 1325 reference to two Friar Minors with the men of Ghent see *Chronicon Comitum Flandrensium*, I:198.
[241] For the Battle of Mons-en-Pévèle see *Annales Gandenses*, 61.

Illustration IV: Flemish townsmen with banners of their guilds

Illustration V: The Flemish battle array on the Groeninge field

adze. The next banner is the lion of Ghent or of the Franc of Bruges. Following this, there are more banners of the guilds: of the smiths with a hammer and horseshoe, the masons with a trowel and square, the brokers, and finally the banner of the Brugeois leader, Pieter de Coninc, with a cross between four flowered crowns, as can be seen on the remains of a seal that belonged to the knight.[242]

The difference between the surcoats worn by the two princes and the doublets worn by the townsmen is clear. As represented in the description of the battle positions given by the narrative sources, the soldiers with *goedendags* were positioned next to or just behind those with pikes. The *goedendag* had a shorter rod or handle than the pikes intended to be stuck in the ground, as Guy de Namur is depicted doing.

As in illustration IV, there are soldiers from the towns who are wearing short coats of mail, since they have sleeves with mail. They are all, even the princes, wearing open helmets, neck-coverings, thick padded doublets and iron gloves.

To the left of the above, a knight is being attacked by three townsmen. One of them is thrusting his sword into the breast of the horse and another is attacking with his pike. The knight has as his coat of arms a saltire between four trefoils. It is the Lord of Sijsele, near Bruges. The banner of the Lord of Lens, commander of the French garrison, is flying in the wind above the heads of the Flemish soldiers.

Illustration VI

Illustration VI represents the sortie made by a section of the garrison stationed in the Courtrai fortress.

To the left, at the edge of the depiction, part of the castle has been cut off. Two towers are still fully depicted. A man is descending by a rope from one of the towers. It is doubtful that this was Willem van Mosscher since he was not reported as having been in the garrisons.[243] There is an observation point on top of the tower and between both towers there is a section of a trebuchet – a machine catapulting heavy stones. On the tower, to the right, the banner of France in simplified form and the banner of the Lord of Lens are flying. A tun filled with pitch is fastened above the gate.[244]

The iron portcullis in front of the gate has been drawn up and a knight is charging out. His shield has a cross and five rings of which one of the circles is above the cross. It is not known which French nobleman is being portrayed here.

The men of Ypres are all wearing the coat of arms of the town, which is also portrayed on the town seal.[245] Moving from left to right, there is a pavis or large

---

[242] There is a good reproduction of this in Fris, *Vlaanderens vrijmaking in 1302*, 137. See also Pirenne, *Histoire de la Belgique*, I:246.
[243] ffoulkes, 124. ffoulkes was of this opinion, but Willem was not mentioned as being in the garrison with several known noblemen. See *Chronique artésienne*, 44–5.
[244] ffoulkes, 125.
[245] See a reproduction of this seal in Blockmans, *1302, vóór en na*, pl. 12.

Illustration VI: The sortie of the French knights out of the castle of Courtrai

shield, with two arrows in it in the midst of the ranks of the men of Ypres. It is one of the *targen* or shields used by the crossbowmen and carried by *garsoenen*, their helpers, during the battle. Right next to the shield, and to the right of the castle gate, there is a soldier with a falchion, a weapon with a very wide blade and sharp point. One of the soldiers is using a small round shield. At the front, in the centre, there is a soldier with a finely reproduced *goedendag*. One can very clearly make out the steel pin in the wood of the thick club bound together by means of a fastening ring enabling the soldiers to hammer hard with the weapon while protecting the wood. The *goedendag* is shorter than a pike but longer than a knight's sword, as seen very clearly here.

Illustration VII
The depiction presents the collection of booty before and after the dead were stripped. Everything that they possessed was taken from them, and the bodies were left there, naked, on the battlefield until they were buried. One sees that the dead had been terribly wounded and mutilated, this being the result of the merciless battle waged by the Flemings with very heavy weapons.

Illustration VII: Collecting the booty after the battle

Conclusion[246]

As shown in the depictions on the chest, as well as the mural paintings in the Ghent Leugemeete chapel, the Flemings had uniforms: soldiers from each guild had tunics of the same colour and also had relatively expensive weapons. The heavy and long arms with which the townsmen awaited the charge of the knights and squires were chosen as being most suitable for the type of battle to be fought. The long pikes, whose rods were stuck into the ground, were to stop the charge of the noblemen and, at the same time, inflict heavy losses on the enemy. The men with *goedendags*, who held their weapons with both hands, stood either beside the soldiers with pikes or just behind in the space between two men with pikes. They attacked the knights and their warhorses as soon as they passed through the wall of pikes.

Although not all the Flemish soldiers wore a coat of mail, all of them had a helmet, neck-covering, iron gloves and sturdy weapons. They were thus not as well protected as the noblemen but on the other hand had longer weapons with which they could attack their enemy at a distance. This gave them a considerable advantage when fighting at close quarters.

It is thus completely erroneous to portray the Flemish soldiers as poor devils armed with ploughshares stuck to rods. When the Italian Villani presented the Flemish townsmen as poor and lowly characters the intention was to emphasise the contrast. On the one hand, there were the poor devils from the towns who had to defend themselves and attack with the very same weapons. On the other, there were the rich and splendidly armed noblemen who were to fall at the feet of such lowly townspeople. The flower of nobility against the lowly masses: the Italian took much pleasure in being able to disparage the arrogant French noblemen in this manner. However, greater significance should not be attached to the comparison. A convincing portrayal of the excellent quality of the Flemish weaponry is to be found in the lengthy description of the Flemish battle array given by the French eyewitness and soldier, Guillaume Guiart, who sincerely admired the power of the Flemings.[247] The Flemings were rightly proud of their sturdy weapons and such pride was presented by foreigners as arrogance.

A quick look outside the county of Flanders indicates that all foot-soldiers who were successful in the Middle Ages against armies of knights had weapons based on the same principles. The Scotsmen used long pikes and powerful battle-axes. The Swiss had their heavy halberds that were used to pierce, as were the

---

[246] R. H. Marijnissen, 'De "Chest of Courtrai": een vervalsing van het pasticcio-type', *Mededelingen van de Koninklijke Academie voor Wetenschappen, Letteren en Schone Kunsten van België*, 40 (1978), no. 3, believes that the chest is a fake. Refutation of Marijnissen's views is found in B. Dewilde, A. Pauwels, J. F. Verbruggen, and E. Warlop, 'De kist van Oxford', *De Leiegouw*, 22 (1980), 163–256. See also Brian Gilmour and Ian Tyers, 'Courtrai Chest: Relic or Recent: Reassessment and Further Work: An Interim Report', in *Papers of the "Medieval Europe Brugge 1997" Conference*, vol 5: *Art and Symbolism in Medieval Europe* (Bruges, 1997), 17–26.

[247] Guiart, 287–8, vv. 20,155–69; 291–2, vv. 20,573–8. See also an example in the description of the battle.

goedendags, and due to their weight enabled the heavy armour of the knights to be hacked through and their horses to be killed. The foot-soldiers stopped the charge by means of their pikes and lances which kept the enemies at a distance and prevented them from penetrating the close and compact ranks. After this, the other soldiers attacked with powerful weapons that were shorter than the pikes and lances but much longer than the short swords used by the noblemen. The terrible wounds inflicted by such weapons, and the savagery of the foot-soldiers, made the weapons famous. Each of the three types of foot-soldiers referred to above mercilessly killed the knights. Following the Battle of the Spurs, this clearly influenced the knights' tactics in subsequent expeditions. The French knights simply did not realise, before the Battle of Courtrai, the force and strength of Flemish foot-soldiers, and the townsmen for their part were not yet conscious of the fact that they could resist, and defeat, the most celebrated army of knights of their time.

5

From the Bruges Matins to the Battle of the Spurs for freedom, equality and fraternity

An unbridgeable chasm arose between the King of France and the Flemish town of Bruges in the early hours of 18 May 1302, known as the Bruges Friday. The blood of 120 noblemen and royal foot-soldiers destroyed all hope of peaceful settlement to the conflict that had broken out.[1]

Simple weavers, fullers and other artisans suddenly became the powerful rulers of the richest town in Flanders.[2] They were aware of the gravity of the massacre committed and of the crime of lèse majesté that called for revenge: it was clear to them that they could no longer avoid responsibility, and that the struggle would have to be waged to its very end. A victory, or terrible death as punishment, was for their leaders, as well as for a large number of the rebels, the only choice presented to them. They fought for classic ideals of the highest value through the ages, an inspiration to countless men of supreme sacrifice: equality, fraternity and liberty. From the beginning of the protest in Bruges, the members of the guilds gathered under the banner of Pieter de Coninc, the representative of the guild with the most members. The artisans of the wool industry – weavers, fullers, and shearers – wanted to become the equals of the members of rich trades, like brewers, sellers of wool cloth or butchers, and the equals of the patricians who were the masters of the town. The weavers wanted to buy their wool and to sell the cloth they had made. The equality would have to lead to economic independence and social prestige. They wished to have the same rights as the rich in the government of the town. They wanted to be small and independent entrepreneurs in a guild where they could elect their deans and other leaders. In these guilds the members called themselves brothers. This fraternity was extended to the friends and the allies of the other towns and the peasants of the country. Alliances were closed between the towns and the communities of the county: everybody would pay his part of the cost of waging war against the King of France. Every man was a brother in arms. It was not permitted to kill him. During the war the law would be the same for everybody: an eye for an eye, a limb for a limb, a life for a life. Equality and fraternity: the same penalty must be applied for noble, rich and poor men. Everybody would be

---

[1] *Chronique artésienne*, 43.
[2] The town of Bruges had the highest income of all the Flemish towns at that time. See H. van Werveke, *De Gentsche stadsfinanciën in de middeleeuwen*, Académie royale de Belgique, Classe des Lettres, Mémoires, 34 (Brussels, 1934), 349.

free to choose his craft, or trade or commerce. The artisan and the peasant fought for his private liberty, and for the liberty of his town, his community and the county. The liberty of Bruges and Flanders must be won. The Count, Guy de Dampierre, his sons and the noble prisoners in France must be free again.

Fortunately for them, higher commanders appeared who seemed capable of assuming this important task and by their characters showed themselves to be worthy of leadership in this epic battle. They succeeded in providing the essential direction and driving force without becoming entangled in the small details of daily administration. They acted intelligently and, although belonging to the nobility, they granted the necessary freedoms and privileges so as to keep the masses enthusiastic. Since artisans were also sharing in the execution of political power, first in Bruges and later in other towns, they believed that the era of equality in law had dawned, thus spurring them on to make the utmost sacrifices. Neither Willem van Jülich, nor Guy de Namur, Jean de Namur or Philip of Chieti were to deem it necessary to write the following, as had Guy de Dampierre in 1298, bitter and fully lacking in political foresight: 'And do not forget, my beloved son, that the privileges and freedoms that we granted during this war in order to win the favour of our good towns, having not served us well, must be destroyed.'[3]

Willem van Jülich immediately returned to Bruges together with Pieter de Coninc. On 23 May, he held a second triumphant entry,[4] and the common people were not lax in their ardent welcome for the young cleric. The youthful nobleman, who had rushed from the east to help the rebels, was welcomed even more passionately than several weeks earlier. He wore the lion of the Count of Flanders over his coat of mail, this being the symbol of the power that he sought to restore. He went immediately to Moerzeke to fetch the armour and sword of his grandfather, Count Guy de Dampierre, who was being held prisoner in France. While returning to Bruges, the armour was carried in front of the prince. Is there any clearer indication of the fact that only the force of arms was capable of securing a favourable course of events in the risky enterprise which had been embarked upon? And it was certainly a perilous undertaking, waging war against the powerful King of France with a handful of rebels. The Lord of Moerzeke constantly pointed out to Willem van Jülich that it was folly to hope for victory against such an enemy as Philip the Fair. The fact that the grandson of the Count was leading the rebellion could, according to the lord, not fail to endanger the life of Guy de Dampierre and his sons, held captive in France.[5]

However, Willem van Jülich did not let himself be influenced by the hesitant and faint of heart. He took upon himself the task of *ruwaerd*, governor of Bruges, and immediately gained the support of the Flemish knights, of whom some had already taken the side of the town prior to the Bruges Matins.[6] Willem van Jülich's eloquence, his beauty, youth and the renown of his noble origins and name quickly

---

[3] Funck-Brentano, *Philippe le Bel*, 245; and Delfos, *1302 door tijdgenooten verteld*, 98 n. 16.
[4] Wyffels and Vandewalle, 808.
[5] Lodewijk, II.1.IV:276, c. 17, vv. 1176–205.
[6] Wyffels and Vandewalle, 827, 74–5.

made him an idol for the common people.[7] The rebels understood that the young man was not fighting for his own interests but was, in their eyes, taking revenge for his brother, Willem van Jülich, the elder, who was so badly wounded at Furnes, in 1297, that he died several days after the battle. Nothing was refused to this leader who had come to save their cause and not to enforce his power upon the town. The most expensive horses, the most splendid weaponry, the finest garments were all given to him at the expense of the town. In a period of several weeks, immense sums were spent, thousands and thousands of pounds on the prince and his increasingly more powerful entourage. Willem led a princely existence and spent his money with the true generosity of a knight.

The presence of a relative of the lawful Count, joined shortly afterwards by a son of the prince, Guy de Namur, exerted a powerful influence upon Flemish noblemen who supported the Count and were still living in the county. They understood that something more was happening than a mere town rebellion instigated by the guildsmen against the patricians. The most brave among them rushed to help, and Willem van Jülich called upon his friends for assistance too. Among them, as one of the first to answer the call, was Hendrik van Lontzen who had already fought in Flanders under Guy de Dampierre. He came now, once again, as did his nephew and an entourage of knights and squires. Willem van Jülich appointed Hendrik Marshal of Bruges, with the town paying him generously and reimbursing all expenses incurred by his entourage.[8]

Pieter de Coninc also appeared in his home town together with Willem van Jülich. The poor weaver only had his eloquence in common with the prince, his exceptional skills as a speaker. It is difficult to imagine a greater contrast between the young, beautiful and gifted nobleman and the small, penniless, aged weaver of lowly origins.[9] The leader of the common people was taking the side of the representative of the Count's house, the lawful authority. Could there have been a better guarantee for the defence of the interests of his fellow townsmen and of the artisans?

Aside from these two renowned leaders and Guy de Namur, a third element appeared, somewhat in the shadow of the great men: the new town magistrate of Bruges. The three types of leaders show the various tendencies present at that time in the rebels' camp. For Willem van Jülich and Guy de Namur the battle was being waged, first of all, to restore the power of the Count and to make Flanders independent once again under the rightful administration of the house of the Count. Pieter de Coninc was the leader of the common people, the man of the artisans, emerging from their midst and knowing their problems. While the two princes represented above all the national aspect of the struggle, a man such as Pieter de Coninc, and the success of his actions, ought to be seen as embodying the powerful current that dictated a social aspect to the rebellion. The Bruges town administration added a further element: the conscious attempt to gain leadership in the

---

[7] *Annales Gandenses*, 19, 41; and Lodewijk, II.1.IV:255, c. 10, vv. 664–74.
[8] Wyffels and Vandewalle, 82, 870.
[9] *Chronique artésienne*, 37–8; and Lodewijk, II.1.IV:254, c. 10, vv. 643–53.

county, or at least the paramount position among the towns, and, if circumstances permitted, the exertion of actual power in Flanders. Since the new town administration also included representatives of the guilds that were now acting as political bodies, once again the social forces in the politics of the Bruges town administration that spurred the artisans on in the battle can be seen. They fought for freedom, equality and fraternity. One should, moreover, note the complex nature of the conflict: a mixture of national, political and social tendencies that rapidly evolved into a national struggle against the King and even against the French. This became clear following the battle of 11 July 1302.

The young princes who following the Bruges Matins led the decisive campaign acted first and foremost as military commanders and paid less attention to the political aspects of the situation in the county. This can certainly be considered as guaranteeing the success of the rebellion, and they let the Bruges town administration have its own way in that area. They were rewarded by the town administration, and the great masses of artisans, with such loyalty and trust that the incompetent actions taken by Guy de Dampierre against Bruges were immediately forgotten. For their part, the princes closed their eyes concerning the position of Bruges on the side of Philip the Fair in the period 1297–1301.

The powerful military leadership given by Willem van Jülich and Guy de Namur and the trust they placed in the rebels gave great impetus to the formation of such personal loyalty into a national identity. If a political leader such as Jean de Namur had appeared in the county, at that point the cooperation with the Bruges town administration would probably have been less enthusiastic, since Jean would have noticed more quickly that power in the county had in fact fallen from the hands of the representatives of the prince.

Numerous entries in the Bruges town accounts indicate the feverish energy shown by the town administration. Behind the scenes to this brilliant display of successful military leadership shown by both princes, the Brugeois aldermen and the members of the council took over political power in Flanders. After Courtrai, it was obviously impossible to react: Jean de Namur and Philip of Chieti understood that and were obliged to let the town administration have its way.[10] Any other form of action would only have alienated them from the common people, and how could they have resisted without any material resources?

The Bruges town administration naturally had full control of financial policy which was, all said and done, practically the same as the real power in the county. The town's receipts were increased by their administration of the properties of Flemish noblemen who supported the King and of patricians in Bruges and the Bruges Franc. All receipts from the above went to the town treasury,[11] which from

---

[10] Funck-Brentano, *Philippe le Bel*, 418–19, 448.
[11] Wyffels and Vandewalle, 11–53, 871–86; and Verbruggen, *Vlaanderen na de guldensporenslag*, 13–24.

then onwards had direct control over a significant portion of receipts in the county.[12] On the other hand, other large towns such as Ypres were to carry part of the costs of the war. Those French and Flemish noblemen captured during the Bruges Matins, as well as several Bruges patricians and even several extremely rich bankers from Arras, were obliged to pay very high ransoms.[13] Money was also borrowed from rich burghers, clergymen and the guilds, as well as from those in other towns.[14] During the expeditions the *pointinghe* (burghers' tax) was raised to recover some of the costs.[15]

The town was thus able to recompense the Flemish noblemen and pay the foreign mercenaries; Willem van Jülich and Guy de Namur were paid from the Bruges town treasury just as other hired soldiers. This is also the case with some members of the high Flemish nobility: Zeger van Gent and his son were already enlisted from 8 May 1302.[16]

When Guy de Namur called upon the clergymen, in order to win their support, the Bruges town administration was on the side of the prince.[17]

The messengers sent by the town, often accompanied by an alderman or member of the council, travelled all over Flanders in order to win all the towns over the side of the rebels; they went to Aardenburg, to Courtrai, to Ghent and to Ypres.[18] One visit to Aalst on 29 June was actually followed by the considerable sum of 5000 pounds sent to the same town.[19] A visit to Hulst from 25 to 30 June with the knight, Zeger van Gent, the bailiff of Bruges, Gillis uten Broeke, and Willem de Repre was followed by a new journey by Willem de Repre 'to the Zeelanders'.[20] On 8 July, Jan van Renesse received a payment from the town.[21] On 3 July, a messenger was sent to Jean de Namur,[22] and, on 7 July, representatives were sent from Bruges to Nieuwpoort and other towns, patently to raise further troops. On 12 July money was transported to Oudenaarde.[23]

Meanwhile, no time was being lost and action was being taken astonishingly quickly. As early as 31 May, Willem van Jülich and Pieter de Coninc left the town at the head of an army.[24] They lay siege to Wijnendaal, just before the solid castle gates. As a castle of the Count, it ought to have been freed at once; however, no

---

[12] Bruges was the richest town, paying 15.21% of the taxes, Ghent 13.85%, the Bruges Franc 13.37%, and Ypres 10.72%.
[13] Wyffels and Vandewalle, 56–8; and J. De Smet, 'De gezindheid van de Vlaamse ridders in 1302', 145–7.
[14] Wyffels and Vandewalle, 60–7; and Gilliodts-van Severen, I:110–11, no. 169.
[15] Wyffels and Vandewalle, 58–9.
[16] Ibid., 74–5, 827.
[17] Kervyn de Lettenhove, ed., *Codex Dunensis sive Diplomatum et Chartarum Medii Aevi* (Brussels, 1875), 310–11.
[18] Wyffels and Vandewalle, 115–18.
[19] Ibid., 116.
[20] Ibid., 116.
[21] Gilliodts-van Severen, I:98, no. 165.
[22] Wyffels and Vandewalle, 116.
[23] Ibid., 116.
[24] Ibid., 810

time was wasted on a lengthy siege, and the expedition immediately moved on. The siege of the fortress continued, and later favourable conditions were even granted to the French garrison.[25] On 1 June, Willem van Jülich and Pieter de Coninc arrived with their troops at Gistel. Nieuwpoort was reached the following day. By 5 June, they were already in Hondschote from where they advanced towards St Winoksbergen, freeing the town on 6 June. The garrison in the town fled: the hundreds of knights and Flemish supporters of the King of France did not even attempt to resist, since the soldiers did not trust the local people who had all chosen the side of the rebels.[26] The French occupation had occasioned those Flemish noblemen who supported the King to react severely against the local inhabitants. The wrath of the common people now rushed back, not only against the noblemen, but also against their French allies.

On 9 June, Willem van Jülich's and Pieter de Coninc's campaign of liberation came to an end. For the first time they then met with powerful resistance. The town of Cassel was still recaptured without any difficulty, but the fortress could not be taken immediately. It was being defended by the Lords of Haveskerke, Jan and Gillis, two Flemish supporters of the King of France who since November 1298 had been receiving a yearly fee from Philip the Fair.[27]

Since they were not far from the southern border of the county, and almost all of maritime Flanders had been liberated, Willem van Jülich and Pieter de Coninc considered it necessary to capture the strategically very important position. Siege equipment was set up, and a full siege began. However, the fortress was very difficult to storm and had sufficient provisions to resist the rebels for weeks.[28]

Meanwhile, at the beginning of June the people of Bruges had enthusiastically welcomed another representative of the Count's house. Following the merry news of the Bruges Matins, Guy de Namur had left distant Namur and come to take command of the rebellion himself. Grass was strewn in the streets of Bruges, as customary for a prince, and the bells of the town gave a cheerful welcome.[29] At once, Guy appealed, together with the Bruges town administration, to the clergymen of the county, asking them for pious prayers and processions so that heaven would grant victory to the soldiers.[30]

After this, Guy advanced to liberate the county, bringing to a successful end the siege of Wijnendaal where the bailiff of Torhout, a Flemish ally of the French, was beheaded following the surrender of the fortress.[31] Messengers from Ypres then came to report the entry of the town. On 14 June, Guy was once again in the same

---

[25] *Annales Gandenses*, 25–6.
[26] Ibid., 26; and *Chronique artésienne*, 44.
[27] Godefroy, V, nos. 4129, 4130, 4218, 4219. Jan van Haveskerke received a yearly payment of 600 Parisian pounds. See also a further document in Funck-Brentano, *Philippe le Bel*, 353 n. 5.
[28] *Annales Gandenses*, 26; *Chronique artésienne*, 44; and Lodewijk, II.1.IV:281–3, c. 20.
[29] Wyffels and Vandewalle, 103.
[30] Kervyn de Lettenhove, ed., *Codex Dunensis*, 310–11. See also Delfos, *1302 door tijdgenooten verteld*, 43.
[31] Lodewijk, II.1.IV:279–80, c. 19, vv. 1299–304.

fortress as he had had to transfer to the brother of the French King on 21 May 1300, after resisting for the longest period of all of the Count's sons.[32] However, in Ypres, supporters of the King were in power, and the help offered by the town was limited to a contingent of somewhat more than five hundred members of the militia.[33] Ypres was obviously immediately freed from any payment of fines set by the King, and the town's freedoms and privileges were confirmed by the son of the Count.

Guy then learned that the fortress at Courtrai was still held by a French garrison and immediately 'called for an expedition to free it'.[34] The rebels' army was to be drawn to Courtrai. Guy gathered the soldiers together there, and all nobles of the area who had remained faithful to the Count rushed to him. Guy, like Willem van Jülich, was a young and impressive knight, a powerful and experienced soldier who together with his relatives kept up morale, inspiring the confidence of the Flemish soldiers and bringing out the most courageous nature in them.[35]

However, Ghent, the largest and most populous town in the county, did not follow the rebels. The supporters of the King were still in power there and since St Pol had made concessions there was no immediate reason to rebel. Still, entrances to the town were now completely blocked by the men of Bruges and their supporters. At Oudenaarde, the Scheldt river was blocked and Ghent was severely struck by famine.[36] The supporters of the King and the rich burghers were continually afraid of fines that could be imposed upon the town or of the confiscation of their property by the King. However, they succeeded in convincing the artisans, who wanted to join the men of Bruges, and kept them in Ghent. Despite this, there was still the constant threat of an uprising. Only several hundred people secretly left the town, being immediately exiled by the town administration.[37] They went to Courtrai, placing themselves under the command of the exiled Jan Borluut, who lived in Tournai because of a feud with other Ghent patricians.[38]

The two well-constructed fortresses of Cassel and Courtrai had in the mean time brought the triumphant advance of Willem van Jülich and Guy de Namur to a standstill. However, the leaders were intelligent enough to put an end to such a dangerous dispersion of their forces. While Guy advanced towards Courtrai, he sent a messenger to Willem van Jülich, summoning him to Courtrai. Willem van Jülich and Pieter de Coninc immediately followed the call, all the more since they saw that the Lords of Haveskerke were ready to resist at all costs and would not

---

[32] Funck-Brentano, *Philippe le Bel*, 349, 397–8.
[33] *Annales Gandenses*, 26–7.
[34] Lodewijk, II.1.IV:280, c. 19, vv. 1323–4: 'dedi gebieden herevard, / Dapperlike te Cortrikeward.'
[35] *Annales Gandenses*, 26.
[36] Lodewijk, II.1.IV:27, c. 18, vv. 1235–8.
[37] *Annales Gandenses*, 29.
[38] F. Blockmans, 'Een patricische veete te Gent', 607–8, 630.

surrender without a bloody assault upon the castle.[39] On 24 June, they left the town, reaching Poperinge that very same day. On 26 June, they arrived in Courtrai, reinforcing Guy de Namur's troops.[40] The whole rebel army had now been brought together for the decisive battle and an important step had been taken on the road to victory.

The Strategic Problem

No serious French threat had, in fact, arisen for both of the Flemish armies as of 23 June. At that time the Count of Artois was still in the town of Arras with those French troops that had already been brought together.[41] According to the *Chronique artésienne*, the siege of Courtrai began on 23 June, that is on the same day that Guy summoned his nephew, Willem van Jülich, from Cassel.[42] The Count of Artois was planning to advance to Cassel. This is logical, since this previously had been the only besieged location where a French garrison was holding out. Whether he was already on his way to the fortress is difficult to determine,[43] and is, all said and done, of lesser significance. In this case, either Guy de Namur's summoning or the advance of the French army would have induced Willem van Jülich to leave Cassel. Other narrative sources, however, presented this movement incorrectly, claiming that it occurred when the Flemings saw that the Count of Artois was advancing to Courtrai.[44] In fact, comparison of the information indicates that Guy de Namur had only arrived in Courtrai on 23 June and summoned Willem van Jülich to Courtrai that very day without being aware of the danger approaching from the direction of Cassel.

However, bringing together the whole army beneath the walls of Courtrai was a strategic measure of the utmost significance, forming the first step towards the great victory there: the rebels' move obliged, or at least prompted, the French to advance to Courtrai.

The concentration of all forces in Courtrai appears so logical and obvious that previously no attention has been paid to the problem. We are thus mostly confronted with incorrect presentations of the event. The importance of the matter will no doubt be clarified when we compare the general operations in 1302 with those of 1297, 1328 and 1382.

In 1297, Guy de Dampierre's troops were hopelessly dispersed in the major

---

[39] Lodewijk, II.1.IV:283, c. 20, vv. 1392–402; and *Chronique artésienne*, 44. See also *Annales Gandenses*, 28.
[40] Wyffels and Vandewalle, 813–14.
[41] According to evidence given by the well-informed and anonymous Artesian chronicler (*Chronique artésienne*, 44).
[42] *Chronique artésienne*, 44.
[43] Ibid., 44. According to this source, he was on his way. In the accounts, he was in Lens on 30 June from where he could advance to Cassel as well as to Lille.
[44] *Annales Gandenses*, 28; *Anciennes chroniques*, 377; *Chronographia*, I:103–4; and Villani, 385.

towns of the county. In Lille, they were under the command of Robert de Bethune, where there was a strong garrison, in Douai, under the command of Willem van Dendermonde and in Ypres under the command of Jean de Namur.[45] The Count certainly wanted to keep the above towns until his ally Edward I of England arrived with his army. Later, in 1300, the same situation obtained for Damme, which was being defended by Willem, for Ghent, occupied by Robert de Bethune, and for Ypres, which was being defended by Guy de Namur. This is without mentioning the garrisons in the towns along the Zwin river and in other small fortresses. No troops were left over in 1297, and certainly not in 1300, for a large-scale battle on an open field. For this reason, the Count's troops were in the final event weak everywhere, and they very soon suffered military defeat.

In 1328, during the rebellion in the coastal areas of Flanders, the strategic situation was almost the same as that of 1302. The men of Bruges and the soldiers from the Flemish coast had to fight against French troops who were able to count upon the help of the town of Ghent. However, the rebel's camp lacked capable military leaders. Instead of waiting for the enemy in a well-chosen position with the whole army, they thought it possible to close off the three traditional approaching routes. The men of Bruges and of the Bruges Franc had to hold back the Ghent militia and the enemy in Biervliet. The troops from Ypres, Courtrai and the surrounding areas of these towns guarded the approaches from Lille. Finally, the troops from the Flemish coast were to hold the third approach at Cassel, from St Omer towards Ypres. Therefore only the troops from the castellanies of Furnes, St Winoksbergen, Broekburg, Cassel and Belle were left to face a very powerful enemy army.[46]

The campaign of 1382 differed from those of 1302 and 1328 because the French showed excellent strategic skills when called upon to fight against the men of Ghent, led by Philip of Artevelde. They marched straight to Bruges, thus avoiding the rebel army instead of approaching it while it was laying siege to Oudenaarde. Philip of Artevelde was then forced to rush as quickly as possible to block the path of the enemy.[47] In 1382, the French army of knights executed operations on its own terms. In 1302, however, Artois arrived with the French army at that point where the Flemings most wanted him, at Courtrai, with the towns of Bruges and Ypres being protected by both the River Lys and the fortress at the same time. If the enemy troops sought to advance towards Ghent, they would have to do so past the Flemings.

It will be seen that the leaders not only positioned their army excellently, but also chose a very good battlefield at Courtrai. Moreover, the general political situation was favourable to the Flemings. They had by then very quickly liberated a great part of the county, and everything indicated that the rest of Flanders would also fall into their hands. Furthermore, they were threatening the Courtrai fortress, the fall of which would bring with it that of Cassel, thus making an advance towards Lille and Douai possible. Thus the Count of Artois had no time to lose.

---

[45] Pirenne, *Histoire de Belgique*, I:241; and Nowé, *La Bataille des éperons d'or*, 49.
[46] J. Sabbe, *Vlaanderen in opstand*, 67–8.
[47] Lot, *L'Art militaire*, I:451.

Since all the rebels were gathered together at Courtrai, Artois suddenly saw the chance to destroy the insurgents in one battle and to take revenge for those who had fallen in the events of Bruges Friday, at the same time freeing the French garrison.

On 30 June, Artois was still in Lens from where he was able to send troops to Cassel, either passing by Bethune, Aire and St Omer or passing by Lille to reach Courtrai. On 1 July, however, the French army reached Seclin to the south of Lille. This time there was no doubt: Artois was to advance towards Courtrai. By 2 July, the army had already reached Marquette, but it was kept there until 8 July by ditches which first had to be filled before the troops could move on.[48] On the evening of 8 July, Artois arrived with his army, setting up camp on the Pottelberg hill just to the south of Courtrai.[49]

Since the royal army was camped before the fortress, the Count of Artois immediately attempted on 9 July to storm the Tournai gate. The following day the Lille gate was attacked heavily.[50]

Both attempts failed completely. There was one solution left for the commander to free the castle: to enjoin in battle against the Flemish rebels in their very favourable position on the Groeninge field where they blocked the entrance to the castle from the north-east.

It should not be thought that the problem of a battle on the Groeninge field first appeared to Artois and his advisors on the morning of 11 July. The French commander was aware that the garrison had already been under siege for a long time, having few soldiers and provisions only for a few days. It is naïve to imagine that the commander would wait for two days before forcing an outcome of a battle when this could have been done on 9 July. There is only one solution to the matter: Artois hesitated, and attempted first to conquer the town. This was in fact a fruitless undertaking against a determined opponent since a strong fortress defended by a powerful field army was at that time impossible to conquer.

Aside from engaging in open battle, there was also the possibility of advancing further into Flanders towards Ghent, which was still on the side of Philip the Fair. However, in the mean time, the castle of Courtrai would have fallen, and how would Artois find the necessary provisions for his army so deep in Flanders? Furthermore, a retreat after his army had faced the rebels would have made as bad an impression as a defeat. The rebels would have drawn great advantage from this and would have faced a battle in the future with even more confidence.

Advancing on Bruges made even less sense. The powerful fortress, where the town ramparts had been partially destroyed in 1301, would naturally have been repaired. The town would be defended vigorously and would be just as difficult to conquer as Courtrai. Since his army was at Courtrai, Artois was obliged by the general situation to bring about an outcome by force of arms. Since such an outcome had not been attained by storming the town gates, it had to be reached by battle on the Groeninge field.

---

[48] For the itinerary taken by Artois see Funck-Brentano, 'Mémoire', 311–17.
[49] Funck-Brentano, 'Mémoire', 311–17.
[50] Lodewijk, II.1.IV:286–7, c. 21, vv. 1450–92.

The question was: how would the Flemings defend themselves in their good position? In 1297, Artois had already defeated them at Furnes, despite having to cross a waterway that was being defended by the Flemings and their mercenaries.[51] Would the rebels actually confidently await the force of the impact of heavily armoured knights? Would these foot-soldiers who had almost no military experience dare resist the most splendid army of that time? The events of 11 July would answer these questions, which certainly weighed on the minds of the French commander and his advisors.

---

[51] *Chronique artésienne*, 15.

6

11 July 1302

The night passed and the sun arose. In the castle of Courtrai the Viscount of Lens waited impatiently to be liberated. Two full days had already passed since the Count of Artois had set up his camp on the Pottelberg hill, and the defender of the castle was in the dark about the plans of the French commander. He sought to point out to Artois how, and along which path, it would be possible to free the garrison rapidly. His soldiers carried a burning torch around the fortress walls to indicate that the Groeninge field was the most suitable place to free the castle. They stopped in front of the Flemish troops, near the Grey Nuns' abbey, and after giving a sign in that direction, they threw down the blazing torches beside the fortress ramparts. Other soldiers in the garrison tried to give signs with their swords, the steel of which shone in the morning sun.[1] They all pointed to the low-lying area that was intersected by the Groeninge and Grote Beek streams and was bounded by the damp Lys marshes and the abbey buildings to the north. To the south the area was bounded by the Courtrai town ramparts. This was the only way left to the Count of Artois to set free the garrison.

The commander saw the signals of the garrison and rode towards the camp of the Flemings on the Groeninge field to take reconnaissance. He realised that he would have to engage in battle and at around 6 o'clock he gave the necessary orders.[2] Trumpets sounded the call to arms, and the French troops were gathered together. The noblemen put on their coats of mail and plates; their horses were harnessed, saddled and completely prepared for battle. The feverish activity on the Pottelberg hill could not fail to escape the attention of the Flemings.[3] On the Groeninge field and in the town of Courtrai the townsmen were called up. They broke down their tents and thousands of soldiers put on their armour, preparing themselves for the approaching battle.

The noblemen in the royal army were divided into ten formations, or *bataelgen*, of knights, with an average strength of 250 knights in heavy armour. The noblemen were positioned beside their relatives and those of their region. They would ride into battle led by their lord or a specially chosen leader who had been deemed best suited on the basis of his military experience. The *bataelgen* were a grouping of banners or *conroten*, smaller units, that formed the basic element in an army of

---

[1] Lodewijk, II.1.IV:289–90, c. 22, vv. 1528–60.
[2] Ibid., II.1.IV:291, c. 23, v. 1584.
[3] *Annales Gandenses*, 29.

knights, being composed of the entourage of a powerful lord, a baron, banneret or a prominent knight who commanded around twenty noblemen. Such units often took up a rectangular position: one body of troops consisting of twenty-one men on horseback would consist of three ranks of seven men each.[4] Elsewhere, battle was waged with units comprised of two rows of knights. At times, the *conroot* would be composed of only one rank, allowing all the knights to use their weapons well during the charge, as well as being able to engage in battle immediately.

The first *bataelge* was placed under the command of Jean de Burlats, seneschal of Guyenne and grand master of the crossbowmen. In his formation of knights, there were mercenaries from the south of France, Navarre, Spain and Lombardy.[5] The second *bataelge* was commanded by the two French marshals, Gui de Nesle and Renaud de Trie. The third was under the command of Raoul de Nesle, the constable of the royal army. Robert d'Artois, the supreme commander, was in charge of the fourth *bataelge*. The fifth was under the command of the former governor, Jacques de St Pol, who had meanwhile been removed from that post due to the great incompetence he had shown.[6] The sixth *bataelge* was led by Louis de Clermont, and the seventh by the Count of Eu, the Lord of Tancarville, both from Normandy, and the Count of Aumale, from Ponthieu. The eighth *bataelge* was led by Mathieu de Trie. The ninth, with the men of Brabant and the troops of his son, Jean de Vierson, the Viscount of Tournai, was commanded by Geoffrey de Brabant. The tenth *bataelge* of knights was to be charged with keeping the rearguard and hence it was numerically stronger than the others. This formation was led by two counts: Guy, the Count of St Pol, and Robert, the Count of Boulogne and Auvergne, who had just been appointed as the new representative of the King of France in the county of Flanders.[7]

Much time passed before all the soldiers had put on their armour. They still had to take a light breakfast and attend a mass. In the mean time, the Count of Artois sent out scouts to see what the intentions of the Flemings were and how their troops were positioned. Because of their functions, the two marshals were charged with this task and saw that the enemy was positioned behind a long and marshy waterway.[8] Moreover, the rebels were protected in the rear by the River Lys, so that they could not be attacked from behind. They only noted a few noblemen whose banners were flying in the wind above the Flemish troops: Guy de Namur, son of the Count, Willem van Jülich, grandson of Guy de Dampierre, and Jan van Renesse, who had a large flag depicting a lion. The great majority of the army consisted of artisans from the towns and peasants from the country.[9]

---

[4] J. F. Verbruggen, 'De slag bij Woeringen', *Het leger. De natie*, 5, nos. 5–6 (1950), 252. See the French army in 1300 above: one banneret per twenty men on horseback.
[5] Villani, 386. The list of units is based on a combination of data given by Lodewijk and Villani. On this see the discussion of these accounts above.
[6] Funck-Brentano, *Philippe le Bel*, 406.
[7] Ibid., 407.
[8] *Anciennes chroniques*, 377; *Chronographia*, I:105; Lodewijk, II.1.IV:297, c. 25, vv. 1716–20; and Guiart, 238, v. 15,010.
[9] Lodewijk, II.1.IV:298, c. 25, vv. 1728–40.

Since the report given by the marshals about their scouting mission indicated that the Flemings were prepared to wage battle in their favourable position, Artois decided to hold a war council to discuss the tactical objections arising from an attack on such terrain.[10]

The Council of War Held in the French Camp

As usual in a council of war held in an army of knights, all the prominent commanders were able to freely express their opinions and explain their objections. The constable, Raoul de Nesle, noted that it would be very dangerous to engage in battle after crossing the waterways, with the streams behind them. If the noblemen had to retreat in order to charge once again, or had to draw back from the enemy, then the ditches might prove to be fatal since, if a man were to ride into them, he would have great difficulty in getting out again. The best solution would be to tempt the Flemings out of their favourable position.[11] But how could that be achieved? The enemy would obviously not be so stupid. The grand master of the crossbowmen, Jean de Burlats, however, proposed attacking the enemy with the foot-soldiers. He was so certain of victory that he thought his crossbowmen would force all the Flemings to retreat. This would then be the moment to employ the closely ranked *bataelgen* of knights. As soon as any sign of weakness was noted in the Flemish ranks, then the charge would have to be undertaken. This would be the *coup de grâce*, crowning the series of skirmishes and attacks made by the foot-soldiers.[12] Geoffrey de Brabant proposed the same tactic of wearing down the Flemings, who were to be obliged, following their meagre breakfast, to remain the whole day without food and unable to quench their thirst.[13] He even proposed not engaging in battle on 11 July, but waiting until the following day. After a full day in the hot July sun in their heavy armour suffering from hunger and thirst, the Flemish artisans and peasants would certainly lose their bellicose spirit. Tired as they would be, they might refrain from any further resistance the following day.

Some of the noblemen took account of the fact that the Flemish commanders had not only chosen a strong position but that they had at the same time positioned their troops in such terrain that they must either die or gain victory.[14] Retreating, or even fleeing following a defeat would be impossible since the River Lys flowed behind the Flemish troops, and all entrances to the town were blocked since the only gate was too close to the front line positions and was too narrow for a fleeing army of thousands of soldiers.

The majority, however, declared themselves to be for an attack.[15] The rebels had

---

[10] *Anciennes chroniques*, 377; and *Chronographia*, I:107.
[11] Guiart, 238–9, vv. 15,018–30.
[12] Villani, 386.
[13] Lodewijk, II.1.IV:298–9, c. 25, vv. 1741–60.
[14] See, for example, Villani, 386: 'The Flemings stand there as hopelessly determined men.'
[15] *Anciennes chroniques*, 377; and *Chronographia*, I:107.

to be punished terribly and destroyed in one blow; the garrison had to be freed. Would the Flemings really dare to resist vigorously? Was their fearless appearance not just bravado, the arrogance of troops who had never engaged in battle? The terrain was susceptible to being crossed, and preventative measures would be taken. The crossbowmen and the *bidauts* would prepare the attack and advance towards the obstacles. If the knights followed at a certain distance, the Flemish crossbowmen would retreat.[16] As soon as they had been driven back sufficiently the moment would have come to cross the stream and begin the decisive charges. Crossing the stream would naturally be a critical moment but the Flemings surely would not dare attack at that moment. Foot-soldiers without any major military experience would certainly not attack on an open field. Why should that happen here? One strong charge would most probably immediately lead to a decisive outcome. The foot-soldiers would not resist the powerful advance of the closely ranked formations of knights in heavy armour.[17] They would penetrate deep into the Flemish ranks and break through them with one powerful thrust.

The tactical objections proffered by several commanders were thus rejected. An easy method of doing so was to doubt the personal courage of such noblemen, explaining their advice not to wage battle was due to their fear of death. The classical response that followed was: 'If you penetrate into the enemy ranks as far I, then you will be a very brave knight.'[18] However, once the discussion had been finished and the decision to attack taken, they all attacked equally courageously and many were to meet their death.

Artois made the decisive comment in the council of war, saying:[19]

What can such common people do against us? Even if there are many of them, one hundred knights are worth a thousand men on foot! The more vigorous the enemy defends himself the more honour shall fall to us on the battlefield. We have not advanced here to kill and pursue defenceless men!

In the mean time, the knights in heavy armour were prepared for battle and took up their positions in the formations. The army was already descending from the Pottelberg to the fields, full of confidence in the show of force that would bring honour and avenge the fall of Bruges.

---

[16] Geoffrey de Paris, 100, vv. 1164–75.
[17] The French underestimated their enemies. See *Chronicon Comitum Flandrensium*, 169.
[18] Lodewijk, II.1.IV:300, cc. 25–6, vv. 1769–88; Villani, 387; and Geoffrey de Paris, 100, vv. 1186–205.
[19] This conclusion has been reached based on Lodewijk, II.1.IV:300, c. 25, vv. 1769–80. For the council of war, use was made of all the sources, although the discussions were taken as having occurred at the same time in the deliberation before the battle. It is, however, possible that the chroniclers each gave a fragment of the actual discussion. The whole series of information reproduces practically all possible objections that were certainly discussed.

Preparations in the Flemish Army

The Flemings had occupied the open field next to the town since the early morning. Their camp was protected by the stream and the River Lys. They were also preparing themselves for battle. Anyone still in Courtrai was called outside when the trumpeters blew the call to arms. The crossbowmen immediately took up their positions behind the stream to prevent it being crossed. All bridges had long been destroyed.

Very little was eaten just before the battle; some had taken bread dipped in wine.[20] It also took a long time before the thousands of men were fully armed and the tents had been taken down and put away. As everyone was ready, the waiting seemed even longer. The soldiers were now completely equipped with a neck-covering of fine mail over the head which protected the throat, neck and part of the shoulders, with a small open helmet, a thick doublet and iron gloves. This equipment of the common soldier in the Flemish army was complemented by a strong weapon, a sturdy *goedendag*, a long pike, a hooked spear, a sword and a small shield or even a falchion with a very wide blade and sharp pointed end. The men must have suffered much from the heat under the burning sun of a July morning. The wealthiest soldiers were even more heavily armed, having short coats of mail, breastplates, or body irons, and mail stockings.[21]

Waiting for the enemy made the soldiers nervous, above all as they knew that their opponents enjoyed the glory of forming the best and most splendid army of that time. The Flemings were, for their part, fearful of the great battle that was to follow.[22] Undoubtedly, many of them at that moment would have much preferred to be far away from the battlefield. Any escape was, however, impossible: the wide River Lys ran behind them, where there were also two more army corps, the men of Ypres and the reserve corps under Jan van Renesse. Once the enemy had completed the advance, then any chance of fleeing from the front would be impossible. However, those who had advanced with the men of Bruges took note of the fact that they were in the end quite numerous. They stood there from the town ramparts to the abbey in large groups encouraging each other. They confessed and sought salvation in prayer. Friars Minor gave encouragement to them and blessed the troops.[23] The men closed in tightly against their fellow soldiers, spurring each other on. They talked in an exaggerated manner of the plundering and the misdeeds of the enemy in order to incite the soldiers to revenge.[24] For the peasants, the great

---

[20] Lodewijk, II.1.IV:342, c. 39, vv. 2802–5.
[21] See above section on the Oxford Chest.
[22] Lodewijk, II.1.IV:303, c. 26, vv. 1834–5; *Chronicon Comitum Flandrensium*, 169; and illustration IV of the Oxford Chest.
[23] It was normal for soldiers to attend a mass in the morning. For the Battle of Mons-en-Pévèle see *Annales Gandenses*, 65. The picture sketched by Villani (385) of the priest and the communion with the earth has, however, not been confirmed by any of the three pro-Flemish sources. Given its epic character, this appears to be a literary addition.
[24] *Annales Gandenses*, 28–9, 31.

day had come during which they would settle scores with their noble enemies who had previously exploited them. Many had suffered greatly during the raids committed by the French troops, from 1297 to 1300, during the military expeditions and the long period of so-called truce.[25] The townsmen were gathered together in their guilds, in one of those great families of men that defended the interests of the fellows and now provided mutual trust. There were also sufficient competent commanders; all Flemish noblemen fighting with the rebels had of their own free will rushed to join them. The noblemen still had a score to settle with their enemy, many of whom had received part of their properties. Many of the knights and squires had a brother to avenge, who had fallen in 1297 or 1300, or was still being held captive in France. This was the case for the princes; among others Willem van Jülich had a brother to avenge, and Guy de Namur's father and two brothers were still being held captive in a royal fortress. Rogier de Lille had lost his possessions during the period of truce.[26] Thomas and Iwein van Vaernewijck were still being held prisoner in France while Simon van Vaernewijck fought on the Groeninge fields.[27] This was also the case for Alard van Roebaais, with Geraard van Roebaais fighting at Courtrai.[28]

The intrepid nature of the two young princes gave confidence to all. Guy de Namur and Willem van Jülich, both wearing the foot-soldiers' open helmet,[29] rode before the front ranks of the troops and encouraged them.[30] They formed the Flemish ranks together with the Flemish noblemen and the heads of the guilds. The soldiers had long pikes that could be planted into the ground to stop the charge of the heavy knights' horses. Next to them, there were men with shorter *goedendags*. Such soldiers were to attack the knights and their warhorses as soon as the horses had been brought to a standstill, thrown to the ground or killed.[31] The most sturdy, brave and best-equipped soldiers were placed shoulder to shoulder in the two front ranks.[32]

Guy de Namur rode in front of the battle array speaking to the soldiers:

> A cloud now covers the sun; we shall therefore have no difficulty from its rays. We shall gain victory, I am certain of this. Beware, noble Flemings! Stand firm, because the enemy will ride towards you with much force. Call upon the help of God. He will certainly stand by us.

Willem van Jülich unfolded his banner and also gave encouragement to his troops. Jan van Renesse, the commander of the reserve corps, explained how he

---

[25] Ibid., 26.
[26] Funck-Brentano, *Philippe le Bel*, 307 n. 2.
[27] Lodewijk, II.1.IV:246, c. 7, vv. 486–7; and Wyffels and Vandewalle, 75, 85.
[28] Lodewijk, II.1.IV:245, c. 7, v. 472; and *Chronique artésienne*, 53.
[29] See Oxford Chest, illustration V.
[30] Lodewijk, II.1.IV:311, c. 29, vv. 2027–9.
[31] *Chronicon Comitum Flandrensium*, 168–9; Villani, 385; and illustration V of the Oxford Chest.
[32] This was general practice. See *Chronicon Comitum Flandrensium*, 198–9; and Guiart, 248, vv. 16,052–3.

would come to give assistance to the long battle array. He gave the last and most noble advice:

> Do not let the enemy break through your ranks. Do not be frightened. Kill both horse and man. 'Flanders, the Lion' is our battle cry. When the enemy attacks Guy's corps we shall come and help you from behind. Every man who penetrates into your ranks or breaks through them shall remain there, dead. Go now all of you and make your confessions.[33]

The announcement was then made in the Flemish army that no one was allowed to pick up booty, even if it lay at his feet. Whoever saw a fellow soldier gathering up a precious object was to kill the man. The same fate would fall to those who retreated or fled: 'Above all slay the horses and kill the enemy; it is forbidden to take prisoners.'[34]

Before the front lines of the full army Guy de Namur knighted the most deserving leaders of the common people. Such an honour fell upon Pieter de Coninc and his two sons, as well as around thirty other men of Bruges and Jan Borluut, the leader of the men of Ghent.[35] What better proof was there for the artisans that something had changed and that merit now led as much as the rights of birth to the greatest honours? As good commanders who know how best to encourage their troops, Guy de Namur and Willem van Jülich had their horses taken away to Courtrai, where the horses of all the other noblemen had been brought to safety.[36] They entrusted the supreme command to Jan van Renesse of Zeeland, who was less well-known to the Flemings, albeit a faithful ally of the Count for many years.[37] The two young princes both took one of the favourite weapons of the rebels, a sturdy *goedendag* or pike, and took up positions among their troops in the front rank.[38] This act of the purest courage shown by the two princes gave further encouragement to their troops. Their leaders, noblemen with much experience of war, were to fight on foot in their midst, having sent their horses far away. They had of their own free will chosen to share the lot of the

---

[33] Lodewijk, II.1.IV:303–4, c. 27, vv. 1844–61; II.1.IV:305–6, c. 27, vv. 1894–903. The commanders' speeches have not all been combined. This would make for a long speech that was certainly not given in virtue of the extension of the Flemish front. The commanders, riding before the front lines, gave short pieces of advice in full accordance with the military situation. They did not make any general observations. The general orders were announced and well reproduced by the pro-Flemish sources. Such advice and orders were the best that could be given. One finds similar information and advice being given elsewhere, notably at Crécy in 1346 by Edward III, King of England, to his troops. See Jean le Bel, II:106.
[34] Lodewijk, II.1.IV:306, c. 27, vv. 1904–9; *Annales Gandenses*, 31; and *Chronicon Comitum Flandrensium*, 168.
[35] Lodewijk, II.1.IV:306, c. 27, vv. 1910–17; Villani, 385–6; and Wyffels and Vandewalle, 84: '31 rode sindale ter niewer rudders boef.'
[36] *Chronicon Comitum Flandrensium*, 168; Lodewijk, II.1.IV:311, c. 29, vv. 2037–40; *Annales Gandenses*, 30; *Chronique artésienne*, 51; Villani, 385; le Muisit, 66; and *Chronographia*, I:106.
[37] *Chronique artésienne*, 51.
[38] Lodewijk, II.1.IV:311, c. 29, vv. 2039–40. According to the Oxford Chest, Guy de Namur had a pike and Willem van Jülich had a *goedendag*.

common man, braving all the dangers of the battle with them after giving the most competent advice and the strictest orders. For this reason, the common soldiers were able in full confidence to await the battle. During the battle, the reserve corps would if necessary rush to their aid, and the men of Ypres could also help them. The soldiers still stood nervously and impatiently, but they were ready to wage battle as soon as possible in order to free themselves from the oppressive and nerve-racking tension.[39]

The men of Ypres were positioned in front of the castle on the battlefield and, in part, in the town, either so as to prevent an outbreak of the enemy garrison or to resist it. The crossbowmen and their helpers, pavisers or *garsoenen*, were positioned just behind the two streams. The *garsoenen* were carrying the large shields, the pavises, behind which the crossbowmen were to span their bows. Moving from the town ramparts to the abbey, in the following order, one could see the Brugeois contingent, the soldiers of the Franc of Bruges and those from East Flanders. The strong Bruges corps were rallied around the banners of the town and of Willem van Jülich and were gathered a little further behind the Grote Beek stream. The men of the Franc were positioned in a curved line, facing the stream, which also followed the course of the obstacles. Its left wing stretched back behind the Groeninge stream where the Flemish ranks continued with Guy de Namur's troops. The soldiers of the Oudenaarde area, from Aalst and Courtrai, together with the Ghent corps, led by Jan Borluut, were to fight under Guy's banner. The banner of Guy de Namur flew in the wind as did that of the town of Ghent carried by Zeger Lonke.[40]

The long and very deep battle array formed in the middle a slight curve facing the Frenchmen and staying as close as possible to the stream, although far enough to escape being seriously impaired by the bolts of the enemy crossbowmen. This powerful battle array, with the hundreds of banners and pennants representing the guilds and noblemen, and with the shining steel weapons of the closely ranked soldiers, must have been a magnificent and commanding sight. The Frenchman, Guiart, who fought against the Flemings in 1304, described such a position in full admiration:

> It will be no easy thing, and will perhaps be impossible, to break through it. We can see so many sharp swords, so many shields, so many pennants, so many bucklers, so many helmets, so many sturdy beech rods, so many *goedendags*, so many hooked lances, neck-coverings and short coats of mail that their battle array is shining. Above all the front ranks, the wall of lances and *goedendags* gleam when the sun shines upon them. Whoever has seen the Flemings positioned in such a manner can say that they are animated by great pride. They stand packed so close to each other and their commanders continually repeat that they have to keep the packed ranks firmly closed. They must not let any person penetrate. That is the most important piece of advice they keep giving.[41]

---

[39] Lodewijk, II.1.IV:306, c. 27, vv. 1918–19; II.1.IV:297, c. 25, v. 1715: 'gewillech genoech te stride' (ready enough to fight). See also *Annales Gandenses*, 29–30.
[40] Lodewijk, II.1.IV:318, c. 32, vv. 2219–20. On the battle see Chapter I: terrain and map.
[41] Guiart, 287, vv. 20,131–60. The pride of the Flemings, a consequence of victory gained at

The Battle Array Chosen by the French Forces

In the mean time, the Count of Artois's splendid army had completed its approach from the Pottelberg to the Grey Nuns' abbey. The crossbowmen and the light foot-soldiers were positioned at the front and immediately spread out towards the two waterways, the Groeninge and the connecting stream, which protected the front line of the Flemish troops. The final preparations for battle for the formations of knights were made behind the shield of foot-soldiers. The most courageous and best-equipped knights here were also positioned in the front rank of the formations. The others were placed in the second rank. It is most probable that the formations formed as wide a front as possible so as to more easily overcome the obstacles. This would unleash the maximum number of soldiers at the very same moment onto the enemy as a living wall of warhorses and lances.

As soon as the Count of Artois had taken note of the Flemish battle array, observing that it was comprised of one large formation, he reformed his original ten formations of knights into three larger formations each comprised of different bodies of knights positioned next to each other. Two formations were to attack, one across each stream, with the third formation serving as a rearguard.[42] The third formation was to be ready to exploit the victory and to pursue the defeated enemy with fresh force. The first large *bataelge* took to its position facing the Grote Beek stream, the second, under Artois's command, was positioned in front of the Groeninge stream from the abbey to the stream that connected the Groeninge to the town ramparts.[43] The rearguard stayed further back on the Lange Mere and was comprised of the formations of knights under the command of the counts of St Pol and of Boulogne-Auvergne with, in addition, a formation under Louis de Clermont.[44] It appears from the course of the battle that the deployment of forces in the first *bataelge*, from left to right, was probably the following: the formations of knights under the command of Jean de Burlats, of Geoffrey de Brabant, who was to fight against Willem van Jülich, and of Raoul de Nesle, who was also the commander of the whole formation and finally the formation under the two marshals. These formations were positioned from the town ramparts to the Groeninge stream.[45] The first *bataelge* was to attack across the Grote Beek the men of Bruges and a section of the position held by the men of the Bruges Franc. The second *bataelge* was comprised, moving from south to north, of formations under the Count of Eu, the Lord of Tancarville and the Count of Aumale, then

---

Courtrai and of the success of the war from 1302 to 1304; and even after that, made a deep impression on those living at the time. Most presented it as arrogance. See, in addition to Guiart, Villani's text, cited above (388).

[42] *Annales Gandenses*, 30.
[43] This appears from Lodewijk's work. See the discussion above on Lodewijk's account.
[44] Guiart, 239, vv. 15,074–81; *Chronique artésienne*, 48; *Anciennes chroniques*, 379; *Chronographia*, I:112; Villani, 388; and Lodewijk, II.1.IV:334–5, c. 37, vv. 2615–18.
[45] For Geoffrey de Brabant and the two Lords of Nesle see Lodewijk, II.1.IV:314, c. 30, vv. 2106–19. For Jean de Burlats, who was probably fighting on the left wing, with Artois on the right see Guiart, 239, vv. 15,050–2.

Jacques de St Pol and finally the contingent from Champagne and Lorraine under the command of Mathieu de Trie.[46] From the account of the battle, it appears that Artois and his formation took up a position in the second line,[47] probably because the front line facing the Groeninge from the source of the Grote Beek stream to the abbey was not wide enough to allow all the formations to open out fully.

The battle commenced with skirmishes between the light foot-soldiers and the Flemish crossbowmen, situated on the other side. This was before the formations of knights had finished taking up their positions.[48]

The Battle of the Crossbowmen

The French light foot-soldiers, composed of crossbowmen, *bidauts* and also shield-bearers of minimal fighting power, all advanced towards the streams just after Guy de Namur and Willem van Jülich had taken their place in the long Flemish ranks.[49]

This was somewhat before midday and, luckily for the Flemings, the sun was hidden by a cloud.[50] The crossbows were spanned on both sides and shot through the air. Hundreds of short darts were shot from the crossbows while the *bidauts* stood there ready to throw both spears and stones. The Flemish crossbow men defended themselves courageously behind their great shields and returned the shots. The enemy was, however, more numerous and moreover was followed at a distance by the powerful formations of knights, who could begin their charge at any moment. Under the pressure of the enemy crossbowmen and the threat of the knights, the Flemish crossbowmen gave way, very slowly moving back from the streams towards the tightly packed Flemish ranks.[51] In moving back, the first ranks of the Flemish troops also came under pressure, although the short bolts shot by the enemy crossbows lost the major part of their force at such a distance. The bolts brushed off the helmets or stuck in the thick doublets, shields and bucklers.[52] No heavy losses were suffered, certainly not among the well-protected Flemish crossbowmen[53] whose only task was to prevent the enemy crossbowmen from getting too close to the Flemish position. The French foot-soldiers advanced, full of courage, shooting their arrows until some of the crossbowmen's quivers were

---

[46] For the Count of Eu see Lodewijk, II.1.IV:326, c. 34, v. 2399.
[47] Ibid., II.1.IV:321, c. 33, vv. 2285–6. Artois was right of centre in the battle array. See Guiart, 239, v. 1559.
[48] *Chronographia*, I:107.
[49] Lodewijk, II.1.IV:311, c. 29, vv. 2037–43.
[50] The battle took place between midday (12:00) and noon (15:00). Lodewijk, II.1.IV.303, c. 27, v. 1847; II.1.IV:342, c. 39, v. 2795: 'Tusscen middach ende none', and *Annales Gandenses*, 30: 'parum ante nonam'. For the Friar Minor, noon was 12:00; Lodewijk, however, used it as being church noon (between 14:00 and 15:00). See also *Annales Gandenses*, 18, 22, 65, 66.
[51] Guiart, 239, vv. 15,082–93; Geoffrey de Paris, 99–100, vv. 1125–39; le Muisit, 66; *Chronicon Comitum Flandrensium*, 169; and Lodewijk, II.1.IV:311–12, c. 29, vv. 2041–6.
[52] Lodewijk, II.1.IV:312, vv. 2047–57.
[53] Wyffels and Vandewalle, 95; and Verbruggen, *Vlaanderen na de guldensporenslag*, 145–6. The Bruges Town Accounts do not mention a single leader as having fallen. For other battles, this was the case.

completely empty. However, when they reached the two streams and in their over-confidence wanted to cross over, the Count of Artois, as well as several lords in his entourage, saw the moment as having come to send the knights and squires over the stream.[54] The Flemish crossbowmen were at that moment quite far from the stream and as soon as they saw the cavalry advancing they retreated. It appeared too dangerous to allow the French crossbowmen, with the other light foot-soldiers, to cross the stream. It would after all have been much more difficult to call them back afterwards, and they would also have hindered the charge of the knights. Furthermore, it was still possible that the Flemings would suddenly attack the lightly armed French soldiers, crushing and pushing them back in the stream without the knights being able to help. This would then bring the Flemings to a position just behind the streams, which would subsequently make any attack by the knights impossible. Moreover, rapid action needed to be taken, not only in crossing the stream, but also to take advantage of the preparations to the battle and the consequences of the attack made by the crossbowmen.

'Foot-soldiers, withdraw!' Artois commanded, and he immediately had the banners brought in front of the formations of knights in order to begin the attack. 'Forwards!'[55] The seven formations of knights, with the standard-bearers at the front, rode towards the stream. The larger *bataelge* on the left wing, led by Raoul de Nesle, advanced somewhat ahead of the formation on the right wing. Not all of the foot-soldiers heard the orders and some were at a later date to speak of marvellous deeds in their skirmishes, since they had in fact gained some success that day. Others did not know why they were being called back, but they all took to their heels as soon as they noticed that the knights were approaching. Some men stumbled in their haste, others were thrown over by the horses as they were not steady enough to move out into the space between the units of knights.[56] Most of them, however, were able to retreat along the side and in the space in between.

The Charge of the French Left Wing

The whole *bataelge* under Raoul de Nesle on the French left wing advanced as rapidly as possible across the Grote Beek. The *bataelge* included the four formations under the command of Jean de Burlats, Geoffrey de Brabant, the constable himself and the marshals. The other three formations of knights also advanced to the right but this *bataelge* advanced more slowly and crossed the Groeninge stream in a less agitated manner. The three metre wide stream was, however, a significant impediment for the great sea of weighty warhorses with knights in heavy armour

---

[54] Guiart's representation of the events is erroneous (239, vv. 15,106–18). See also Geoffrey de Paris, 100, vv. 1151–205; Wodsak, 59; and Delbrück, 443.
[55] Guiart, 239, vv. 15,119–20; Geoffrey de Paris, 100, vv. 1206–7; *Chronographia*, I:108; and *Anciennes chroniques*, 378.
[56] Guiart's depiction contains much exaggeration (239, vv. 15,122–7), as does Geoffrey de Paris (100, vv. 1210–26). See also le Muisit, 66.

on their backs. Some horses would, at first, not cross and had to be forced to make the jump; others stumbled and their riders fell from the saddle. Some warhorses were stuck for a while in the marshy edges of the stream or missed their jump.[57] Still, in general the crossing took place rapidly, although, so as not to be surprised by a Flemish attack, the noblemen quickly reformed their formations once on the other side.[58] The four units on the left wing, in thinner formations than was normally the case, began their charge against the men of Bruges and part of the Flemish centre positions with the soldiers from the Franc of Bruges.

Now that the charge of the knights had begun, the Flemish crossbowmen quickly cut the strings of their bows and threw the weapons to the ground.[59] Their helpers hastily fled with the heavy shields, and all of them moved behind into the space between the large corps in the battle array and alongside the flanks.

The hundreds of knights in heavy armour, spurring on their horses and approaching rapidly, formed an impressive and terrible picture for the men of Bruges and of the Franc of Bruges who were facing this attack.[60] Instinctively, the soldiers pushed closer together in their ranks. The foot of the pikes or lances were held firmly in the ground, and the pointed end was directed towards the breasts of the horses. The heavy *goedendags* were lifted, ready to crash down upon the heads or feet of the warhorses.[61]

The loud sound of trumpets blowing the charge agitated the horses. Their neighing, all the terrible noise and the approaching front of splendidly equipped knights fully protected by coats of mail and plates and with their long lances couched under their upper arm – this all put the Flemish soldiers to a very hard test.[62] Never in their lives had they experienced such distressing moments. However, the most bitter surprise awaited their enemies. The wall of pikes, lances and *goedendags* did not give way. The noblemen of the royal army had never experienced this in the course of their profession and countless victories. The weavers, fullers and artisans of all types, peasants with hands hardened by work, the men with blue nails, did not flee but remained at their posts.

The bravest and most experienced knights were able at the last moment to force their horses to ride into the living wall formed by the Flemish battle array. Others, however, hesitated, knowing that their priceless warhorses, and perhaps they themselves, would meet a certain death in the charge. Their horses slowed down, and

---

[57] This has to be accepted from the otherwise exaggerated presentations given by Geoffrey de Paris, 100, vv. 1262–6; le Muisit, 66; and *Chronographia*, I:108.
[58] *Anciennes chroniques*, 378; and Villani, 387. Guiart also had the knights cross the stream without much difficulty (239, vv. 15,047–9, 15,075–6).
[59] Lodewijk, II.1.IV:312–13, c. 29, vv. 2067–74. However, during the Battle of Mons-en-Pévèle, the soldiers from Bruges and the Bruges Franc did not throw away their bows any more, as they had come to understand that it was more useful to keep them. They had, above all, concluded since 11 July 1302 that the men with pikes could repel the enemy's charge and that the crossbowmen could still play a role at a later point in the battle.
[60] See *Chronicon Comitum Flandrensium*, 169.
[61] Ibid., 169; Villani, 385; Geoffrey de Paris, 101, vv. 1242–5; and *Continuatio Chronici Guilelmi de Nangiaco*, 585.
[62] *Chronicon Comitum Flandrensium*, 169.

they did not force their way in between the grounded pikes and the *goedendags*. Nevertheless, most of the noblemen continued the charge with the courage and bravery shown on countless occasions by knights in general and the French knights in particular.

The charge met with undeniable success on one side of the front. In the centre, there was a greater room for manoeuvre, allowing the knights to develop the charge from a sturdy run to a gallop. It was there that the noblemen attacked with their celebrated vigour, and a section of the men of the Franc of Bruges gave way. Many knights rode into the ranks, and the battle raged intensely. The deep penetration threatened to develop into a breakthrough; some of the men of the Franc of Bruges fled.[63]

The men of Bruges did more than defend themselves successfully. They met the charge of the knights with the tenacity that was to characterise them during the war of 1302–4. Geoffrey de Brabant, one of the heroes of the Battle of Worringen (1288), who had brought about a decisive breakthrough of the enemy cavalry,[64] hoped to repeat this feat of strength at Courtrai. He even unwittingly knocked Willem van Jülich to the ground with his horse, causing the banner to fall to the ground. However, this brave attack made by the man of Brabant was answered by the *wederstoot* or counterattack of the masses into which he had penetrated. His horse, halted by the long pikes used by the men of Bruges, reared up and fell backwards. Geoffrey was killed immediately. Raoul de Nesle also died in the first clash of the charge. Willem van Jülich and his standard-bearer, Jan Ferrant, sprang once again to their feet, and the soldiers worked miracles with their *goedendags*. As soon as the charge had come to a standstill on account of the sturdy pikes, the soldiers courageously attacked the noblemen and their warhorses. They held the rod of the thick iron-clad clubs and struck so relentlessly that the horses reared up, full of fear. The rods of some of the *goedendags* broke or split as the men hit so hard with them. The slender Willem van Jülich faced his opponents intrepidly. First hit in the breast by an arrow that did not penetrate his coat of mail, and then knocked over by Geoffrey de Brabant, he was now striking back so vigorously with his *goedendag* that he was soon exhausted. Blood poured from his nose and soldiers from his entourage quickly carried him from the thick of the battle. His servant, Jan Vlaminc, however, put on the prince's coat of arms, temporarily replacing his master, and shouted 'Jülich is still here'.[65] Even though the battle still raged ferociously, the most dangerous moment had passed. The French charge had been stopped, and the knights and squires had been brought under control.

---

[63] Lodewijk, II.1.IV:313, c. 29, c. 2085–95. Lodewijk pardoned the men of the Bruges Franc for this by pointing to the useful effects of Jan van Renesse's intervention. See also *Chronicon Comitum Flandrensium*, 169.

[64] Jan van Heelu, *Rijmkronijk*, ed. J. F. Willems (Brussels, 1836), 225, vv. 6052–5. See also Verbruggen, 'De slag bij Woeringen', 308.

[65] Lodewijk, II.1.IV:314–16, c. 30: 'Guulke is nog hier.' See also Villani, 387.

The Charge of the French Right Wing

The French knights triumphantly penetrated the ranks of the soldiers of the Franc of Bruges in the centre. They were, however, brought to a standstill by the men of Bruges. It was at this point that the three formations of knights on the French right wing attacked on the other side of the Groeninge stream. With unfurled banners, the counts of Eu and of Aumale, Jacques de St Pol and Mathieu de Trie, together with their formations, charged against the troops under Guy de Namur. The formations had certainly begun their charge a few minutes later or crossed the Groeninge stream less rapidly since they saw that the Flemings did not dare attack them. For this reason they made their charge somewhat later than their fellows in arms on the left wing. The charge was carried out with well-ordered and closely packed formations and was undoubtedly the most expertly executed attack. However, Guy de Namur's soldiers gave way even less than the men of Bruges. Despite the many knights thrusting deep into the Flemish ranks, the battle array as a whole was untouched; whoever penetrated the ranks quickly met his death. The standard bearer of Ghent, Zeger Lonke, was knocked to his knees, but like his fellow standard-bearer on the Flemish right wing, he stood up once again. Boudewijn van Popperode, the brave Viscount of Aalst, distinguished himself at Guy de Namur's side and fully understood, together with the young prince, how to encourage the troops by his own example. 'He may be named with honour wherever knights come together, as he threw himself into the breach both night and day for the honour of Flanders.' The intrepid knight, Willem van Boenhem, with an entourage from the Four Ambachten, also performed many glorious feats of arms.[66] Like the right wing, the Flemish left wing resisted vigorously, and the soldiers succeeded in expelling the enemies from their ranks or killing them.

At the moment the general charge was taking place – on the left wing across the Grote Beek and on the right wing across the Groeninge – the Viscount of Lens, the commander of the French garrison in the Courtrai castle, made preparations to break out to attack the Flemings from behind. In order to divert the attention of the men of Ypres who had remained in the town he set fire to one of the most beautiful houses in Courtrai,[67] as he had repeatedly done during the days prior to the battle.[68] When all seemed to indicate that the French knights would break through the centre of the Flemish battle array, the gate of the castle suddenly opened wide and a troop of knights and squires charged out, while the men of Ypres came under heavy fire from on top of the fortress.[69] The latter, however, had taken precautions, and their crossbowmen shot back from behind their high shields. The heavily armoured foot-soldiers courageously resisted the knights who were pushed back into the fortress.[70] The sortie made by the Viscount of Lens ended in complete failure.

[66] Lodewijk, II.1.IV:317–18, cc. 31–2.
[67] *Annales Gandenses*, 30; and Guiart, 240, vv. 15,144–60.
[68] *Chronique artésienne*, 45.
[69] Oxford Chest, illustration VI.
[70] *Annales Gandenses*, 30; and *Chronicon Comitum Flandrensium*, 169.

The Intervention of Jan van Renesse

The attack of the two larger *bataelgen* meant that the greater part of the royal army had been thrown into the battle. The situation was critical at one point in the long Flemish front. The men of the Franc of Bruges defended themselves bravely, although some soldiers could not resist the terrible charge and had given ground. A breakthrough had not yet occurred, but the French knights did not give up and courageously moved further forwards. Their penetration of the Flemish lines grew deeper and deeper.

The menace of a breakthrough that could quickly lead to defeat at the beginning of a battle fought by an army of inexperienced soldiers did not escape the attention of Jan van Renesse. He had perhaps remained on horseback[71] in order to be able to choose, as he looked down from the Ghent road, the best moment to intervene with his reserve corps. Now that the two major French formations were engaged in close combat, he considered the moment to have come and arrived rapidly with his troops.[72]

With his fresh formation, he immediately strengthened the corps of the Franc of Bruges, whose ranks had grown thin and weak. The men had not given way entirely and fought on bravely.[73] The situation now turned around completely. The excellent French knights who with their entourage were trying to break open the enemy position were then frontally attacked at the centre of the Flemish ranks by the men of the Franc of Bruges as well as by Jan van Renesse's soldiers who had already gained more confidence after seeing that the Flemish left and right wings had resisted superbly. It was, however, possible that the reserve corps of the leader from Zeeland consisted to a great extent of noblemen from Zeeland and other countries who were able to employ their lengthy experience to the advantage of the Flemish foot-soldiers. The French knights were crushed by the ranks into which they had penetrated.[74] This occurred at a time when they thought, triumphantly, that they were creating a breakthrough and winning the battle.

Jan van Renesse's intervention was, however, not just limited to defeating a few smaller French bodies of knights. He continued the attack with the men of the Franc of Bruges and his corps, and the Flemish centre advanced with *goedendags* hammering down hard on the heads of the warhorses and on the knights, who now had to give way themselves.

All around there was a fierce hand-to-hand mêlée. Here the Flemings had a great advantage. The superior force of a hundred knights, equalling that of a thousand soldiers fighting on foot, melted as snow in the sun. The rebels were now fighting in their thousands at the same time. Three to four thousand soldiers were hammering away with their long pikes or their terrible *goedendags*, while the knights, fourteen to fifteen hundred strong, were clearly in the minority. They did try to free themselves from the mêlée by turning back in smaller bodies, *conroten*

---

[71] *Chronique artésienne*, 51; and *Chronographia*, I:106.
[72] Lodewijk, II.1.IV:313, c. 29, vv. 2094–7.
[73] Ibid., II.1.IV:313, c. 29, vv. 2089–90.
[74] Ibid., II.1.IV:313–14, c. 29, vv. 2098–102.

(banners), and making a short charge. Nevertheless, in doing so they were closely followed by the Flemish troops on the right and left wing. In the mean time, the centre under Jan van Renesse's command advanced further and pushed the enemy noblemen before them back towards the two streams.[75]

A Flemish victory became ever more likely. Everywhere the townsmen were resolutely moving forward. The resistance given in their positions and the mastering of the general charge, due to the wall of pikes, had given them confidence.[76] It was now the soldiers' task to strike the squires and knights from their horses or to kill their warhorses.

The knights tried in vain to free themselves from the mêlée, following the usual tactic of turning around in order to charge again. The Flemings attacked so tenaciously that they prevented any tactical withdrawal by the French noblemen, who were now retreating and fighting at the same time. Along the whole front, from the town ramparts to the monastery, the veterans of European battlefields had to give way under the powerful pressure that was pushing them slowly but surely back towards the two streams.

The Charge Led by Robert d'Artois

The Count of Artois did not take part in the general charge and saw the alarming turn the battle was taking for the French noblemen. At once he gave the necessary orders for his formation of knights to undertake the ultimate charge before it was too late, hoping that such an intervention could avert the catastrophe. Thereby the rearguard would have more time to rush to provide assistance.

One knight from Champagne who was in their midst warned the supreme commander about the deep Groeninge stream into which several French knights had already been thrown.[77] However, Artois understood that he had to intervene immediately. The trumpets once again sounded the charge.[78] The Count spurred his splendid horse and the animal carried him across the Groeninge stream with a powerful jump. He was immediately followed by his knights.[79] Thus he charged towards the soldiers of Guy de Namur who, on recognising Artois's coat of arms, advanced with the men of Ghent in the direction of the enemy knights. The long run of the powerful battle horse led the French supreme commander deep into Guy de Namur's troops. He penetrated as far as the banner, part of which he grasped with both hands, thereby ripping the flag.[80] The Flemish soldiers, however, rushed to him from all sides. They hit out with a multitude of *goedendags* and clubs. Artois resisted most bravely, and his battle horse broke through the small group of

---

[75] Ibid., II.1.IV:314, c. 29, vv. 2104–5.
[76] *Chronicon Comitum Flandrensium*, 169.
[77] Lodewijk, II.1.IV:321, c. 33, vv. 2285–90.
[78] Ibid., II.1.IV:322, c. 33, vv. 2294–5.
[79] Ibid., II.1.IV:322, c. 33, vv. 2299–312.
[80] Ibid., II.1.IV:322–3, c. 33, vv. 2313–29.

Flemish soldiers. Once again the able knight carried out a charge against other soldiers. Much time passed before the supreme commander of the army of knights could be overcome.[81] There were, however, two sturdy men on the battlefield who were renowned for their physical force:

> Their equal could not be found,
> Each could bind a bear.

One of the men was a monk from the Abbey of Goes in South Beveland who had left his monastic order: the other was a lay brother from Ter Doest near Lissewege, Willem van Saaftinge. He had rushed to the battlefield with a horse that he exchanged there for a *goedendag* and was now performing great feats of arms in the Flemish ranks.[82] Willem van Saaftinge succeeded in approaching Artois and striking down the Count's battle horse with a powerful blow, carrying the Count with it in its fall. Artois was surrounded, and many *goedendags* were raised to kill him; he asked in vain that his horse be spared.[83] The exhausted commander fell, covered in wounds.[84]

Artois's final attempt had failed completely. Everywhere the French noblemen were being slain and forced back into the streams. They defended themselves boldly and bravely in an attempt to escape their fate. Some noblemen tried in vain to surrender, since they saw that the battle was lost. However, no prisoners were taken. For many artisans and countless peasants the moment had come for merciless revenge. The battle had drawn to an end and the massacre began on the banks of the two fatal streams.

Crisis and Conclusion

The charge of the supreme commander and the subsequent approach of the rearguard caused, however, a short-lived crisis among Guy de Namur's troops. The soldiers had already experienced the most powerful charge, and their ranks had now become much less compact due to the counterattack. The men were not so well protected against the charge of knights as when they had motionlessly awaited the charge with grounded pikes. Alarm broke out along a section of the front when Artois penetrated as far as Guy de Namur's banner, and the soldiers noticed at the same time that the French rearguard was approaching. Guy was fully taken up by this attack. He was not able to continue the fight against Artois and could not take

---

[81] Ibid., II.1.IV:323, c. 33, vv. 2331–4.
[82] Ibid., II.1.IV:323–4, c. 33, vv. 2335–49: 'Men conste haers gelike niet vinden / Elc soude enen bere binden.' See also *Annales Gandenses*, 91–2.
[83] Lodewijk, II.1.IV:324, c. 33, vv. 2350–64.
[84] *Continuatio chronici Guilelmi de Nangiaco*, 585: according to the monks who buried him, Artois had more than thirty wounds on his body. Delfos noted correctly that it was not very likely that Artois asked for mercy, as presented by Lodewijk (II.1.IV:324–5, c. 30, vv. 2360–86) and in the *Anciennes chroniques* (378) and *Chronographia* (I:109). See Delfos, *1302 door tijdgenooten verteld*, 110, n. 52.

the supreme commander captive – for he wanted to spare him.[85] Those fleeing left their weapons on the battlefield. Some even wanted to swim across the River Lys, while others attempted to save themselves by fleeing to Courtrai. Guy called them back, as new enemies were approaching.[86] The faithful Flemish noblemen rushed to help him. Together with Jan Borluut, Goswin van Gossenhoven, Willem van Boenhem, Boudewijn van Popperode, Geraard Ferrant and Bangelijn van Aardenburg, he succeeded in restoring the battle array and regrouping the men in units.[87] The men of Ypres, who in the mean time had defeated the troops under the Viscount of Lens, now helped to drive those fleeing back to the front.[88]

The battle was then carried further along the banks of the two streams where the relentless Flemish counterattack threw back the knights in heavy armour. Many knights drowned in the streams without being wounded. Others were slaughtered mercilessly there.[89] In vain they offered the hilts of their swords to the victors.[90] With remarkable discipline and cruel bitterness, they refused to have mercy upon their enemies. It became a hideous massacre, and not even the horses were spared.[91]

As seen elsewhere, the common people, so despised by the noblemen, took cruel revenge as soon as they had the chance of gaining victory in favourable circumstances. The clearest example of this was given by peasants of the county of Berg in slaying the knights of the archbishop of Cologne at the Battle of Worringen.[92] The Flemings were as merciless towards their enemies as the Swiss foot-soldiers were against the Austrian noblemen.[93] Not one of the commanders who led the charge with their formations escaped alive: Raoul and Gui de Nesle, as well as Geoffrey de Brabant, had already fallen during the attack.[94] Jean de Burlats shared the same fate.[95] The Count of Eu, the Count of Aumale, the Lord of Tancarville and finally Robert d'Artois all fell. There is one single exception: Mathieu de Trie was taken captive,[96] certainly at the end of the battle by the streams, when victory had long been gained.

---

[85] Lodewijk, II.1.IV:331, c. 35, vv. 2526–8; and *Chronographia*, I:113–14.
[86] Lodewijk, II.1.IV:329, c. 35, vv. 2484–93.
[87] Ibid., II.1.IV:330, c. 35, vv. 2505–9.
[88] See *Chronicon Comitum Flandrensium*, 169, although this was taken to be at another point in the battle.
[89] Lodewijk, II.1.IV:314, c. 29, vv. 2104–5; II.1.IV:317, c. 31, vv. 2199–203; II.1.IV:321, c. 33, vv. 2288–90; II.1.IV:328, c. 34, vv. 2469–71; II.1.IV:333, c. 36, vv. 2576–80.
[90] Ibid., II.1.IV:315, c. 30, vv. 2128 33; *Annales Gandenses*, 31; *Anciennes chroniques*, 378; and *Chronicon Comitum Flandrensium*, 169.
[91] *Annales Gandenses*, 31.
[92] Verbruggen, 'De slag bij Woeringen', 308.
[93] Delbrück, 665. This also took place, in the Swiss example, by order of the commanders.
[94] Lodewijk, II.1.IV:314, c. 30, vv. 2106–19.
[95] *Chronique artésienne*, 50; and *Chronographia*, I:111.
[96] *Chronique artésienne*, 49–51; *Chronographia*. I:110–11; le Muisit, 68–9; *Annales Gandenses*, 31–2; and Lodewijk, II.1.IV:326, c. 34, vv. 2399–400; II.1.IV:339–41, c. 38, vv. 2722–69.

At the end of this desperate struggle of the noblemen on the marshy banks of the Groeninge and the connecting stream some men were in fact taken captive, most of whom were wounded. Raoul de Grantcourt was thus spared after resisting heroically.[97] But for the Flemish supporters of the King of France there was no mercy; their corpses were even terribly mutilated.[98]

The Flight of the French Rearguard and the Pursuit

At that very moment Artois was seeking to turn around fate and prevent a defeat of the retreating right and left wings, the French rearguard also advanced.[99] However, before they had moved close enough to the streams it was too late. The defeat was complete.

The Count of St Pol, the Count of Boulogne and Auvergne and Louis de Clermont then decided to retreat. However, they first tried to gain time to allow the helpers to clear some of the knights' personal belongings and the army train. It was for this reason that they had the trumpets sound the call for a charge. At that point they were standing alongside the Lange Mere, gathered closely together in their units of knights with beautiful banners and pennants. All of them were ready to attack, yet they did not charge. There was also a formation of Hainaulter noblemen there as well as a Brabantese troop. Yet none of these formations of knights dared undertake a new charge.[100]

The Flemings first restored the order in their ranks so as to be able to meet the attack. However, as no charge was made, they vainly challenged the enemy with their pikes and *goedendags*. But then the men of Bruges crossed the connecting stream and even sought to attack the enemies, who quickly chose to take to their heels with their shields on their backs.[101]

Several noblemen from the formation under the Count of St Pol did not want to outlive their colleagues in arms and above all their commander, Artois. They bravely and desperately advanced to meet the triumphant Flemish soldiers by the Lange Mere, but were killed there immediately.[102]

At tSiexmans, another body of soldiers was overtaken and destroyed. Willem

---

[97] Lodewijk, II.1.IV:326–8, c. 34, vv. 2406–61; and *Chronique artésienne*, 51.
[98] Lodewijk, II.1.IV:329, c. 34, vv. 2478–83; II.1.IV:334, c. 36, vv. 2608–13.
[99] This is concluded from the fact that Guy de Namur called out that fresh enemy forces were advancing (Lodewijk, II.1.IV:329, c. 35, vv. 2491–3), and that he was unable to continue the battle against Artois. Lodewijk's chapter 37, detailing the advance of the rearguard, also argues in this direction. It is indeed evident that the rearguard would also have attacked if this had been possible.
[100] Lodewijk, II.1.IV:334–5, c. 37, vv. 2614–36.
[101] Ibid., II.1.IV:335–6, c. 37, vv. 2637–42.
[102] Ibid., II.1.IV:333–4, c. 36, vv. 2584–602.

van Mosscher was surprised near his house on the Pottelberg and sought in vain to swear his loyalty to the young princes. As a Flemish supporter of the King of France, he was mercilessly beheaded.[103]

Among the fleeing nobles and helpers there were, however, several men of Brabant who, remembering their knowledge of Flemish, now sought to escape from their enemies by also giving the battle cry, 'Flanders, the Lion'. Guy de Namur, however, having been informed of this, gave the following command:

> Kill all... that has spurs on.[104]

The flight of the rearguard turned to panic. The soldiers and their helpers fled head over heels as fast as their feet could carry them along all roads that led south: towards Zwevegem, St Denijs, Tournai and Lille.[105] How misfortunate were those whose horses refused to be of any more service or collapsed exhausted! They were mercilessly slaughtered. Many soldiers and helpers of the foot-soldiers were overtaken and killed.

The pursuit appears to have incited the Flemings so much that they hunted down their enemy as far as Zwevegem, St Denijs, and Dottenijs, more than 11 kilometres from the battlefield. Frenchmen were even killed as far away as Dottenijs.[106]

From the towers of the church of Our Lady at Tournai, of the abbey of St Martin and of the town gates the astonished inhabitants of the royal town could that evening see the pitiful remains of the flower of French nobility rushing towards them. Along the roads, through fields and hedges, the vanquished and fleeing soldiers rushed on in such masses that it appeared unbelievable for those who did not witness it. The town administration did not understand what was happening and gave the order to close the town gates. Even the Count of St Pol was not able to seek refuge in the town and was forced to spend the night in the abbey of St Nicholas. In the surrounding villages and dwellings outside the town walls a great multitude of men on horseback and foot-soldiers arrived, all absolutely exhausted, hungry and panic-stricken. Some men gave away their expensive weapons for a little bread. However, most of them were in such a state of apprehension and shock that they could not eat for fear.[107]

The Flemings returned to the battlefield completely exhausted. In the space of three hours, between midday and 3 pm, they had practically destroyed the most splendid army in the whole of Western Europe.[108] Engaging in the decisive battle

---

[103] Ibid., II.1.IV:334, c. 36, vv. 2603–13.
[104] Ibid., II.1.IV:336 7, c. 37, vv. 2656 81: 'Slact al doct! hets volc verbannen / Wat dat sporen heeft gespannen!'
[105] Ibid., II.1.IV:336, c. 37, vv. 2650–5; and le Muisit, 67.
[106] Lodewijk, II.1.IV:336, c. 37, vv. 2650–5; and le Muisit, 67.
[107] Le Muisit, 67–8. See also Lodewijk, II.1.IV:337, c. 37, vv. 2690–1.
[108] Lodewijk, II.1.IV:342, c. 39, v. 2795. It is difficult to determine how many Flemish soldiers fell. The *Annales Gandenses* (32) spoke of barely one hundred who fell, although there were many who were wounded. Lodewijk (II.1.IV:333, c. 36, v. 2574) noted in passing that the West Flemish knights and those from the surrounding areas of Ghent lost less than twenty men. It is probable that several hundred men fell in total (500–700?). It is certainly possible that there were

against the two larger *bataelgen* as well as repelling the enemy forces probably took less than an hour. The full destruction of the enemy, delayed by Artois's intervention, must have taken two hours. However, the soldiers had been standing on the battlefield from as early as 6 am. Following a nerve-racking period of waiting, they fought ferociously for three hours and many subsequently covered a distance of 20 kilometres in pursuit of the enemy and in returning to the battlefield. Even though they were very happy on account of the great victory, they said little to each other since they all suffered from thirst. Many soldiers could no longer close their stiff hands after having clasped their *goedendags* and pikes too firmly during the battle. All of them were also very hungry, as they had hardly eaten anything that morning. Food was collected all around them. The first bread came from Ename. Guy de Namur and Willem van Jülich were so exhausted that they retired to sleep, leaving other commanders to guard the battlefield. The day after the booty and spoil was collected.[109] Following an old custom of that period, the fallen enemy soldiers were fully stripped and remained on the battlefield until they were buried.[110] The booty collected from the French camp on the Pottelberg was so great that Lodewijk called it the 'Berg van Weelden', the mountain of luxury.[111] More than five hundred pairs of golden spurs were gathered from the battlefield, and numerous banners and pennants were hung as trophies next to the castle in the church of Our Lady at Courtrai.[112] First, however, the banners were used to show the French garrison what further resistance would lead to,[113] and on 13 July the Viscount of Lens surrendered the fortress.[114]

Great celebrations took place on 12 and 13 July; the clerk who kept Willem van Jülich's accounts was no longer able to say from whom he bought meat for the prince's entourage nor how much he paid for it. He was also not able to state how much food was bought the following day nor from whom.[115]

However, some inhabitants of Courtrai were forgotten in this flush of victory. When the Viscount of Lens, in all haste following the Bruges Matins, began prepa-

---

fewer Flemings than French noblemen who fell, since the Flemish soldiers' excellent and long weapons allowed them to inflict heavier injuries on the enemy.

[109] Lodewijk, II.1.IV:338–9, c. 38, vv. 2700–21; II.1.IV:342–3, c. 39, vv. 2798–829.

[110] Ibid., II.1.IV:343, c. 39, vv. 2830–3. See also the Oxford Chest, illustration VII. This was also the case at the Battle of Woeringen (Heelu, 332, vv. 8815–17) and at the Battle of Hastings (1066) after William the Conqueror's victory (E. Maclagen, *The Bayeux Tapestry* (London and New York, 1945, pl. 76–9).

[111] Lodewijk, II.1.IV:287, c. 21, v. 1487.

[112] Where they were removed by the French on 1 December 1382 following the Battle of Westrozebeke. See Jean Froissart, *Chroniques*, ed. S. Luce and G. Raynaud (Paris, 1899), XI: 61–2, 70. On the same occasion the bell and beautiful clock, then the most beautiful in Flanders according to a chronicler, were taken from the belfry to Dijon by Philip the Bold. See *Istore et croniques*, II:253. See also II:181, 217–18.

[113] *Chronographia*, I:112.

[114] *Chroniques artésienne*, 52. See also the publication of the act by E. Gachet, *BCRH*, 2nd ser., 2 (1852), 16.

[115] Gilliodts-van Severen, I:122, no. 171. Legend has it that there were blood stains on the parchment with the entry for 12 July. See the photograph of the accounts in Blockmans, *1302: vóór en na*, pl. 16.

rations for the defence of the Courtrai Castle, he quickly demanded the necessary provisions for the garrison. Grain, wine, bacon and all manner of provisions were taken from the people of Courtrai without any compensation being given. After the surrender of the castle, the prince promised to compensate the poor who had been robbed. A list was even drawn up of all that had been lost. Still, it appears from a complaint made by the 'poor people' of Courtrai that they still had not been paid after the Battle of Mons-en-Pévèle (18 August 1304).[116] They humbly asked Guy de Namur to have the monies owed sent to them: 'Otherwise we will lose everything and will have to leave the country due to bitter poverty: Have mercy upon us.'[117]

---

[116] Rijksarchief of Ghent, Fonds Gaillard, no. 820. See also V. Gaillard, *Inventaire analytique des chartes des comtes de Flandre* (Ghent, 1857), 121, no. 820. However, in the examination given this was erroneously taken as being addressed to Count Guy. The document was not dated, although it was drawn up following the death of Willem van Jülich who fell at the Battle of Mons-en-Pévèle. It is addressed to Guy de Namur: 'Li povre gent de Courtray' (The poor people of Courtrai) complained that they still had not been compensated. The document was written in French.

[117] This is the end of the plea: 'Nous pierdrons tout et il nous convenra viider le paijs de fine poverté. Si aiés pitiét de nous.'

General Conclusion

With the Battle of Courtrai, the epic story of the Flemish townsmen began. They liberated the rest of their county and held out against the most powerful monarchy of their time for two years. A new punitive expedition by Philip the Fair led to a disorderly retreat. The military expeditions followed on from each other at a very quick tempo and the example of the men of Bruges merits special citation here. After the decisive expedition to Wijnendaal, Cassel and Courtrai they were, for the time being, left in peace while liberating Lille and Douai. However, on 30 August 1302 a communal army once again marched towards Douai and Nieuwendijk to stop the King's advance. The men remained under arms for a period of forty-one days.[1] On 14 October, the aldermen took part in a military expedition to Gravelines, and, on 2 November a new communal army followed.[2] During the winter, the whole frontier was defended by garrisons, and at the end of February or beginning of March 1303 they advanced again, this time in an offensive against Hainault. It was there that Lessines was conquered on 2 April with the Count of Hainault not even daring to attack those laying siege. On 23 April the men of Bruges sailed to Zeeland, with men for relief and reinforcements following them on 15 May and 11 June. A subsequent expedition led their army to Cassel, and they finally lay siege to Tournai in an expedition that lasted forty-seven days.[3] The Artesian chronicler wrote: 'Never had such a great army laid siege to a fortified town for so long.'[4] In 1304, a small expedition was organised against Hainault from 20 February to 6 March, and the offensive began again in the north while a truce was in force with the King. For this reason a new expedition was undertaken with the fleet to Zeeland and Holland, lasting from 18 March to 3 May. During this expedition they quickly penetrated to the heart of Holland, to Utrecht and to just short of the town of Haarlem.[5] Following the failure of the enterprise, they returned immediately on 11 May to Zierikzee, which was besieged until their defeat in the two-day naval battle (10–11 August) against a powerful French fleet reinforced by several ships from Holland. In the mean time, they had sent an army to the southern border, where they fought the Battle of Mons-en-Pévèle on 18 August.[6] The Flemings also suffered a defeat here, but they once again equipped a new army that immediately advanced to Lille with completely new material that astonished the enemy. It was then that a provisional treaty was concluded.

---

[1] Wyffels and Vandewalle, 97.
[2] Ibid., 99.
[3] Ibid., 172–3, 186–8, 214, 215, 217.
[4] *Chronique artésienne*, 73.
[5] Niermeyer, 304; and Wyffels and Vandewalle, 359–62, 362–9.
[6] Wyffels and Vandewalle, 466–70, 487–95.

As can be seen from this concise and summary list of events, the townsmen did not sit back on their laurels. Their fervent activity and energy can only be explained by recourse to the powerful forces driving them on.

One prime factor was the social element to their struggle. The great victors of 11 July were without a doubt the members of the guilds from Bruges, and the artisans and peasants of the county in general. The guilds then became independent professional organisations endowed with political power and administered by the artisans themselves. At the same time, they gained an immense role in the administration of the towns and complete control of the finances. In one fell swoop, they had achieved their political objectives; rarely had a feat of arms given rise to such far-reaching social and political consequences. The artisans now hoped that they would in future be left to their own devices and that an end could be put to economic exploitation for all time. In the Flemish towns a 'democratic' system of government was established, as far as the word is applicable to the circumstances of that period. At the same time, the five major towns continued to play their role in the administration of the county and all the more so as the young princes of the house of Dampierre had to follow their will completely. The artisans participated, via their aldermen, in the administration of the county.

The young princes came to understand that they had access to forces that had previously never been employed. They encouraged guildsmen by giving them concrete advantages. Consequently the power of the guilds also grew steadily during the war. No sacrifice appeared too great for the common people and nothing could discourage them. Even though they suffered two defeats in 1304, they did not consider themselves defeated. When, at a later point, a peace agreement was concluded at the expense of the common people, they resisted tenaciously and delayed the execution of the agreement. No one dared attack the guilds openly since they had become too powerful. They were prepared once war broke out again. It was only in 1319 that the military operations came to end.

In the introduction it was indicated that there was an immense difference between the position taken by the common people in 1297–1300 and that in the years 1302–4. Aside from the social element another factor behind those fighting in 1302 had a great influence: national sentiment.

The sentiment of Flemish national identity had long existed in the county of Flanders. In 1297 and 1300 it did not, however, lead to any reaction that was significant enough to be noted down by chroniclers of the time. The most probable explanation for this is the fact that the Count had alienated himself from the common people on account of his incompetent politics at home. The complaint made by Gilbert van Outere remained the pious wish of a clerk. The fact that the commoners of Bruges and Damme stood by and let the towns surrender to the King proves, in any case, that national identity was not powerful enough at that time to lead to a reaction in favour of the Flemish Count. Even in 1300, there was not a single trace of such a reaction.

However, the imprisonment of the Count, the return and actions of the Flemish supporters of the King, as well as the lack of political foresight shown by the French governor, all contributed to galvanising the sentiment of national identity.

St Pol's arbitrary and severe actions were clearly seen in 1301 during a local social conflict between the common people and the burghers in Bruges and caused the people to become hostile to the governor. In the countryside he already stood in their bad books on account of his assistance to Flemish supporters of the King against the peasants and those noblemen favourable to the Count. The Count's sons exploited this dissatisfaction in Bruges and sent Willem van Jülich, who had no personal interests in the county but was a symbol of the struggle against the King since his brother had fallen in Flanders in 1297. He was to turn the conflict between St Pol and the commoners of Bruges, now strengthened by several discontented patricians, into a rebellion against the King. He was able to count upon the help of noblemen such as Willem van Boenhem, Willem de Visch and Zeger van Gent and his son. The first attempt failed, but Willem took the common people of Bruges, led by Pieter de Coninc, so far that they could not go back any more. The Bruges Friday brought about a definitive break and initiated the rebellion. The appearance of Willem with the communal army and several noblemen made the peasants and Flemish noblemen who supported the Count rush to them. The arrival of Guy de Namur reanimated the old and loyal sentiments of affection towards the Count's house. National identity began to throw its weight into the scale, although it was not yet powerful enough to incite a rebellion in all places: Ghent still remained a neutral town in the midst of Flanders. The noblemen retained their doubts, and this was disbelief about the possibility of successful rebellion. And, as in any uprising, it was in the end the common man who had to do the dirty work. But an unexpected and brilliant victory was gained on 11 July. National pride was flattered and stirred up. Those who had not yet contributed now sought to do so, and those who formerly supported the King of France were now converts to the Count's cause. Ypres and Ghent did not want to remain second to Bruges and carried the heavy burden of the following expedition that liberated the whole of Flanders. In Douai and Lille, the commoners stood on the side of the rebels. This new Flemish victory against the King of France himself raised national sentiment even higher. In fact, national sentiment was so high that the Flemings in 1303 decapitated the statue of St Louis in the marketplace of Térouanne, while at the same time attempting to free the country from the spiritual oppression exerted by the French bishops in Térouanne and Tournai. The complete independence of Flanders was their goal.

National identity thus received a great boost due to the military successes while this itself acted as a source of encouragement for the troops. This is also the case for the social forces at work. Due to the high population of the Flemish towns the old county suddenly gained a new military power. The communal armies were able to replace the knights who had since the end of the twelfth century been surpassed by the more powerful armies of knights of the French King. Due to the division of the Flemish communal army into guilds and the existence of rural communities, the common people gained the necessary cohesion and essential confidence in themselves. The artisans fought beside their fellows in the same guild, under one banner, and these groups formed large families. The finances had already prior to this allowed for the corps of soldiers to be provided with necessary materials such as tents; and now the guilds paid their soldiers. The wealth of an individual artisan provided him with expensive and superb weapons. The guilds also provided weapons. The mutual confidence and cohesion of the corps of soldiers supplied the excellent morale that drew new force from the victories gained.

The consequences of the Battle of Courtrai as a feat of arms have already been pointed out. The impression made upon those living in that period was so great that many, even in foreign countries, believed that the Flemings overcame the powerful enemy troops with small militias. In reality, the power of the Flemings lay in their organisation, morale and, above all, their strength of numbers. The French were astonished that a county could raise such powerful armies, and the defeat made a great impression upon them. The tactics employed by the townsmen were something new for the French, and their brutal power both disturbed and bewildered the nobles. The commoners were thrown into battle against a qualitatively excellent professional army, albeit rather small in size. The most terrible element for the French nobles was, however, the fact that the fearless townsmen, who could call upon thousands of soldiers in their towns, did not grant mercy in the battle, preferring to slay the noblemen rather than take prisoners. The war could thus lead to the exhaustion of knights in the kingdom. Since the frontal attack made by the heavy horsemen failed at Courtrai, the noblemen avoided such bloody charges and sought to wage artful war with their enemies by encircling them or attacking them from the side. When such manoeuvres failed against the defensive circular positions taken by the Flemish troops, they sought to attack the smaller Flemish units, as they were not so powerful as the larger divisions. Against such small Flemish corps they gained some successes, but all their attempts against the larger armies failed, even on a terrain that was favourable to cavalry. It went so far that the knights systematically refused to engage in a major battle. They chose to retreat in September 1302 and on the eve of the first anniversary of the Battle of Courtrai on 10 July 1303. In the great Battle of Mons-en-Pévèle, it was the Flemings themselves who had to force the battle on a favourable terrain where the French could manoeuvre as they desired. The knights, however, applied their new tactics integrally and gained a victory, albeit so narrowly that the townsmen did not recognise it. The men of Bruges, supported by units from other towns, led such a powerful attack that they broke through to the French camp and could leave the battlefield unhindered. After the Battle of Mons-en-Pévèle, the town armies still commanded sufficient respect to avert a new battle, while the most turbulent elements of the common people even demanded that an attack take place from the beginning of the battle, or at night by full moon. The common people remained prepared to continue the war although their young and able leaders of 1302 had already fallen, as had Willem van Jülich, or were being held captive in France, as was Guy de Namur.

The Flemish townsmen only gained one major victory. However, one should not, in the final event, forget that this did not only depend upon themselves. Their opponents who on occasions had previously been seen as reckless French knights did belong to the most powerful state of that time. Moreover, they had been applying very cautious tactics since September 1302. The Flemings won a second victory at Arques on 4 April 1303. The Flemish defeat at Mons-en- Pévèle could, with some luck, have turned into a splendid victory. At a later time the French still appeared to be cautious and even let the Flemings take the initiative in attacking. At Cassel (1328) and Westrozebeke (1382) the Flemish rebels fought without any experienced commanders. There was much less unity than in 1302. The independence of the county was not directly threatened. Furthermore, the townsmen had become careless due to the lack of able commanders. Instead of awaiting the attack in a defensive position, they advanced themselves. Their superiority to the French foot-soldiers and even the French heavy cavalry was still apparent, as is shown by the superb victory gained at Enguinegatte in 1479.

The Battle of Courtrai was the first of a series of major victories in Western Europe gained by foot-soldiers against knights. The victory was followed by those of the Scottish foot-soldiers against the Anglo-Norman noblemen at Bannockburn (1314), by the first significant victory gained by the Swiss against the Austrian knights at Morgarten (1315), and by the victory of the peasants of Dithmarschen over the knights of Holstein (1319). However, on foot-soldier tactics, the Flemings were still not superior to the foot-soldiers of the Italian towns and above all those of Milan in the twelfth century, or to the indomitable and triumphant Frisians. Despite this, neither the Frisians nor the Italians gained such a sensational and significant victory as that of 1302. The Italian foot-soldiers were always supported by their own knights who continued to form the central element of the army. The foot-soldiers never gained a significant victory solely due to their own forces. At the beginning of the fourteenth century, the Flemings overtook them in military matters as well as in organisation with the recognised and autonomous guilds that took part in the administration of the towns. The Frisians were aided in their victories against armies of knights by the terrain that was extremely unfavourable for such armies. Furthermore, they did not have to fight against the larger armies that the French knights could raise.

The Battle of Courtrai stands alone among the four great victories at the beginning of the fourteenth century in the power of the enemy forces that were defeated and the unexpected nature of the victory at a moment that the French monarchy had become so strong. The Scottish foot-soldiers were able to resist their enemy for a longer period as the English King was not as powerful at that point as the King of France. Still, they were to give way following the new tactics used by the Englishmen. The knights of the King of England also changed their tactics, although the solution was to employ archers supported by noblemen on foot and knights who remained on horseback as a reserve force. Morgarten was a battle where, in comparison with the two previous battles, the nature of the terrain was infinitely more favourable to foot-soldiers than was the case at Courtrai and Bannockburn. The Austrian army was surprised by a flank attack made by the Swiss in a mountain pass alongside a lake. The Swiss soldiers fired rocks down on their enemies from the mountain and then attacked them at a point where the knights could not deploy their troops. Morgarten was, however, the beginning of a long series of Swiss victories that showed the foot-soldiers of that region to be the best in the whole of Europe in the late Middle Ages and the beginning of the modern period. This military development was, nevertheless, aided by the nature of the terrain and by the special position of the country between two rather weak neighbours. When they actually came into conflict with the French King (in 1444), a Swiss army of two to three thousand men was completely destroyed by the French cavalry, and the rest of the Swiss army retreated. The French achieved their objectives in a single day of combat.[7]

The feat of arms, so important for the evolution of military tactics, also had territorial and political consequences. The towns of Lille, Douai, Bethune and surrounding areas were given as a guarantee for the execution of the Treaty of Athis-sur-Orge (1305). The area, that is all of French Flanders, fell into the hands of the King, who gained definitive possession of the region in 1312. However, this territorial mutilation of the county led to the principality becoming as early as 1305 a monolingual area, thus enhancing the specificity of Flanders and deepening the gulf with the kingdom of France that had arisen due to the war.

Finally, the Battle of Courtrai and the military power of the towns preserved the independence of the principality. At no other moment in history would the situation be so desperate as in 1300. The independence of Flanders was certainly threatened in the years following the war, but the tenacity with which the military operations were carried out in the years 1302–4 provoked much thought. A serious check to French expansion in the south of the Low Countries had been given. The plans attributed to the French King by two pro-Flemish sources of that time, the Ghentenaar Friar Minor and Lodewijk van Velthem, have already been noted in passing. Philip IV allegedly intended to replace Jan II, Duke of Brabant, with his uncle, Geoffrey, who was a willing instrument of the King. Brabant would then, after Flanders, have been brought into the French sphere of influence just like his allies Hainault, Holland and Zeeland. The Battle of the Spurs, however, put an end to that. By ensuring the independence of Flanders, the rest of the Low Countries were protected at the same time, and the Dukes of Burgundy were able to carry out their programme of territorial unification.

---

[7] See Lot, *L'Art militaire*, II:73–4.

Bibliography

Abbreviations

BCRH   *Bulletin (Compte rendu des séances) de la commission royale d'histoire* (in both Dutch and French from volume 100 (1936): *Handelingen van de Koninklijke Commissie voor Geschiedenis*)
CRH   Publications of the Commission royale d'histoire
CTEH   Collection de textes pour servir à l'étude et à l'enseignement de l'histoire
MGH, SS Monumenta Germaniae Historica, Scriptores, ed. G. H. Pertz, Hanover, 30 volumes, 1826–96. There is also a Nova Series.
RBPH   *Revue belge de philologie et d'histoire* (in both Dutch and French for volumes 20 to 23 and again from volume 25: *Belgisch tijdschrift voor philologie en geschiedenis*)
RHF   Recueil des historiens de la Gaule et de la France, ed. Dom Martin Bouquet and from volume 14 by the Académie des inscriptions et belles-lettres, 24 volumes, Paris, 1737–1904
Rolls Series   *Rerum Britannicarum Medii Aevi Scriptores*, 224 volumes, London, 1858–96
SHF   Société de l'histoire de France

Narrative Sources

Anciennes chroniques de Flandre, ed. N. de Wailly and L. Delisle. RHF, vol. 22. Paris, n.d.
Annales Gandenses, ed. and trans. H. Johnstone. Medieval Classics. London, 1951.
Annales S. Jacobi Leodiensis, ed. G. Pertz. MGH SS, vol. 16. Hanover, 1859.
Baudouin d'Avesnes, *Chroniques abrégées, continuation*, ed. Kervyn de Lettenhove. In *Istore et croniques de Flandre*. CRH, vol. I. Brussels, 1879.
Chronicon Comitum Flandrensium, ed. J. J. De Smet. *Corpus Chronicorum Flandriae*. CRH, vol. I. Brussels, 1837.
Chronique artésienne et chronique tournaisienne, ed. F. Funck-Brentano. Collection de textes pour servir à l'étude et à l'enseignement de l'histoire, fasc. 25. Paris, 1899.
Chronique normande du XIVe siècle, ed. A. and E. Molinier. SHF. Paris, 1886.
Chroniques de St Denis, ed. Daunou and Naudet. RHF, vol. 20. Paris, 1840.
Chronographia Regum Francorum, ed. H. Moranvillé. SHF. 3 vols. Paris, 1891–7.
Codex Dunensis sive Diplomatum et Chartarum Medii Aevi, ed. Kervyn de Lettenhove. CRH. Brussels, 1875.
Continuatio Chronici Girardi de Fracheto, ed. Guigniaut and de Wailly. RHF, vol. 21. Paris, 1855.
Continuatio Chronici Guillelmi de Nangiaco, ed. Daunou and Naudet. RHF, vol. 20. Paris, 1840.

Dubois, Pierre, *De Recuperatione Terre Sancte: Traité de politique générale*, ed. Ch. V. Langlois. Collection de textes pour servir à l'étude et à l'enseignement de l'histoire, fasc. 9. Paris, 1891.
Froissart, Jean, *Chroniques*, ed. S. Luce and G. Raynaud. SHF. Paris, 1899.
Genealogiae Comitum Flandrensium, ed. E. Martène and U. Durand. Thesaurus Novus Anecdotorum, vol. III. Paris, 1717.
Geoffroy de Paris, *Chronique rimée*, ed. N. de Wailly and L. Delisle. RHF, vol. 22. Paris, n.d.
Gilles le Muisit, *Chronique et annales*, ed. H. Lemaître. SHF. Paris. 1905.
Giovanni Villani, see Villani, Giovanni.
Les Grandes Chroniques de France, ed. J. Viard. SHF. Paris, 1935.
Guillaume Guiart, *La Branche des royaus lignages*, ed. N. de Wailly and L. Delisle. RHF, vol. 22. Paris, n.d.
Istore et croniques de Flandres, ed. Kervyn de Lettenhove. CRH. 2 vol. Brussels, 1879–80.
Jan van Boendale, *Brabantsche yeesten*, ed. J. F. Willems. CRH. Brussels, 1836.
Jan van Heelu, *Rijmkronijk*, ed. J. F. Willems. CRH. Brussels, 1836.
Jean le Bel, *Chronique*, ed. J. Viard and E. Depréz. SHF. 2 vols. Paris, 1904–5.
Jean des Preis d'Outremeuse, *Ly Myreur des histors*, ed. St Bormans. CRH. 6 vols. Brussels, 1880.
Johannes S. Victoris Parisiensis, *Memoriale Historiarum (excerpta)*, ed. Guigniaut and de Wailly. RHF, vol. 21. Paris, 1855.
Johannes Vitoduranus, *Chronicon*, ed. F. Baethgen. MGH, nova series, vol. 3. Hanover, 1924.
Lodewijk van Velthem, *Voortzetting van de Spiegel historiael (1248–1316)*, ed. H. vander Linden, W. de Vreese, P. de Keyser and A. van Loey. CRH. 3 vol. Brussels, 1906–1938.
Louis of Velthem, see Lodewijk van Velthem.
Ottokar von Stiermarken, *Oesterreichische Reimchronik*, ed. J. Seemuller. MGH, Deutsche Chroniken, vol. V:1, 2. Hanover, 1890–3.
Petrus de Langtoft, *Ex Chronico Rythmico*, ed. F. Liebermann. MGH SS, vol. 28. Hanover, 1888.
Petrus Pictor, *De Laude Flandriae*, ed. J. van Mierlo, SJ. Brussels, 1944.
Pierre Dubois, see Dubois, Pierre.
Récits d'un bourgeois de Valenciennes, ed. Kervyn de Lettenhove. Leuven, 1877.
Sir Thomas Gray of Heton, *Scalachronica*, ed. J. Stevenson. Maitland Club, vol. 40. Edinburgh, 1836.
Triumphus S. Lamberti in Steppes, ed. J. Heller. MGH SS, vol. 25. Hanover, 1880
Villani, Giovanni, *Historie fiorentine*, ed. L. A. Muratori. Rerum Italicarum Scriptores, vol. 13. Rome, 1728.
Vita Edwardi Secundi Auctore Malmesburiensi, ed. W. Stubbs. In *Chronicles of the Reign of Edward I and Edward II*. Rolls Series, vol. 2. London, 1883.
Willelmus Procurator, *Chronicon*, ed. C. Pijnacker Hordijk. Werken uitgegeven door het Historisch Genootschap (gevestigd te Utrecht), 3rd series, no. 20. Amsterdam, 1904.

Unpublished sources

Bruges Town Archives. (*a*) Town Accounts: see L. Gilliodts-van Severen, *Inventaire des archives de la ville de Bruges, Introduction*. Bruges, 1878, pp. 23–5. (*b*) Charters: see L. Gilliodts-van Severen, *Inventaire*, vol. I.

Brussels Algemeen Rijksarchief (General State Archives). Trésor de Flandre, 1st series (inventory on manuscript); Trésor de Flandre, 2nd series (inventory on file cards).

Courtrai Town Accounts (Chambre des comptes, 33.161–4). Courtrai Town Archives; Weeserieboek den Lupaert; Perkamenten Privilegieboek; La Royère, *Corte anotatien ende beschrijvinghe van de stadt Cortrijck*. Codex 504, Box 52.

Ghent Rijksarchief (State Archives). Tresaurie der graven van Vlaanderen; Fonds de St Genois, see J. de St Genois, *Inventaire analytique des chartes des comtes de Flandre . . . autrefois déposées au château de Rupelmonde*. Ghent, 1843–6; Fonds Gaillard, see V. Gaillard, *Inventaire analytique des chartes des comtes de Flandre*. Ghent, 1857; Fonds Diegerick, Fonds Verbaere, Loose leaves, see Inventory on file cards.

Lille, Archives départementales du Nord. Charters of the counts of Flanders formerly kept in the Accounts Chamber, see D. J. Godefroy, *Inventaire chronologique et détaillé de toutes les chartes qui se trouvent dans les archives des comtes de Flandre déposées dans l'ancienne chambre des comptes du Roy à Lille*, vols. I–V, manuscript; C. Dehaisnes and J. Finot, *Inventaire sommaire des archives départementales antérieures à 1790, Nord. Archives départementales, série B*, 9 sections in 10 volumes, and a *Table du tome I* (by M. Bruchet and E. Lancien). Paris, 1872–1931; Lille Town Accounts 1301–2: B. 7.581, see A. Richebé, *Compte des recettes et dépenses de la ville de Lille, 1301–1302* in *Annales du comité flamand de France* 21 (1893).

Paris National Archives J. 543, no. 17; Bibliothèque nationale; MS Latin 6222 c, see N. de Wailly, *Mémoire sur un opuscule, intitulé: Summaria Brevis et Compendiosa Doctrina Felicis Expeditionis et Abbreviationis Guerrarum ac Litium Regni Francorum*, in *Mémoires de l'Académie des inscriptions et belles-lettres*, vol. 18.2 (1855).

Historical Works, Collections of Deeds and Documents, etc.

Atlas des villes de Belgique au XVIe siècle: plans du géographe Jacques de Deventer, ed. C. Ruelens, E. Ouverleaux and E. P. van den Gheyn, SJ. 24 parts. Brussels, 1884–1924.

Blancquaert, E., 'Scilt' en 'Vricnt', in *Album Prof. Dr Frank Baur*, vol. I. Antwerp, 1948.

Blockmans, F., *Het Gentsche stadspatriciaat tot omstreeks 1302*. Rijksuniversiteit Gent, Werken uitgegeven door de Faculteit Wijsbegeerte en Letteren, no. 85. Antwerp, 1938.

——, *1302 vóór en na: Vlaanderen op een keerpunt van zijn geschiedenis*. De Seizoenen, 9. Antwerp, 1941.

——, 'Een patricische veete te Gent', *BCRH*, 99 (1935).

Boutemy, A., *Recueil de textes historiques latins du moyen âge, Coll. Lebègue.* Brussels, 1943.

Buntinx, J., *Het memoriaal van Jehan Makiel.* CRH. Brussels, 1944.

Callewaert, C., *Onuitgegeven aantekening uit het Jaar 1302 over den Guldensporenslag*, in *Annales société d'emulation de Bruges*, 60 (1910).

Colens, J., *Le Compte communal de la ville de Bruges.* Société d'emulation, vol. 35. Bruges, 1886.

Coussemaker, E. de, 'Confiscations dans la Flandre maritime', *Bulletin du comité flamand de France*, 6 (1872–5).

Daniels, E., *Geschichte des Kriegswesens*, vol. II: *Das mittelalterliche Kriegswesen, Sammlung Göschen*, no. 498. 2nd edn. Berlin and Leipzig, 1927.

Degrijse, R., *Vlaanderens haringbedrijf in de middeleeuwen.* De Seizoenen, no. 49. Antwerp, 1944.

Delbrück, H., *Geschichte der Kriegskunst im Rahmen der politischen Geschichte*, vol. 3. Berlin, 1907.

Delfos, L., *1302 door tijdgenooten verteld.* Antwerp, 1931.

——, *Verkenningen door onze Geschiedenis.* Bruges and Utrecht, 1944.

—— ,'Wat betekent "Scilt ende Vriend"?', *Wetenschappelijke tijdingen*, 10 (1950).

Demey, J., 'De vlaamse ondernemer in de middeleeuwse nijverheid: de Ieperse drapiers en "upsetters" op het einde der XIIIe en in de XIVe eeuw', *Bijdragen voor de geschiedenis der Nederlanden*, 4 (1949).

——, 'Proeve tot raming van de bevolking en de weefgetouwen te Ieper van de XIIIe tot de XVIIe eeuw', *RBPH*, 28 (1950).

Devillers, L., 'Notice sur un cartulaire concernant les terres dites de débat (Hainaut et Flandre)', *BCRH*, 4th ser., 3 (1875–6).

Dewilde, B., A. Pauwels, J. Verbruggen and F. Warlop, 'De kist van Oxford', *De leiegouw*, 22 (1980), 163–256.

Diegerick, L. A., *Inventaire analytique et chronologique des chartes et documents appartenant aux archives de la ville d'Ypres*, vol. I. Bruges, 1853.

Dhondt, J., ' "Ordres" ou "puissances": l'exemple des Etats de Flandre', *Annales. Economies. Sociétés. Civilisations*, 5 (1950).

——, *Les Origines des états de Flandre.* Leuven, 1950.

Duyse, H. van, 'Le Goedendag, arme flamande: sa légende et son histoire, *Handelingen der Maatschappij voor Geschied- en Oudheidkunde te Gent*, 3 (1896).

Espinas, G., *Une guerre sociale interurbaine dans la Flandre wallonne au XIIIe siècle: Douai et Lille, 1284–85.* Paris and Lille, 1930.

Favier, J., *Philippe le Bel.* Paris, 1978.

Fawtier, R., 'L'Europe occidentale de 1270 à 1328', in *Histoire générale*, ed. G. Glotz. Paris, 1940.

ffoulkes, C., 'A Carved Flemish Chest at New College, Oxford', *Archaeologia*, 2nd ser., 15 (1914).

Frederichs, J., 'De Slag van Kortrijk', *Nederlandsch museum*, 36 (1893).

——, 'Les Derniers Travaux sur l'histoire et l'historiographie de la bataille de Courtrai', *Messager des sciences historiques de Belgique*, 67 (1893).

Fris, V., 'L'Historien Jean Villani en Flandre', *BCRH*, 5th ser., 10 (1900).

——, 'Récits d'un bourgeois de Valenciennes', *BCRH*, 5th ser., 11 (1901).
——, *De slag bij Kortrijk*. Koninklijke Vlaamsche Academie. Ghent, 1902.
——, *Vlaanderens vrijmaking in 1302*. Willems-Fonds, no. 146. Ghent, 1902.
Funck-Brentano, F., 'Additions au Codex Diplomaticus Flandriae', *Bibliothèque de l'école des chartes*, 57 (1896).
——, 'De Exercituum Commeatibus Tertio Decimo et Quarto Decimo Saeculis post Christum Natum'. Thesis. Paris, 1897.
——, *Mémoire sur la bataille de Courtrai (1302, 11 juillet) et les chroniqueurs qui en ont traité pour servir à l'historiographie du règne de Philippe le Bel*. Mémoires de l'Académie des inscriptions et belles-lettres (Savants étrangers), 1st ser., vol. 10, 1. Paris, 1891.
——, *Philippe le Bel en Flandre*. Paris, 1896.
Ganshof, F. L., 'Aantekening over Lodewijk van Velthem, "Spiegel historiael", IV L., v. 3681–84', in *Album Prof. Dr Frank Baur*, vol. I. Antwerp, 1948.
——, 'Medieval Agrarian Society in its Prime: France, the Low Countries and Western Gerrnany', in *The Cambridge Economic History of Europe*, vol. I. Cambridge, 1942.
——, *Over stadsontwikkeling tusschen Loire en Rijn gedurende de middeleeuwen*. Verhandelingen van de Koninklijke Vlaamsche Academie. Antwerp, 1941.
——, 'Staatkundige geschiedenis, XIIe, XIIIe, XIVe eeuw', in *Geschiedenis van Vlaanderen*, vol. 2, ed. R. van Roosbroeck. Antwerp and Brussels, 1937.
Gilmour, Brian, and Ian Tyers, 'Courtrai Chest: Relic or Recent: Reassessment and Further Work: An Interim Report', in *Papers of the "Medieval Europe Brugge 1997" Conference. Vol 5: Art and Symbolism in Medieval Europe*. Bruges, 1997, pp. 17–26.
Hemelrijck, M. van, *De vlaamse krijgsbouwkunde*. Tielt, 1950.
Houtte, J. A. van, 'Makelaars en Waarden te Brugge van de 13e tot de 16e eeuw', *Bijdragen voor de geschiedenis der Nederlanden*, 5 (1950), 1–30, 177–97.
Les Journaux du trésor de Philippe le Bel, ed. J. Viard. Collection de documents inédits sur l'histoire de France. Paris, 1940.
Koechlin, H., *Chapelle de la Leugemeete à Gand: peintures murales, restitution*. Ghent, 1936.
Köhler, G., *Die Entwickelung des Kriegswesens und der Kriegführung in der Ritterzeit von Mitte des 11. Jahrhunderts bis zu den Hussitenkriegen*, vol. 2. Breslau, 1886.
——, *Ergänzungsheft die Schlachten von Tagliacozzo und Courtrai betreffend*. Breslau, 1893.
Lettenhove, Kervyn de, *Histoire de Flandre*. 4 vols. Brussels, 1847.
Lewis, N. B., 'The English Forces in Flanders, August–November 1297', in *Studies in Medieval History Presented to F. M. Powicke*. Oxford, 1948.
Limburg-Stirum, T. de, *Codex Diplomaticus Flandriae (1296–1325)*. Société d'emulation. 2 vols. Bruges, 1879–89.
Lot, F., *L'Art militaire et les armées au moyen âge en Europe et dans le proche orient*. 2 vols. Paris, 1946.
——, *La France des origines à la guerre de cent ans*. Paris, 1941.
Maclagan, E., *The Bayeux Tapestry*. London and New York, 1945.
Maere d'Aertrycke, M. de, *La Bataille des éperons d'or*. Namur, 1933.

—, *Campagnes flamandes de 1302 et de 1304, ou gloire militaire de Bruges au XIVe siècle*. Ghent, 1901.
—, *De la Colme au Boulenrieu*. Namur. 1935.
—, *Guerre de Flandre de 1302 et de 1304*. 2nd edn. Bruges, 1913.
—, *De slag der gulden sporen*. Ghent, 1899.
Marez, G. des, and E. de Sagher, *Comptes de la ville d'Ypres de 1267 à 1329*. CRH. Brussels, 1909.
Marijnissen, R. H., 'De "Chest of Courtrai": een vervalsing van het pasticcio-type', *Mededelingen van de koninklijke academie voor wetenschappen, letteren en schone kunsten van België*, 40 (1978), no. 3.
Moke, H. G., 'Mémoire sur la bataille de Courtai', *Mémoires de l'académie royale de Belgique*, 26 (1851).
Monier, R., *Le Livre Roisin: documents et travaux publiés par la société d'histoire du droit des pays flamands, picards et wallons*, vol. 2. Paris and Lille, 1932.
—, *Les Institutions centrales du comté de Flandre*. Paris, 1943.
—, *Les Institutions financières du comté de Flandre*. Paris, 1948.
Naibh, Pleimion, *Zannekin en de vrijheidsstrijd van het Kustland*. Tielt. 1928.
Niermeyer, J. F., 'Het sticht Utrecht en het Graafschap Holland in de dertiende eeuw', in *Algemene geschiedenis der Nederlanden*, vol. 2. Utrecht and Antwerp, 1950.
Nowé, H., *Les Baillis comtaux de Flandre*. Académie royale de Belgique, Classe des lettres, mémoires, vol. 25. Brussels, 1929.
—, *La Bataille des éperons d'or*. Collection Notre Passé. Brussels, 1945.
—, 'Fonctionnaires flamands passés au service royal durant la guerre de Flandre', *Revue du nord*, 10 (1924).
Obreen, H., *Floris V, Graaf van Holland en Zeeland, Heer van Friesland (1256–1296)*. Université de Gand, Recueil de travaux publiés par la Faculté de Philosophie et Lettres, fasc. 34. Ghent, 1907.
Oman, Sir Charles, *A History of the Art of War in the Middle Ages*. 2nd edn. 2 vols. London, 1924.
Perroy, E., 'Les Crises du XIVe siècle,' *Annales. Economies. Sociétés. Civilisations*, 4 (1949), 167–82.
—, *The Hundred Years War*, trans. W. B. Wells. Oxford, 1951.
Pieri, P., 'Alcune quistione sopra la fanteria in Italia nel periodo comunale', *Rivista storica italiana*, 4th ser., 4 (1933).
Pirenne, H., 'L'Ancienne Chronique de Flandre et la Chronographia Regum Francorum', *BCRH*, 5th ser., 8 (1898).
—, *Histoire de Belgique* (illustrated edition), vol. I. Brussels, 1948.
—, 'Note sur un passage de van Velthem relatif à la bataille de Courtrai', *BCRH*, 5th ser., 9 (1899).
—, *Le Soulèvement de la Flandre maritime de 1323–1328*. CRH. Brussels, 1900.
—, 'La Version flamande et la version française de la bataille de Courtrai', *BCRH*, 4th ser., 17 (1890).
—, 'La Version flamande et la version française de la bataille de Courtrai, note supplémentaire', *BCRH*, 5th ser., 2 (1892).

Prevenier, W., 'Motieven voor leliaardsgezindheid in Vlaanderen in de periode 1297–1305', *De leiegouw*, 19 (1977).
Putte, F. van de, *Chronica et Cartularium Monasterii de Dunis.* Société d'emulation. Bruges, 1839.
——, *Chronique et cartulaire de l'abbaye de Groeninghe à Courtrai.* Société d'emulation. Bruges, 1872.
Rousset, P., *Les Origines et les caractères de la première croisade.* Neuchâtel, 1945.
Seligman, General, *Les Nivellements en Belgique.* Congrès national des sciences. Liège, 1931.
Sevens, T., *De slag van Kortrijk in 1302.* 2nd edn. Ghent, 1902.
——, 'Hoeken en Kanten op Groeninge', *Bulletijn van den geschied- en oudheidkundigen kring te Kortrijk*, 4 (1906–7).
——, 'De Groeningebeek', *Bulletijn van den geschied- en oudheidkundigen kring te Kortrijk*, 6 (1908–9).
Smet, A. de, 'De klacht van de "ghemeente" van Damme in 1280', *BCRH*, 115 (1950).
Smet, J. De, 'Les Effectifs brugeois à la bataille de Courtrai en 1302', *RBPH*, 8 (1929).
——, 'Les Effectifs des milices brugeoises et la population de la ville en 1340', *RBPH*, 12 (1933).
——, 'De gezindheid van de vlaamse ridders in 1302', *Biekorf*, 51 (1950).
——, *Le Plus Ancien Livre de fiefs du Bourg de Bruges vers 1325, tablettes des Flandres.* Bruges, 1950.
——, 'De inrichting van de poorterlijke ruiterij te Brugge in 1292 en haar indeeling in gezindheden in 1302', *Koninklijke vlaamsche academie, verslagen en mededelingen* (Aug.–Sept., 1930).
——, 'Rond een Brugs poortersgeslacht van de XIIIe eeuw', *Biekorf*, 51 (1950), 10–11.
Stad Kortrijk. Stedebouw. Survey. Courtrai, 1948.
Stevens, C., 'Les Déformations naturelles et récentes du sol belge', *Bulletin de la société royale belge de géographie*, 59 (1935).
——, 'Les Élements directeurs de la géomorphologie de la Belgique', *Bulletin belge des sciences militaires* (July/August 1938).
Strayer, Joseph R., *The Reign of Philip the Fair.* Princeton, 1980.
Thomas, P., *Textes historiques sur Lille et le Nord de la France avant 1789.* Bibliothèque de la société d'histoire du droit des pays flamands, picards et wallons, vol. 2. Lille, 1936.
Tout, T. F., 'Some Neglected Fights between Crécy and Poitiers', in *The Collected Papers of T. F Tout*, vol. 2. Manchester, 1934.
——, *The Place of the Reign of Edward II in English History.* Manchester, 1914.
——, 'The Tactics of the Battles of Boroughbridge and Morlaix', in *The Collected Papers of T. F Tout*, vol. 2. Manchester, 1934.
Vanderkindere, L., *Le Siècle des Artevelde: études sur la civilisation morale et politique de la Flandre et du Brabant.* Brussels, 1879.
Verbruggen, J. F., 'De Brugse effectieven in de slag bij Kortrijk', *Bijdragen voor de geschiedenis der Nederlanden*, 2 (1948).
——, 'De Gentse minderbroeder der *Annales Gandenses* en de krijgskunst in de

periode 1302–1304', *Handelingen der maatschappij voor geschiedenis en oudheidkunde te Gent*, n.s., 4 (1949).

——, 'De organisatie van de militie te Brugge in de XIVe eeuw', *Handelingen société d'emulation te Bruges*, 87 (1950).

——, 'Le Problème des effectifs et de la tactique à la bataille de Bouvines en 1214', *Revue du nord*, 31 (1949).

——, 'Scilt ende vrient', *Revue belge d'histoire militaire*, 23 (1979–80), 311–22.

——, 'De slag bij de Pevelenberg (18 aug. 1304)', *Bijdragen voor de geschiedenis der Nederlanden*, 6 (1952), 169–98 and *Het Leger. De Natie*, 7 (1952), 258–62, 338–42.

——, 'De slag bij Woeringen', *Het leger. De natie*, 5, nos. 5 and 6 (1950).

——, 'La Tactique militaire des armées de chevaliers', *Revue du nord*, 29 (1947).

——, *Vlaanderen na de guldensporenslag*. Bruges, 1991.

Vercauteren, F., *Luttes sociales à Liège (XIIIe et XIVe siècles)*. Notre Passé. Brussels, 1943.

——, 'Het prinsbisdom Luik tot 1316', in *Algemene geschiedenis der Nederlanden*, vol. 2. Utrecht and Antwerp, 1950.

Verriest, L., 'Le Registre de la 'Loi' de Tournai, de 1302 et listes des otages de Bruges (1301) et de Courtrai', *BCRH*, 80 (1911).

Vigne, F. de, *Recherches historiques sur les costumes civils et militaires des gildes et des corporations de métiers*. Ghent, 1847.

Vinkeroy, E. van, *Costumes militaires belges*. Braine-le-Comte, 1885.

Vis, A. J., 'Willelmus Procurator en zijn chronicon'. Dissertation. Amsterdam, 1950.

Voet, L., 'Het Platteland maatschappelijk en economisch', in *Algemene geschiedenis der Nederlanden*, vol. 2. Utrecht and Antwerp, 1950.

Vuylsteke, J., *Uitleggingen tot de Gentsche stads- en baljuwrekeningen, 1280–1315*, ed. V. van der Haeghen and A. van Werveke, in *Oorkondenboek der stad Gent, 1e afd.: rekeningen*, vol. 2. Ghent 1906.

Wagner, R. L., 'La Bataille de Courtrai (1302): essai de critique des sources françaises', *Mémoires de l'académie nationale des sciences, arts et belles-lettres de Caen*, n.s. 10 (1942).

Wailly, N. de, 'Mémoire sur un opuscule, intitulé: Summaria Brevis et Compendiosa Doctrina Felicis Expeditionis et Abbreviationis Guerrarum ac Litium Regni Francorum', *Mémoires de l'académie des inscriptions et belles-lettres*, 18, 2 (1855).

Warnkoenig, L. A., *Flandrische Staats- und Rechtsgeschichte bis zum Jahre 1305*. 5 vols. Tübingen, 1835–42.

Warnkoenig, L. A., and A. E. Gheldolf, *Histoire de la Flandre et de ses institutions civiles et politiques jusqu'a l'année 1305*. 5 vols. Brussels, 1835–64.

Werveke, A. van, *Het godshuis van St Jan en St Pauwel*. Maatschappij der Vlaamsche Bibliophilen, 4th ser., no. 15. Ghent, 1909.

Werveke, H. van, 'Avesnes en Dampierre: Vlaanderens vrijheidsoorlog, 1244–1305', in *Algemene geschiedenis der Nederlanden*, vol. 2. Utrecht and Antwerp, 1950.

——, 'De opbloei van handel en nijverheid', in *Algemene geschiedenis der Nederlanden*, vol. 2. Utrecht and Antwerp, 1950.

——, 'De steden', in *Algemene geschiedenis der Nederlanden*, vol. 2. Utrecht and Antwerp, 1950.

——, 'Het bevolkingscijfer van de stad Gent in de veertiende eeuw', in *Miscellanea L. van der Essen*. Brussels, 1947, pp. 345–54.

——, *Gand. Esquisse d'histoire sociale*. Collection Notre Passé. Brussels, 1946.

——, *De Gentsche stadsfinanciën in de middeleeuwen*. Académie royale de Belgique, Classe des lettres, mémoires, vol. 34. Brussels, 1934.

——, *De koopman-ondernemer en de ondernemer in de Vlaamsche lakennijverheid van de middeleeuwen*. Mededelingen Koninklijke Vlaamsche Academie. Antwerp, 1946.

——, *De omvang van de Ieperse lakenproductie in de veertiende eeuw*. Mededelingen Koninklijke Vlaamsche Academie. Antwerp, 1947.

Wittenberg, R., 'De waarheid over den guldensporenslag', *Handelingen van den koninklijke geschied- en oudheidkundigen kring van Kortrijk*, n.s., 15 (1936).

Wodsak, F., 'Die Schlacht bei Kortrijk'. Berlin dissertation, 1905.

Wyffels, C., 'Les Corporations flamandes et l'origine des corporations de métier', *Revue du nord*, 32 (1950).

——, *De oorsprong der ambachten in Vlaanderen en Brabant*. Verhandelingen Koninklijke Vlaamse Academie. Brussels, 1951.

——, and J. De Smet, *De rekeningen van de stad Brugge (1280–1319). Eerste deel (1280–1302). Eerste stuk*. CRH. Brussels, 1965.

——, and A. Vandewalle, *De rekeningen van de stad Brugge (1280–1319). Tweede deel (1302–1306)*. CRH. Brussels, 1995.

Index

Aalst 7, 40, 215, 229
Aardenburg 8, 24, 25, 166, 215
Aardenburg, Bangelijn van 177, 179, 239
Adrianople, Battle of xv
Agincourt, Battle of xv
Aigremont, Anselm van, Guardian of Tournai 168
Alexander the Great 109
Alisant 107
Anciennes chroniques de Flandre 30, 37, 66, 70–76, 115–18, 120–22, 132–34, 150
Anjou 188, 192
Annales Gandenses 26, 29, 31, 33, 42, 53, 57, 83–88, 96, 111, 114, 121–23, 133, 152, 162, 176, 178, 182, 188, 192, 193, 199, 249
Antwerp 89
Apremont, the Lord of 93, 189
Archises (Attiches?) Robrecht van 166, 172
Arques, Battle of 53, 59n, 247
Arras 10, 46, 47, 53, 54, 57, 115, 124, 215
Artevelde, Philip van, Ghentenaar Leader 219
Artois, Robert of, Count of xxiii, 17, 44–48, 55–57, 61–62, 65, 67–69, 72, 73, 76, 78, 80, 82, 83–85, 91–94, 98, 104, 105, 107–10, 115, 116, 118, 122, 123, 131, 182, 183, 189, 193, 218–24, 230, 232, 237–40
Athis-sur-Orge, Treaty of 64, 249
Auberchicourt, Baudoin d', Guardian of Tournai 19, 165, 166, 191
Aumale, Jean I, Count of 56, 57, 67, 93, 117, 190, 192, 223, 230, 235, 239
Austria xxiii, 51, 248
Avesnes, Jean I d', Count of Hainault (Jan II, Count of Holland) 13, 15, 18, 56, 83, 96, 117, 118, 164, 182, 191, 244
Axel 8, 104
Axel, Philips van, Lord of 174, 176, 177, 179
Bachrach, Bernard S. (historian) xii
Bannockburn, Battle of xxiii, xxiv, 36, 114, 248
Bataelgen 100, 103, 105–8, 110–12, 117, 118, 120, 192, 222–24, 230, 232, 236

Baugelijn. See Aardenburg, Baugelijn van
Bavaria, Ludwig of, Holy Roman Emperor 89
Beatrice, daughter of Guy de Dampierre, wife of Floris V of Holland 8
Beckine, Jacob van den 154, 155
Bel, Jean le (Chronicler) xxiv
Belle, Pieter van 176, 180
Belle, Zeger van 176, 180
Benevento, Battle of xxiv
Berry 164, 192
Bersaques, Louis de 135, 138, 139, 141–43, 147, 150
Bersaques, Pierre de 141, 143
Bethune 8, 220, 256
Bethune, Mathilda of, first wife of Count Guy de Dampierre 8
Bethune, Robert de, son and heir of Count Guy de Dampierre 6, 8, 18–20, 84, 96, 165, 219
Bidauts 66, 194, 225
Biervliet 8, 219
Biest, Veys van der 154, 155
Black Death 1, 63
Boechoute 8, 104
Boenhem, Willem van 108, 109, 235, 239, 246
Boniface VIII, Pope xxiii, 9–11, 17, 18, 44n, 45, 79
Borluut, Jan, Mayor of Ghent 104, 108, 109, 152, 153, 177, 179, 217, 228, 229, 239
Boulogne, Godefroid de 93, 190
Boulogne, Robert, Count of Boulogne and Auvergne 47, 60, 73, 93, 105, 109, 117, 188, 191, 223, 230, 240
Bourges 43, 81, 113
Burgundy 62, 188
Bouvines, Battle of xv, xxiii, 121
Brabant xxv, 4, 16, 68, 85, 86, 89, 96, 109, 114, 162, 188, 192, 223, 241
Brabant, Geoffrey de, brother of Duke Jan I 56, 57, 68, 92, 96, 105–7, 110, 117, 182, 191, 192, 201, 223, 224, 230, 232, 234, 239, 249
Brabant, Jan I, Duke of 13
Brabant, Jan II, Duke of 15, 96, 119, 249

Branche des royaus lingnages, La. See Guiart, Guillaume
Brittany   188, 192
Brittany, Jean II, Duke of   93
Breucq, Pierre du   22, 25, 92, 96, 168
Broukerke, Wouter van   171, 172, 174
Bruges   1–3, 4, 10–14, 17–26, 40–42, 58, 64, 66, 73, 78, 81, 82, 84, 87, 94, 109, 114, 131, 152, 153, 156–61, 163, 173, 175–77, 182, 197, 199, 211, 212, 214–17, 219, 220, 228, 229, 233–35, 240, 244–47
Bruges Franc   40, 56, 58, 91, 102, 103, 107, 109, 112, 131, 152, 161, 173, 206, 214, 219, 229, 230, 233, 235, 236
Bruges Friday. See Bruges Matins
Bruges Matins   xxvi, 26, 34, 42, 46, 49, 84, 95, 158–60, 167, 173, 182, 194, 197, 211, 212, 214–16, 220, 242, 246
Brunembart, Jean le Brun   109, 190
Burlats, Jean de, Seneschal of Guyenne, Master of Crossbowmen   6, 47, 56, 67, 68, 92, 105, 117, 182, 190, 192, 223, 224, 230, 232, 239
Carson, Patricia (historian)   xi
Cassel   66, 85, 154, 156, 167–70, 173, 178, 183, 217–20, 244
Cassel, Battle of   122, 248
Cassel, Siege of   175
Castracani, Castruccio, Lombard Condottiere   66, 194
Champagne   4, 46, 62, 85, 108, 188, 192, 193, 231, 237
Châtillon, Gaucher, Lord of   43, 184
Châtillon, Jacques de. See St-Pol, Jacques de
Chieti-en-Loreto, Philip, Count of, son of Count Guy de Dampierre   8, 66, 212, 214
Chronicon comitum Flandrensium (Genealogiae comitum Flandriae continuatio Clarismariscensis)   30, 31, 88, 110–13, 121, 123, 134
Chronicon of Willem Procurator. See Procurator, Willem
Chronique artésienne   29, 32, 35, 45–49, 51, 83, 113, 117, 124, 133, 162, 182, 188, 192, 193, 218
Chronique Normande du XIVe siècle   30, 70, 71, 193
Chroniques de Saint-Denis   54
Chronographia regum Francorum   30, 33, 61, 93, 94, 100, 115–19, 132, 133, 134, 150, 182, 193
Clairmarais, Abbey of   30, 111, 114

Clermont, Louis de   47, 56, 60, 67, 69, 73, 93, 105, 117, 183, 191, 223, 230, 240
Cleves, Lord of   191
Clokettes, Michiel as, solicitor of Count Guy de Dampierre to the Pope   77, 79
Coninc, Pieter de, Brugeois Leader   21, 22, 24, 61, 63, 64, 67, 72, 106, 117, 197, 206, 211–13, 215, 216, 228, 246
Conroten   222, 236
Contamine, Philippe (historian)   xii
Continuatio prima Guilelmi de Nangiaco chronici. See Nangis, Guillaume de
Cortenuova, Battle of   121
Courtrai   12, 21, 25, 40–44, 46, 59, 64, 67, 71, 78, 79, 86, 127–51, 154, 157, 160, 173, 215, 217, 218, 226, 228, 229, 235, 242–44
  Berg van Weelden. See Courtrai, Pottelberg Hill
  Bloedbeek   150
  Bloedmeers   98, 150
  Canonic Gate   136
  Castle   74, 100, 131, 149, 152, 153, 207, 216, 217, 219, 220, 222, 235, 243
  Doornikpoorte. See Tournai Gate
  Groeninge Bridge   147
  Groeninge field   44, 48, 88, 220, 222, 227
  Groeninge monastery, Our Lady of Groening, Cloister of the Grey Nuns   47, 48, 79, 105, 111, 113, 130, 131, 133, 135, 141, 150, 151, 222, 230
  Groeninge Stream (Groeningebeek)   37, 57, 58, 81, 92, 97–103, 110, 116, 128, 129, 131, 132, 134–36, 138–50, 222, 230, 231, 235, 237, 240
  Grote Beek (St-Jansbeek)   33, 37, 55, 57, 58, 98–103, 110, 116, 128, 132, 135, 138–40, 143, 222, 229–32, 235
  Harelbeke Street   136–38
  Hoge Vijver   100, 128, 132, 135, 136–40, 147, 149, 150
  Lage Vijver   137
  Lange Mere   98, 109, 116, 132, 135, 136, 138–40, 147, 150, 230, 240
  Lange Mere Street (Lange Meersch Street)   136, 137
  Lille Gate (Rijselpoort)   116, 130
  Mossenborch   104, 130
  Mosscher Stream (Mosscherbeek or Klakkaertsbeek)   57, 58, 98, 100, 135, 147–50

Neveldries 135, 150
Our Lady Church (Onze Lieve Vrouw Kerk) xi, 104, 242
Pottelberg Hill, Berg van Weelden 97, 99, 104, 120, 130, 131, 220, 222, 225, 230, 241, 242
St Jan's Bridge 136–38
St Jan's Church 148
St Jan's Gate 138
St Jan's Stream. See Courtrai, Grote Beek
tSiexmans 109, 130, 132, 240
Tournai Gate (Doornikpoort) 116, 130, 147, 150
Vierschaar ten Akker 147–50
Crécy, Battle of xv, xxiv, 77, 194
Créquy, Jean, Lord of 190
Dammartin, Renaut, son of the Count of Dammartin 73
Damme 4, 8, 17–20, 24, 25, 166, 219, 245
Dampierre, Guy de, Count of Flanders xi–xii, xxvi, 5–6, 8–11, 14–20, 44, 53, 66, 69, 78, 89, 90, 158–60, 163, 164, 172, 173, 199, 212–15, 218, 219, 223, 245, 246
Daniels, E. (historian) 121
Delbrück, Hans (historian) xii, 36, 121
Delfos, Leo (historian) 34, 128, 129, 142, 179, 195
Deventer, Jacob Roelofs van 128, 129, 135, 139–43, 147, 149, 150
Ditches (*grachten*) 42–45, 47, 48, 50–52, 55–59, 65, 69, 72–76, 79–83, 88, 97, 98, 101, 107, 108, 113, 129, 131, 132, 134, 147
Dixmude, Jan van (Chronicler) 113
Dorez, Gilbert 172, 173, 186
Dottenijs 79, 88, 109, 118, 132
Douai 2, 11, 14, 17, 18, 40, 41, 154, 156, 160, 177, 179, 219, 244, 246, 249
Dreux, Jean II, Count of 163
Dubois, Pierre, Royal Counsel xxiv, 13
East Flanders 152, 161, 229
Edward I, King of England 15, 17, 77, 89, 90, 219
Edward II, King of England 8, 14
Egmond, Abbey of 30, 80
England xxiii, 2, 4, 11, 14
Eu, Jean de Brienne, Count of 56, 57, 68, 93, 105, 108, 117, 188, 190, 192, 223, 235, 239
Falkirk, Battle of 121
Ferrand of Portugal, Count of Flanders xi, 10

Ferrant, Gerard 179, 239
Ferrant, Jan, Willem van Jülich's Standard-Bearer 107, 109, 234
Ferraris (geographer) 135, 143, 147, 150
ffoulkes, Ch. (archaeologist) 195, 196
Fiennes, Guillaume II, Lord of 189
Flamenc, Raoul VI le, Lord of Cauny-en-Verpillière 190
Flanders the Lion (*Vlaanderen de Leeuw*), Battle-Cry 106, 107, 109, 228, 241
Flines 42–45
Floris V, Count of Holland 8, 9, 14, 15, 18
Flote, Pierre, Chancellor and Councillor to King Philip IV 11, 25, 26, 57, 61, 62, 189
Forez, Jean I, Count of 184
Four Ambachten (*Vier ambachten*) 24, 104, 152, 235
Frachet, Girard de (chronicler) 82, 134
France, Louis of, brother of King Philip IV 183
Frederichs, J. (historian) 33, 34, 36, 58, 98, 99, 127–29, 140
Fris, Victor (historian) xvii, 33, 36, 58, 99, 100, 127, 129, 138, 140
Frisians 248
Funck-Brentano, Frantz (historian) xix, 32, 35–38, 59, 97, 127, 128, 129, 138, 140–42
Furnes, Battle of 17, 20, 53, 71, 166
Gaier, Claude (historian) xii
Garter, Colard de 154, 155
Gascony 164, 188
Genealogiae comitum Flandriae. See *Chronicon comitum Flandriae*
Gent, Zeger van, the elder 179, 215, 246
Gent, Zeger van, the younger 215, 246
Germany xxiii, 2, 4, 9, 13, 51, 52
Ghent xxv, 1–4, 10, 13–24, 40, 41, 50 , 67, 78, 83, 86, 89–91, 99, 104, 107–9, 116, 131, 132, 135, 136, 147, 152–54, 215, 217, 219, 220, 228, 229, 236, 237, 246
Ghent, Leugemeete Chapel 195, 202, 208
Ghentenaar Friar Minor. See *Annales Gandenses*
Gistel, Jan, Lord of 22, 165, 166, 170
goedendag, Flemish weapon 41, 53, 64, 65, 69, 82, 87, 104, 111, 112, 116, 195, 199, 202, 206–9, 226–29, 233, 234, 236, 237, 240, 242
Gossenhoven, Goswin van 86, 109, 162, 179, 180, 239
Grandes chroniques de France 82, 95, 115, 134

Grantcourt, Raoul de   101, 108, 190, 240
Gravelines   7, 53, 160
Gruuthuus, Ghildolf, Lord of   5, 158, 171
Guelders, Reinout van, Count of   8, 9, 13
Guiart, Guillaume (chronicler)   29, 33, 36, 37, 44, 52–60, 63, 81, 83, 85, 98, 99, 110, 115, 119, 121, 123, 133, 194, 205, 209, 229
Guyenne   11, 182
Hainault   18, 46, 68, 82, 83, 85, 109, 111, 188, 192, 244, 249
Halewijn, Wouter, Lord of   166, 168, 171, 172
Hangest, Jan van   173, 190
Harcourt, Jean, Lord of   164, 184
Hastings, Battle of   xv, 121
Haveskerke, Gillis van   167, 216, 217
Haveskerke, Jan van   167, 173, 216, 217
Hazebrouck, Aelipdis, widow of Hendrik, Lord of   173
Hazebouck, Hendrik, Lord of   166, 169
Hazebrouck, Jan van   169, 173
Heelu, Jan van (chronicler)   13, 89
Holland   xxv, 8, 13, 18, 30, 80, 244, 249
Holland, Jan II van, Count of Holland. See Jean d'Avesnes, Count of Hainault
Holy Roman Empire. See Germany
Hondschote, Diederik van   86, 162, 165, 177, 179, 181
Hondschote, Wouter, Lord of   165, 166, 170, 172
Hulst   8, 104, 215
Hundred Years War   76, 114, 193
Isabella, daughter of Count Guy de Dampierre   8
Istore et croniques de Flandre   30, 33, 61, 74, 75
Johanna, daughter of Count Guy de Dampierre   8
Jülich, Willem van, the elder, brother of Willem, the younger   23, 213
Jülich, Willem van, the younger, son of the Count of Jülich, grandson of Count Guy de Dampierre   8, 23, 24, 41, 42, 66, 67, 69, 72, 80, 82–86, 95, 101, 102, 104–12, 117, 118, 123, 131, 132, 153, 154, 156, 162, 176, 178, 181, 199, 201, 205, 212–18, 223, 237–31, 234, 242, 246, 247
Katzenellenboghe, Everard, Count of   178
Kervyn de Lettenhove (historian)   30, 70
Köhler, G. (historian)   31, 33, 35, 36, 58, 127, 129, 140
La Haignerie   52, 54
Lauwaerd, Jan, Ballif   5, 23, 167

Leeuwergem, Robrecht van   86, 162, 177, 179, 181
Legnano, Battle of   64, 121
Leliaarts   xxv, 16, 19, 86
Lembeke, Jan van   174, 175
Lembeke, Michiel van   174
Lens, Jean de, Viscount   48, 57, 59, 112, 113, 197, 206, 207, 222, 239, 242
Lichtervelde, Rogier van   167, 171, 172
Liebaarts   105
Liège   xv, 8
Liège, Jean de, Bishop of, son of Count Guy de Dampierre   8
Lille   xxv, 2, 12, 14, 16, 17, 21, 40–42, 71, 79, 86, 112, 164, 165, 166, 219, 220, 241, 244, 246, 249
Lille, Jan V, Viscount of   25, 165, 172, 191
Lille, Rogier de   162, 179, 227
Lille, Thomas de   176, 177, 180
Limburg   86, 197
Lodi, Henry, Count of, son of Count Guy de Dampierre   8
Lombardy   68, 194, 223
Lombards   66, 194
Lontzen, Hendrik van, Marshal of Bruges   72, 86, 116, 117, 153, 162, 178–80, 197, 199, 205, 213
Lontzen, Hendrik van, nephew of the Marshal of Bruges   181
Lonke, Zeger, Ghentenaar Standard-bearer   108, 229, 235
Lorraine   188, 192, 231
Lorraine, Ferri de, son of the Duke of Lorraine   68, 117, 118
Lorraine, Mahieu de   117, 189
Lot, Ferdinand (historian)   37, 38, 98, 99, 104
Louis IX, Saint, King of France   6, 62, 85n, 246
Luxembourg, Isabella de, second wife of Count Guy de Dampierre   8
Lys River   57, 62, 63, 64, 67, 71, 78, 99, 107–9, 112, 116, 131, 132, 134, 135, 139, 147–49, 151, 219, 222, 224, 226, 239
Maere d'Aertrycke, M. de, Baron (historian)   31, 104, 127, 129, 130, 134
Maerlant, Jacob van (poet)   89, 96
Maldegem, Rogier van   136, 137
Mansurah, Battle of   62
Manzikert, Battle of   xv
Margareta, daughter of Count Guy de Dampierre, wife of Jan I, Duke of Brabant   8

Maria, daughter of Count Guy of Dampierre, wife of Count Willem van Jülich 8
Marigny, Enguerrand de, Councillor to King Philip IV 11, 12
Marquette 47, 48, 220
Massemen, Geraard van 174, 180
Matte, Joris van der, the elder 158, 159
Melun, Treaty of 9, 15, 163
Menen, Jan van 174, 175, 179
Menen, Pieter van 175, 180
Milan 248
Milvian Bridge, Battle of xv
Moen 109, 132
Moerkerke, Lonis van 167, 171, 172
Moerzeke, The Lord of 199, 212
Moke, H. G. (historian) 58, 127, 129, 140
Molaines, Drieu de, The Lord of Mello 189
Mons-en-Pévèle, Battle of ix, xix, xxiv, 8, 12, 39, 53, 55, 58, 63–65, 71, 83–85, 87, 88, 94, 95, 110, 111, 121, 122, 133, 160, 194, 202n, 243, 244, 247
Montigni, Robert of, Lord of 165, 166, 168
Moor, Geraard de, Lord of Wessegem 5, 83, 84, 165, 174, 175
Moranvillé, H. (historian) 70
Morel, horse of Robert of Artois 94, 108
Mortgarten, Battle of 51, 248
Mortagne, Willem van, Lord of Dossemer 164, 165, 174
Mosscher, Willem van 97, 109, 120, 130, 132, 168, 207, 240, 241
Mote, Boudewijn van 173, 184
Muisit, Gilles le (chronicler) 30, 76–80, 97, 116, 118, 122, 123, 133, 162
Musciatto, Guidi di Francesi, Financier and Councillor of King Philip IV 66
Namur xxv, 8, 16
Namur, Guy de, son of Count Guy de Dampierre 8, 19, 23, 24, 41, 42, 67, 72, 80, 84–86, 96, 97, 99–102, 104–6, 108, 109, 111, 112, 117, 118, 132, 154, 156, 162, 181, 182, 199, 201, 205, 212–19, 223, 227–29, 231, 235, 237–39, 241–43, 246, 247
Namur, Jean de, son of Count Guy de Dampierre 8, 23, 41, 42, 106, 123, 162, 163, 178, 212, 214, 215, 219
Nangis, Guillaume de (chronicler) 30, 33, 81–82, 115, 134
Navarre 66, 223

Navarre, Johanna of, Queen of France and wife of King Philip IV 21, 84
Nesle, Gui de, Marshal of France 56, 57, 92, 105, 117, 184, 189, 223, 239
Nesle, Raoul de, Constable of France 19, 20, 47, 55–57, 67, 68, 73, 92, 105, 107, 117, 182, 189, 223, 224, 230, 232, 234, 239
Neuville, Eustaes van 164, 172
Nevele, Willem van 166, 174, 179
Nevele, Wouter van, Viscount of Courtrai 165, 175
Nieuwpoort 7, 215, 216
Nogaret, Guillaume de, Councillor to King Philip IV 11, 45
Normandy 12, 46, 85, 188, 191–93, 223
Oesterreichische Reimchronik. See Stiermarken, Ottokar von
Oman, Sir Charles (historian) xii, 36, 37, 195
Oostburg 8, 25
Orléans 52, 53, 55, 194
Ostrevant 13–15
Oudenaarde 139, 147, 150, 164, 215, 217, 219, 229
Oudenaarde, Arnulf van 164, 175
Oudenaarde, Jan van, Lord of Rosoit 164, 172
Oudenburch, Clais van 154, 155
Outere, Master Gilbert of 21, 245
Oxford, Chest of 117, 195–210
Paris 1, 14, 30, 54, 70, 73, 76, 81, 89
Paris, Geoffrey de (chronicler) 29, 33–37, 44, 52, 60–63, 76, 80, 115, 118, 119, 134, 188
Pene, Jan, Lord of 171–73
Pene, Willem van, Brother of Jan van Pene 173
Philip III, King of France 10
Philip IV, King of France xi, xxvi, 9–22, 26, 29, 34, 37, 40, 42, 43, 45, 46, 50, 53, 57, 61, 64, 65, 71, 72, 77, 78, 81–85, 90, 96, 152, 159, 160, 163, 166, 172, 173, 182, 194, 211, 212, 214, 216, 217, 223, 240, 241, 244–46, 249
Philippina, daughter of Count Guy de Dampierre, fiancé of Edward, son of King Edward I of England 8, 14, 15
Pietersheim, Hendrik van 179, 180
Pirenne, Henri (historian) 31, 32, 34, 35, 37, 38, 61, 64, 98, 195
Planke, Baudouin de le, Lord of Thiennes, Steenbecque, and Heuchin 167, 173

Plasian, Guillaume de, Councillor to King Philip IV   11, 45
Plateel (or Plateil), Jan   167, 180
Poitou   85, 113, 188, 192
Pont-à-Vendin   58, 176
Ponthieu   191, 223
Popperode, Boudewijn van, Viscount of Aalst   86, 96, 108, 109, 123, 162, 177, 179, 181, 235, 239
Praat, Jan van, Lord of   5, 165
Procurator, Willem (chronicler)   30, 80–81, 134
Récits d'un bourgeois de Valenciennes   82–83
Renesse, Jan van   18, 59, 72, 80, 82, 86, 91, 101–3, 105–11, 116–18, 123, 124, 132, 152, 161, 162, 178–81, 215, 223, 226–28, 236, 237
Rhine River   2, 68
Roebaais (or Roubaix), Alard van   175, 176, 179, 227
Roebaais, Geraard van   227
Roland, Marcher Lord of Brittany, hero of the *Song of Roland*   107
Rome   xxiii, 9, 17, 76, 77
Roncevalles, Battle of   107
Rosebeke, Battle of. See Westrozebeke, Battle of
Rupelmonde   12, 96, 152
's Hertogenbosch   xxv
Saaftinge, Willem van   84, 91, 123, 238
St Denijs   88, 109, 118, 132, 147, 150, 241
St Denis Abbey   30, 54, 57, 60, 70, 81, 82, 116, 117
St Omer   xi, 13, 30, 111, 182, 219, 220
St Pol   21, 25, 26, 62
St Pol, Guy IV, Count of   60, 68, 69, 73, 79, 86, 105, 109, 111, 117, 188, 191, 223, 230, 240, 241
St Pol, Jacques de (also named Châtillon)   12, 20, 22, 23, 47, 56, 57, 68, 91, 92, 105, 112, 117, 155, 160, 183, 188, 189, 217, 223, 231, 235, 246
Saint-Victor, Jean de (chronicler)   192
St Winoksbergen   216, 219
St Winoksbergen, Gilbert, Viscount of   6, 164, 172
Sancerre, Etienne II, Count of   68, 118, 188
Scheldt River   13, 109, 132, 135, 217
Scilt ende vrient (Shield and Friend)   25
Scots   xxiii, 121, 209, 248
Sevens, Th. (historian)   127, 129, 130, 138, 140, 143, 150

Sijsele, Jan van, Lord of   24, 166, 170, 197, 206
Spiegel historiael. See Velthem, Lodewijk van
Steenhuize, Otto van   162, 176, 179
Steppes, Battle of the   95
Stiermarken, Ottokar von (chronicler)   30, 49–52, 113, 134
Switzerland and the Swiss   xxiii, 51, 52, 209, 248, 249
Tancarville, Robert de, Chamberlain of Normandy   57, 68, 82, 93, 190, 192, 223, 230, 239
Tanghe, Zeger   135–37, 140
Ter Doest Abbey   84, 108
Termonde, Willem of, Lord of Crèvecœur, Son of Count Guy de Dampierre   8, 19
Tournai   xxv, 4, 11, 22, 42, 53, 76–80, 97, 109, 116, 118, 123, 132, 153, 155, 157, 165, 217, 241, 246
  Church of Our Lady   79, 241
  Abbey of St Martin   76–79, 241
  Abbey of St Nicholas   79, 241
Tournai, Siege of   77
Trie, Mathieu de   93, 105, 189, 192, 223, 231, 235, 239
Trie, Renaud de, Marshal of France   67, 93, 105, 117, 189, 192, 223
Tyrol   xxiii, 49
Uitkerke, Geraard van   175, 179
Uitkerke, Pieter van   175
Utrecht   xxv, 244
Vacrnewijck, Iwein van   175
Vaernewijck, Simon van   176, 180, 227
Vaernewijck, Thomas van   174, 175
Valenciennes   13–15
Valkenburg, Walram van   89, 164
Valois, Charles of, brother of King Philip IV   18, 20, 50, 65, 90, 183, 193, 199
Velthem, Lodewijk van (chronicler)   29, 31, 33–35, 38, 57, 59, 88–111, 115, 116, 118–24, 129, 130, 131, 134, 147, 150, 153, 181, 182, 188, 192, 193, 199, 249
Vertbois, Geraard van   165, 174
Vidame, Gui le   57, 189
Vienne   193
Vier Ambachten. See Four Ambachten
Vierson (or Vierzon), Jean de, Viscount of Tournai, son of Godevaart van Brabant   95, 182, 188, 191, 223
Villani, Giovanni (chronicler)   xxiii, 30, 37, 63–70, 91, 92, 94, 95, 100, 110, 115–20, 122, 132–34, 147, 149, 150, 162, 192, 194, 208

Vitry-en-Artois 42, 45, 71
Vlaanderen de Leeuw, Battle-Cry. See *Flanders the Lion*
Vlaminc, Jan, Squire of Willem van Jülich 107, 123, 234
Volcard, Jan 154, 155
Waas, Land of 19, 104
Wagner, R. L. (linguist) 35, 36, 38, 47, 48, 59, 62
Walepaièle 56, 82
Wavrin, Robrecht van, Lord of St Venant 6, 166, 173
Wederick, Willem 154, 155
Westrozebeke (Rosebeke), Battle of xi, 122, 248
Wijnendaal 154, 156, 215, 216, 244
Winterthur, Jean de (chronicler) 30, 49, 51–52, 113, 134
Wodsak, F. (historian) 36, 37, 121

Worringen, Battle of 89, 234, 239
Ypres 2–4, 11, 14, 17–21, 40, 57, 58, 79, 86, 106, 111, 112, 133, 152, 153, 161, 196, 197, 207, 215–17, 219, 226, 229, 235, 239, 246
Ypres, Bernard of (chronicler) 30, 111
Zeeland 8, 14, 18, 53, 72, 80, 86, 102, 161, 162, 167, 178, 215, 228, 236, 244, 249
Zeggherscappel, Boudewijn van 167
Zieriksee (Zerikzee), Battle of 53, 55, 84, 160, 244
Zottegem, Geraard van, Lord of, Viscount of Ghent 165, 179
Zoutenaaie, Hendrik van 167, 173
Zoutenaaie, Jan van 167, 173
Zoutenaaie, Willem van 167, 173
Zwevegem 88, 109, 118, 132, 241
Zwin River 7, 18, 25, 178, 219